Aftershock

Kieran Cashell is Lecturer in Critical and Contextual Studies at the School of Art and Design, Limerick Institute of Technology.

'Kieran Cashell discusses artists who use everything from soiled bed linens to blood to dead sharks in their works. Drawing on an impressive array of philosophical ideas, Cashell helps viewers tackle the messy details of art by Damien Hirst, Orlan, Marc Quinn, Tracey Emin, and more, as he provides a probing and subtle defence of the moral value of such recent "transgressive" art.'

Cynthia A. Freeland, Professor & Chair, Department of Philosophy, University of Houston, Texas

To Martin,

Best Wishes,

AFTERSHOCK

THE ETHICS OF CONTEMPORARY TRANSGRESSIVE ART

Enjoy!

KIERAN CASHELL

Kieran

I.B. TAURIS
LONDON · NEW YORK

Published in 2009 by I.B.Tauris & Co Ltd
6 Salem Road, London W2 4BU
175 Fifth Avenue, New York NY 10010
www.ibtauris.com

Distributed in the United States and Canada Exclusively by Palgrave Macmillan
175 Fifth Avenue, New York NY 10010

ISBN 978 1 84511 524 1

A full CIP record for this book is available from the British Library
A full CIP record is available from the Library of Congress

Library of Congress Catalog Card Number: available

Typeset by JCS Publishing Services Ltd, www.jcs-publishing.co.uk
Printed and bound in India

For Rachel and Benjamin
with all my love

CONTENTS

List of Illustrations ix
Acknowledgements xi

0 Introduction 1
The Incompatibility of Aesthetics and Contemporary Art 1
Transgression: The War Against Disinterestedness 5
The Ethics of Transgressive Art 12

1 Everybody Hates a Tourist 17
The Ethical Analysis of Contemporary Art 17
Disinterestedness and Cultural Tourism 18
The Ethical Evaluation of Art: Autonomism versus Moralism 27
A Difficult Case: Marc Quinn and Alison Lapper 32
Transgressive Art Meets the Autonomist–Moralist Model 42
Quinn and Lapper Revisited: A Contextualist Analysis 46
Conclusion 49

2 Carte Blanche 51
Marcus Harvey's *Myra* 51
Preliminary Approaches to the Ethical Analysis of *Myra* 56
'Suffer Little Children': The Facts of the Case 58
Myra: Portrait of a Serial Killer 61
Postmodernism and the Absence of the Referent Thesis 66
Contextualist Ethical Analysis of *Myra* 68
Myra and Merited Response Theory 79
Conclusion 84

3 Atrocity Exhibition 87
Aesthetic Defences of the Work of Jake and Dinos Chapman 87
The Canonic Defence and the Chapmans' *Disasters of War* 90
The Transgressive Defence of Transgressive Art 97

Hans Bellmer, Bataille and Authentic Transgression 101
The Trivial Pursuit of Psychoanalysis 107
Evaluation of Aesthetic Defences of Transgressive Art 109
Acknowledging the Immorality of the Chapmans' Work 114
Contextualist Ethical Evaluation of *Zygotic Acceleration* 116
Conclusion 121

4 Fearless Speech 123
Tracey Emin's Ethics of the Self 123
'With Myself Always Myself Never Forgetting': The Structure of Ethical Subjectivity 129
Exposure Without Reserve: Emotional Response and its Moral Significance 138
Shame: An Existential Analysis 145
Concluding Ethical Evaluation: Tracey Emin's Fearless Speech 151

5 Horrorshow 159
The Transvaluation of Morality in the Work of Damien Hirst 159
Obscene Objects of Pleasurable Fascination 162
Non-Human Animals and Ethical Inclusion 167
Attending to the Other of the Animal: Art and the Ethics of Care 172
Exquisite Corpse: Death and the Sublime 176
Cognitive Immoralism 179
The Artistic Transvaluation of Morality 182
Aftershock: Tragic Sympathy and Meta-Ethical Significance 188
Conclusion 196

Notes 201
Further Reading 241
Index 249

ILLUSTRATIONS

1	Richard Billingham, *Ray's A Laugh (Untitled)*	23
2	Richard Billingham, *Ray's A Laugh (Untitled)*	24
3	Marc Quinn, *Alison Lapper Pregnant*	33
4	Marc Quinn, *Self*	34
5	Marc Quinn, *Self* (detail)	35
6	Marcus Harvey, *Myra*	52
7	Myra Hindley, custodial photograph	61
8	Marcus Harvey, *Dudley, Like What You See? Then Call Me*	69
9	Marcus Harvey, *Julie from Hull*	70
10	Jake and Dinos Chapman, *Zygotic Acceleration, Biogenetic De-sublimated Libidinal Model (enlarged x 1000)*	88
11	Jake and Dinos Chapman, *Great Deeds Against the Dead*	92
12	Goya, *Grande Hazaña con Meurtos*	95
13	Tracey Emin, *If I Could Just Go Back and Start Again*	124
14	Tracey Emin, *Everyone I Have Ever Slept With 1963–1995*	130
15	Tracey Emin, *My Bed*	133
16	Tracey Emin, *Why I Never Became a Dancer (1)*	139
17	Tracey Emin, *Why I Never Became a Dancer (2)*	140
18	Damien Hirst, *When Logics Die*	160
19	Damien Hirst, *The Physical Impossibility of Death in the Mind of Someone Living (1)*	163
20	Damien Hirst, *Mother and Child Divided*	164
21	Damien Hirst, *The Physical Impossibility of Death in the Mind of Someone Living (2)*	177
22	Damien Hirst, *A Thousand Years*	189
23	Damien Hirst, *This Little Piggy Went to Market, This Little Piggy Stayed at Home*	193

ACKNOWLEDGEMENTS

I would like to express my gratitude to several people whose assistance was invaluable to the realisation of this project. My former editor at I.B.Tauris, Susan Lawson, supported my proposal and her detailed commentary on the early states of the manuscript was crucial. Sara Macdonald and Sophie Greig at the White Cube Gallery, Annabel Fallon at the Saatchi Gallery, Maria Stathi at the Anthony Reynolds Gallery, and Robyn Katkhuda at Other Criteria secured permission to reproduce the images discussed in the book. Philippa Brewster, at I.B.Tauris, took up the project at a critical stage and, with the assistance of Victoria Nemeth, shepherded the project to its final publishable form. A particular word of thanks is due to Jessica Cuthbert-Smith for her forensic copy-editing, and to artists Marcus Harvey and Richard Billingham who personally gave me permission to reproduce their work in this book.

I would also like to acknowledge the help and encouragement of my colleagues, John Scaggs, Alice Bendinelli, Brian Coates and Dara Waldron. I sincerely thank Professor Christopher Norris and Professor Daniela Carpi for their mentoring assistance; thanks also to Professor Cynthia Freeland for reading and commenting on the final draft. Projects like this would be unfeasible without the support of family and friends; and I want to take this opportunity to extend very special (and long overdue) thanks to Pat and Anne Cashell.

But in acknowledgement of the exceptional debt of gratitude I owe to Rachel and to Benjamin (who was born during the red-eye period of writing), I dedicate this book to them.

Finally, as the sole author of this work, I remain responsible for any errors or omissions that may have escaped detection, and for this I apologise in advance.

That coming autumn, the Royal Academy would be staging a most audacious exhibition of the most controversial contemporary British artists. Dorian, who was involved on the publicity side, was in the middle of a planning dinner at Quo Vadis in Soho with the Academy's director, when things began to go awry.

Will Self, *Dorian* (2004)

0 INTRODUCTION

The Incompatibility of Aesthetics and Contemporary Art

> Certain techniques of shock are embedded in the way we determine right from wrong.
>
> *Jake Chapman*

Contemporary art has caused controversy for its uncompromising and sometimes extremist strategies. Even where these strategies are revealed as necessarily radical interventions in ideological cultural enclaves, or ultimately prove profound in other ways, much that is valued as art remains shocking, disturbing and problematic. Such art has been endorsed with the generic descriptor *transgressive* – suggesting that this art shocks only by virtue of its uncompromising mission to interrogate conservative views and subvert conventional moral beliefs. However, many consider that this mission has become excessive. Transgression 'goes too far'; it violates the remit of enlightened culture to the extent that it becomes impossible to engage with transgressive practices *as art*.

Yet the fact remains that transgressive practices have genuinely expanded the horizon of artistic expression. Associated with the cultural project of postmodernism, transgressive art (which includes sub-generic tendencies such as abject art[1]) continues to constitute an important aesthetic force in post-twentieth-century vanguard culture. Professional critics have therefore been faced with a challenge: either support transgression unconditionally or condemn the tendency and risk obsolescence amid suspicions of critical conservativism. This explains the widespread phenomenon that one commentator has correctly diagnosed as the 'unreflective contemporary endorsement of the transgressive'.[2]

Aesthetic transgression can be defined as any act of violation presented under the alibi of art. More than an aesthetic genre it more accurately nominates a general 'oppositional practice' that includes many sub-genres and assumes a multiplicity of variations.[3] In the most comprehensive *tour de horizon* of transgressive art, Anthony Julius[4] distinguishes the aesthetic of transgression as an art committed to violating socio-consensual, but importantly non-legal, taboos: under the auspices of the 'constructive nihilism' of Friedrich Nietzsche and, in the spirit of the 'expenditure without reserve' developed in the 'erotism' of Georges Bataille, 'Taboo-breaking artworks put under threat certain under-articulated or unspoken sentiments and beliefs to which their audiences may be taken to adhere.'[5] The threats associated with transgressive art are thus directed at the audience; the viewer is meant to be affected by the violation of taboo symbolised by or enacted in the work.[6]

Bataille defines taboo as one of an economy of prohibitions that outline and protect the structure of the socio-symbolic realm.[7] And given this definition, we can characterise the transgressive act as a perceived assault on rationality. In its pursuit of the 'irrational', art has become negative, nasty and nihilistic. Influenced by the dark troika Nietzsche–Freud–Bataille, artists scrutinise what transcends the moral good–evil spectrum by openly 'discrediting the institutions of morality',[8] or, in challenging the psychoanalytic theory of sublimation, some artists openly expose and display 'unconscious' repressed instincts.[9] Some explore the erotic thrill of the irrational in itself in a disconcertingly indulgent way; some examine practices of destructive, demoralised and vicious impulses for their own sake, unrestrained by any moral constraint or self-critical censure – *le mal pour le mal*.

Thus, when certain artists encourage exposure to pathogenic motifs through an uninhibited exploration of their own traumatic neuroses (Vito Acconci, Janine Antoni and Jana Sterbak) or when they engage in acts of debasement without rationale or purpose (Mike Kelley and Paul McCarthy), or when artists appear intent on publicly unleashing libidinous and violent instinctual energy (the *Wiener Actionismus* artists Hermann Nitsch, Otto Muehl and Gunther Brus), or, finally, when artists inflict elective harm on themselves in a programme of public para-suicidal performances (Bob Flanagan, Marina Abramović or Franco B), we acknowledge the violation of a socio-consensual taboo in the Bataillean sense and recognise that we are dealing with transgressive artistic practices.

Transgression becomes a valued cultural practice, Chris Jenks explains, because the uncompromisingly honest confrontation with the less salubrious aspects of the human condition is assumed, according to a tacit but widespread adherence to atmospheric post-Freudian tropes, to be a healthy social regulative.[10] The burden has fallen on contemporary culture to put in place the creative conditions that make it possible to experience abandonment and excess safely and to give (at least vicarious) expression to the impulsive attraction to the instinctual urge towards the amoral and the irrational involved in this post-Freudian commitment.[11] Thanks to transgressive art practices, we can experience excess, and identify with possibilities of life liberated from all social constraints and moral judgement, at an acceptable imaginative distance.

Do transgressive cultural practices enable audiences to access neuroses indirectly and, by vicarious experience of violation, become psychologically enriched by the process? As the Viennese Actionist Hermann Nitsch, director of the Orgiastic Mystery Theatre (founded in 1958) claims, spectacles of horror and sacrifice become cathartic mechanisms for releasing potentially psycho-pathological repressions. 'Our intellect is repressed energy,' he says, and inevitably, the drawing out of such repressions is going to appear 'orgiastic, as violent as it is obscene'.[12] Nitsch assumes, he says, 'all that appears negative, unsavoury, perverse and obscene, the lust and the resulting sacrificial hysteria, in order to spare YOU the defilement and shame entailed by the descent into the extreme.'[13]

Perhaps this explanation goes some way towards the critical justification of transgressive art's 'predatory relation with what is forbidden'.[14] Indeed, art critics have defended the disturbing – unsavoury, perverse *and* obscene[15] – performances of Californian artist Paul McCarthy as not only artistically significant but also enriching, because he enables audiences to experience violent regression vicariously, without becoming directly involved. Similar to the cathartic relationship developed between the agonists of ancient Greek tragedy and their audience, McCarthy acts out his personal traumata in public so we don't have to. Or perhaps not.

As Cynthia Freeland has observed, this theorisation fails to explain the negative impulse behind transgressive art completely; it fails because, unlike the Dionysian ritual catharsis at the origin of Greek tragedy, there no longer exists a shared community-unifying belief system according to which the transgressive act can arrogate a general socio-cultural value.[16] 'Many people', Fenella Critchton agrees, 'are sceptical as to whether or not it is possible to re-animate those myths at the end of the 20th century.'[17] When Nitsch claims to spare us the defilement of the descent into the extreme, sceptics like Julius can simply counter: 'no you do not'. For how can we become true participants in such ritual catharsis if there is no consensual agreement as to the value and significance of the transgressive act as required for ritual behaviour?[18] 'Far from audiences coming to feel part of a group, sometimes they get shocked and abandon the community.'[19] The question therefore remains: just why *has* vanguard art become so nasty and nihilistic?

Addressing this question, Jake Chapman's recent documentary, *Artshock: Is Bad Art for Bad People?*[20] suggests that post-holocaust society, altered irrevocably by the obscenities witnessed during two world wars, now suffers from a kind of global traumatic neurosis. Referring to the Freudian theory of repression, Chapman proposes that extreme culture emerged in the aftermath of the war as a kind of public 'abreactive'[21] therapy, whereby confrontation with the original source of trauma is assumed to result in a kind of beneficial catharsis for the neurotic. He claims that, as shock is used for positive ends in psychoanalytic therapy, so extreme culture tries to shock society out of its paralysing hysteria by cruelly confronting it with 'de-sublimated' transgressive imagery.[22]

Certainly, the artists associated with Viennese Actionism, whose performances included public acts of hysterical regression (Brus's performances included urination and defecation with faecal play as well as acts of self-directed insult including self-mutilation), may appear more reasonable in light of this explanation; Nitsch, as we have seen, defends his spectacles of excess, claiming that it is for cathartic ends that the primordial impulsive darkness repressed in the collective organisation of civilised social existence is 'unleashed'. Exposing culturally suppressed barbarism can perhaps be defended as necessary for the psychic health of artificially civilised humanity. So, according to this picture, in order to overcome global trauma following the experience of atrocity, it is necessary for the critical project of Western culture to turn antagonistic in order, paradoxically, to preserve the project of affirmative humanism. Therefore, it is only for the sake of the critical principles of culture that art has rejected the traditional affirmative values of culture – and has become, in the process, negative, nasty and nihilistic.[23]

Is this explanation plausible? Certainly, it seems slightly absurd to suggest, for instance, that Paul McCarthy's artistic programme should be linked to a post-traumatic hangover of collective guilt in the wake of global atrocity. Although there have been repeated attempts to contextualise his transgressive practices in relation to Actionism, what he has appropriated, if anything, from the Viennese Actionists is a simulated mimesis of excess, a *style*.[24] This crucial stylistic aspect of the transgressive aesthetic demonstrates that if it is to be adequately addressed it will become necessary to narrow the field of focus and avoid the ambitious temptation to provide planetary answers to localised questions. In respect of this caveat, I will claim that what contemporary transgressive art – more aggressively than any previous cultural practice – has actively sought to do is *invalidate the principles of institutional aesthetics*. To this end, the principal target of transgressive antagonism will be discovered to be the paradigmatic concept of philosophical aesthetics, namely, the so-called 'disinterested' mode of aesthetic contemplation.[25]

Transgression: The War Against Disinterestedness

Disinterestedness, long considered the fundamental motif of traditional art discourse, has its foundations in the philosophical tradition of the eighteenth century and its associated prioritisation of the category of beauty for aesthetics.[26] As a prescribed aesthetic concept, however, disinterestedness receives its most rigorous analysis in the work of the German philosopher Immanuel Kant who argued in the *Critique of Judgment*[27] (*Kritik der Urteil*, 1790) that a form of contemplation *disengaged* from all practical contexts – and dissociated from all *emotional*, *sexual* or *moral* feelings – is the only objective form of perception appropriate to the rational appreciation of (artistic) beauty.

In order for a judgement of aesthetic value to have universal validity, Kant decided that it must be 'independent of all interest'.[28] And in the aesthetic context *interest* is identified as any motivation towards the object that involves *desire*.[29] Thus aesthetic appreciation should not driven by any purposive urge to satisfy an intentional appetite.[30] According to Kant, beauty can become accessible as a phenomenon of transcendental ('objective') aesthetic judgement only as a result of a mode of contemplation that has been sanitised of desire.[31]

For instance: to appreciate the nude in a manner sensitive to its aesthetic value one must learn to suspend any erotic desire that may be provoked by the sight of the model's naked figure. For, if the body becomes the object of sexual desire, then it is not possible to dwell exclusively on, and thereby completely appreciate, the aesthetic significance of the nude, because one has not engaged the conditions of disinterested perception that enable the artistic value – the *beauty* – of the naked human body to emerge and be comprehended as an end in itself (and *not* as a means to satisfy sexual appetite, or as a vehicle to express erotic passions, or whatever). When we disinterestedly consider the naked body as an abstract design that stimulates a kind of pleasure completely unlike the visceral thrill of erotic desire, only then can we begin to contemplate it, in the disinterested mode relevant to Kant's theory, as an aesthetic form: the nude.[32] And every authentic judgement of aesthetic value is only made on the basis of such emotionally detached contemplation, unsullied by means–ends motivation.

Disinterestedness, following the psychological revision of the Kantian standard in the modern era,[33] has become generally understood in the philosophy of art as a specific modality of perception that, in 'disengaging' our normal responses, imaginatively removing practical concerns and emotional reactions and, crucially, suppressing any *moral* responses,[34] becomes sensitised to what makes an object qualify as art. This is the assumption that the distinctively aesthetic value of the art object only discloses itself to a particular kind of perception that is not our 'normal' attitude to ordinary objects. Key to this sensitive perception is the requirement that the subject of the aesthetic experience (i.e. the person experiencing it) be in a special kind of *state*, a contemplative or abstract state that, responsive to the harmonious expression of pure forms, enables the category of beauty to emerge and be recognised as transcendental, that is, shared by everyone with the subjective capacity for aesthetic judgement.

Because it apparently supplies an objective criterion for artistic value, enabling critics to distinguish aesthetic value from mere opinion, Kantian disinterestedness has had an overwhelming influence on the subsequent philosophy (and criticism) of art. It has been centrally upheld, reinforced and repeatedly recommended by post-Kantian institutional aesthetics, and it continues to exert a palpable magnetism on philosophers of art; present as a tacit commitment, it also informs the writing of many contemporary art critics. Yet it is precisely this concept that much important contemporary artistic practice actively tries to sabotage by engaging with the 'extra-aesthetic' contexts of the very emotional, sexual and especially *moral* life-worlds prescriptively disengaged by the dogma of disinterestedness.

Consider, for instance, Paul McCarthy's *Bossy Burger* (1991), the first in a repertoire of combination performance and video installations that, taken together, constitute a grievous assault on the sensibility of taste institutionalised by post-Kantian aesthetics. A synthetic environment, made up of plywood studio sets from an axed television sitcom is the setting of *Bossy Burger*. In the claustrophobic confines of this studio set, the artist, dressed in a chef's overalls, yellow rubber gloves, an apron and hat, and wearing a mask of Alfred E. Neuman (from *Mad* magazine), shambles, evacuating plastic ketchup and industrial mayonnaise containers of their contents. Grumbling and moaning, he squeezes and splatters, smearing every surface, filling every available vessel with the viscid ooze. Narcissistically absorbed in his purposeless business, and finally, completely covered in the mess, he kneels on the table and begins to apply coats of the coagulating ketchup to a tatty armchair.

Witnessing McCarthy's acts of unscripted regression is extremely distressing. 'Mayonnaise goes on a chopstick and gets shoved into the ketchup' (as one observer reported); '"Fuck it up the butt," [McCarthy] yells and puts the chopstick up his ass, then back into the bottle.'[35] Such excessive behaviour without purpose is paradigmatically transgressive in the Bataillean sense because it constitutes a pure expression of primordial irrationality that exceeds sense, meaning and, of course, *every traditional measure of aesthetic value*. 'The removal and separateness, the passive attention we associate with contemplation have little place here.'[36]

Yet this should not be taken to mean that transgressive work (such as McCarthy's) does not count as art. Rather such transgressive ART renders orthodox aesthetics redundant because the leitmotif of aesthetic theory, the concept of disinterested contemplation – and especially its purported universal application – is exposed as deficient in application to it: *but it is still art*.

In post-Kantian aesthetic theory, beauty, as we have seen, is centrally positioned as a transcendental category: 'Without beauty, no theory of aesthetics can have', Ruth Lorand observes, 'a reasonable [meaning "objective"] explanatory power.'[37] What about its opposite? A judgement of aesthetic value takes place when, according to the disinterested mode of perception, a certain object is recognised to possess the necessary formal aesthetic criteria to result in pleasure, and the rational, if irresistible, judgement of beauty. What happens, on the other hand, when an *ugly* object causes *displeasure*? Does the category of ugliness have equal rights in an aesthetic evaluation? For orthodox post-Kantian aesthetics, the answer is emphatically NO: 'If beauty is characterised as a quality that is perceived by disinterestedness, then the opposite [ugliness] produced by negating this characteristic would be an instrumental, non-aesthetic value which is [detrimentally] informed by interest.'[38]

Emotions of displeasure – disgust, repulsion, nausea – solicited by the sheer ugliness of McCarthy's aesthetic refuse to be acclimatised to the disinterested mind-set: we cannot become emotionally detached, or indifferent to the existence of the object, for it is impossible to disengage emotional responses completely and coolly detach ourselves from physical sensations that are involuntarily produced by the performance. In being affected viscerally by scenes of primal-infantile regression, it is impossible to suspend our normal attitude and engage the disinterested perspective. The possibility of ignoring our immediate adverse emotional reactions in order to contemplate the work's purely formal characteristics is cruelly retracted by the ugliness of the scene.

Example: the abject amorphousness of the materials employed by McCarthy cannot be translated to significant form because they (and how they are being used) refuse to settle into typical aesthetic categories (unlike static, dried paint, glazed on a surface). Although constantly aware that they possess the status of simulacra – they are not the real thing – using these products to act out psychodramas in the way McCarthy does means that they become over-determined – polymorphous with perverse possibilities.[39]

However, I would argue that the traumatic associations McCarthy's products assume depend *not* on what they come to symbolise (for instance, blood, body-fluids, excreta etc.). Ketchup and mayonnaise (and the other 'fluxes' he uses, hand-cream, milk etc.) are not transubstantiated by McCarthy into their referents; they are not, in fact, meant – despite what critics may suggest – to represent blood or other body-fluids. Rather they remain intractably what they are. In this way, the ketchup and mayonnaise, as displacements, phobic substitutes for personal neuroses, devoid of any general significance, utterly contingent, arbitrary and horrifically inconsistent, become *more* disturbing, more abject and more traumatic – precisely *as* ketchup *and* mayonnaise –

than any intentional deployment that aimed at direct reference to blood or semen.[40]

First shown in LA, the work was presented as an installation: the stage sets and their contents remained as McCarthy had left them post-performance (surfaces covered in stale sauces and decomposing meat). Crumpled like shed skins, the costume and mask lay discarded in a corner. A video loop of the performance played continuously on two television screens installed in the scaffolding outside the sets. 'Reeking of violence, the scene conjured the aftermath of a barbaric assault'; but the only assault here is the threat to our ability to assimilate the obscene field of McCarthy's art into aesthetic categories – zero tolerance for any orthodox aesthetic value.[41] The aftermath of the performance remained for the duration of the exhibition. What began as mildly noxious became so unbearable that it was, apparently, impossible to enter the shuttered studio rooms. 'Every time you went back you were agreeing to be more nauseated.'[42] To repeat: decomposition and the physical reaction it incites – disgust – are, in principle, intransigent to the aesthetic attitude of disinterestedness.

Other authors have admittedly taken into account the specific challenge to disinterestedness posed by contemporary art. In a recent study that confronts traditional aesthetic values with contemporary artistic tendencies, Matthew Kieran grants that there is 'something fundamentally wrong with Kant's conception of aesthetic value'.[43] He quotes from the sections of the Third *Critique* where Kant argues that it is impossible to render beautiful 'that which excites *disgust*', for the disgustingly repulsive, in provoking an immediate emotional response, cannot be assimilated to disinterested contemplation. In the Kantian aesthetic tradition, that which causes a visceral reaction is necessarily in conflict with a form of aesthetic appreciation that depends on the attitude of critical (or emotional) distance.[44]

Kieran refers in this context to the 'abject art' of US artist Cindy Sherman. He cites a series of photographic images produced in late 1980 dedicated to the theme of repulsion. The so-called 'disgust series', which memorably features post-mortem (de)compositions with human remains incompletely buried among other debris in the displaced earth of a shallow grave, 'seem driven by a practical artistic attempt to investigate Kant's claim that disgust is beyond the pale of an aesthetic response'.[45] As argued, all transgressive art, abject or not, is driven by a similar intent to menace the emotionally distanced perspective associated with the aesthetic attitude, by deliberately provoking emotional responses or visceral reactions that refuse to be assimilated to the disinterested mode of perception. However, Kieran (with reference here to a series of violently misshapen photographs of British artist Jenny Saville squashed up against plate glass) argues that, despite the challenges of transgressive art, it may be possible *nevertheless* to appreciate the repulsive aesthetically. In the case of

Saville's self-portraits, for instance, Kieran stubbornly insists that it is the very obscenity of the image that paradoxically 'grabs our aesthetic interest'.[46] And thus the transgressive artistic impulse, however 'disgusting, grotesque, ugly and incoherent' it may prima facie appear, can be processed and domesticated for aesthetic contemplation.[47]

In a similar vein, Cynthia Freeland discusses the work of controversial US artist Andreas Serrano.[48] Again, acknowledging the difficulties that transgressive art present to traditional paradigms of aesthetic judgement, she considers various approaches to his work. She concedes that recent art practice seems utterly remote from eighteenth-century aesthetic ideals. 'Art includes', she recognises, 'not just works of formal beauty to be enjoyed by people with "taste", or works with beauty and uplifting moral messages, but also works that are ugly and disturbing, with a shatteringly negative moral content.'[49] When confronted with the transgressive photographic work of Serrano, for instance, it is simply not possible to assume a distanced attitude and remain indifferent to its disturbing content.

A significant challenge to the historical legacy of disinterestedness has come from feminist philosophy. Associating the disinterested attitude with an aspiration that is specifically masculine in character,[50] for instance, Peggy Zeglin Brand, in 'Disinterestedness and Political Art', takes issue with the alleged objectivity, universality and 'neutrality' involved in the notion of disinterestedness.[51] Detecting in these concepts the outlines of a phallocentric grand narrative, she argues that certain kinds of postmodernist art demand, on the contrary, an *interested* approach. This is particularly the case, she says, with interventional feminist art.

In exploring her hypothesis, she uses the example of the controversial French performance artist known as Orlan. Since 1990, Orlan has voluntarily undergone facial transformation with the help of intensive surgical reconstruction.[52] She arranged to have the series of operations filmed while under local anaesthetic and transmitted live via satellite to various venues in Europe and North America. The result is an on-going performance entitled 'The Reincarnation of St Orlan' in which she attempts to demonstrate, in the most severe and uncompromising manner, the absurd futility of striving to achieve the elusive ideal of beauty established by (the gendered discourse of) classical aesthetics.

Following a physiognomy grafted of features appropriated from art historical paradigms of beauty: 'the chin of Botticelli's Venus, the Fontainebleau school's Diana, the lips of Gustave Moreau's Europa, the nose of Gerome's Psyche, the brow of Leonardo's Mona Lisa',[53] Orlan's extended performance, Brand concludes, 'is meant to discourage women from reconstructive surgery'.[54] Her material, the site of her expression, the surface on which her transformative project unfolds, is her own suffering body; but her face, far from achieving any paradigmatic beauty, has been distorted into a ghastly parody – a Frankenstein's monster – of classical beauty. Thus the aesthetic paradox is cruelly, monstrously, demonstrated: Orlan's attempt to achieve ideal beauty in reality results in ugliness; even if we are *theoretically* aware that all efforts to achieve beauty by physical intervention based on the notion of perfect aesthetic form are vain (in both senses), to see the ocular proof of this is profoundly shocking. 'If the parts of seven different ideal women are needed to fulfill [*sic*] Adam's desire for an Eve made in his image,' Barbara Rose observes, 'Orlan consciously chooses to undergo the necessary mutilation to reveal that the objective is unattainable and the process horrifying.'[55]

To the extent that viewers may recognise Orlan's effort to make a point about masculine-determined stereotypical notions of feminine beauty and to the extent that they may admire the extreme lengths she is prepared to go for her beliefs (like McCarthy, her work has been contextualised in relation to Viennese Actionism[56]), and to the extent that those critics may identify with the pressure she feels placed under to conform to a hegemonic concept of beauty largely conditioned by male desire, such responses to the work cannot, according to Brand, be disinterested. Rather, the work of Orlan is an instance of art that, on the contrary, provokes an *interested* response.[57]

However, drawing on Wittgensteinian aspect-seeing, Brand goes on to develop the counter-argument that, despite this conclusion, it *is* possible to appreciate the extreme acts of transgressive art disinterestedly.[58] Employing the ambiguous duck–rabbit sketch from the *Philosophical Investigations* (two distinct figures in one design that, depending on the aspect attended to, can be seen as either one figure or the other: i.e. now it is a duck, now a rabbit),[59] she argues that it is possible to toggle between the different modalities of aesthetic perception. Like a stereoscopic card, the work can appear now one way, now another: now individual woman suffering mid-term pain and discomfort (as well as transformed facial features), now interesting composition and colour, fascinating glistening crimsons and purplish blooms, pink smudges, clinical green-grey textures. Brand's conclusion is 'that although the adoption of a stance of traditional disinterestedness is a masculinist approach to the experiencing of a work of art, it is still a possible and appropriate, useful mode of experiencing art, including feminist art'.[60]

Brand, like many defenders of the aesthetic attitude, as we can see here, has opted for a *prescriptive* (as opposed to *descriptive*) mode of expression to argue for the merits of disinterestedness in the critical appreciation of art. There is a subtle but not imperceptible shift in her analysis from the description of a situation in contemporary art practice to the prescription of how we *ought* to experience such a situation. Such, I would argue, is the magnetism of the concept of disinterested contemplation that even where it is disabled by contemporary transgressive art-acts, and even in contexts where it is explicitly acknowledged to be an outmoded theoretical construct, it has been tacitly committed to all along until finally reparsed as the ideal aesthetic attitude.

It is by emphasising a paradoxical double-aspect modality in 'aesthetic' perception that Kieran and Brand can claim that the categories of traditional aesthetics can and should be preserved for the appreciation of contemporary, and especially, transgressive art. This moral argument seems to suggest that what prima facie incites nausea should ultimately, when attention falls on an alternative aspect of the same phenomenon, be revealed as beautiful. But Will Self's phrase from a critique of art criticism's use of philosophical tropes such as this seems apt here: 'Like clever children playing with one of those stereoscopic postcards [the critics] flick it this way and that, to show the Emperor alternately naked and adorned.'[61] Thus, by flicking our attention this way and that, we can learn to love the obscene. By forcing ourselves to become emotionally detached according to the disinterested mode, what is obscene or unacceptable can be adapted to aesthetic form and thus appreciated as ultimately beautiful.

But is it not to completely miss the point to treat transgressive art in this way? Is it not misdirected in some crucial sense to argue that Orlan's work *should* be contemplated disinterestedly, from an emotionally detached perspective? Is her performance not supposed to affect us emotionally, viscerally, physically? What she is doing is intended to have a direct and unpleasant effect on us. If it doesn't shock, it ceases to have its desired function. Because it is *meant to shock*, it is intended to make us involuntarily exclaim: STOP! *This is wrong*. Yet it is precisely this kind of ethical reaction to art practice that the revisers of disinterestedness attempt to neutralise, because what Orlan is doing is very difficult to defend on a moral level, but, they believe, through exhuming cadaverous aesthetic principles, it can be justified as art. And yet the intensification of this very conflict, I would suggest, constitutes the entire meaning of Orlan's enterprise.

By demonstrating that she is prepared to go to obscene, unacceptable lengths for her convictions, Orlan forces witnesses of her project to accept the morally questionable nature of her volitions (which one critic has condemned as a submission to 'medical barbarism' motivated by 'self-hatred')[62] as artistically meaningful – that is, as an ethically necessary form of cultural transgression. Otherwise the political objective of the work – namely, to disclose the irrationality of the concept of perfect formal female beauty (as determined, again, by Western philosophical aesthetics according to the mode of disinterested perception) by metamorphosing herself into what Parveen Adams has called an 'art-historical morph'[63] – would not emerge so clearly and with such admirable conviction.

The Ethics of Transgressive Art

Against an overwhelming consensus to the contrary, this book will propose that ethical analysis is an effective and critically revealing method of engaging with contemporary transgressive art. I am specifically interested in artists that, like Orlan, challenge the aesthetic attitude of disinterestedness through engaging moral sensibility. Because ethical judgement is institutionally considered to be anathema to aesthetic appreciation, such art can be identified as paradigmatically transgressive precisely because the reaction it provokes is a *moral* reaction.

But what do I mean by moral reaction? The signature of morally transgressive practice is that it proposes engagement with the work on an ethical – as opposed to aesthetic – level. What I have in mind here is art, similar to the work of Orlan, that initially produces a kind of moral shock, a shock experienced, moreover, as a visceral reaction that refuses to be processed according to the disinterested modality. For those willing to accept the challenge of this kind of art – for those who engage with it, in other words – the effect is *moral* and not aesthetic (or at least not exclusively aesthetic).

Typically, reaction to transgressive art assumes the form, THIS IS WRONG: the artist was wrong to have done this. Such work may, however, motivate the subsequent, (re)considered and highly complex, indeed, tortuous response: this is difficult, may appear indeed to be wrong, or immoral, but the artist was ultimately right to engage this difficult and contentious subject-matter – because its overall ethos demands approval and establishes that the transgression the work entails is ethically justifiable. This phenomenon of reflective moral response I shall later identify as the ethical *aftershock* of the work.

My approach not only takes issue therefore with a very powerful art-critical consensus, but also questions Julius's assertion that the 'transgressive aesthetic is not an aesthetic of immorality.'[64] It would be to misconstrue my argument, however, if it were taken to suggest that transgressive art *is* immoral; rather, my position would be parsed more accurately if it were taken to claim that certain kinds of transgressive art practice seem deliberately designed to *engage moral sensibility* by provoking a negative ethical response. But how is ethics being understood here?

Philosophical ethical discourse is the zone of the controversial and the perpetually disputable. Because ethical principles are not objective – moral values do not possess the status of mind-independent facts that can be established with definitive empirical or rational precision[65] – as Martha C. Nussbaum argues, ethical theory 'cannot be a form of scientific knowledge that orders "matters of the practical" into an elegant antecedent system'.[66] Contentious as it may be to claim, it is almost as if the mark of a genuine moral problem is precisely its inconclusive, undecidable status.[67] Thus, with respect to Julius, it is simply not possible to impose a universal moral imperative that applies to all equally.[68] Moral disagreement is a practical *fact* and cannot be spirited away by creative ratiocination.

Ethical pluralism is a model that attempts to address the fact that conflict between mutually opposed yet equally reasonable attitudes arises because moral values are neither exclusively oppositional nor commensurate with each other. Moral concepts cannot be expected to apply to every situation in exactly the same way: 'intractable moral disagreements' may simply 'be the result of moral indeterminacy – there just being no answer to the question of which action is right or preferable in particular circumstances'.[69] Pluralism[70] has been defined as the view that there exist several incomplete (but not necessarily incompatible) value-concepts to which a person can commit without their being reducible to a single supreme belief system.[71] Moral principles are thus characterised by the pluralist as sensitive to specific situations that, to this extent, makes the application of a particular moral hypothesis irreducible to an ultimate ethical standard and yet also, and more importantly for our purposes, resistant to trans-context codification.[72] In practice, this means that whichever moral 'principle' is employed in any given situation, it will be discovered to be case-sensitive; that is, the application of a moral concept will depend on (and must be tailored according to) the specific discriminating factors, conditions or parameters of a particular existential situation.

Pluralism is, therefore, a form of ethical particularism: application of any moral principle will be found to vary on a case-by-case basis. The meaning of individual principles will also change depending on the real-life context in which they are applied.[73] Acceptance of pluralism involves prioritising the existential situation and committing to the ultimate determination of the context in ethical analysis. Yet this acceptance of pluralism, very significantly, respects the ethically crucial ethos of toleration: views that, although incompatible with my own moral commitments, may be equally reasonable, equally valuable and therefore equally deserving of axiological admiration.

The complex philosophical readings of art elaborated in this book are guided by commitment to the attitude that an irreducibly specific event is not amenable to (ethical or aesthetic) evaluation in abstraction from the context in which it occurs. Moral pluralism is crucial to my mode of ethical inquiry because it proves adequate to the ordinary experience of value in everyday life; quotidian evaluations and relationships are, as Berys Gaut observes, founded and delimited by sets of unsystematic and heterogeneous ethical commitments, yet these 'commitments we can disavow only at the cost of abandoning these evaluations and relationships'.[74] Such commitments respect a multiplicity of unpretentious yet non-trivial minimal moral responsibilities perhaps best captured by the non-systematic obligation of *care*, or 'what many moral theorists call "empathy" or "feeling with"'.[75] This is the view that the ethical perspective is motivated by concern or compassion in a manner that cannot be captured adequately by abstract reasoning. For such an ethics of particularity, according to Dwight Furrow, moral thinking 'is a process of deliberation and appropriate feeling developing out of our capacity to care' in which 'emotions are central'.[76]

Secular morality, as understood here therefore, in the words of Robert Solomon, is constituted by 'the emotional sense that what happens to others matters'.[77] Although such obligations may not be, and cannot be made, part of an integrated, rational belief-system, they nevertheless constitute the basic apparatus of what could be called the 'ethical perspective'. And the signature of such a perspective is just this *other-sensitive care*, or, to use the words of Peter Singer (*sans* his utilitarian motivations) the minimal realisation that 'my own interests cannot count for more, simply because they are my own, than the interests of others.'[78]

Ultimately, the challenge of morally transgressive art is to evaluate it in ethical and not exclusively aesthetic terms. This book represents the acceptance of that challenge. It has been necessary, obviously, to limit the amount of works selected in the effort to meet this challenge in the most critically effective way, while at the same time reinforcing the central argument. To that end, I have adopted a selection strategy that is not meant to suggest that the works of the (predominantly) British artists that have been subjected to ethical analysis for this project are the very best examples of morally transgressive art. Neither is this selection strategy entirely arbitrary. The work of the young British artists associated with the 1990s and the private patronage of visual art in a post-Thatcherite UK that had been changed irrevocably by her decade-long administration represents a kind of cluster phenomenon where diverse artists began to produce work that was extremely interesting and exciting, *and* infuriating and problematic, *precisely because it engages moral sensibility* in the manner described above.

The art practice of Richard Billingham, Marc Quinn, Marcus Harvey, Jake and Dinos Chapman, Tracey Emin and Damien Hirst, in that it interrogates the aesthetic attitude of disinterested contemplation, may not be unique; but the precise manner in which these artists transgress taboos to initiate moral shock, and, by this, propose engagement with their work at a ethical level, makes it highly appropriate for the evaluation proposed here. Also, it is not insignificant that all these artists were represented in the controversial *Sensation* exhibitions in the Royal Academy of Arts in London in 1997 and again, two years later, in the Brooklyn Museum of Art in New York. For both exhibitions are now considered *loci classici* in the institutionalisation of transgressive art.

The so-called yBa phenomenon can be considered a generic set in the philosophical sense given to this mathematical concept by the French philosopher Alain Badiou. That is to say, the British art that came to prominence at the very end of the twentieth century constitutes a multiplicity made possible by a kind of fertile matrix that enabled unpredictable variations to occur within its parameters.[79] Although ultimately incommensurable, the individual elements of this set nevertheless share certain characteristic traits. For the specific purposes of this project, what the young British artists discussed in this book share is a form of artistic transgression that, in being morally shocking, is, for that reason, in some way (to be elaborated in the chapters of this book) ethically significant.

'Certain techniques of shock are embedded in the way we determine right from wrong'.[80] This proposition by Jake Chapman can be considered an epigraph for this book: shock is often required for the development of an ethical perspective that is sensitive to the moral distinction between good and bad, right and wrong. The evaluations undertaken in the following chapters take Chapman's proposition as their departure point and reinforce it repeatedly. When confronted with art that shocks as a result of the moral transgression it performs, there is real danger here. Such work shakes us, makes us think twice. The danger is that something fundamental will occur as a result, that we will be changed in some way, that the work will have more than an aesthetic effect. Julius's distinction between taboo and moral value is thereby invalidated in practice: we have already been affected by the work. We've already responded morally to it, already answered: right or wrong.

1 EVERYBODY HATES A TOURIST

The Ethical Analysis of Contemporary Art

In a review of the landmark exhibition of transgressive art, *Sensation: Young British Artists from the Saatchi Collection* at the Royal Academy of Arts in 1997, Kitty Hauser criticises the show, proposing that the artists reminded her of the St Martin's sculpture student in the satirical song 'Common People' by British band Pulp. In the song, a Greek émigré student who has a 'thirst for knowledge' takes the opportunity, while attending the art institution, to carry out some ethnographic research into the authentic British lower classes. Selecting the protagonist of the song as a suitable envoy for her induction, she tells him of her desire to 'live like common people, do whatever common people do'. Before quoting the (last) chorus of the song, Hauser comments:

> Within the cool paradigms of the yBa, where to preach is taboo, no art work could come to the clear conclusions of the song, which is that class and poverty are more than lifestyle choices. Since her Dad [*sic*] is 'loaded' – and also presumably because of her education – the St Martin's student will never 'live like common people'.[1]

According to Hauser, poetry, satire and popularity form a unity of three enviable elements that, however heroically they attempt, must remain beyond the capacity of the Saatchi-generation artists. Not so, she says, for a songwriter like Jarvis Cocker, who, Hauser believes, is capable of mobilising his abilities to engage with a political debate that, while adopting an evident moral stance, does not sacrifice any musical, rhetorical or artistic significance in the process.

However compelling, I disagree with Hauser's critical evaluation of the 'young British art' phenomenon. First, in many respects, the phenomenon paralleled the advent and rise of Britpop in the 1990s. With cross-pollinating creative intersections between the artists and the musicians, Damien Hirst and Tracey Emin, for instance, were engaging a similar audience to that which high-profile, commercially marketed and company-promoted bands like Blur, Elastica, Pulp, Suede, PJ Harvey and of course, Oasis were currently, and deservedly, enjoying. Many of the members of these bands attended Goldsmiths (and other art institutes in London) contemporaneously with Hirst et al.[2] Therefore, the knowing allusions to (alternative) popular culture, music and film seen in the work of the yBas (especially Hirst and Gavin Turk) were being appreciated by a new particular (and, artistically speaking, non-conventional) audience that made this kind of art, contrary to Hauser's critique, uniquely popular with a contrarian British youth culture still emerging from the shadow cast over culture by a decade of economic expediency. The legacy of the post-punk 'golden age' of British counter (post-punk 'indie'-milieu) culture was being assessed in strikingly similar ways in both Britpop and the work of the young British artists.

Secondly, added to this was the new prominence of art school graduate (and post-graduate) artists with working-class or 'lower-class' (I use the term circumspectly, in the interests of making the point) backgrounds in the late 1980s and early 1990s. A survey of the young British artists will reveal quite a striking cohort of Jarvis Cocker's so-called 'common people' among their ranks. Cocker, obviously authoring the song from some measure of personal experience (he enrolled to study filmmaking at Central St Martin's College of Art and Design in 1988[3]), makes the point that he (i.e. the protagonist of 'Common People') is *himself* considered by the Greek émigré student to be one of the common people (from a working-class, or, more accurately, from a Thatcherite economics welfare-class background) that she has selected to be her tour-guide of the still-life of the British underclass, to 'slum it' for a season in the hell-circle of the urban unemployed.[4] But, as Cocker sings in his signature sardonic Sheffield whisper, 'Everybody *hates a tourist*, especially one who thinks it's all such a laugh.'

Disinterestedness and Cultural Tourism

Jerome Stolnitz characterises the disinterested aesthetic viewpoint in terms of a suspension of our natural attitude to the world.[5] This description corresponds uncannily closely to the mechanism of reduction associated with philosophical phenomenology. Formulated by Edmund Husserl as a pure eidetic (conceptual image-forming) method, phenomenology, facilitated by the mechanism of reduction, was capable, he believed, of disclosing the essence of reality and thus furnishing presuppositionless grounding principles of knowledge.[6] Such disclosing of essences was conditional on what Husserl called the *epoche*, by which he meant the 'bracketing' or 'putting out of action' of our natural orientation toward the everyday; it meant adopting a radically alternative attitude to the life-world such that reality appears as it purely *is*, outside all moral, political, psychological accretions, commonsensical conventional interests, relative opinions or socio-cultural schemes.[7]

The aesthetic attitude, as recommended by Stolnitz, constitutes a reduction in this sense.[8] To assume the disinterested attitude in Stolnitz's sense can therefore be understood as an attempt to adopt a disengaged *epoche* that is capable of abstracting the art object from its profile of relative and contingent, social and especially moral presuppositions. This suspension of our natural orientation to reality, as we have seen, is repeatedly and consistently recommended by institutional aesthetics as the only attitude appropriate to the contemplation of art. Yet – and this point will return us to the discussion – the disengaged attitude characteristic of the suspension of the natural ethos in the disinterested *epoche* is identical to the attitude of the tourist. The tourist is content to gaze abstractly at monuments, fountains and façades for a brief time without regard for their practical purposes; for the tourist is on holiday from practical (and moral) commitments and dreads the return to the workaday responsibilities of quotidian reality.

Identifying aesthetic disinterestedness with the attitude of the tourist going native for a temporary period (like Cocker's Greek émigré among the 'common people') makes it possible to observe that it is precisely this ethos that is contested by certain contemporary artists. In an mode analogous to that of Pulp on the album *Different Class*, artists like Richard Billingham, Sarah Lucas and Mark Wallinger have presented equally acrimonious critiques of the attitude of the traditional art appreciator by developing an entirely commensurate 'splenetic' and visually 'articulate tirade' against middle-class consumer fantasies of working-class life.[9]

Paradoxically inhibited by its own official liberal ideology, the middle-class fascination with the idyll of the 'common people' and their unadorned 'lifestyle' is fulfilled by an almost exclusively media-fabricated fictional impression of the working class derived in part from the popular kitchen-sink aesthetic of the 1960s.[10] The ubiquitous popularity of entertainment-industry stylisations of ersatz post-industrial British working-class life, as seen, for instance, in TV soap operas *Coronation Street* and *EastEnders* – but also, more complexly, in critically acclaimed slice-of-life or urban neo-kitchen-sink television dramas such as *Shameless*, *The Royle Family*, *Early Doors* and *The Street* – owes itself to an inveterate, suburban middle-class desire to temporarily inhabit the social milieu of the inner-city 'lower classes'. It has already been suggested by critics that a series like *The Royle Family* epitomises 'how even representations of working-class life have been commodified in the post-industrial or postmodern era'.[11]

In their study of television, Fiske and Hartley[12] have observed that prevailing ideological relations are subject to complex encodings in mediated representations of social class. 'The latent meaning of programmes is usually encoded in the dominant code. Hence a preferred meaning emerges at the connotative level.'[13] Preferred readings particularly appropriate to the genre discussed here, I will argue, are conditioned by a perspective that assumes a shared, but always very vague and ill-defined (hence, latent), scheme of middle-class values. The latent encoding spoken of by Fiske and Hartley is often generated below the threshold of conscious awareness through formulaic framing contexts and repeated simple but effective narrative structures.

Light-hearted, non-serious: the sit-com context within which the British post-industrial working-class lifestyle genres are generally situated ultimately reduces every event depicted to the comic or the melodramatic, simultaneously restoring narrative equilibrium, resolving inner conflict and, most importantly, reinforcing ideology.[14] Such plot resolution reinforces ideology by having the effect of homogenising any serious social (or indeed moral) conflict that would threaten to alienate audiences. Issues such as social exclusion, inequality, disempowerment and class disadvantage raised incidentally by the plot are frequently resolved through what Thomas and Callanan have critiqued as the media myth of the simple life of the 'happy poor' (signifying the tendency in fictional representations to depict poor people as happy – meaning, of course, that because of their simple values they are content with their lot).[15]

Social issues are therefore not avoided in the working-class lifestyle genres; rather they are decontaminated by portraying the stable characters as fundamentally happy (or absurdly eccentric) in a manner that is intended to be experienced as sentimental and quaintly comic from the superior standpoint structurally assumed by the middle-class audience. This suggests a way of addressing concerns over whose version of working-class life we are witnessing in these genres. Such a suggestion is clearly related but ultimately takes issue with previous sociological explanations of the atmospheric 'middle-class values discerned in popular entertainment such as film or television'.[16] Such studies, according to Fiske and Hartley, recognising the increasing affluence of the traditional working-classes, highlighted their aspirations to upward mobility. Thus media representations of 'status groups higher than their own' were consumed by working-class audiences in terms of a flourishing value paradigm that could be aspired to and acquired.[17]

However accurate this thesis of the media reinforcement of social *embourgeoisement* may be, when it comes to the issue of the representation of social classes assumed to be inferior (from the standpoint of a collective acceptance of dominant middle-class liberal values as superior), it begins to attain a moral significance. It is possible to develop this suggestion further by transferring Laura Mulvey's celebrated psychoanalytic model of narrative cinema[18] to the analysis of popular media fictional representations of social class.

In essence, Mulvey's hypothesis (which should not be assumed to be unchallenged) is that a specific, preferred and gendered subject-position is constructed through the narrative structure and visual effect of the Hollywood film. An ideal spectator, assumed to be masculine, is subtly constructed, she argues, through encouraged identification with the principal (male) character. And, through his eyes, an entire erotic regime of fascinated optics is processed for the (male *and* female) audience that encodes the masculine as active looking subject and the feminine as passive looked-at object of 'male desire'.[19]

In an equivalent manner, popular media representations of the working class are based on the assumption that the audience for such genres, as the *embourgeoisement* thesis proposes, is – or aspires to be – middle class, or, more importantly, shares non-specific middle-class values. An analysis of the narrative strategies and visual forms associated with genres that feature this version of working-class life will reveal a preferred subject-position that presupposes a middle-class perspective by acknowledging the assumed superiority of liberalist values.

I would argue, beyond Mulvey's account, that the version of the working class that we witness is an imaginary fabrication, an averaging-out of middle-class preconceptions, sentimental desires and patronising prejudices situated in a once-popular aesthetic form (the kitchen-sink drama). Such a working class no longer exists – and, needless to say, perhaps never did.[20]

Things are more complex than this. The desire of the social tourist to inhabit another world with distanced impunity is less important to media-reinforced middle-class fantasies of the working class than the longing to escape from *their* social habitus, to be liberated from the straitjacket of liberal morality, if only for a fugitive hour of imaginative abandon. And this is the key to these genres, for it determines – more than any strategic, commercially successful narrative structure – the pleasure the genres deliver. This is the fantasy indulged by the media-fabricated image of the working class, repackaged as a lifestyle choice for the consumption of middle-class media tourists. From the security of their modular Semi-D, the tourist-viewer is enabled at once to experience vicariously, temporarily, and via the hallucinogenic vehicle of television, the visceral amorality of the urban under classes who 'dance and drink and screw because there's nothing else to do'. In 'Common People', therefore, Jarvis Cocker critically and economically identifies a significant social and *moral* phenomenon when he diagnoses the middle-class envy of (ironically, a particular ideological middle-class fabrication of) working-class life.

Courtauld Institute art historian Julian Stallabrass has indicated a structural continuity between this media-reinforced middle-class escape fantasy and the romantic pastoral fancy. In the case of the contemporary British urban pastoral, he argues, 'simple rural folk enjoying rustic pleasures have become replaced by the characters of the inner city, similarly devoted in middle-class fantasy to the joys of politically incorrect humour, the circulation of obscenities, the joys of violence, crime and vandalism, carefree sexual encounters and drug-taking.'[21]

Despite the cogency (as well as the enviable political and social acuity) of his analysis of this phenomenon, Stallabrass's identification of the work of British artist Richard Billingham as characteristic of this contemporary pastoral fantasy is tendentious and, as the following discussion of the artist's work will demonstrate, quite dubious.

In 1996, Billingham published *Ray's a Laugh*, a portfolio of photographs documenting – without written commentary – his family life in a claustrophobic West Midlands British council flat. In this series of disquieting images, the idyll of British working-class life that has, as claimed, been largely manufactured by a cynical entertainment industry to indulge middle-class fantasies is, image by image, subjected to systematic attrition.

Jim Lewis's account is worth quoting for the descriptive economy in which it captures Billingham's extraordinary book.

> His primary subject is his father, Ray, an everyday alcoholic who rarely leaves the house; instead he stays in and drinks home brew, puttering around while wearing a series of drunkard's expressions: delighted, dazed, about six inches short of dead. Aside from Ray there's a behemoth mother, a brother who comes and goes peripherally, a dog, and a cat.[22]

Viewing the images in *Ray's a Laugh* does raise legitimate concerns that they encourage the adoption of the voyeuristic perspective we have associated with the tourist (Stallabrass's critique, for instance, makes an indirect reference to 'middle-class porn'); but in actual fact, the connotations of the photographs suggest, as Stallabrass is well aware, that the photographer is himself implicated as an integral and indispensable part of the social environment that his images document.

This is signified most obviously by the deliberate eschewing of (highly putative in any case) formal photographic techniques (composition, framing, lighting etc.) that would be, in Billingham, equivalent to the restoration of narrative equilibrium in the TV drama (and disinterested contemplation in the aesthetic context). Thus, the general domestic catastrophe that commentators claim is so cruelly (and crudely) testified to in the photographs – the abject squalor, the sporadic violence, the grunge, tack and filth – is infused with an unmistakable sympathy, a sense of respect and sometimes even tenderness,

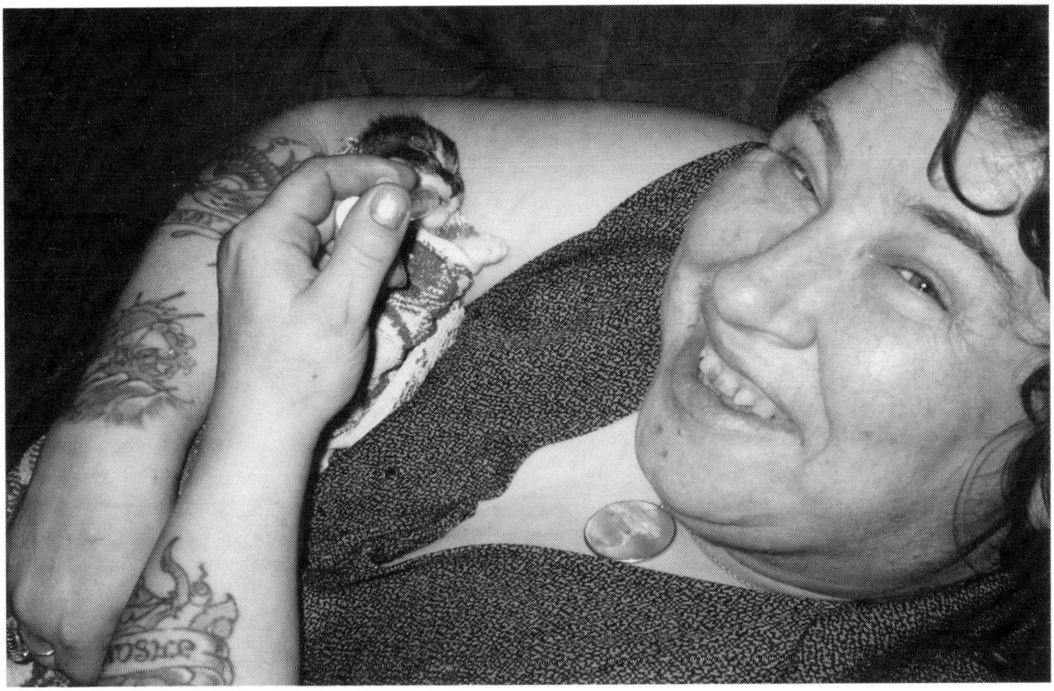

1. Richard Billingham, *Ray's A Laugh (Untitled)*, 1993–5
Colour photograph on aluminium
Courtesy Anthony Reynolds Gallery (London)

something that again has not been overlooked by commentators. For instance, one picture of Elizabeth (Billingham's mother) shows her in maternal circumstance, weaning a blind newborn kitten with a syringe of milk: cradling the tiny creature in her huge tattooed arms, she looks up at the photographer and laughs, clearly enjoying the moment.

This sympathetic mode is, however, also disturbingly offset, it has to be admitted, by images of a morally disquieting nature. Lewis draws our attention to the perplexing image of Ray crashed out on the lavatory floor right beside the freshly stained toilet bowl. He comments: 'one might notice that Billingham chose to photograph the old man and then publish the photograph, rather than immediately picking him up and cleaning him off. One might ask why he chose to do that, and what it implies.'[23] We will return to this question. For now, I want to consider the work of Billingham by situating it in relation to the critique of the disinterested attitude undertaken previously.

Even a superficial consideration of the photographs published in *Ray's a Laugh* can successfully distinguish the work from the usual entertainment

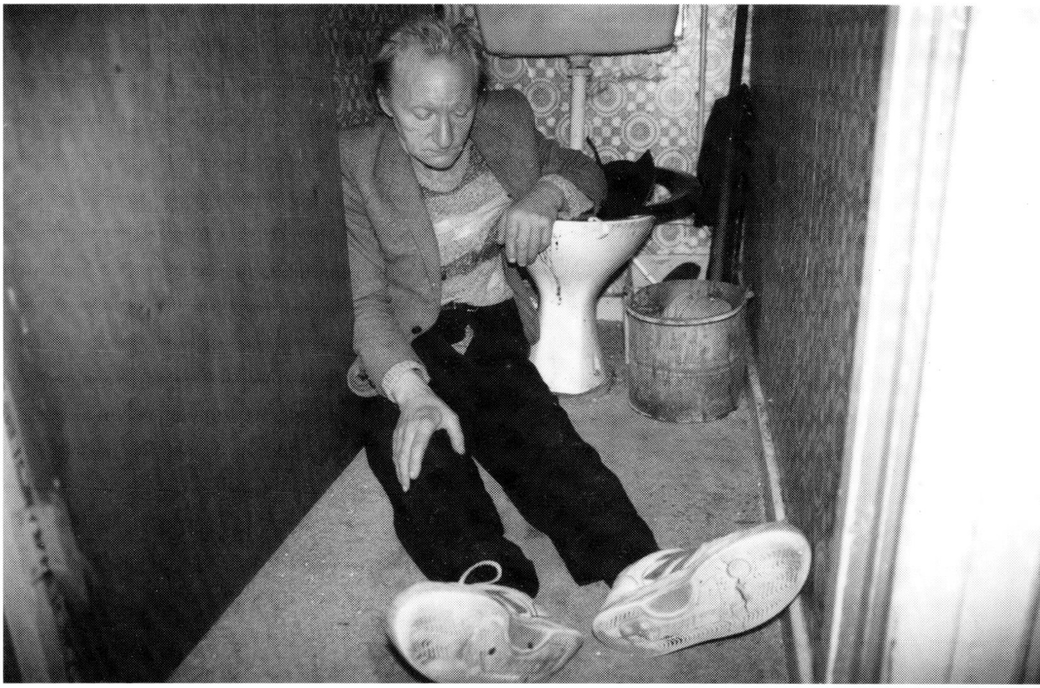

2. Richard Billingham, *Ray's A Laugh (Untitled)*, 1993–5
Colour photograph on aluminium
Courtesy Anthony Reynolds Gallery (London)

industry mediations of working-class life: no effort is made to glamorise the Billingham family's lifestyle (even according to a reactionary aesthetic of the heroin-chic *Trainspotting* variety). Despite the nonsensical efforts of Stallabrass to argue that the images are carefully and formally constructed (and should therefore – according to the simplistic opposition between authenticity and construction that Stallabrass's critique of contemporary art relies on – be considered in effect *fictional*), *Ray's a Laugh* is essentially unedited documentary footage. Incorrigible art historian Stallabrass cannot bring himself to believe that the formal ineptness of the photographs can be anything other than consciously contrived; his work is replete, he says, with 'signs of authenticity', the result of Billingham's 'calculating design'.[24]

As Lewis points out, on the contrary: 'Almost every rule of photography is badly broken: pictures are out of focus, over-exposed, printed with a grain so visible that the image beneath is almost completely obscured. Half of them are absurdly framed . . .'[25] Billingham's work is *merely*, not *conspiratorially*, substandard. His snaps are, Lewis continues, 'as formally bad as my own';

they are 'marred by red-eyed subjects, with the focus fixed on some corner of furniture when the main image is blurred, with the glare of the flash reflected in a window'.[26] He concludes of the most formally botched efforts in the series that Billingham must have been half-cut on Ray's homebrew himself when they were taken. How can it be that art so formally substandard can yet be so artistically compelling? Lewis addresses this conundrum with reference to the provision of fucking up: 'Such is the aesthetic of our times: there is a desire in effect, almost a policy, of fucking up so completely, yet with such confidence and control, that one's medium expands.'[27] And Billingham, he says, is 'better at fucking up than any [other] photographer'.[28]

However, the reason why his work is so formally bad, so absolutely 'fucked up', is not *only* due to the artist's rejection of formal conventions; it is therefore not *completely* captured by the destructive desire to subvert all aesthetic formality. Rather the key to the formal awkwardness is to be found in Billingham's desire to render the medium as transparent as possible, to reduce the anaesthetising effects of form and make the images more immediate, more visceral, and more violent.

'Looking at the work again and again,' Lewis remarks, 'I've found myself feeling an almost physical pain.'[29] Clearly, to defend the artistic value of this work with reference to its 'exquisite formal properties' or its aesthetic qualities (as defenders of the problematic content of the photographic work of Robert Mapplethorpe and Andres Serrano have done) is quite redundant: the work does not possess any conventional aesthetic qualities. In fact, such possible aesthetic defences are rendered doubly implausible because Billingham's work actively undermines precisely these aesthetic conventions. It is not possible to experience such formally fucked-up work aesthetically, primarily because it is impossible to adopt the attitude of disinterested contemplation in the face of – to remain emotionally distanced from – the content of such work.

And yet, here's the paradox: this is precisely the reason why his work is artistically significant. Billingham's work resists the recommendation of objective or impartial looking, challenges the suspension of the natural attitude and invalidates the adoption of a form of perception other than our normal outlook. To look at these images is to feel something for the situation and people in it that it is morally right to feel: concern, compassion, sympathy, pity, shame, guilt – to the point indeed of physical pain in Lewis's case.

Yet, despite what was claimed above, Billingham's imagery is not entirely incommensurable with media-generated stereotypy. His work *does* draw, perhaps unconsciously, on the conventions of the entertainment industry semiotic of working-class life. I will argue, though, that it only does this to undermine this semiotic more thoroughly, and more profoundly. Perhaps years of artist and audience introjection of such semiotic conventions and media stereotypy makes it futile to subvert them directly. In any case, as is by now well documented, any representation is destined to be interpreted, *consumed*, according to habitually inured, already-read, still-born representational codes. However, what is artistically compelling about Billingham's work is the way in which the artist has exploited these codes and semiotic conventions to critique the very voyeuristic tourist structure on which such codes and conventions are founded. We are invited to become tourists by Billingham's work, invited to take a temporary tour around an unfamiliar yet media-familiar social stratum. And the codes we engage to experience images like this are already firmly, transcendentally, in place; we may approach his work, for instance, the way we would approach a carefully edited and always tendentious documentary as it guides us toward its narrative closure. Billingham's work may appear to resemble the kind of cultural products that we are incessantly offered to consume with complete impunity, with ethical amnesty.

This is the difference: *it isn't*. His work is categorically different. Yes, Billingham may invite us to adopt the attitude of the cultural tourist. When we do, however, we are shocked to find ourselves morally uncomfortable with the role: for he makes us aware of having adopted a cold, invasive, ultimately unethical approach to his family, to his life, to *him*. And thus, ultimately, we find ourselves shocked into questioning the distance associated with the disengaged attitude we are conventionally encouraged to adopt by orthodox aesthetics. Unlike the work of American photographer Diane Arbus, for instance – whose work has been criticised for degrading her subjects and encouraging the spectator to gaze with sideshow impunity at the 'freaks'[30] they would be ashamed to stare at in reality – Billingham, on the contrary, makes the viewer ashamed for looking, ashamed for trying to suspend the natural attitude, ashamed for assuming the ethical immunity of the cultural tourist. My point here is that this reaction is produced by his work, the sense of *shame* generated by his work is actually structural to it.

Susan Sontag describes Arbus's acceptance of the appalling in her work as 'sinister'.[31] For, she says, 'it is based on distance, on privilege, on a feeling that what the viewer is asked to look at is really *other*.'[32] But, as James Lingwood suggested to Billingham, his work is a document of his relations with his family: in the context of his family, he is *there*; he is one of the Billinghams – the one who takes the photos. He is the artist. Because, despite the intensive scrutiny of his work, Billingham does not alienate his family or estrange them by aesthetic mediation; Ray, Liz and Jason (and domestic animals) are not reduced to aesthetic form, nor are they reduced to entertainment industry stereotypes. It is in fact the viewers who, in attempting to reduce his imagery to such media-generated generic codes (because they intuitively believe that this is what they are supposed to do), are ashamed when they realise that, having prompted this reduction, the photographs ultimately treat it with contempt.

Therefore I would argue that, unlike the aesthetic tendency to, in Sontag's words, 'suppress, or at least reduce, moral and sensory queasiness',[33] Billingham's work precisely intensifies moral and sensory queasiness by shocking and embarrassing us for looking at his family in that way, for approaching his family and home with the repulsive attitude of the cultural tourist. His work makes us uncomfortably conscious of the fact that, as someone disengaged practically from a culture temporarily inhabited and, enjoying moral immunity from the lives of the indigenous population, everybody *hates* a tourist.

The Ethical Evaluation of Art: Autonomism versus Moralism

To propose that moral inquiry may be relevant to the evaluation of art is to engage the terms of an internecine debate in contemporary philosophical aesthetics. In *Values of Art*, a major study of orthodox aesthetics, Malcolm Budd isolates, as one of the fundamental principles associated with the field, the presupposition that any reaction to art should be disengaged from whatever moral position it may involve.[34] This principle, with which we are by now over-familiar, clearly goes hand in glove with the related dogma of aesthetic disinterestedness I have put in question above; it suggests that whatever ethical status a work of art may possess is entirely irrelevant to its aesthetic significance. Yet, as analysis of Billingham's work has demonstrated, certain kinds of art (particularly, but not exclusively, contemporary transgressive art) are artistically interesting and yet remain problematic precisely because, to use Noël Carroll's phrase, 'such art engages the moral life of its audience'.[35]

Thus, it is obvious that (not all but certainly some) works of art evidently do involve the activation of moral responses. And, as we have already demonstrated, and will proceed to consider at some length, it is philosophically untenable to separate the *ethical* aspects of morally transgressive art from its *aesthetic* aspects; for this means ignoring its most artistically significant characteristics. It also means suppressing the very aspects that make such works transgressive in the first place.

Now, in the philosophy of art there are at least two important ways in which the relationship between aesthetic value and moral value has been modelled.[36] On the one hand, there are those philosophers of art (habitually of a formalist stripe) convinced that the spheres of aesthetic value and moral value are *absolutely distinct*, necessarily separate and independent axiological dimensions; and, if there is any significant relationship between them, it is simply not relevant to the artistic merits (or demerits) of any individual work that is evaluated.

This partition of artistic and moral value, which, since R.W. Beardsmore's[37] characterisation, has become standardised under the rubric of *autonomism*, basically renders all art indemnified from evaluation in moral terms. Beardsmore situates the first clear articulation of this view in Oscar Wilde's proposition that 'the critic should be able to recognise that the sphere of art and the sphere of ethics are absolutely distinct and separate.'[38] Beardsmore's autonomist, *à la* Wilde's aesthete, will therefore canvass the absolutist thesis that moral and aesthetic value always correspond to two completely incommensurable modes of human experience. According to this view, each domain, art and ethics, is considered to possess its own unique and irreducible criteria of evaluation; and it is simply inappropriate to apply the criteria associated with ethical evaluation to art. To do so is somehow to erode the intrinsic significance of art and risk compromising the exclusivity of the aesthetic experience.

The term autonomism captures the tendency to maintain a theoretical and normative commitment to the view that moral value is – and should remain – necessarily distinct from aesthetic value. It is imperative for the autonomist that the domain of the aesthetic remains hermetically isolated from issues of moral concern; but this is argued for even in those artistic instances *where morality may appear relevant* to the complete aesthetic evaluation of the artwork under consideration. Yet, because it fails adequately to acknowledge or account for works of art that possess ethical significance, autonomism, it seems, is compelled to treat any works that do as hybrid deviations, as art mutations that cannot be considered purely artistic.

Defenders of aesthetic autonomy[39] characteristically advocate the separatist thesis that theoretically maintains an absolute axiological partition between aesthetic value and morality; typically, this view entails a more or less explicit commitment to the identification of aesthetic value with artistic form. Thus aesthetic value will be found to consist in 'a work's internal, formal, organic character, upon its inner system of relations, upon its structure and its style, and not upon the morality it is presumed to recommend'.[40] All the salient features associated with the doctrine of autonomy are captured succinctly by Curtis Brown when he recommends that art objects

> *should* be studied and appreciated as objects in their own right, without regard to the causes of their production, their historical context, their effects on an audience, or even their relation to the (rest of the) real world, and, moreover, that the contemplation or study of artworks should appeal *only* to some of the properties of the artwork, namely, its aesthetic properties – as opposed especially to its moral properties . . . [41]

In this prescriptive manner, autonomism raises the antithesis of aesthetic value and moral value to a structural level by conveniently mapping its terms onto the ready-made dualism of form and content. Accordingly, anything aesthetic in the art object will be identified with *form*, while everything un-aesthetic will remain, by tacit opposition, associated with *content*. Ultimately, the effect of such an artificial cartography is to expatriate artistic content, and especially morality, from the realm of the truly, purely, aesthetic. We could put this in another, less salubrious and more overtly moralistic way – form: *good*, content: *bad*.

However, the autonomist commitment to aesthetic value contradicts recent tendencies in art practice, especially those that, as we have seen, aggressively challenge exactly these arbitrary ideological divisions. To discuss contemporary art without reference to its causes of production, its historical context, its audience effects or its relation to the rest of the real world, reveals a serious misunderstanding of its aesthetic significance. For, according to the autonomist's formal recommendations, the work of an artist like Billingham (who 'fucks up' form) cannot be considered artistically significant. Yet contemplation of transgressive art practices will find that the features proscribed by the autonomist are the very properties that are responsible for the artistic significance of Billingham's work. As claimed, such art practices actually target the ideology of aesthetic autonomy by focusing transgressive attention precisely on conceptual oppositions such as art/morality as well as on the identification of aesthetic value with form.

Therefore, I shall enquire: if art practice engages so vividly with precisely the elements proscribed by autonomism, how is it possible to maintain that aesthetics continue to evaluate art in isolation from them? If it can be shown, contra the autonomist model, that the moral value of at least some profound and compelling works of art is inseparable from aesthetic value, then, in such – admittedly marginal, yet for just that reason, exceptional – artworks, it becomes critically necessary to evaluate them from an ethical perspective. Far from a category error, as Carroll suggests, transgressive art 'engages the moral understanding and can be assessed in terms of the efficacy of that engagement'.[42]

In recognition of the intertwinement of value dimensions in certain art objects, there is a branch of the philosophy of art committed to the view that moral value and aesthetic value are necessarily related. Most commentaries cite David Hume as the progenitor of this view. Hume's 'Of the Standard of Taste' (1757)[43] incorporates the classic formulation of aesthetic moralism: in a work of art that conflicts with ethical sensibility or that provokes moral indignation by describing 'vicious manners' in the absence of their 'being marked with the proper characters of blame and disapprobation', Hume says, 'this must be allowed to disfigure the [art], and to be a real [aesthetic] deformity.'[44]

In a significant contribution to this debate, Daniel Jacobson has labelled the offspring of views associated with this perspective *Humean* moralism, and has finessed its central principle: 'Moral defects in a work of art are aesthetic flaws; insofar as they are present, the work's aesthetic value is diminished.'[45] Diametrically opposed to autonomism, Humean moralism can be characterised negatively as rejecting the absolutist thesis that 'moral defects are irrelevant to a work's aesthetic value.'[46] Moralism argues the converse of this thesis, namely that the morality of art has a direct impact on its aesthetic value. However, it derives from this argument an absolutist thesis of its own: the morally defective work is *inevitably* aesthetically flawed as a direct consequence of this.

Concerned that moralism is on the increase in the philosophy of art, Jacobson cites the work of at least three committed contemporary proponents of this view.[47] Among them, it is Berys Gaut who, for Jacobson, provides the most cogently argued defence of Humean moralism in the modern context. Gaut proposes that because artistic creation involves the manifestation of an attitude, ethical evaluation is an entirely relevant analytical procedure for the complete aesthetic estimation of the work of art.[48] He argues that this hypothesis leads inevitably to the normative claim that, should a particular work of art manifest an attitude considered to be deeply offensive (because it conflicts with conventional ethical standards), and that is therefore found to be morally repugnant, the work should be judged to be aesthetically prejudiced as a result. In so far, therefore, as morally transgressive art manifests any ethically questionable attitudes, it will be found, according to Gaut's ethicist thesis, to be necessarily aesthetically flawed.

A problem case such as Vladimir Nabokov's celebrated novel *Lolita* puts the moralist's hypothesis under severe strain. Written in a formally exquisite, infinitesimally wrought, picturesque and richly allusive prose, *Lolita* is the diary of an opportunistic and unrepentant paedophile. Equally beautiful and disgusting, therefore, the novel constitutes, and was intended by Nabokov to constitute, a sublime artistic paradox: 'we find ourselves repelled by [Humbert Humbert] and his desires but also transfixed and transported,' Colin McGinn confirms.[49] *Lolita* has 'completely bamboozled our habitual reactions to good and evil, the ugly and beautiful'. It is a work of both 'aesthetic and moral trespasses. What is in effect', McGinn concludes, 'child sexual abuse is rendered in terms of high poetry.'[50] Finding himself in the impossible position of having to condemn Nabokov's ethically reprehensible yet aesthetically beautiful novel as artistically flawed – or to agree to assume the schizoid state he had previously argued was psychologically dysfunctional to maintain – artistic transgression (in the sense of a deliberate intention to subvert aesthetic value by moral value) plays havoc with the moralist's arguments.

Noël Carroll's already-mentioned critique of autonomism also qualifies as a version of moralism for Jacobson; it comprises a defence of Hume's thesis in negotiated form. Qualified as 'moderate', Carroll's moralism hopes to establish a kind of dialectical 'third way' that avoids both the myopic suppression of content associated with aesthetic formalism and the deterministic dangers inherent in Humean moralism (which can easily resemble an egregious philistinism when applied to canonical art that conflicts with the critic's moral standards). Carroll moderates the central principle of moralism to the thesis that in cases where moral value *is* significant to a work of art, it is therefore also relevant to the aesthetic value of that work. He contends that the morality of a given work is therefore response-dependent; that is, the moral value of art is established by the response of the viewer to the interpreted intention of the artist. This pro-intentional view enables him to argue, like Gaut, that if a work fails to invoke the moral response intended by its producer, this constitutes 'a failure in the design of the work, and, therefore, is an aesthetic failure'.[51]

The example he uses to illustrate this thesis is instructive. Bret Easton Ellis's novel *American Psycho* is aesthetically compromised, he argues, because the author's intention that the work be interpreted as a satirical critique of 1980s yuppie culture and Reaganomics failed aesthetically because readers were unable to reprocess the lurid and baroque descriptions of the protagonist's serial murders in ironically detached satirical terms. It was not possible, Carroll argues, to get beyond the affective level of the 'clinically meticulous dismemberments' to a level of critically informed, second-level, ironic reflection. Thus, 'a great many of the readers of *American Psycho* reacted to the flawed moral understanding of [the novel], and rejected it aesthetically.'[52] The failure to inspire the moral response that was intended by the artist therefore has a negative impact on the artistic value of the work. 'Thus, an artist whose work depends upon a certain moral response from the audience, but who has proffered a work that defies moral understanding, makes a structural, or as they say, aesthetic error.'[53]

In such instances where moral and aesthetic values appear inextricably alloyed, according to Carroll, it is entirely appropriate to subject an artwork to ethical analysis; indeed, to evaluate the work in moral terms is *pari passu* to pass aesthetic judgement on it. Carroll's 'moderate moralism' therefore maintains that the aesthetic value of a work of art is index-linked to its moral value but *only if the moral constitution of the work is relevant to its artistic condition*; that is, if an ethical problem is identified in the artwork by a 'morally sensitive' viewer, then, depending on the nature of the problem (whether it constitutes, for instance, a serious moral violation), this will be found potentially to compromise the aesthetic value of the work.

A Difficult Case: Marc Quinn and Alison Lapper

The applicative potential of the ethical analysis of art can be examined by considering a recent case of controversial public art. In 2003, in response to a call for proposals to suggest a monument for the fourth plinth in London's Trafalgar Square, Marc Quinn submitted to install his sculpture of a disabled female nude on the vacant site.[54] Requested by the commissioning committee to tender a small-scale maquette of his intended sculpture, Quinn's proposal was accepted in 2004.

As part of a series of sculptures of people with disabilities, Quinn had previously cast the body of fellow artist Alison Lapper in 1999[55] (then in the final trimester of her pregnancy), and the artist's proposal for Trafalgar Square involved scaling up the original life-size piece to monumental scale in proportion to the plinth; he made arrangements to have it sculpted by craftsmen from a single block of white Alpine marble in a studio in Pietrasanta, Italy. *Alison Lapper Pregnant* (2005) is 3.5 metres in height and weighs 12 tonnes. It took over a year to create (three months to locate the block and ten to sculpt it). Installed in the site on 15 September 2005, and supposed to remain on the fourth plinth for a term of fifteen months, the sculpture remained in situ until October 2007.[56]

Born in 1965, Lapper suffers from a condition known medically as *phocomelia*, a congenital chromosomal deformity affecting in-utero limb development, which left her without arms and with diminutive legs. Upon delivery, doctors advised her mother to give Alison up to institutional care. She relates how her mother never saw her but was given to believe that her baby also suffered severe mental disability and would not survive very long: 'she thought I was a monster . . . she was allowed to believe that.'[57] Alison spent her childhood and adolescent years in a residential home among other children suffering from a range of physical and mental disabilities. Despite these adverse conditions, and what we can only imagine she had to endure as a result of her disability, she went on to study art, graduating from Brighton University with a first-class honours degree in Fine Art in 1986.

Lapper's mobility, as for many people with disabilities, depends on wheelchair assistance (her access to public spaces, as well as her home, is made possible only through assistive ergonomic technology). Needless to say, she finds everyday tasks that able-bodied people take for granted – and mostly aren't even aware of – extremely demanding. Life, for Lapper, as for many other disabled people, has been a constant struggle to overcome dependency and social stigmatisation. 'I'm considered to be ugly and grotesque and deformed . . . And I've heard myself described as these things.'[58] She has, however, proved to be highly adaptive, successfully overcoming the associated

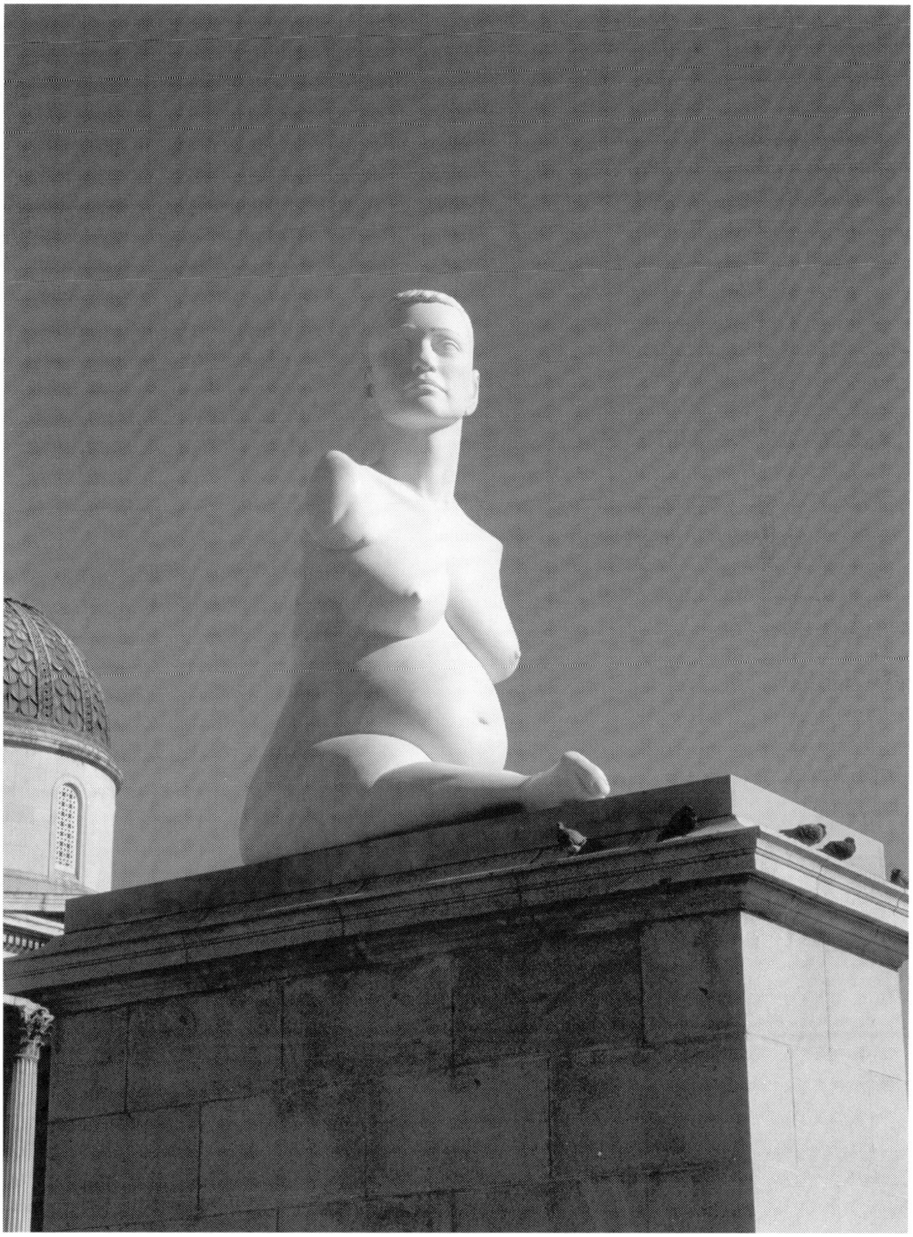

3. Marc Quinn, *Alison Lapper Pregnant*, 2005
Marble, 139 3/4 x 71 1/16 x 102 3/8 in (355 x 180.5 x 260 cm)
Photo: Marc Quinn Studio. Courtesy Jay Jopling/ White Cube (London)

difficulties of her disability, and enjoying an independent and productive life. She lives in London with her son Parys. I fill in this background to demonstrate that, preparatory to her further achievements, it is itself already a remarkable achievement for Lapper to assert and sustain the kind of independent existence the able-bodied majority treats as a basic entitlement.

High-profile contemporary British artist Marc Quinn came to the attention of the art world in the early 1990s with a cycle of morbidly fascinating introspective studies. *Self* (1991), a life-mask cast in his own blood became the leitmotif of his project when it was shown to critical acclaim in the 1997 *Sensation* exhibition (and the New York show two years later).[59]

A refrigeration system is necessary to sustain the solidity of Quinn's transfused likeness. To prevent haemorrhage, the cast must be coated in silicone and cryogenically maintained at a constant -20°C. Atop its stainless-steel appliance, protected behind a transparent showcase, although scabbed, deeply fissured and peeling, Quinn's haematoma seems alive but asleep – a dormant 'brain-in-a-vat' awaiting reanimation.[60] The artist apparently makes a new one every five years, arranging to have nine pints of blood extracted (over a nine-month period) for the purpose.

4. **Marc Quinn, *Self*, 2001**
Blood (artist's), stainless steel, perspex and refrigeration equipment
$80\,^{11}/_{16} \times 25\,^{9}/_{16} \times 25\,^{9}/_{16}$ in (205 x 65 x 65 cm)
Photo: Stephen White. Courtesy Jay Jopling/ White Cube (London)

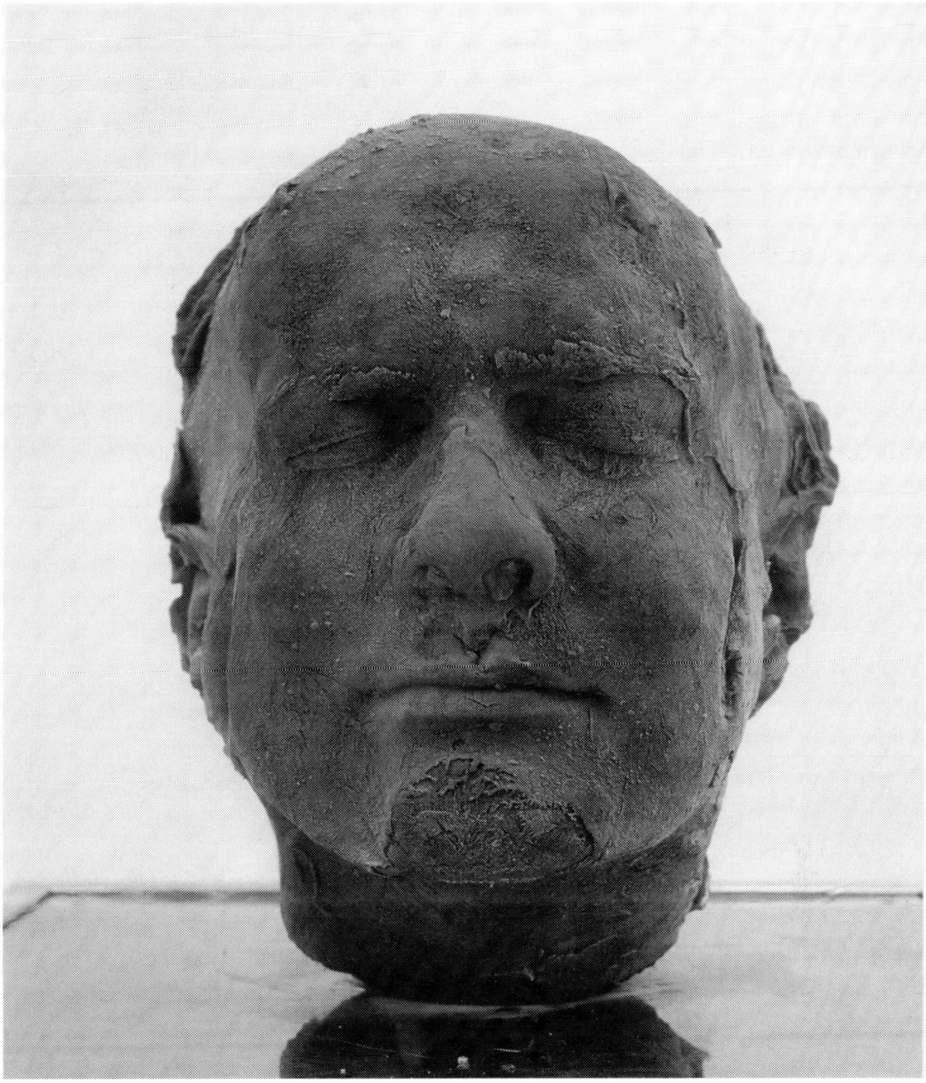

5. Marc Quinn, *Self* (detail), 2001
Blood (artist's), stainless steel, perspex and refrigeration equipment
80 11/16 x 25 9/16 x 25 9/16 in (205 x 65 x 65 cm)
Photo: Stephen White. Courtesy Jay Jopling/ White Cube (London)

In general, Quinn's work thematises the human condition as encountered in the state of embodiment and the concomitant consciousness of mortality: hence the entropic physicality and imperfection of the non-traditional substances he relies on to reify his existential concerns. However, I want to emphasise another aspect of his work that is important for the present context. Quinn's work can be considered a dramatisation of the metaphysical agonism between interior experience and exterior appearance; his practice enacts a conflict between mental and physical aspects of the self. His post-*Self* sculptures attempt to dramatise the experience of this mind–body conflict by expressing it physically on material extrusions of his own body.

His work is paradigmatically transgressive in that its resultant ugliness contravenes conventional aesthetic principles of beauty and formal integrity. Contorted, distended and excoriated, twisted by the anatomy of pain, his sculptures express emotional anguish in physical form, and can be considered as the infliction of inadequately sublimated self-harm. In this context, Will Self correctly observes that Quinn's work is a manifestation of disgust.[61] He renders his own unremarkably average body grotesque either by sub-violent physical manipulation or by the abject[62] nature of the materials he uses – a project motivated, Self suggests, by a kind of self-disgust. 'The body's inside', Kristeva's analysis of the role of abjection in the crises of personal identity maintains, 'shows up in order to compensate for the collapse of the border between the inside and the outside.'[63] This explains Quinn's psychosomatic concentration on sites of transgression where the physical borders that differentiate the inside from the exterior are breached or permeated. Precisely because they signify ambiguous sites where the distinction between interior and surface is weakened or damaged, body fluids and faecal matter (which Quinn has explored as sculptural materials) become, Kristeva suggests, semiotic indexes of 'repugnance, disgust, abjection'.[64] Because their ontological status is rendered ambiguous when excreted, such substances become pregnant with phobic power. 'Urine, blood, sperm, excrement then show up in order to reassure a subject who is lacking its "own and clean self".'[65]

In this context, Quinn's transition to the exploration of his concerns on other people in 1999 can be considered an artistic breakthrough. When he turned to the body of the other (in the strong political sense of that term, i.e., the Other) he cast volunteers – people with disabilities – people who, unlike Quinn himself, had no need to make their bodies appear ugly or grotesque, for they lived with their specious 'abnormalities' exposed or, indeed, inscribed inescapably as an exterior part of their own embodiment. Disturbingly, Kristeva postulates that such a transition to the symbolic Other often appears as a stage in the psychodynamic economy of abjection where the significance attached to the phobic object is therapeutically displaced onto another person and thus 'the abject [is transformed] into the site of the Other.'[66] Is this what happened with Quinn? In the present context, I shall merely emphasise that the figures of his series of people with disabilities, in complete contrast to his previous work, are modelled in the classical idiom. Tailored to the perfect standards of traditional Hellenic form, Quinn's figures are colourless, featureless and coldly, generically, figurative. In November 1999, a cast of Alison Lapper's body was made for the ninth sculpture in this series. And it was with his proposal to erect a monumental version of this sculpture[67] on the Trafalgar Square site that Quinn secured the fourth plinth commission.

'No group in society', moral philosopher Martha Nussbaum observes, 'has been so painfully stigmatised as people with physical and mental disabilities.'[68] Quoting Goffman, she claims that for those marked out and ostracised because of an overt physical disability, the stigma is made into the defining feature of the person. An entire personality – or identity – is thereby reduced to the feature of impairment, such that, under the gaze of the able-bodied majority, the disabled 'person's full humanity' is compromised and our shared human condition 'cannot come into focus'.[69]

Nussbaum argues that this tendency is irrational for, from a wider vantage point, it is possible to ask: who can confidently claim complete physical 'normality'? According to the hegemonic ideal of perfection, an ideal that we have already seen Orlan accuse of being unachievable in reality, everyone fails (or will inevitably fail when the stigmata of age set in) to measure up to that particular standard. 'Human beings are in general disabled: mortal, weak-eyed, weak-kneed, with terrible backs and necks, short memories and so forth.'[70] For many citizens, provision of the assistance necessary for their access to the public world has not been made because certain disabilities are considered uncommon or abnormal by utilitarian majority consensus. More alarmingly, disability is increasingly stigmatised as a result of what Nussbaum diagnoses as a particularly American obsession with 'aesthetic' physical perfection that carries micro-god-like connotations of 'self-sufficiency, competence and (the fiction of) invulnerability'.[71] However, Nussbaum goes on to suggest that this pseudo-ideology of aesthetic perfection is in reality a dolled-up *hegemony of the average*, deployed to keep those with atypical disabilities out of sight. And out of mind.

This suggestion leads to the disquieting implication that it is in fact our own all too human vulnerability – the vulnerability of the normal – that we attempt to conceal from ourselves by forcing those with disabilities outside the pale of an arbitrary normality. People with disabilities – through non-provision of assistance or through shame – are more than excluded, they are concealed from (public) view by what Jenny Morris calls the 'tyranny of perfection'.[72] She comments: 'Such false ideas of perfection and defect have as their consequence the creation of two worlds: the public world of the ordinary citizen and the world of people with disabilities, who are implicitly held to have no right to inhabit the public world.'[73]

Marc Quinn's sculptural project, in a similar mode to Orlan, can be construed as an aesthetically motivated attempt to intervene in this political/ethical debate. His work, by engaging with this theme, constitutes an on-going visual argument to render people with disabilities visible by publicly revealing their existence; his work metaphorically insists on their rightful place in social discourse. He confronts the idealised 'normal', aesthetically conditioned, tyranny of perfection with the reality of disability.

To place his sculpture of Lapper in such a significant public location is precisely to argue, by way of the site-specificity of the work, for the rights of people with disabilities to be included in the social contract, to be provided with access to the public realm, to be treated as valuable citizens, to be provided with the assistance that makes possible their participation and involvement in social and cultural life, and to be acknowledged without prejudice or discrimination. Trafalgar Square is the centre of the *polis* – the navel of the political culture of the British nation. As Will Self points out, it is:

> The nexus between the power of the military and the power of the state and the power of the crown . . . which makes it an enormously significant site. So a statue of Alison Lapper at that point on the fourth plinth becomes, to my way of thinking, deeply subversive.[74]

What, therefore, if anything, is ethically problematic about Quinn's sculpture? Aside from some unenlightened (and sometimes vicious) public reaction to the project (which I will not consider for this evaluation), is there any moral issue here? A certain moral uneasiness is occasioned by the worry that the artist may have used Lapper's body – and by extension, people with disabilities – as a conduit for his own personal aesthetic programme. If this is the case, if Lapper has been treated as an instrument or objectified in the realisation of Quinn's artistic agenda (to make politically charged, confrontational, cutting-edge contemporary art that transgresses the aesthetics of beauty), then this may be considered to violate one of the most venerable ethical principles of moral philosophy, namely, the Kantian categorical imperative.[75]

Kant considered the following injunction to represent the categorical imperative: 'Act in such a way', he puts it, 'that you always treat humanity, whether in your own person or in the person of any other, never simply as a means, but always at the same time as an end.'[76] And as a practical rendering of the kind of abstract behavioural self-surveillance associated fairly with the imperative, Kant recommends the following reformulation: it is *always* unethical to treat the other in Machiavellian mode as a means to further one's own ends.[77] In other words, my obligation to other people is to ensure that I respect them unconditionally as ends. What Kant intends by the strange locution 'end' is that every person ought to be respected as valuable *in their own right*. In my relationships with others, it is morally necessary to see beyond their useful status for furthering any motive I might entertain.[78] To consider something valuable as a means, according to Downie and Telfer's study of respect, on the other hand, 'is to regard it as valuable merely for what we can get out of it'.[79] Something that is considered not solely as a *means* but as an *end* in the Kantian sense is, rather, 'valuable in itself'.[80] The categorical imperative is meant to demonstrate that this is how we *should* regard persons: we ought to treat others as valuable in themselves, for we can recognise with justifiable resentment when we are treated as conduits for the satisfaction of another's aims. This kind of relationship, whatever the circumstances (even in the case of a masochist who desires to be treated as a means) Kant suggests, is morally destructive to both parties. Thus Downie and Telfer argue that the attitude of respect for others encapsulated in Kant's principle is '*morally* basic'.[81]

As conscious, autonomous, goal-directed, and sensitive emotional agents, we are all motivated by interests, desires and projects – or, in Kant's idiom, ends. Seeing these as intrinsic to who we are, we care (sometimes passionately, sometimes jealously) about these ends, often considering them, at the limit, constitutive of personal identity. An essential formative phase of moral understanding is the extension of this self-knowledge in the recognition that everyone possesses their own personal ends and that these may sometimes conflict with ours. If our personal ends are obstructed, we feel hurt; if we obstruct someone else's, we should therefore, according to Kant, feel guilty.

With Kant's principle, the intrinsic value of every person – including what I may reasonably request of others – is thus established, respected and morally protected. The intrinsic nature of this value Kant encapsulates with the charged noun, *dignity*.[82] This marks the inviolable value embodied in each person. Dignity is what makes each individual unique and 'irreplaceable' and it is what demands our respect.[83] The respect demanded by the acknowledgement of human dignity, as exemplified in every individual person, in this sense therefore forms the basis of our moral obligation to others. Indeed, this respect for others through 'active sympathy' has been characterised as 'the ideal moral attitude'.[84] Respect for others may, as Richard Norman remarks, thus require cooperation with others to help realise *their* ends; 'but what it does more basically, is to set limits on my own pursuit of my own ends'.[85] And the moral concern with the sculpture of Alison Lapper is that, in using her body to make a highly charged statement, Quinn did not set limits on the pursuit of his own ends. But did he help her to realise her ends? Does his sculpture involve objectifying Lapper, and therefore disrespecting her? Let us attempt to address these difficult questions.

Lapper, as mentioned, is also an artist. And, like Quinn, her body is the main site of her artistic practice. Unlike her portraitist, however, her work is confrontational because it reflects how others (the able-bodied majority) regard her. Because she herself is disabled, establishing her body as the principal motif of her art practice challenges the tendency to reduce her to her physical disability or identify her with her bodily appearance. Thus, unlike the 'freaks' captured by Arbus's lens or the intentionally sub-humanised entities of Joel-Peter Witkin's amputee pornoramas (encouraging subject-positions of voyeuristic impunity and morbid fascination respectively),[86] Lapper makes viewers of her work uncomfortable for witnessing dominant attitudes to people with disabilities pictorially dramatised and reflected back to them. Her work confronts us with the inured social codes (of) regarding the disabled.

As a result, the viewer, in a manner entirely consistent with Richard Billingham's work, for instance, is made to feel guilty for looking: we cannot look with what I earlier called 'sideshow impunity' at her work. What is disturbing about Lapper's work rather is that she – the model . . . the artist – subverts orthodox objectifying representational attitudes because, as the object of her own representation, she also insists on encoding a subjective perspective that remains intractable to normative subject-positions.[87]

As we regard her thus she regards us. Subject and object intersect at the frontier of the depiction process. Obviously, this strategy is not unique to Lapper's work. Cindy Sherman has also deconstructed the subject-vs-object conventions of representational logic. Through her work, however, Lapper has developed a mode of reflexively challenging assumed normal subject-positions; and thus her compositions construct an alternative position through which others who have suffered similar social exclusion and stigmatisation as a result of their perceived 'disability' can identify. Her work is empowering in the same way as Billingham's because it refuses to accede to the tourist gaze: 'I'm no longer somebody else's object,' she says. 'I like the way I look, I'm very comfortable with my body – be it dressed or nude.'[88]

This, she adds, 'has taken a long time', however.[89] And the moral problem with Quinn's sculpture of Lapper, to draw the conclusion, is that she has become 'someone else's object' again. Reduced to the content of a representation, identified yet again with her disability, we cannot ignore the fact that Quinn is not someone who has been affected by the stigma and psychological harm endured by people with disabilities. Rather he is someone who, from an external perspective, is using the issue to make an artistic statement. This is dangerous because it may be taken to be ultimately exploitative of Lapper (infiltrating her life, affecting her view of herself etc.), having the potential to change her life in radical and unpredictable ways.

Appropriating the techniques of the classical tradition to represent the physically deformed body, Quinn engages critically, but also respectfully, with the history of art. He announces his aesthetic programme thus: 'Disabled bodies are hardly represented in the history of art and when they are, they are usually interpreted as something "other" or negative. To see these different bodies reproduced in the material of beauty and heroism, marble, involved a celebration of a wider notion of beauty and humanity.'[90]

But this motive can be considered in an alternative manner: the employment of a regnant traditional form (as well as process and material) can also be regarded as an attempt to 'beautify' or aestheticise the disabled somatic, rendering it more palatable to a liberal art audience.[91] A dramatic tension, the sense that a contradiction between 'ugly' content and 'beautiful' form, precisely as that which is celebrated in the work of Mapplethorpe and Serrano, has also been achieved in Quinn's sculptural series – a visual contradiction, produced from the fact that real bodies fail to achieve the transcendental values associated with classical morphology, is accentuated by the failure of the dysmorphic content to inhabit the form comfortably.

As the matrix, the generic standard that still must in some way be aspired to, Quinn's choice of form cannot be regarded as neutral in this context. Disabled bodies articulated in classical formal conventions cannot be processed as anything other than striving to achieve but ultimately 'falling short of' the traditional aesthetic principles – a relationship that is dependent on the very canonical and conservative ideology it evidently subverts. An aesthetic ideology is thereby critically engaged with in a way that, according to our discussion above, is conducive to the transgressive impulse. Yet, if this engagement takes place from a position of privilege and superiority, then is the aesthetic ideology not simply reinforced?

Quinn's work is critically acclaimed and commercially valuable in the art market. 'What is frustrating', Lapper comments, 'is that he's managing to do it as an able-bodied artist – and I and my other fellow-artists can't do it.'[92] Two works sold at her solo exhibition in the Eyestorm Gallery in London in 2004.[93] David Grob, director of the gallery,[94] remarked that the reason why Lapper has found it difficult to make an impression in the art world is explained by the 'unsettling' content of her work. 'She is the subject of her own work and that poses a lot of complicated questions for us all and the way we react to it – it is always going to be difficult.'[95] People do not want, he added, to have to continually justify the art they purchase.[96]

According to Alison Lapper, Quinn's sculpture for the fourth plinth has 'created a huge dilemma' for her.[97] Here she is: but this is not her work. Fame is found, not as the artist but as the subject of the artist's work. Yet all her own work is about herself and her personal experiences as someone with a physical disability. 'Where the hell do I go from here? Nothing I do about me is going to match this.'[98] What, if anything, can the autonomist–moralist paradigm contribute to addressing the ethical concerns raised here?

Transgressive Art Meets the Autonomist–Moralist Model

Autonomism claims that an ethical problem in an aesthetic context is simply not a problem. Even if there is a moral aspect to a given work of art, if this work is acknowledged to qualify as art, it is rigorously maintained even by advocates of 'moderate' autonomism that its morality is not directly relevant to its aesthetic evaluation (unless it has an adverse effect on its artistically valuable characteristics[99]). As we have seen, Quinn has ensured that his disabled sculptures accord formally with the highest historically endorsed aesthetic codes. It would therefore be nonsense to attempt to argue that they do not qualify as art. However, this is precisely what autonomism would be compelled to admit. A noted corollary of the autonomist's hypothesis (that morality is not relevant to aesthetic value) is that any work of art that intentionally engages with a moral or political agenda thereby somehow denigrates its aesthetic status. Implicit in the normative recommendations of autonomism is the idea that art should predominantly concern itself with formal questions and ignore moral, social or political issues because these extraneous elements ultimately have an adverse affect on aesthetic value.[100] Marc Quinn, according to autonomism, has compromised the artistic value of his work by violating its aesthetic autonomy: he has 'corrupted' a formal statement with a moral agenda and used it to make a political assertion in a public venue.

Yet, as we have considered, this agenda and this assertion are crucial to whatever artistic significance Quinn's work possesses. In other words, these aspects cannot be ignored or dismissed (in the manner recommended by autonomism) as a kind of superficial non-artistic excrescence that ultimately has no bearing on the aesthetic value of his work. By insisting that the content of his work is crucial to its *artistic* significance and cannot be distinguished from its form in any conventional sense, Quinn's work can be understood, in the transgressive mode, as representing a challenge to the autonomist's identification of aesthetic form with artistic value. As argued in relation to the transgressive aesthetic, Quinn's work similarly cannot be experienced according to the disinterested attitude recommended by the aesthetic tradition. As with all transgressive art, his work undermines the autonomist approach, an approach – in that it advocates the disinterested attitude alongside its basic concept, the autonomy of art – that is ultimately indistinguishable from orthodox (Kantian) aesthetics.[101] When confronted with works of morally transgressive art, autonomism is rendered redundant as an explanatory model of art practice. Because, if morality can be demonstrated to be relevant in a non-trivial sense to any work of art that yet retains its aesthetic value (just like Quinn's work, as we have seen) – or actually results in an *increase* in aesthetic value – then autonomism (which is presented, incredibly, as a general theory of art) is disqualified in application to transgressive art.

Moralism, being the antithesis of autonomism, is no more congenial for the evaluation of difficult cases. The moralist's grounding thesis is that the moral value of art is relevant in a non-trivial way to its aesthetic evaluation; therefore if any work of art is shown to be immoral then it will be aesthetically discredited as a necessary consequence of this. Now, as it is not at all clear that Quinn's work is aesthetically flawed in any way, cases like this put moralism (at least in this Humean interpretation) under severe stress.

As demonstrated, Quinn's work intentionally acquiesces to the conventions of the classical aesthetic idiom. Therefore, any argument that his work is 'aesthetically flawed', whatever the reasons for this, will be very difficult to sustain credibly in any circumstance. Any moralist defending this view would have to be prepared to argue that a work in the canonical style of *David* or indeed, Rodin's *Kiss*, and in fact made of the same material as Michelangelo's sculpture (white Carrara marble), *could* be *aesthetically* flawed. Yet moralism appears committed to the view that if a moral defect is detected in even the most consummate work of art, then its aesthetic value is depreciated as a result.

A debilitating weakness in the moralist's approach is hereby exposed. If it proves impossible – or counter-intuitive, absurd, nonsensical etc. – to argue that a given work of art is aesthetically defective because it remains artistically 'beautiful' (formally exquisite etc.) despite its immoral aspects, then does this compel the moralist to argue that the work cannot, either, be considered unethical? Hypothetically, let us imagine that, in relation to a certain widely accepted ethical concept, doubt can be cast on the morality of an artwork that is also widely considered to be of the highest aesthetic value. Then this demonstration has, according to the moralist, actually resulted in the depreciation of its aesthetic value. Yet nothing, everything else being equal, has changed. By their own abstract thesis, moralists are cornered into the counter-intuitive acceptance that, if it can be shown to be morally problematic, Marc Quinn's work, for instance, is *by that reason alone*, artistically compromised. If we insist on demonstrating that Quinn's work cannot be considered artistically defective in any way, the moralist will be forced to accept that there cannot be any moral problem with it either, despite what is revealed about it. Or, on the other hand, the moralist will be forced to continue, despite evidence to the contrary, to claim that its artistic value is adversely affected by its immorality. As an explanatory theory of art, moralism therefore is as ineffectual as autonomism. Because it is compelled to accept that a work of art is morally good (even if it is immoral), moralism cannot credibly maintain that an aesthetically valuable work is made defective as a result of its unethical disposition.

In acknowledgement of this situation, there have been attempts to formulate plausible – more sophisticated, less entrenched in eighteenth-century norms – theoretical models adequate to the challenges posed to aesthetics by contemporary art. For instance, Karen Hanson,[102] recognising that different value dimensions may be more intimately enmeshed than can be acknowledged by traditional aesthetics, challenges the normative aesthetic ideology that art should remain immune from ethical estimation. By raising ethical concerns and provoking moral reactions therefore, the work of certain contemporary artists demonstrates that the different value dimensions are 'more intimately interrelated than we admit, and our analytical separation of value areas may simply disclose the partiality of our perspective, our ignorance of the ways in which our "distinct" value "types" affect and depend upon one another.'[103] In many respects, this is the principal characteristic of contemporary transgressive art; it challenges the separatist ideology of autonomism, especially in relation to the partition of aesthetic value and moral value.

A notorious problem case for the relationship of aesthetic and moral value, Leni Riefenstahl's mesmerising cinematic synthesis of beauty and evil in *Triumph of the Will* (*Triumph des Willens*, 1935), has given philosophers of art much grief. Kendall Walton,[104] for instance, in an eminent example of Humean moralism in practice, famously admitted of Riefenstahl's film of the 1934 Nuremberg Nazi Party rally that, although the 'obnoxious message' fails to completely deflate its aesthetic value, nevertheless it makes the film 'morally inaccessible'. That, he continued, in familiar Humean mode, 'may be counted as an aesthetic as well as a moral defect'.[105]

However, Daniel Jacobson has demonstrated that, with regard to problematic instances like *Triumph of the Will*, moralists are twisted into an exact mirror-image of their autonomist opponents.[106] For, in order to account for the 'objective' artistic quality of immoral art, they are, paradoxically, compelled to 'adopt a formalist approach to the work's aesthetic value'.[107] The moralist's dilemma, when confronted with the problem of immoral art, is either to rescind its aesthetic value altogether, thereby denying it artistic status, or to continue somehow to accept it as art while remaining unmoved by – or disgusted by – its offensive moral message. In light of this paradoxical discovery, Jacobson critically revises the definition of Humean moralism to take into account its commitment to the belief that the ethical deficiencies of immoral art necessarily impede its (aesthetic) appreciation. Yet, if this is the case, then, in relation to an immoral art object, its ethical deficiencies must necessarily preclude its appreciation as art. But, clearly, if Riefenstahl's film can still be regarded as art, even to a minimal extent, then the moralist is logically compelled to justify whatever property of the work allows us to consider it of aesthetic value despite its obviously immoral 'message'. Therefore, if the artistic dimension of the film can be distinguished and thus appreciated in isolation from its ethical value, then, evidently, the morality of the film has minimal effect on its aesthetic value.

Clearly, the 'poverty of this approach', Jacobson devastatingly concludes of moralism, 'demonstrates why the Humean moralists' thesis is inadequate even to their favourite case'.[108] Jacobson establishes that neither autonomism nor moralism can adequately accommodate the possible permutations of the aesthetic and ethical dimensions and their unpredictable intersections in practice. As has quite dramatically been revealed in application to Quinn's work: 'both theories are false, even in their best and most moderate formulations.'[109] He then proceeds to develop a theoretical position that, in opposition to both standpoints, has been termed 'immoralism' by Berys Gaut and Matthew Kieran.[110]

For the purposes of the present discussion, 'immoralism' can be taken to suggest the provocative idea that the ethically problematic characteristics of certain transgressive artworks can contribute positively to their artistic value. Jacobson writes: 'while intrinsic moral defects in art *can* be relevant to its aesthetic value (contra autonomism), they *need not* be aesthetic defects – not even when they are aesthetically relevant (contra moralism).'[111] Unhappy with the false impression that moral defects are automatically aesthetic merits that the term 'immoralism' connotes, Gaut has re-titled it 'contextualism', and finessed the position thus: occasionally what makes a morally questionable work unethical may be found to contribute positively to the artistic value of that work. However, *it depends on the work*.[112]

Gaut's contextualism is attractive because it can accommodate difficult and challenging works of transgressive art that involve paradoxical relationships between their aesthetic and moral dimensions (as in the cases considered above): 'if art sometimes subverts our moral values,' Gaut enquires, 'could it not be *ipso facto* good?' He answers: it depends on the context. Indeed, Kieran has argued, in relation to transgressive art, that it is actually important for our ethical development to engage with shocking images and immoral perspectives – to appreciate moral goodness it may be crucial to understand the provenance of unethical acts and evil dispositions.[113]

Gaut agrees with this cognitive approach. However much transgressive art may severely challenge moral attitudes, this does not automatically signify, by default, that it supports immoral beliefs. This reinforces our view that the ethical evaluation of transgressive art requires a pluralist critical approach. Ethical pluralism can provide a kind of critical engagement that recognises the sensitive dependence of moral principles on specific instances and attempts to accommodate this in application; different ethical concepts will be discovered to have different weights relative to the dimensions of particular circumstances.

Aesthetic moral 'contextualism' advocates such a pluralist approach – the deployment of whatever principle may be required in the particular circumstances. According to this perspective, something that might be thought unethical may ultimately have to be adjusted in relation to other or more urgent moral considerations; and, relative to these considerations, the local immorality may be significantly diminished.

Quinn and Lapper Revisited: A Contextualist Analysis

Although Quinn's sculpture could be criticised for reducing Lapper to her disability (by making it the defining feature of her personhood), and although the artist could be accused of using another person as a means to his artistic ends[114] and although it is not irrational to suggest that his choice of form may remain morally problematic (in that classical form encourages the disinterested attitude and ultimately re-emphasises, by antithesis, any dysmorphic content it contains), I will nevertheless argue that these moral concerns are for the most part significantly mitigated when the fine-grained details of the work are taken into account in the manner of ethical contextualism.

There are two contextual aspects that must be taken into consideration in any ethical evaluation of Quinn's sculpture, two factors largely neglected by the partial analysis undertaken above: namely, its placement, and the pregnant condition of the depicted figure. First, the site-specificity of the sculpture may worryingly be considered to encourage the tourist gaze we have associated with the disinterested attitude. Will Self's admiration of the subversive site-specificity of the sculpture fails to recognise that Trafalgar Square is now a locus of tourist appeal as much as it once was a nexus of imperial power. Therefore, the context tends on this occasion to codify the figure as a public *spectacle* – something to be looked at.

However, it can also be reasonably argued that, just as in Billingham's work, the tourist gaze that its locus encourages becomes subject to a powerful critical reversal by the public placement of Quinn's work. Because the sculpture is so prominently sited in the British agora, a space typically decorated with historically significant figures and national monuments, and populated by tourists looking up, 'doing cultural Britain', what the sculpture of Lapper subverts may not be the power of the crown but rather the attitude of the tourist. Thus, although the classical form adopted by the artist may encourage the disinterested gaze (as suggested), the placement more effectively undermines it. Because the sculpture is so public, so prominent and *open* that it almost represents the idea of openness itself, the viewer is made to feel guilty for being tempted to adopt a disinterested (and therefore disrespectful) attitude towards the sculpture – and by extension Lapper and (by further extension) people with disabilities.

Transformed into a commanding icon of moral resistance to the status quo therefore, through the critical reversal of disinterestedness, the monumental sculpture impugns social attitudes to disability and demands our respect. Our resultant incapacity to adopt the disinterested attitude towards her reflexively marks our obligation to, in the words of Martha Nussbaum, 'devise ways to recognise and support . . . full humanity and individuality' for people with disabilities.[115]

Quinn and Lapper (and the work should be considered a collaborative project), in this way, effectively criticise the entire history of the manner in which citizens with disabilities were treated as inferior and dehumanised, stripped of dignity, victimised, and shamed, as Nussbaum observes, into concealing themselves from society. By making the statement so close to Whitehall, in Trafalgar Square, a zone thoroughly marinated in the flux of history, politics and national identity, the artists make disability officially visible in a way that effectively but subtly – subtly, because rendered in the monumental classical form – impugns past and prevailing socio-political attitudes to people with disabilities. In this sense, the site-specificity of the sculpture represents a political call for the extension of the concept of national identity to include people with disabilities, for a wider concept of social justice, and for official ideology to be amended. It represents a visual and non-didactic, subtle, but insistent, argument to put ethics, accessibility, tolerance and social inclusion into political practice, to shape the future of civic policy. As Deborah Orr argued, in this sense, *Alison Lapper Pregnant* is 'just as valid as a reproach as it is a celebration'.[116]

'There is no document of culture that is not at the same time a document of barbarism.'[117] One of Walter Benjamin's most critically sobering aphorisms is relevant in many respects to the ethical modality of *Alison Lapper Pregnant*. Here Benjamin testifies to the fact that any cultural icon of national identity and historical pride may appear less deserving of respect to the critic cognisant of the fact that history (that is, the interpretation of past facts that *survives*) is always conditioned by the viewpoint of the victorious, the alpha conqueror who has ensured consolidation of power through violence and oppression. Injustice is morally justified after the fact by official historiographers of the new regime who, as Shoshana Felman observes, unconsciously identify with 'the discourse of the victor'.[118]

According to Benjamin's critically reversed perspective, the truth of history can only mean 'the traumatised by history', the dispossessed 'who are oppressed by the new victory', who have, Felman says, been 'constitutionally deprived of voice' and, we could add with reference to the sculpture in question, deprived of *visibility*.[119] The cultural monuments of a glorious past meant to evoke a sense of the glorious present can only be considered with extreme scepticism; indeed, Benjamin says they can only be regarded 'with horror'. In light of this pessimistic attitude they become the 'products of class injustice, social and political oppression and inequality'.[120] Large public statues, in particular, represent 'a notable example of monuments of culture that are at the same time, and indissociably, monuments of barbarism celebrating war and massacre'.[121]

Regarding its placement, *Alison Lapper Pregnant* significantly functioned as a moral intervention in this discourse of power and disenfranchisement; restoring visibility in the most non-violent and passive way (a site-specific work of art) to those who have been constitutionally dispossessed of it, the work critically interrupts what Michael Löwy calls 'the continuity of oppression'[122] and performs a kind of passive, continually gentle, yet insistent, ethical vengeance for victims of historical and social exclusion.

Secondly, the fact that Lapper is depicted in a state of pregnancy is highly significant for the moral evaluation of the sculpture. She was well into the third trimester when Quinn cast her in 1999. She subsequently gave birth to her son Parys in 2000. Mitigating the concern that Lapper has been reduced to her disability, the pregnancy cancels the generic status of the sculpture. The sculpture is pregnant – in both senses of the term, literally (with child) and metaphorically (with meaning). It has already, copiously, been pointed out that pregnancy symbolises the future.[123] Therefore if, as suggested, the piece indicts past attitudes to people with disabilities through dramatising the rejection of the tourist gaze, the pregnant state of the figure precisely represents hope for an alternative, better, future. More importantly, the future that the sculpture so efficiently symbolises has become the present and thus awareness is relayed – that is, consciousness is directed in indexical mode – to the existence of Lapper's son: what *was* the future is *now* the present and the hope signified by the sculpture has been realised. This gives renewed hope for the actualisation of the other future referred to: the future of changed attitudes.

Finally, the fact that she is pregnant makes one consider Lapper's role as a mother (and motherhood generally) and her relationship with her child (and childcare generally). Not only do Quinn and Lapper effectively raise consciousness about the ubiquity of disability in human life – a visual polemic concerning the importance of the concepts of accessibility, tolerance and inclusion in social and political policy – but they also dramatise a deeply, but non-sentimental humanistic celebration of maternity. It could be seen in terms of a kind of response to Mark Wallinger's previous sculpture for the fourth plinth, *Ecce Homo* (an updated depiction of the figure of Christ shown to the populace). Quinn and Lapper's '*Ecce Femina*', therefore, symbolises motherhood as well as disability, giving it at once a further dimension of richness and depth, the sculpture becomes an icon of the maternal relationship. And this is highly significant because all these factors, taken together, transform the piece into a non-propositional metonym generally representative of the *ethics of care*. The maternal relationship refers above all to care. This extraordinary and powerful work is, therefore, ultimately about care.

Conclusion

Disinterestedness indemnifies the morally corrupt work. Because of this, it has been suggested that adopting the aesthetic attitude to morally problematic works of art *is itself* morally problematic.[124] According to Mary Devereaux, one of the reasons why *Triumph of the Will* can be considered morally corrupt is precisely because it encourages a non-judgemental disposition to be assumed in relation to its subject.[125] She concludes that the autonomist partition of aesthetic and moral value, facilitated by the mechanism of disinterestedness, dangerously inhibits any adequate understanding of the artistic value of morally problematic works of art. Bracketing the moral vision that *Triumph of the Will* communicates aesthetically removes us from an 'essential dimension of the film', namely, its artistic vision: 'its particular, utterly horrifying vision of Hitler and National Socialism'. Such a vision, she concludes, constitutes 'the *essence* of the film' – i.e. the site where moral and aesthetic values intersect – and this precludes the dream of a *purely* aesthetic, impartial, morally immune appreciation that abstracts structurally from all moral concerns.

What makes Riefenstahl's film fascinating from an aesthetic point of view, Devereaux argues, is *precisely* what makes it disturbing from a moral standpoint. *Triumph of the Will* represents Nazism (an uncontroversial evil) *as* aesthetically pleasing; it is transformed into a beautiful, enthralling and alluring vision.[126] Engaging with the work means to confront its difficulty – its disturbing vision, what Susan Sontag correctly calls its fascinating 'Fascist visuals'[127] – and the appalling coalition of beauty and evil that Riefenstahl successfully constructs. This means engaging with the moral issue it raises and not ignoring it, setting it aside, suspending or otherwise bracketing it, through the conceptual mechanism of aesthetic distance.

This chapter has argued that the theories of autonomism and moralism are equally inadequate to the ethical evaluation of contemporary morally transgressive art practice. Richard Billingham's work undermines aesthetic conventions because it is very difficult to experience such fucked-up work according to traditional aesthetic categories. His work shocks us into questioning the disengaged attitude conventionally recommended by the dominant autonomist aesthetic paradigm by inviting us to adopt the attitude of the cultural tourist and then making us morally uncomfortable with the role. Ultimately, this raises consciousness to the fact that it is unethical to adopt the attitude of disinterested, emotionally distant contemplation in relation to his work.

In the later sections of the chapter, I claimed that contextualism, because it defends a pluralist approach to the ethical evaluation of art, is a useful practical alternative to the dominant historical solutions to the problem of morality and art. Taking the contextual aspects of Marc Quinn and Alison Lapper's sculpture for the fourth plinth in Trafalgar Square into consideration enabled us to develop the argument that, although the artist could be reasonably accused of using another person as a means to his artistic ends, nevertheless, because the sculpture is public, the viewer is made to feel guilty for adopting an unethical disinterested attitude towards people with disabilities. In this application I showed how the placement of the work subverts the tourist gaze. Lapper's pregnant state is also a contextual detail that is crucial to the ethical evaluation of the sculpture. I concluded that this detail allows us to consider the work as a monumental icon of the ethics of care. Unique in the transgressive aesthetic, Quinn and Lapper's sculpture, although it remains difficult, is ultimately a morally affirmative work. In that it contests normative attitudes and conventional morality (including, as we have seen, the Kantian categorical imperative), it is paradigmatically transgressive – its challenge, although uncompromising, is ultimately celebratory and affirmative – but not in a way that is crass, sentimental or condescending. Possibly, for some, moral problems remain; but I believe that Quinn's efforts to alleviate these by meeting and befriending Lapper, as well as consulting her at every stage of the process, significantly mitigate whatever problems may be associated with the project.[128] Quinn and Lapper's sculpture is affirmative at the same time as challenging and deeply subversive; this makes it a unique work in the transgressive canon and a remarkable artistic *and* ethical achievement.

2 CARTE BLANCHE

Marcus Harvey's *Myra*

> An exclamation of horror broke from the painter's lips as he saw in the dim light the hideous face on the canvas grinning at him. There was something in its expression that filled him with disgust and loathing.
>
> *Oscar Wilde*[1]

Nothing captures the ambivalence of Charles Saatchi's aesthetic taste more precisely than Marcus Harvey's painting *Myra* (1995). Measuring almost four metres in height and just over three in length (396.2 × 320 cm, 156 × 126 in[2]), it is a very large work, its size somehow appropriate to the magnitude of the statement it appears to make. It is immediately recognised as a super-sized enlargement of the infamous custodial photograph of Myra Hindley, co-convicted with Ian Brady in 1966 for the murder of two juveniles and a seventeen-year-old man in the Manchester area between 1963 and 1965. The artist has reconstructed her huge monochromatic face from a composite of small grey, white and black handprints.

For many who saw the work, the duplicated handprint was the demoralising detail: for an image that had come to represent the epitome of crimes against children to be scaled-up using the body part of a child was considered exploitative of the suffering of the victims of this crime in particular and insensitive to the victims of child abuse in general.[3] When the painting first appeared in the Saatchi Gallery in 1995, incensed relatives of children killed by Hindley and Brady condemned it.[4] One of those who called for its removal was Winnie Johnson, mother of Hindley–Brady victim Keith Bennett (whose body has never been recovered despite Brady's boasts that he could, with his 'mental map' of the moors, easily locate the boy's remains[5]); she commented at the time that the 'idea of using a child's handprints to make a picture of this evil woman is beyond belief'.[6]

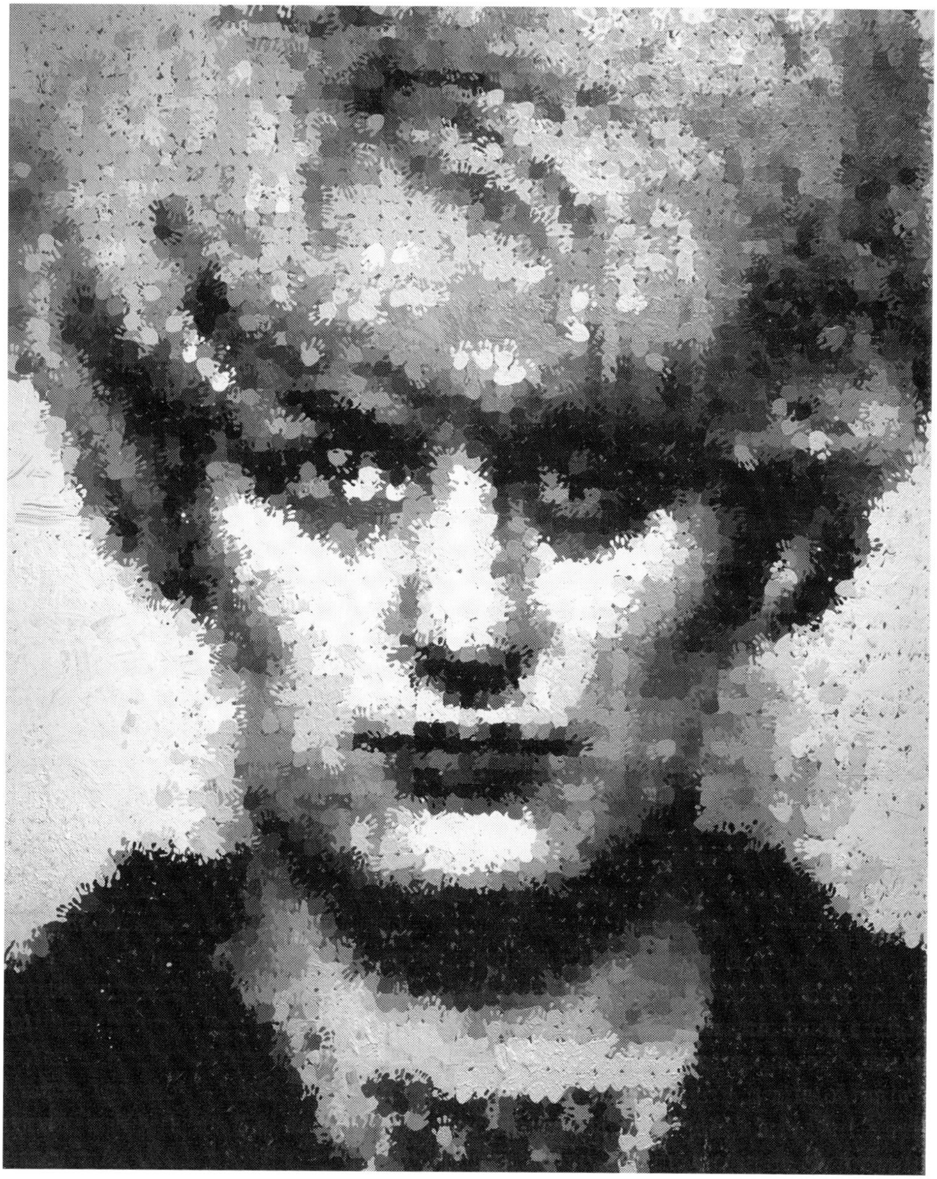

6. Marcus Harvey, *Myra*, 1995
Acrylic on canvas
156 x 126 in (396.2 x 320 cm)

Photo: Stephen White. Courtesy Jay Jopling/ White Cube (London)

In his analysis of transgressive art, Julius explains that this detail is responsible for the moral shock elicited by the image. For, whatever the artist's creative solution, the implication of the handprint is that the image was made by children, that children were somehow involved in its formation: 'given the subject's crime, getting children to help in creating her image seems a violation of them.' He continues: 'the picture horrifies in its implicit subordination of Hindley's victims to their tormentor. It is as if they were being compelled to praise her. For her image to be constructed out of a child's palm print is to enlist her victims in its creation.'[7]

Defending the work on its debut public outage at the Saatchi gallery, Harvey claimed that his intentions were purely – disinterestedly – aesthetic in nature; he simply wanted, he said, to re-establish 'physical recollection' by informing the image of Hindley with 'a children's [*sic*] innocence'.[8] Referring to the infamous photograph that constitutes the painting's obvious prototype, Harvey observed that the image is powerfully ambiguous: it possesses, he said, a 'hideous attraction' that he hoped to 'bring back to textural reality' by scaling it up with handprints.[9] He explains how his original intention was to cast the hands of several children in preparation for the work, but everyone he approached with the idea declined; 'so eventually I asked some friends if I could use their four-year-old daughter.'[10] So, making a mould of the little hand, he employed a plaster prosthetic to summon – in hypnotically repeated prints, in indirect touches – the ghostly traces of disembodied children hauntingly to the surface of his work.

Since the high-profile trial and their conviction, the case of Myra Hindley and Ian Brady has been associated with extreme public emotion. As news of their crimes percolated through to a dulled and confused nation in the 1960s, there was a widespread sense that this incident signalled a benchmark episode that, given the specific nature of the crimes, foreshadowed the end of a kind of innocence. Thus it was no surprise that Harvey's image (a recognisable version of the familiar photograph of Hindley released at the time of the trial and circulated incessantly in media networks ever since) became the source of a new wave of shock and outrage.

To art critics, though, it was perhaps puzzling when *Myra*, a figurative impression executed in what is widely considered to be a conservative (or even outmoded) genre, was the cause of such controversy that ensued when it was later shown in (a special over-eighteen-rated gallery of) *Sensation: Young British Artists from the Saatchi Collection* at the Royal Academy of Arts in 1997.[11] The controversy was described by one reporter as 'the most divisive in the Academy's 229-year history'.[12] However (as many commentators indicated at the time), the role the Royal Academy played in the controversy was far from purely aesthetic or disinterested.[13]

John Molyneux contended that Harvey's painting was employed by the Academy like a brand in an advertising stratagem. 'This was the sign, under which the exhibition was marketed, its logo, its shop window display, its loss leader,'[14] while Naomi Siderfin ironically enquired: 'whose PR acumen was responsible for insisting that Marcus Harvey's *Myra* was included in the selection?'[15] Due to its establishment (indeed bureaucratic) profile, the central presence of *Myra* in a Royal Academy-endorsed high-status show was considered not only offensive but also premeditated, strategic and entrepreneurial: 'here it was to be shown in a blockbuster exhibition to hundreds of thousands of people, and in an apparent effort to create controversy, producing publicity for the Saatchi collection and money for the Royal Academy.'[16]

Indeed, Mark Wallinger, writing in *Art Monthly*, went further, claiming that the Academy's agenda was one of cynical media manipulation and self-promotion: 'The Royal Academy pre-empted sensational reporting by cynically promoting the Myra Hindley portrait.'[17] Both Winnie Johnson and Ann West, mother of Lesley Ann Downey (murdered by Hindley and Brady in 1965) and member of child-protection organisation Kidscape, alongside other agencies, held organised protests against *Sensation*, recommending that the show be boycotted.[18] But it wasn't. When it closed in December, the Academy announced record attendances for an exhibition of contemporary art (allegedly over 284,734 people paid the £7 admission price to visit the show).[19]

On the first day (18 September) of the exhibition, Harvey's painting was vandalised in two separate incidents.[20] First, Peter Fisher (an artist) smeared blue and red ink onto the painting before attempting to pull it down. He explained that he was 'taking a stand' against the attitude expressed by a work that he believed to be 'glorifying the crimes of a monster'.[21] Later, Jacques Rolé (another artist) managed to fire 'three or four' eggs at the painting, before being restrained by a passer-by (who happened to be an off-duty policeman).[22] Both men were arrested.

In mitigation of his conduct, Rolé explained: 'There are moments when you must do something about it. Otherwise next time we will have even worse, we will have a picture of the actual torture.'[23] The painting was taken away for restoration and, despite protests against its replacement (one request that the painting be permanently removed was communicated to the RA from Myra Hindley's representatives), reinstalled three weeks later. It remained for the duration of the exhibition protected by sheet plexiglass and extra security personnel.[24]

Critical responses to controversial works of art such as *Myra* have generally avoided ethical analysis, preferring instead to deflate any moral provocation by adopting a measured insouciance against the suggestion that certain images may have a shocking impact.[25] To such a liberal sensibility, developing the ethics of such an intimidating work might appear futile or even perverse.

However, as the work provokes a moral reaction and therefore obliges the viewer to adopt a position in relation to the attitude it represents, this chapter argues that ethical assessment is critical for understanding three principal aspects structural to artwork that, like *Myra*, may be experienced as morally problematic.

First, in explicitly addressing the provocation of the work, an ethical assessment – unlike more customary art-critical or aesthetic evaluations – has the capacity to engage with morally transgressive art without seeking to neutralise its shock value and thereby critically overlook an aspect considered central to its meaning. In opposition to the deflationary tendencies of the standard art-critical approaches to transgressive art, therefore, the ethical evaluation of *Myra accepts* that Harvey's painting is a shocking image. Thus, it is possible to maintain that adverse responses to the work, far from being irrational or philistine can be regarded as the sincere reactions of people who 'took it seriously as a representation of a particular individual, and so also took seriously the reactions of those who had been wronged by that person'.[26] In order to understand fully why the work occasioned such extreme reactions, it is necessary, in other words, to consider the work from the viewpoint of those 'who took it seriously' as an affront to the morality of those directly affected by Myra Hindley's crimes.

Second, by taking the morally problematic structure of the work seriously, ethical analysis avoids polarisation into either of the unconstructive critical factions that have dominated discussion of Harvey's work. Controversial artwork is typically defended, on the one side, by a discourse of non-judgemental (and, above all, non-moral) approbation. While, on the other side, the reactionary rejection of controversial work is largely based on the demotic misinformation of public opinion as promulgated by journalist reviewers and agitated by popular press sensationalism.

Third, with reference to Gaut's ethicist schema, an ethical approach to controversial artwork has the capacity to acknowledge the work of art as the 'manifestation of an attitude'.[27] Explicated as 'a work's displaying pro or con attitudes toward some state of affairs or things',[28] this concept appears highly encouraging for the ethical evaluation of art. However, despite Gaut's important concession that the attitude manifested by the work is often inexplicit, latent (and therefore anything but 'manifest'), it is frequently extremely difficult, if not impossible, even by the investigative critical analysis canvassed by Gaut, to expose the work's 'real' attitude from behind what it only *apparently* affirms.[29] And I would emphatically argue that this is especially, indeed radically, the situation with regard to transgressive art. Nevertheless, I shall conclude that, even if Gaut's 'manifest attitude' concept may be inadequate for the evaluation of morally transgressive art (it makes the ethical analysis of art into an *ad hominem* moral judgement of the artist and therefore falls foul of the intentional fallacy), it proves highly effective as a regulative concept for the ultimate ethical evaluation of such a disturbingly ambivalent and non-judgemental work as Harvey's *Myra*.

Preliminary Approaches to the Ethical Analysis of *Myra*

A truly horrific image, *Myra* is traumatic – the psychological analogue of an invasive surgical procedure. This is perhaps because the painter manages to *realise*, that is, he finds effective pictorial means to substantiate, and thus bear witness to, the transgressions associated with Hindley's crime. However, the work is considered transgressive not because it manipulates a familiar photograph until it begins to connote the multiple traumatic violations associated with a high-profile serial murder. Rather, the work counts as transgressive principally because it remains *reticent* precisely about the issues surrounding Hindley and her crimes – issues that the work itself might be considered to provoke. The painting, Julius says, does not 'cause us to ponder that sanctification of childhood, one that leads to the demonising of its violators'.[30] Nor does the work question the justice of Hindley's punishment. This apparent reticence is also perhaps the reason why Stallabrass has characterised Harvey's painting as an 'extraordinarily mute work'.[31] It makes 'no statement', he says, it 'solve[s] no problem'; it simply presents a quandary and, thus, as a result, induces a 'mild panic'.[32] 'The work itself', Stallabrass concludes, remains *split* morally, 'dislocated from the response it elicits'.[33]

Neil Mulholland, in a review of *Sensation*, suggests that this reticence is precisely an important feature of transgressive art. Split undecidability of response makes it difficult (if not impossible) to decide whether the transgressive artist is 'exposing forms of exploitation' to scrutiny or simply reproducing ideological stereotypes completely devoid of any critical or investigative mediation. That is to say, there is nothing in the transgressive work itself according to which we can decide whether the work is critical or celebratory of its subject matter.[34] 'It is hard to decide,' Stallabrass agrees, 'and artists, determined to have it both ways, exploit the difficulty.'[35] This structure of undecidability is a precise indication of the ambivalent or *non-committal* attitude of the transgressive artist; the work irresponsibly perhaps affords no possibility of disproving that the artist is implicated 'in what [he] ostensibly criticise[s]'.[36] *Myra*, Stallabrass concludes, 'a good exemplar of the "present a dilemma and let the viewer decide" school of art, is as ambivalent as the artist'.[37]

However, in defence of the work, liberal reviewers claimed that *Myra* neither celebrates nor condemns because, like other related contemporary transgressive artwork, it merely 'presents' and therefore transfers the responsibility of deciding the meaning of the work, and how it is to be judged, to the viewer. Michael Archer, writing for *Art Monthly*, argued in defence of this strategy, claiming that it represents a legitimate and 'deliberate guarding against a work's reception being either subsumed under, or shaped by, any one interpretive agenda';[38] thus *Myra*, as exemplar of this transgressive artistic strategy, presents a 'difficult reality', in the words of Tom Lubbock, and proceeds to 'leave it there, as a confrontation'.[39] Similarly, John Molyneux, in a review of *Sensation* for *International Socialism*, argues that the confrontation associated with such a transgressive strategy has the result of forcing 'one to choose: for or against'. Works like *Myra*, Molyneux maintains, are therefore unique in the history of art in that they make an *ethical* (as opposed to aesthetic) claim on the viewer: they demand that one judges whether or not they are 'in good faith'.[40] Referring to the kind of moral difficulties raised by the photographs of Richard Billingham, Molyneux claims that such art uniquely pressurises one into adopting a position: we have to decide, he says, whether the work empathises with or victimises those it involves, those on the receiving end of the crime, those who most acutely *feel* its after-effects. 'In this case that means trying to decide on the nature of the relationship between the work and the subjects it depicts. Is it, fundamentally, a work of solidarity and sympathy or a work of exposure and exploitation?'[41]

This dilemma is structural to morally transgressive art (such as Billingham's or Harvey's) and ultimately involves an ethical response on the part of the viewer to those perceived to be on the receiving end; we ask ourselves: is the work supportive or discriminatory of the subjects it depicts or the people it affects?

> With *Guernica* in 1937 a number of questions arose. Does it work as a painting? Is it moving? . . . Does it help the anti-fascist cause? But not, is the painting in solidarity with those on the receiving end of the bombing or is it relishing and exploiting their suffering?[42]

In order to assess Harvey's *Myra* from an ethical perspective it will be necessary therefore to assume the responsibility of deciding the meaning of the work and how it might be judged, by moving beyond the physical surface of the art object to encompass what this surface refers to, to consider the historical atmosphere that has accrued around the work. I will argue that it is necessary therefore to take into account the reactions of those who had been affected by the crime and who considered themselves further wronged in some way by Harvey's painting. This will make it necessary to 'leave the realm of art' in order to appreciate fully why Harvey's work is shocking. For, ultimately, the work can be considered to be about the 'enduring reality of images in people's minds'.[43] The responsibility of judgement leads directly to the referent that the work represents, more vividly and palpably than its attitude.

In acknowledging the provocation that the work makes, an ethical analysis of Harvey's painting, far from being categorically mistaken, perhaps constitutes the critical attitude most appropriate to it. As the analysis of Quinn and Lapper's work undertaken in the previous chapter demonstrates, a contextualist perspective – in correcting the relative inadequacies of the traditional approaches to the ethical evaluation of art; has the unique ability to reveal the relevant characteristics of morally problematic art. Adopting the contextualist approach in the ethical evaluation of *Myra* will entail surveying the entire context in which the work is embedded, a context that ultimately constitutes its difficult and disturbing referent (not just Hindley but the trauma that haemorrhages through the surface like a gross surplus content). Taking into account its appearance, its painterly treatment and its place in Harvey's pictorial project, I acknowledge that the painting's form has more than an aesthetic significance: it can be shown to possess moral value also.[44] First, let us consider some of that gross surplus content.

'Suffer Little Children': The Facts of the Case

From 19 April to 6 May 1966, a jury assembled at Chester Assizes heard evidence following which Myra Hindley was found guilty and sentenced to two concurrent life sentences for her part in the murder of Lesley Ann Downey (10) and Edward Evans (17). She was sentenced to a further seven years as an accessory to murder for assisting Ian Brady in the killing of John Kilbride (12). Twenty years later, from prison, Brady confessed to killing two further children missing since 1963 and 1964; and Hindley, perhaps hoping her sentence would be commuted, agreed to cooperate with a police search team to help locate their remains.[45] In July 1987, the police discovered and exhumed the remains of Pauline Reade (16) on Saddleworth Moor outside Manchester. The body of Keith Bennett (12), known to have been murdered by the couple and believed to be buried on the moors, has never been recovered.

Accounts of their *modus operandi* make grim and unpleasant reading.[46] Brady, aware that children's initial reservations were diminished by the presence of a woman, used Hindley to provide the appearance of stability suggested by a couple. Hindley thus supplied the false sense of security that enabled him to gain the trust of their initially suspicious victims. A period of sexual violation and extreme physical insult followed (committed principally by Brady). These sessions of violence resulted in the victim's inevitable death. Burial of the dead bodies in shallow graves on the moors outside Manchester earned the couple the gothic nickname the 'Moors Murderers'. In fact, at the time of the trial, an intensive search was still in progress on the moors for at least two more children reported missing from the Manchester area during the significant period (but, having discovered nothing, it was eventually called off). During the trial, the all-male jury were subjected to exhibits of forensic evidence, including photographs of Hindley and Brady on the moors. One of these in particular, which showed Hindley posing with her pet dog beside a makeshift gravesite, was used by the police to help triangulate the burial place of their victims.[47]

Perhaps the most distressing items of evidence presented to the jury, however, related to the murder of ten-year-old Lesley Ann Downey. Abducted on her way to a funfair in Ancoats, preparatory to killing her, the couple documented their victim's suffering in a series of photographs that were found during the inquest in suitcases deposited in Hindley's name at a left-luggage unit in Manchester Central Station.[48] The suitcase also contained a cassette-recording that was played to the horrified jury (it was also played to her bereft mother, Ann West, for identification purposes).[49] For seventeen minutes a plaintive voice was heard pleading with her captors to allow her to return home.

Despite this display of evidence, neither Brady nor Hindley displayed any trace of emotion throughout the trial. Both pleaded not guilty to the charges; both remained deadpan when the sentences were handed down. This unrepentant attitude added an extra depth-charge of shock to the public trauma already registered by the couple's crimes. 'Obliterating all subsequent images', Peter Stanford, writing for the *Guardian* in 2002 remarked, this 'complete lack of remorse' was something that, given their particular transgressions and the nature of the evidence associated with them, was beyond any possibility of civic forgiveness. 'As the woman of the pair, Hindley shouldered the greater part of the public outrage.'[50]

Indeed, apropos of the evidently inferior role she played in the *folie à deux*, the public hatred directed toward Hindley is notable in relation to Harvey's painting.[51] A process of teratogenesis (whereby Hindley was inflated to the point of monstrosity in the public imagination) occurred in the wake of the trial that has been sustained (largely by the mass media) ever since. Despite her transgressions (which were appreciably smaller than Brady's[52]), Chris Jenks proposes that Hindley's status as monster relates principally to her 'natural' (but in reality, cultural) status of womanhood: 'what perhaps shocks our taken-for-granted typologies most', he writes, 'is that Hindley is a woman, and was at the time, an attractive young woman.'[53] So, according to Jenks, the transgression that Myra Hindley represents is not so much associated with her crimes as with a widespread sense of the violation of consensually set cultural categories – apparently instinctive symbolic and normative social frameworks that condition how things should be and according to which men and (particularly) women should behave. Such social categories are not designed to cope with something that exceeds their symbolic frames of reference; this explains why the public reaction to Hindley's crimes in particular was so extreme.

Representing an upsetting disturbance of the socio-symbolic order, Hindley became a benchmark symbol of violation and *desecration* per se. And therefore, for the sake of the integrity of symbolic categories that constitute the social structure, the teratogenesis of extreme (female) criminals such as Hindley becomes, according to Jenks, a socially necessary process. 'In this sense, by refusing women who commit acts of supreme violence acceptance within the category of woman (they become monsters), the public was reaffirming to itself the essence of what women are. Thereby also reaffirming its commitment to a 'shared' social order.'[54]

An unconscious reminder of the arbitrary condition of this shared social order, Hindley was reified into a threatening icon of contagious evil. Therefore the necessity of expelling this symbol of social disturbance became urgent: she must be put away, consigned to oblivion, repressed because, again according to Jenks's analysis, 'the system of classification stays intact [only] by resisting the "defilement" of the abhorrent case.'[55] This social repression, facilitated by projection onto a convenient scapegoat, represented 'a way to restore the primary image of the innate maternal and caring dispositions of womankind through relegating some would-be women (those who commit acts of atrocity) to another category essentialised through images of evil or pathology'.[56] However, as Carol Anne Davis accurately speculates in her study of female serial killers, perhaps 'if she had turned against [Brady] and become a witness for the prosecution, she would have been released years ago.'[57]

As things turned out, however, she was never released; on 15 November 2002, having served thirty-six years in prison (eleven more than the tariff recommended by the judge), Hindley died of respiratory failure in a West Suffolk Hospital.[58] Strangely, however, as we shall see, her status as a scapegoat of evil never went into remission; like the repressed in general, Hindley continually returned to haunt public consciousness in one form or another through her long incarceration.

Myra: Portrait of a Serial Killer

Myra was one of the forms in which Hindley reappeared during her absence. Harvey's painting cannot really be considered a portrait of Hindley in the traditional sense, however. The artist did not request to visit his subject in Durham Prison in order to have her sit for preliminary sketches, he didn't make photographic studies, he did not ask his subject's permission to paint her. Nor did he spend time in Hindley's company so that the finished work would possess that sense of personal intensity or presence associated with successful portraits. This is because none of the conventional procedures associated with portraiture apply to Harvey's *Myra*. Why?

The painting is a scaled-up simulacrum of the custodial photograph released by the police at the time of Hindley and Brady's arrest. As well as massively enlarging the scale the photograph is usually seen at, Harvey has also agitated the image in other notable ways: he has cropped the original photograph which has the effect of focusing exclusive attention on the huge face. Harvey has also 'digitally' reprocessed the black-and-white photograph as a kind of bit-map interference pattern of handprints that follows the stark chromatography of the original. Many critics recognised the debt this enlargement-and-atomise

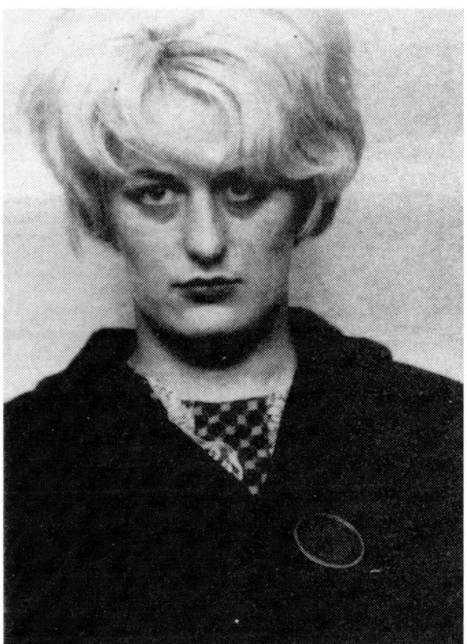

7. Myra Hindley, custodial photograph, 1966

technique (without the hands) owed to American artist Chuck Close.[59] However, the deployment of Close's technique in this instance was to make purposeful reference to the familiar 'original' photograph. Using the technique in a knowing and reflexive way, Harvey effectively, if implicitly, indicates that the intended subject of his work is *not* Myra Hindley in person but rather the *photographic image*. 'The whole point of the painting', he has claimed, 'is that photograph. I don't really want to get beyond that.'[60]

The 'terrifying' (Harvey's own word) potency of this photograph of Hindley is in large part due to its subject's inscrutable look. This look has been interpreted in various ways. Described as 'menacing in its impassivity' by Anthony Julius, Allan Hall says that it 'shows a hard, grim vanity', while for Stallabrass it expresses an 'apparent malevolence'.[61] According to Carol Anne Davis, Hindley explained to Peter Timms that, following their arrest, she and Brady had agreed to 'look coldly at the police camera, to show no sign of emotion. It was important to Ian that they seem to be above society, filled with disdain.'[62]

Head tilted slightly forward, Hindley presents a pale expressionless face to the lens. From under a heavy white fringe she observes the viewer with her black eyes. The studied vacuity of the look makes it difficult to read: the mouth is set and slightly upturned at the corners. There is a dark crescent under the severe angle of the jaw and there are deep shadows under the eyes. The severity of the photograph (and its capacity to disturb) has not been diminished despite its compulsive mass-media reproduction. The point here is that the photograph that constitutes the original matrix of Harvey's painting is *itself* already a shocking image; it is shocking because, far from presenting the image of contrite remorse (which we might be conditioned to expect), there is a sense that the woman in the photograph is silently judging *us*.

As indicated, Julius's short analysis of *Myra* regards the painting to be exemplary of the transgressive aesthetic in contemporary visual culture. Classifying the work as transgressive certainly represents one possible defence of the artistic integrity of the work and marks the beginning of an argument for its aesthetic justification. As Julius clarifies at the beginning of his study, 'the concept of the transgressive lives its real life in contemporary cultural discourse, where it is highly regarded and much deployed.' He explains that to 'describe an artwork as "transgressive" is to offer it a compliment'.[63] Transgression in this sense is valued in art because, as we have seen, it is identified with the avant-garde challenge to the cultural status quo: 'The transgressive challenges received ideas,' Julius explains, because the transgressive artist dares to explore taboo subjects, thereby subjecting prevailing ideological and established mythical norms to necessary critique.[64] 'Taboo-breaking', understood in this sense, is respected as a critical activity, 'a valuable form of truth-telling and a means of including the hitherto excluded'.[65] Because it 'offers us glimpses of an existence unconfined by rules or restraints', according to Georges Bataille, 'the transgressive is the utopian aspect of every artwork'.[66]

There is, however, very little evidence of the utopian in Harvey's artwork. Its nightmarish visage a vision of dystopia, *Myra* certainly exposes repressed social taboos but, contra Bataille, does so in a non-affirmative, negative way. And, in a manner strangely appropriate to the subject of his work, we immediately sense that Harvey has transgressed a limit or exceeded a boundary.[67] But is the work not experienced as a violation only because its represented subject happens to signify a paradigmatic case of breaching the 'limits set by a commandment or law or convention' that Jenks's study has identified with the act of transgression?[68] If this is the case, Harvey's painting may be considered to dramatise the transgressions associated with the Moors Murderers, and thus, with reference to the violation of her crimes, the work disturbs by reopening the scabs of the traumatic breaching of social and ethical prohibitions – thereby reversing the scapegoat status – by compelling awareness of several related taboos associated with this benchmark case.

First is the implicit prohibition against causing harm to children and the social responsibility to protect them: a twin principle, Julius says, that is 'supported by a belief in the sanctity of childhood'.[69] Therefore, against the normative status of this taboo, any crime against children will appear in contravention of an a priori prohibition. As Jenks perhaps unnecessarily emphasises, 'the deliberate harming of children strikes at the most vulnerable part of our collective affects.'[70]

Second and third are the sexual and sadistic dimensions of the crime. Aware that Hindley and Brady's victims (with the exception of Edward Evans) were juveniles, it also emerged during the trial that they were subjected to pre- (and perhaps post-) mortem sexual molestation; this aspect of the crime, as Jenks observes, is doubly transgressive, for not only does it supplement a sexual dimension to the prohibition against harming children, it also indicates that their offences 'were no commonplace acts of paedophilia'.[71] Indeed, as the evidence presented by the prosecution confirmed, 'the cruelty and experience of domination appeared to provide an erotic ecstasy exceeding the actual physical sexual abuse that took place.'[72] And perverse attachments between sexuality and death, as Bataille never tired of iterating, are considered paradigmatically transgressive.

Fourth, and most important for the present context, is the perverse suppression of instinctual parental concern. This taboo is specific to Hindley and is exclusively responsible for the otherwise inexplicable disproportionate public abhorrence directed towards her compared to Brady. Above all, Hindley's sex is the issue here. It emerged during the evidence, as we have seen, that Brady, cognisant that potential victims were more willing to trust a woman, used Hindley to gain the confidence of the children. Her principal role in the partnership was thus, as we have considered, to bait the victim. That she lured the children and had prior awareness of their ultimate fate was generally understood at the time, with widespread horror, as inhuman and hideously deviant, a vicious rejection of 'the innate maternal and caring dispositions of womankind'.[73]

Finally, the lack of remorse Hindley and Brady demonstrated throughout the trial (and as the sentence was passed) was taken as a further, supplementary violation – a sign of the most heinous feature of the crime: the suspicion that they enjoyed their dark work. And this lack of remorse (which was possibly antic), along with the suspicion of enjoyment, is figured precisely in the custodial photograph of Hindley in which her facial expression, in its horribly inscrutable physiognomy, and in the context (which is, of course, vital to the impact of the image), appears cold and cruelly self-satisfied; it represents therefore a visage commensurate with the standard personification of evil in the collective imagination.

In the wake of the Moors Murders, the custodial photograph thus became, in Cohen's celebrated term, a vehicle of 'moral panic'. That is, the image came to mark 'a threat to society'.[74] But my argument suggests that the horrified public actually *required* such an image of displacement that seemed a fitting simulacrum of Hindley and Brady's inexplicable and apparently motiveless crimes.[75] A face thus over-mapped the ineffable violation of the crime. Reified and condensed into a synecdoche of evil, Hindley's photograph became *the* scapegoat image in civic consciousness. For good or ill, this vacuous physiognomy was now filled with the capacity to represent something intangible and nightmarish and profoundly disturbing; it became the prototypical analogue of that transgressive exceeding of social categories that Jenks indicates in relation to perpetrators of off-the-radar 'acts of supreme violence',[76] its ubiquitous presence, iterated through perpetual mediation, serving to actually protect the social conscience from the contamination of radical evil.

Eventually, therefore, this photo becomes powerful: grotesquely pregnant with the semiotic capacity to stand not simply for the woman Myra Hindley but for her transgressions; it becomes a vehicle of radical evil,[77] a 'measure that must itself be unmeasurable', as Alain Badiou observes.[78] Radical evil must always be *presented* as 'unique, unrivalled – and in this sense transcendent' and yet, Badiou argues, it must constantly be *re*-presented, measured, repeatedly evoked, 'compared, used to schematise every circumstance in which one wants to produce, among opinions, an effect of the awareness of Evil'.[79]

Such, precisely, was the case with this popular photograph of Myra Hindley: it was recycled ad nauseam in the popular media as if the hysterical reproduction of compulsively accumulated mediations of the image would somehow eventuate in collective public catharsis. A caveat marking the profile of radical evil, the image of Hindley thus became, in Jenks's apt formulation, a 'transgressive projection for us all'.[80] The image became, in the Freudian and, even more interestingly, the Marxian senses of the term, a *fetish*. That is, it was transformed into something psychologically invested with a preternatural potency, an uncanny *thing* having a 'phantasmagorical'[81] power it does not, or cannot, naturally possess. Through its evolution 'into an emblem of pure evil in a secularised culture where conventional religious images have all but lost their symbolic value' (as Jake Chapman's commentary[82] puts it), the photo acquired the quasi-sacred properties attributed to the fetish object in the psychological interpretations of Marxian economic fetishism.[83] Except that, in this particular case, the preternatural properties invested in the image, being utterly malignant, become 'sacred' in an entirely negative sense, until finally a perverse respect, the innate respect for the scapegoat, is commanded by the image.

My argument is that Marcus Harvey's *Myra* can be considered to *materialise* this process of negative sacral fetishism. The painting has subjected the photographic fetish to a physical augmentation that very effectively lends a kind of tangible reality to the virtual teratogenesis of Hindley in public consciousness, reifying thereby the respect that the scapegoat commands. 'The amplification of Hindley into a monster', according to Jenks, 'has arisen in large part through the exponential accumulation of her transgressions; her excesses both numbed the emotions and severely destabilised the categories of understanding.'[84]

Representing this process of teratogenesis in a grotesquely literal way, Harvey's painting is monstrous. He has accumulated Hindley's excesses in the exponential accretion of the handprint pixels that compose the face and has thus successfully – in an aesthetic sense – reactivated 'the horror of a tired and over-familiar photograph'.[85] The horror is activated again through two key formal features of Harvey's painting: the massive, indeed *hysterical* scale of the painting and, of course, the re-iterated child's handprint that, in its indexical function, refers directly back to the victims of the crime and acts as a hypnotically repeated traumatic mnemonic of their violation.

These features of Harvey's painting implicitly and effectively dramatise the transgression of the several taboos associated with Hindley's crime and are responsible for galvanising the shock of a photograph which was fetishised into a malignant yet perversely respected agent in civic consciousness. Yet the hysterical media iteration can also be considered in terms of a compulsive effort to master this pathogenic process retroactively. But it fails: whatever malignant properties the photograph had acquired over the years of its repetition, this paradoxically bestowed on the image itself the strange untouchable, auratic quality associated with the subliminally venerated taboo. And, in that he has dared to expose the malignant social process responsible for transforming this image into a venerated fetish, Harvey's treatment of the photo appears in itself a violation because it audaciously confronts this taboo by exposing a profoundly respectful attitude to it. By doing so, *Myra* reactivates the shock of the object by manifesting the *process* of its subsequent fetishisation and thereby our perverse respect for it. The painting thus constitutes the socio-psychological *aftershock* of the original photograph. Is it possible, however, to speak of an 'original' in this context?

Postmodernism and the Absence of the Referent Thesis

Insisting, as Harvey does, that the original photograph is the subject of the painting in the effort to de-contextualise the image by emphasising the arbitrary nature of representational systems relies on the received anti-realism slackly identified with postmodernist theory. By way of the latter, Harvey's dark work can be dissociated from the necessity of being accountable to the reality of Hindley, her crimes, as well as, of course, the entire context just considered (not to mention the political controversy apropos her prolonged unlawful incarceration that was being publicly debated contemporaneously with the *Sensation* exhibition).

Under the influence of pictorial postmodernism as theorised by a series of high-octane US critics in the early 1980s,[86] the view that representations are pure floating signifiers liberated from 'subordination' to transcendentally grounding signified concepts (a basic principle of Continental post-structuralism) has been commuted to a full-blown anti-realist challenge to the referential function of representation and has attained the status of an orthodox credo in recent mainstream art criticism. Images are understood, according to this orthodoxy, as detached from (and independent of) what they represent. This largely implicit but yet quite widespread theoretical view suggests that it is only a naive pictorial realism that causes unsophisticated viewers to tend to *reduce* the representation to what it represents. Emphasis is thus placed on the absence of the referent (what the representation represents) from the entire representational relationship, an emphasis that encourages us to celebrate the independence or self-contained *presence* of the buoyant representation liberated from the oppressive anchor of its object of reference.[87]

Applied to Harvey's defence of *Myra*, the postmodernist absence of the referent thesis amounts to the accusation that applying to the reality that the image refers to is to miss the point of the signifying enterprise. However, it is easy to see that such appeal to received anti-realism doubles as an effective way of abrogating the responsibility to treat adequately the ethical and political, contextual and referential ramifications of the morally provocative painting. Harvey's insistence on the photograph as the true subject of his work therefore amounts to the claim that his work should be considered an autonomous sign, irreducible to the reality that the photo, inescapably (because the photograph is an indexical sign[88]) refers to. As an indexical sign, however, the photograph of Hindley cannot be parsed as autonomous in relation to the reality that constitutes its inescapable referent; neither – even despite Harvey's express wishes – can his painting be reparsed as autonomous in relation to this reality, even less so because he has effectively, to defer to postmodernist terminology, re-*presented* the absent referent back to the photo in all its vainglorious obscenity.

In the same way that the theory of autonomism cannot account for the complex relationship between aesthetic value and moral value in morally transgressive art therefore, neither can postmodernist anti-realism, its contemporary avatar. For what seems to have entirely escaped the attention of postmodernist art critics is that, at least in the context of visual art, postmodern anti-realism is, ironically, entirely compatible with traditional formalism[89] and its conservative notion of aesthetic autonomism. Both commitments rely on an intransigent refusal to accept that art can be morally significant. Yet, all that denials of the moral significance of transgressive art (based on received anti-realist beliefs about the autonomy of imagery or the absence of referents) achieve is to stress *even more emphatically* the socio-political, psychological and ethical incorrigibility of the reality to which such culturally super-saturated images inevitably return us. John Tozer's analysis of contemporary painterly practice reinforces this critique: 'If we search for meanings *in* these paintings,' he observes, 'we don't find them in their *seductive surfaces*. Instead they are sited beyond the object, within the relationships the viewer has with his or her perceptions of the myths and histories that have accrued around [them].'[90] Such is precisely the case with Harvey's painting.

Myra presents a situation that, in the process of effectively transgressing the closure of the postmodernist theory of the self-referential status of the irreducible representation, dramatically – indeed, I would suggest, traumatically – breaches the closed realm of aesthetic autonomy. It impairs this closure forever because Harvey's treatment of the 'original' photo can, according to the terms of the postmodernist critique, be considered effectively to return materiality – the absent referent – to the small photograph of Hindley. To claim therefore that the painting is a completely reflexive surface simply because it refers to a photograph (and simply because it is a painting) and not to its underlying 'original' reality is as absurd as claiming that *Myra* is as self-referential as the prototypical abstract modernist painting.[91] Granted: it is a painting. Yet it is *not an abstract painting*, even if what it ultimately depicts is horribly abstract; abstract, that is, in the terrible sense. And here's why: even the marks on the surface of his work, the accumulated marks that exponentially compose the huge face, *even these marks* possess a direct, indexical reference.

Contextualist Ethical Analysis of *Myra*

Harvey's interpretation of the motif of Hindley cannot be construed as of exclusively aesthetic significance for it has an inescapable moral dimension that has to be acknowledged. Understanding the work is not just a matter of recognising *who* the painting depicts but also, as suggested above, *what* Harvey's formal treatment of the Hindley motif connotes and what it adds to who it depicts. When its individual shape is recognised, each pixel of the bitmap pattern in the painting is realised to possess more than a formal significance. As indicated, it represents an encoded statement with moral implications. I will argue that these implications take on a disturbing explication when *Myra* is considered within the context of Harvey's aggregate work. For, although the painting may appear anomalous in relation to the rest of his work, when relativised as part of a continuous pictorial project, the connotative aspects of *Myra* can be brought to light in ways that clarify their moral relevance.

Harvey showed two other paintings in *Sensation* that were more directly representative of his pictorial concerns at the time. *Proud of his Wife* (1994) and *Dudley, Like What You See? Then Call Me* (1996) are enlarged renderings of images of women taken from pornographic magazines; they are painted in a manner that knowingly references the action painting style associated with American abstract expressionism. What is unusual (and aesthetically interesting) about this work, however, is the application of paint. Harvey applies the paint with his *bare hands*, resulting in surprisingly opulent surfaces. In these works, this painterly treatment is reserved exclusively for the figures. Backgrounds, probably screen-printed or otherwise stencilled on the canvas, are reduced to schematised patterns and repeated to resemble wallpaper – thus providing a restrained foil for the messy incontinence of the hand-rendered figures.

With the exception of *Myra*, Harvey's contemporaneous work is related in both form and content to these paintings. *Doggy* (1993–4), *Julie from Hull* (1994) and *My Arse is Yours* (1993) are large-scale paintings of photographs also sourced from top-shelf porno magazines. However, the figures in these paintings are routinely reduced to a stylised outline, the uniform contours of which are achieved by laying adhesive masking-tape down over a black background prior to the anarchic application of pigment (again hand-smeared onto the surface without modulation). When the painted surface has dried sufficiently, the tape is removed, thus exposing the uniform outlines of the

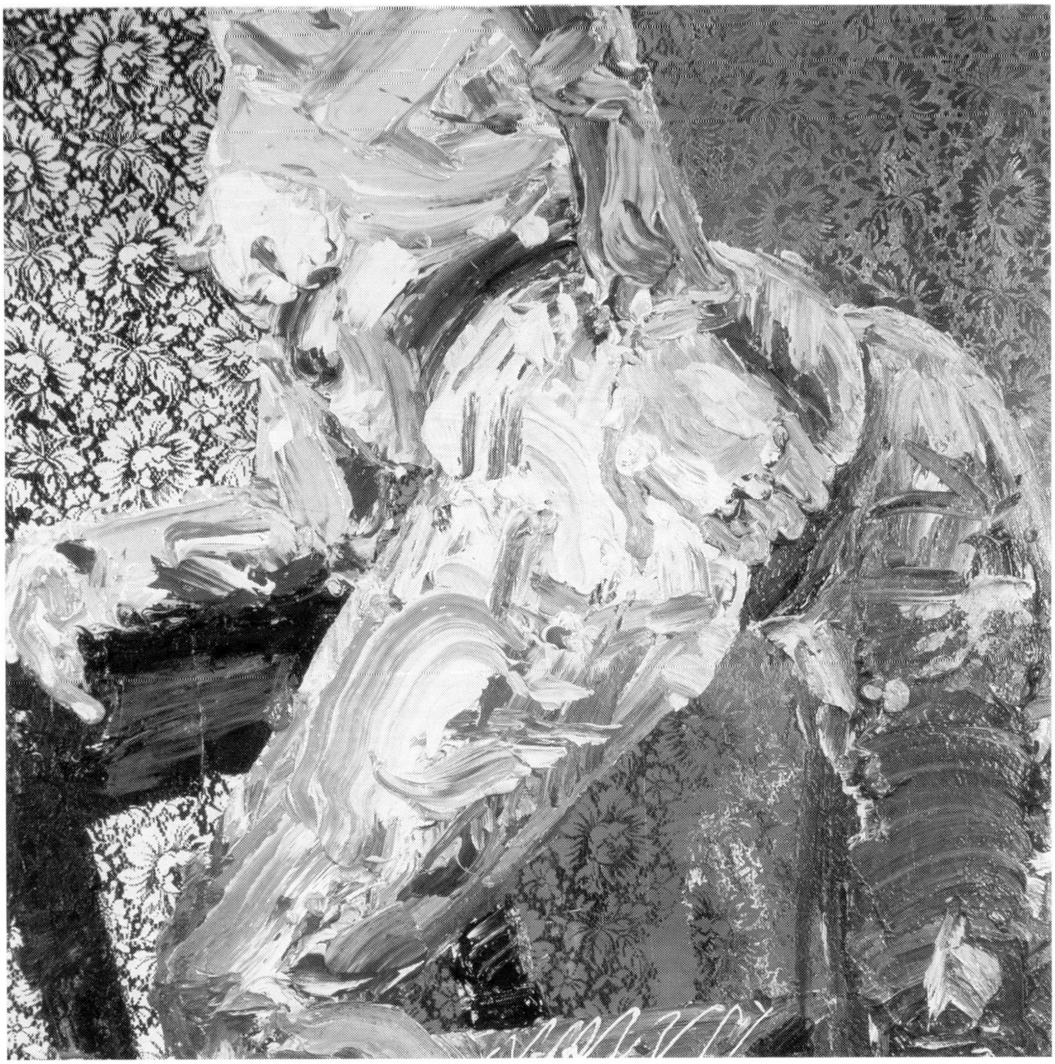

8. Marcus Harvey, *Dudley, Like What You See? Then Call Me*, 1996
Acrylic on canvas
6 1/2 x 6 1/2 ft

Courtesy Jay Jopling/ White Cube (London)

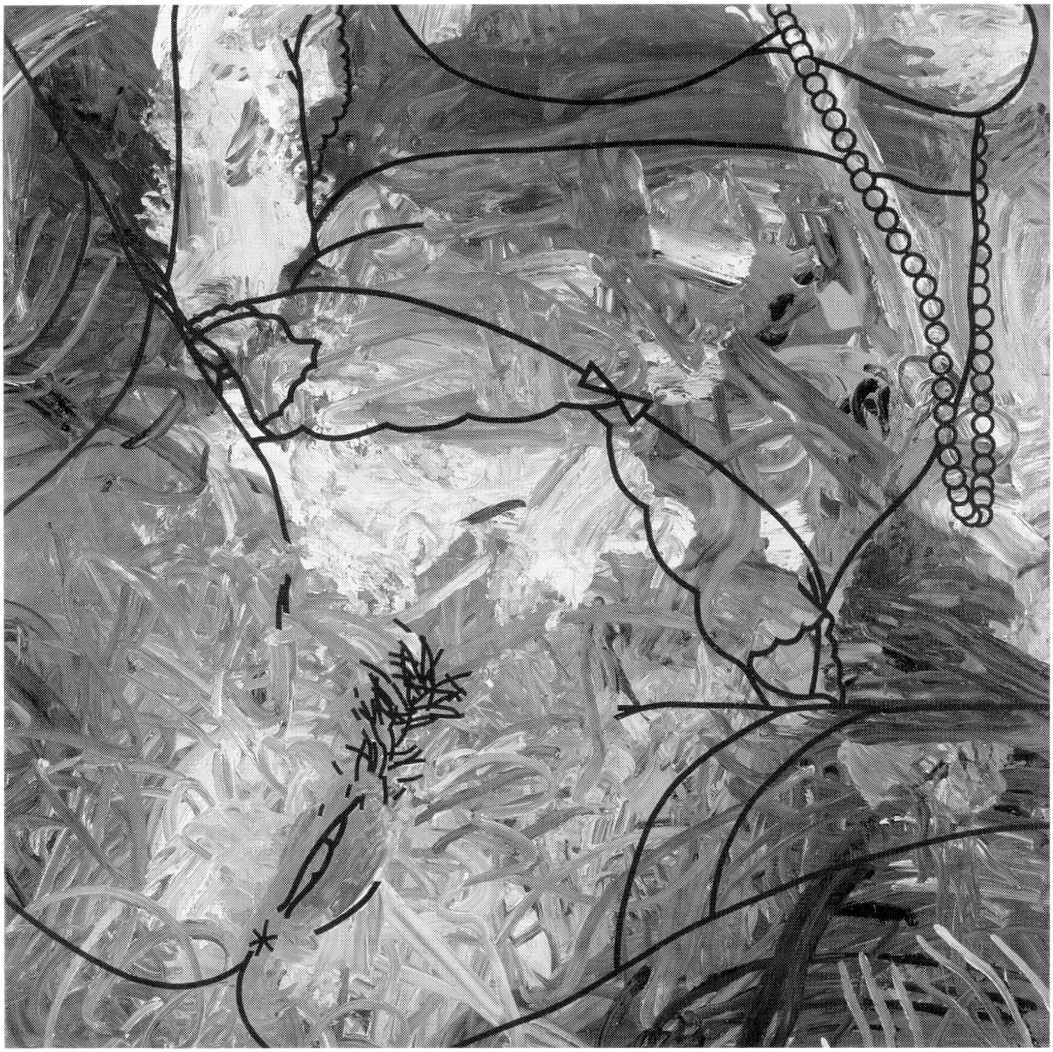

9. Marcus Harvey, *Julie from Hull,* 1994
Oil and acrylic on canvas
96 x 96 in (243.8 x 243.8 cm)

Photo: Stephen White
Courtesy Jay Jopling/ White Cube (London)

figure.[92] In a rhapsodic response to this work, Sarah Kent claims that Harvey considers the physical experience of painting to be 'orgiastic', like the 'animalistic and cannibalistic [?] aspects of sex'; the act of painting for Harvey, she says, signifies the 'abandonment of control'.[93]

That the paintings in this series are immediately recognisable as pornographic images is due to the typically submissive poses of the women in them. Each image displays the female body reduced to genital sections. To quote from Kent's essay, the 'images delineate a crotch, an anus, a pair of tight knickers, suspenders, stocking tops, labia and pubic hair.'[94] The overall sense of subordination (that many critics have associated with the pornographic image) is consummated by the fact that, in each image, the face is concealed, cropped or turned away from the viewer. According to Stallabrass, it is remarkable that Kent, usually so cynical in relation to masculine sexuality, has written an extended defence of such depersonalised, transparently pornographic images. She quotes a passage from the writings of Bataille identifying sex with violation to justify the work by suggesting that it is part of an imaginative cultural exploration and celebration of Dionysian sexual licentiousness. She describes Harvey as an 'unrepentant' painter as well as a 'sexual predator' and attempts, albeit by negation, to associate Harvey's work with the tradition of the nude. Although she moralistically condemns the nude as 'an unacceptable subject' for a contemporary artist and admits that 'Harvey equates art with pornography,'[95] it is astonishing that she is prepared to contradict her own judgement and endorse Harvey's porno-pictures as nudes that, when 'the shock has worn off . . . look as elegant as Roy Lichtenstein's swooning blondes'.[96]

Several cultural feminists and art historians have demonstrated the continuity of the European tradition of the nude with the viewing conventions of pornography.[97] Essentially, the nude, in this interpretation, is exposed as crypto-porn concealed under the alibi of a respectable and time-honoured 'high-art' genre. For such a critical perspective, much of the pictorial tradition of Western culture can be impugned for engendering a specific modality of vision that is determined by a conception of the presumed viewer as virile as well as heterosexual in orientation. Thus exposed as promoting dominant but disguised masculine interests founded generally on the subordination of women, this (now far from uncontroversial) early feminist critique, Matthew Kieran writes, reveals what was formerly concealed behind the undisputedly virtuous façade of culture as a cheap and tacky sublimation of sleazy desires. The Western tradition is thereby 'condemned for aesthetically camouflaging morally pernicious pleasures'.[98] If accurate, the result of this critique means that certain superior cultural treasures that were formerly appreciated with pride can now only be contemplated with shame.

Whatever the debatable merits of this critique, my argument here is that it is a critical error to view Harvey's work – despite what Kent seems to believe –

as continuous with the genre of the nude. By way of the feminist critique, the pictorial genre of the nude is revealed as encoded by a set of viewing conventions that hypocritically *disguise* its gendered subject-position and sanitise its crypto-pornographic content under the aspect of the disinterested gaze. According to these conventions, the viewer is not supposed to become sexually aroused (or feel desire for) the female form as delineated by the artist in the artistic context. Viewed seriously from this perspective (and this is what Kent fails to realise), Harvey's porno-pictures, in their deliberate and direct sourcing from top-shelf adult magazines (determined, despite the feminist critique of the tradition of the nude, by a set of entirely different conventions), if anything, aggressively, and with awareness of this critique, seriously contest the aesthetic tradition of the nude and its normative conventions of subject-position, context and content. The shock doesn't wear off.

For the same reasons that *Myra* cannot be considered a portrait, it is critically challenged to classify Harvey's porno-pictures under the genre of the nude because, by drawing on pornographic imagery (and the hand-application of paint), they represent de-sublimated activations of libidinous excess. Many contemporary artists engage directly with pornographic material precisely because it has been traditionally considered anathema to 'legitimate' or 'important' art. Contemporary art often makes reference to the photographic condition of sex-industry pornography precisely because this practice is transgressive.

According to a venerable distinction associated with establishment aesthetics, that which is considered pornographic can *never* be considered to be art, and vice versa. Pornography is commonly distinguished from art *aesthetically* because, being entirely reducible to its characteristic features of sexual explicitness and intention to arouse prurient interest, it cannot be, so the argument goes, of aesthetic value. Pornographic imagery, according to Kieran, is therefore incompatible with the aesthetic definition of art because it 'threatens the assumption' that all art is edifying and civilised; 'because it speaks directly to sexual instincts', it has been traditionally excluded from the domain of genuine art (which not only is necessary to be contemplated disinterestedly but which also must be made with this intention).[99] With pornography the disinterested mode of appreciation is viscerally disabled, because the 'attention is directed towards . . . body parts to solicit an objectifying interest which gives rise to sensuous thoughts and arousal.'[100] Often merely calling some work of art pornographic is enough to condemn it.

Involuntary erections inhibit the disinterested attitude. And this is what Kieran (and other commentators) fail to acknowledge (and it is important not to be hypocritical or dishonest about this): pornography, as commonly understood, is entirely of instrumental value; its function is to generate a certain prescribed form of sexual interest that demands physical relief. Its value is completely contingent on the success of this visceral reaction. Whatever (highly putative) aesthetic value sex-industry porn might possess, this value is nominal, strictly incidental, indeed completely, *perversely*, negligible in relation to this primary purpose.

Yet, and by now this should be obvious, this is precisely why pornography becomes transgressive in the aesthetic context. Harvey's work, crucially, is *not* pornography.[101] His paintings cannot be considered pornographic because they are not created with the (commercially profitable) intention to arouse sexual interest (or as assistive supplements to sexual activity, or whatever definition is used, it doesn't matter): they are paintings that adhere to the highest stylistic standards and are made for public exhibition – we would not expect, for instance, to find an audience at a public exhibition masturbating while ogling his work. But neither, by exclusion, as claimed, should his work be distinguished as a postmodern exemplar of the *classical nude* that, to employ the standard bromide, continues while questioning the genre. That is because his work enacts the corruption of both orders by each other. Indeed, it is possible to consider this corruption of typically exclusive orders as a central concern of Harvey's work in general: as the indulgent plastering of the painterly expression is corrupted by the reserved leading of the linear statement, the abstract is corrupted by the figurative, the excessive expression is corrupted by the restrained graphic, as thematically, the aesthetic value is corrupted by the pornographic imagery until eventually – corrupting the orthodox porn/art opposition – the mutually exclusive definition of art as not-porn and vice versa is comprehensively stunned and disturbed. As we remain by his work even when the shock has worn off.

It is in this respect, that is, as both formal and thematic corruption, that Harvey's work can be considered effectively transgressive. For, as Michel Foucault in his famous essay on Bataille[102] observes, the act of transgression carries a contradictory moment: it 'forces the limit', he says, 'to face the fact of its imminent disappearance, to find itself in what it excludes',[103] but in this very exclusion zone, where one order desires the elimination of the other, we are in fact just made more conscious of the mutual limiting categories of the order. In that 'outpouring which leaves us spent'[104] we become more aware, that is, of precisely what the contours of the limiting structure normally hold in place. 'Transgression, then, is not related to the limit as black to white, the prohibited to the lawful, the outside to the inside, or as the open area of a building to its enclosed spaces. Rather their relationship takes the form of a spiral that no simple infraction can exhaust.'[105]

He likens this phenomenon to a bolt of forked lightning splitting a uniformly black sky. Emphasising the darkness of the riven night, the crack of white imparts a more profound 'black intensity to the night it denies'. And yet, Foucault continues, the incandescent severity of the lightning depends on the surrounding darkness for 'the stark clarity of its manifestation, [for] its harrowing and poised singularity'.[106] Exactly in this way, the clarity of the schematic figures in Harvey's work depends on the intensity of the smeared passages for their singularity; while the abundant regions of paint depend on the angular schemas for their opulence.

Harvey's porno-picture series is transgressive in more than a formal sense however. Drawing on sex-industry pornography, this work could be reasonably – if fatuously – construed as a reification of a gendered fantasy determined by male sexual desire. Nevertheless, because enacted in the context of a formal artistic transgression, the resultant images cannot (and should not) be identified (or indeed condemned) as pornography. And therefore, according to the standard institutional opposition, his porno series must, by exclusion, necessarily be counter-identified as *art*.

Yet, is it not to miss something here to suggest, as Neil Mulholland observed of Harvey's paintings, that they 'allow the viewer conveniently to keep separate the categories of high art and pornography (the joke *requires* the distinction)'?[107] Is it not more accurate to argue – with reference to Foucault's definition of transgression – that Harvey's pictorial reference to the photographic condition of pornography, by virtue of the corruptive processes he deploys, results in the miscegenation of the standard aesthetic porn/art exclusion? For it is through this transgressive miscegenation – specifically, by infecting 'high art' (aesthetically valuable art) with its excluded other – that Harvey's corruptive strategies ultimately reveal the arbitrary nature of such theoretical, aesthetic (and, importantly, moralistic) distinctions. Indeed, one only has to consider the incontrovertibly aesthetically valuable work of artists that is characterised by features of sexual explicitness to appreciate the arbitrary nature of the opposition: Courbet's *Origin of the World*, Degas's monoprints, Egon Schiele's drawings, Hans Bellmer's *poupées*, late Picasso, Mapplethorpe's photographs, even some of Rodin's sketches, in that they depict standard sex poses with the attention focused on genital erogenous zones, all deviate from 'classical nude studies in order to evoke sexual stimulation by sexually explicit means'.[108]

Therefore, it cannot be claimed that – unlike sex-industry pornography – such 'pornographic' art should be morally impugned simply because it is sexually explicit or gratuitously graphic. Similarly, Harvey's porno-paintings cannot be criticised because they *appear* pornographic in content. Given what we have argued so far, it should be evident that the work is artistically interesting, sophisticated and complex enough to be considered of significant aesthetic value. Indeed, Harvey's corruptive technical strategies are artistically effective precisely because they dramatise the act of transgression simultaneously at formal and thematic levels.

Is there any way to tell from Harvey's pictures whether (to use Lynne Tirrell's terms) they endorse or protest against that which they depict?[109]

In these images, again, like *Myra*, it is extremely difficult to distinguish endorsement from criticism. However, in relation to what has been argued so far, it is reasonable to conclude that although Harvey's work does not explicitly condemn sex-industry pornography, this does not, by eliminative opposition, automatically mean that it should be assumed to celebrate it. Understanding contemporary art (especially transgressive art) requires the renunciation of such simplistic oppositions; indeed, as we have considered, much recent (transgressive and, indeed, abject) art is actually dedicated to challenging such either/or logical, aspect-seeing exclusions. But I will argue that this aspect ambivalence can be addressed by focusing on the significance of *the hands* in Harvey's painterly practice.

What is it about the hands? With reference to the porno-pictures, the use of hands to apply paint connotes the tactile sensuality of the caress or the 'polymorphous' physicality of the sexual grope. However, in the context of such a direct reference to pornography, Harvey's manipulation of paint clearly refers to autoerotic stimulation and hence connotes the onanistic private purpose of pornographic imagery. His pictures disappear in the face of the apparent functionless nature of public 'high' art in relation to the direct, visceral function of porn. What remains behind, branded through the frenzied activity of the masturbating hand, however, is a melancholy after-image, now reduced to a schematic scaffold. Therefore it is not quite correct to call his paintings porno-pictures as I have (and will, for obvious reasons, continue to do): they could more accurately be identified as *wank*-pictures.

Now the significance of the hand-smeared paint in this context comes to light. For this work is less about pornography than masturbation. Harvey's series constitutes a kind of resigned, remorseful and perhaps even guilty acceptance of sex-industry porn couched in a schematic after-image of its solitary masturbatory function. And because this aspect of his work is responsible for indirectly representing *men* – more so, paradoxically, than *women* – in a degrading way, it appears less shocking perhaps than depressing. Men, in the words of Sarah Kent, are portrayed in this work (even more so perhaps than the Sarah Lucas piece of which Kent makes the remark) as 'sex-obsessed wankers'.[110]

Work of his own hands: this painting is narcissistic in the sense of being auto-erotic.[111] However, through implicitly presenting themselves as regretful after-images of masturbatory behaviour (images branded quasi-indelibly through the blurred frenzy of moving hands), his paintings, in fact, may connote a sense of post-onanistic shame, the first whisperings of admonishment issued from a persistent super-egoic agency, or perhaps the first tugging of an *ex post facto* conscience interrupting the solitude of studio work. Thus, the porno-picture series could equally be interpreted as morally significant aftershock images of 'guilt or self-loathing'[112] associated with the consumption of pornography.

Perhaps. My point is that, according to this interpretation (which will become important for our ultimate reading of *Myra*), what may at first appear to endorse an industry devoted to the imaginary normalisation of the sexual subordination of women (or whatever), Harvey's paintings can also, simultaneously, be considered to represent a (perhaps even an overly moralistic) condemnation – but a regretful if resigned and accepting condemnation – of exactly the same thing.

What is it about the hands apropos *Myra*? The reason I have focused so intently on the porno-pictures is to provide ballast for the argument that Harvey's painting of Myra Hindley ought to be considered continuous with this series. Although it may appear a conceptual (and ultimately perhaps disturbing) leap to contextualise *Myra* as isomorphic with Harvey's porno-picture series, I believe it is critically important to do so. For, when the work is relativised within the context of Harvey's other work, certain key features come to light that are crucial to the ethical assessment of *Myra*.

Admittedly, most of the porno-picture paintings referred to above precede *Myra*. However, the later date of *Dudley, Like What You See? Then Call Me* (1996) strongly suggests that the painting of Hindley is part of a morphologically and thematically homogenous suite of work. This is because *Myra* is also painted with hands. Only, in the latter case, Harvey obviously did not use his own hands but employed a cast taken from a four-year-old girl to imprint the pigment on the canvas.

Although it may not be easy to accept, by informing the hands that compose *Myra* with a related iconological interpretation as that suggested above, I mean to suggest simply that it is not possible to read the handprint in Harvey's painting of Hindley as value-neutral. It may be considered to supplement the monstrous image of Hindley with a subtext of innocence, as Harvey suggests. Yet the handprint in *Myra* is not itself innocent. Inevitably perhaps, the connotation of the hands is that Harvey desires the image to be read as if it were made by a chorus of children. And, as we have seen, this detail, for many, wrongly, had the rhetorical effect of exploitation: children become accessories in the production of a fetish-image that signifies their grave abuse. Precluding any disinterested aesthetic appreciation of this painting as a generic still-life, or piece of cultural ornamentation,[113] the handprint may be considered to connote the 'subordination of Hindley's victims to their tormentor'.[114] I will propose that, however compelling, this interpretation is too simplistic and one-dimensional to have much critical currency for the full-blown ethical analysis of Harvey's painting that I am pursuing here.

Interviewed by Jake Chapman for the *Artshock*[115] documentary, Harvey referred to his morbid fascination with the photograph of Hindley as analogous to his contemporary interest in pornographic imagery: in its supersaturated, hysterical mediation, the scapegoat photo had perversely, according to Harvey, attained the simultaneously revered and reviled status of 'a piece of pornography'.[116] Earlier statements by Harvey reinforce the suspicion that the attraction of the image is, somehow, abjectly *erotic*: 'I was very aware', he claimed at the time of its exhibition in *Sensation*, 'that the pull of the image was a sexual thing and that is part of the taboo that increases its appeal.'[117] Therefore, although it may appear distinctly different, these associations suggest that *Myra* is, in fact, commensurate with the porno series. Mention of *sexual appeal* in this highly charged context has, perhaps understandably, disturbed many critics.[118]

There are further relevant details that, however disturbing, need to be cited in this context. In her account of his work for the Saatchi Collection catalogue, Kent makes a point of referring to Harvey's morbid fascination with the cleaning of his hands after work: 'It's like being a murderer,' he says.[119]

> When I was a student the bloke next to me got angry and scraped his painting off his canvas with his hands; it was thick oil paint and he couldn't wash it off under the tap. He panicked a bit and said 'I feel like I've got the hands of a murderer.'[120]

I am not suggesting that the porno-pictures are morally problematic but rather pointing out that when *Myra* is considered within the context of his other work, the attraction of the subject for Harvey finally becomes clear: his references to the perverse erotic appeal of the photograph and the stained hands of murder indicate that the hands in *Myra* are meant to add a kind of appalling surfeit to the image – a supplement that finally acts to codify and synthesise the violent and sexual dimensions of Hindley's transgressions.

Relative to Harvey's porno series, therefore, the little handprints that disturb the surface of *Myra* provide a subtle and suggestive amplification, yet also a very distressing indexical expression of the aspect of violent erotic ecstasy associated with Hindley's transgressions that, according to Jenks, exceeded the first-order physical abuse for the murderers.

Harvey's activation of the surface transforms the photo into a radically over-determined image. However uncompromisingly, however appallingly, this is ultimately appropriate to represent the process of its amplification into a negative-sacral fetish in public consciousness. It also possesses the extraordinary ability to return the unwanted gift of reference to the photo. The hands supplement the image with a super-saturation of sexualised horror that, ironically perhaps, was responsible for the social outrage precipitated by the painting. Therefore, the artist's reference to the erotic nature of the image need not be interpreted as narrowly as above, but rather read, in relation to our critical interpretation of his contemporary engagement with pornography, as a dramatisation of the manner in which the inert photo of Hindley had become subject to a (psychodynamic) process of projected erotic fetishism in the Freudian – as opposed to the previously suggested Marxian – sense of the concept.

In his analysis of fetishism, Freud notes the 'overvaluation' of the object that has replaced the intentional object of normal libidinous energy (cathexis). According to this process, the fetish, in its excessive value 'becomes detached from a particular individual and becomes the *sole* sexual object'.[121] With this excessive overvaluation of the libidinous object, a distinction can be drawn between local variations in sexual preferences and full-blown 'pathological aberrations'.[122] Regarding Harvey's comments apropos the Hindley photo, it would appear that he believes that, through a psycho-social process analogous to the Freudian hypothesis, the image gradually detached itself from Hindley as it metamorphosed into a horribly erogenous fetish; and this process was only facilitated through its hysterical media reiteration.

Harvey's identification of the photograph, therefore, as a 'piece of pornography' refers, in this context, to the manner in which the image, through its incessant reproduction, had slipped under the threshold of civic conscience and was for thirty years being perversely 'enjoyed' as a psychosexual displacement fragment simultaneously revered and despised by the media–public axis. Considered in the full light of this critique, however, Harvey's treatment of Hindley can be alternatively construed in terms of a legitimate reappropriation of the fetish for *moral* use: Harvey, in fact – despite how his work may be defended by the postmodern absence of the referent thesis – by codifying the image with the transgressions of the crime in the manner described here (i.e. through his formal reprocessing of the image), actually returns material (social, historical) *reality* to the image. Thereby – by re-presenting the referent – he ultimately de-fetishises it in order morally to impugn the public for the hypocritical way it allows pictures like this to be powerfully manipulated in order to cash in on the morbid sexual frisson they generate, and to expose the media for cynically capitalising on a contemporary (and also highly sexualised) fascination with the figure of the serial killer. Thanks to this process of de-fetishisation, the shock will never wear off.

However, I still believe that the hands that shape the face of *Myra* remain morally suspect for other, perhaps even less evident, reasons. Having the desensitising effect of introducing a cold forensic distance between the real-life victims and the act of creation, Harvey's prosthetic application of paint to the canvas becomes disquieting in itself. The little prints appear as marks left by a cold, speculative intelligence, touching without touching, laying print upon print down in chill grisaille, until slowly, methodically – and inevitably – the cruel, grey face materialises. Indeed, John Tozer identifies the moral significance of Harvey's technique in this instance as a gesture of abrogation:

using the prosthesis, he says, allows Harvey to 'vitiate the potentially indexical nature of the artist's brushstroke'; this transference ultimately has the dual effect, he continues, of conveying 'the problematic responsibility of authorship to the child and discrediting painting by using it in an unconventional manner toward what some may see as immoral ends'.[123] I agree.

More troublingly again perhaps is that, in this reconstruction of Harvey's creative technique, the little prosthetic hand is vividly pictured as analogous to a severed body part. In colours desolate as moorland loam, the implication is that, under the earth there are hands reaching out and grasping only clay, and for Winnie Johnson, whose son Keith remains buried somewhere on the moors, this must have represented an unacceptable and unforgivable detail.

Myra and Merited Response Theory

In displaying a confidence untroubled by doubt about his ability to comment on such inflammatory, socially sensitive issues as infanticide, child sex-abuse and serial murder – as well as invoking the politically charged questions of criminal punishment, recidivism and the rehabilitation of prisoners – the inflated dimensions of Harvey's painting seem, for Julius and Stallabrass, to correspond only to the hyperbole of an empty statement. Huge and inert, the statement manifested by *Myra* seems, at least for these critics, somehow conditional on its own renunciation. Perhaps the legitimate strategy of intentionally protecting art against interpretive reduction to single meanings results, in the specific case of *Myra*, in *moral undecidability*.

Has the work *used* the closure and protection of the culture institution as a carte blanche to strip the issues raised by the work of their moral context as Julius and Stallabrass suggest? Yet this is precisely one of the transgression's key procedures, for, as Julius also admits, the transgressive artist typically removes 'from his subject its traditional moral colouring'.[124] Indeed, we could say that this ethical blanching is literally configured in the monochromatic grisaille of Harvey's painting. 'The attention given to the opticality of the surface', Jake Chapman also remarks, 'fuses coldness and cruelty together such that the painting's chilling indifference makes an approximation of the crime.'[125] Again, I agree: it does.

Harvey's painting represents a suspension of judgement regarding the subject of his work. Julius concludes that *Myra* is expressive of a powerful moral 'indifference' precisely in relation to the ethical problems that it raises and exposes and, because of its mute indifference, ultimately exacerbates. With reference to Berys Gaut's framework for the ethical analysis of art, is it possible to identify the attitude manifested in *Myra* as the moral indifference recognised by Julius as structural to the image? According to Gaut, the attitudes of works of art are manifested not in their structure but rather in the responses they prescribe to their audiences.[126] Is it possible therefore to discern an asymmetry between the attitude that *Myra* manifests and the response it prescribes to its audience? Because, although Harvey's painting may be considered to manifest an attitude of indifference, the one thing the viewer who *engages* with this provocative painting *cannot* be is indifferent.

Gaut's theory of artistically expressed moral attitudes is not unproblematic. As we have seen, a non-propositional medium such as visual art rarely expresses any attitude explicitly. However, the 'manifestation of attitude' principle associated with Gaut's merited response argument ought not to be confused with the intentional fallacy (the belief that the intention of the artist can be made available to the viewer in an immediate or unproblematic way). Gaut's principle is directed more towards eliciting the responses that works of art prescribe to their viewers than ascertaining the putative *post facto* intention of the artist. 'The attitudes of works', Gaut claims, 'are manifested in the responses they prescribe to their audiences.' Therefore the attitude a work of art manifests is response-dependent: if it proposes that the audience should react in a certain way, then, it is according to this proposal that we infer the manifest attitude of the work.

A specific work may propose a particular response as part of its ultimate artistic constitution. Yet 'if we fail to respond as prescribed', that is, if we respond to the work in a manner contrary to the response it proposes – because we fundamentally disagree with the (moral) attitude thus manifested – the response to the work is *not* merited, and, at least for Gaut, this results in a deficient moral value and has a negative impact on the work's overall artistic significance. 'What matters', Matthew Kieran remarks of Gaut's ethicist hypothesis, 'is whether or not the responses prescribed by the work are merited.'[127] Therefore, he concludes, 'an actual audience's responses are . . . irrelevant – it is a matter of whether they are merited in responding as they do.'[128] Is this true?

Attitudes, especially in relation to the kind of art that matters most in this context, if ever manifested, are often inscrutable and therefore a matter of non-trivial indeterminacy. Despite the importance of Gaut's work for the evaluation of morally problematic art, he seems to base his ethicist hypothesis on the assumption that art-manifested attitudes are a priori readable. However, it is frequently extremely difficult to be certain whether transgressive art represents a condemnation or an endorsement of what it depicts (this, as we have considered, is characteristic of the transgressive aesthetic); this situation clearly makes it equally difficult to appreciate the response prescribed by a particular transgressive work.

Faced with confrontational art, it is often almost impossible to know quite how to respond to it. This indeterminacy of response is a significant cause of the moral shock that transgressive art has elicited in audiences. Inaccessibility of attitude and the associated difficulty of appreciating the prescribed response are especially pertinent features of Harvey's *Myra*, features that ultimately make any unsophisticated ethicist analysis of the work an intimidating undertaking. Ethicism however, as Kieran points out, *is* a sophisticated hypothesis; its fundamental concern is 'whether we *ought* to react as solicited in terms of what we believe the right responses to be'.[129]

Were those who protested most vociferously and actively against Harvey's painting – were least indifferent – responding as prescribed? Or were their 'actual' responses irrelevant because unmerited? If protest against the morally problematic attitude manifested by a work of art constitutes a merited response, then, yes, the protestors were responding as prescribed and *Myra* was appropriately understood as an expression of a profoundly insensitive, perhaps even malicious, attitude to those affected by the crime. However, if those who found the work insensitive, malicious or even immoral were reacting in an inappropriate manner to the work, that is, if their reaction constituted an unmerited response to that prescribed by Harvey's painting, then 'the work is, in that respect [i.e. in that its merited response is not compatible with its prescribed response], a failure.'[130] According to Gaut's response-dependent ethicism, by virtue of the response of the audience to *Myra*, Harvey's work is either immoral or it is an aesthetic failure.

We have already quoted Stallabrass's criticism that *Myra* remains dislocated from the response it elicits, meaning that the reaction to the attitude of indifference that the painting manifests cannot be indifferent. In Gaut's terms, therefore, the work fails to elicit the appropriate response – reaction to the work is unmerited and the work is, consequently, aesthetically unsuccessful. And yet, is the inaccessibility of attitude we have identified in Harvey's painting not ultimately indistinguishable from the attitude of indifference *Myra* allegedly manifests? Is it not this indifference that horrifies us most about the work? What if the horror elicited by the work is, in fact, the 'merited response'? In other words, what if, as has been suggested above, the extreme reactions of Winnie Johnson, Ann West, Peter Fisher and Jacques Rolé to what they considered to be the immorality of the work, paradoxically, constitute the merited response to *Myra*? Would we not be compelled to conclude, at least according to the merited response argument, that the work is *both* immoral *and* only aesthetically successful because immoral? As demonstrated above, because Harvey has discovered effective – and applied complex and subtle – artistic means metonymically to suggest the multiple violations (including, importantly, sexual violations) associated with Hindley's transgressions, *Myra* is a highly effective, indeed *astonishing* piece of work. Reminiscent of

Edmund Burke's characterisation of the sublime[131] (which many consider the highest aesthetic value) as simultaneously fascinating yet terrible, the painting, although profoundly shocking, *cannot be considered an artistic failure*.

It is also equally important to clarify why the difficulty cannot be settled by precipitously concluding that, because it is aesthetically effective at eliciting merited responses of moral shock, Harvey's painting is an 'immoral' work (at least in any uncontroversial sense) either. Julius observes: 'When we say of an artwork that it is immoral, what we mean is that the maker of the artwork is immoral.' This is because, he continues, 'only human beings . . . can act immorally, and it is only human beings . . . who can be described as immoral.'[132] This fact goes some way towards explaining why art critics have been historically reluctant to subject works of art to ethical analysis. (This is also, as we have pointed out, the problem with Gaut's ethicist theory.) According to this kind of analysis, it would seem inevitable that the author of the work be brought into ethically evaluative consideration; that is to say, a moral analysis is ultimately considered to involve judging the actions or behaviour of a rational agent (considered, in this case, responsible for the attitude expressed in the work) ultimately as *good* or *bad*.

Yet, as we have seen, works of art can continue to manifest ethical attitudes in the absence of any authorial agency. But regardless of the attitude manifested by *Myra*, according to the analysis undertaken above, whatever attitude the painting manifests can only be considered immoral to the extent that Hindley's transgressions *themselves were immoral*; and to this extent, therefore, it may nevertheless be *experienced* as immoral by those who perceive the work as a precise artistic representation of Hindley's transgressions – which, as argued, it very effectively is. It is what this non-abstract image of Hindley and its compositional elements represent (the entire historical, cultural and political heritage condensed within its over-determined matrix) that makes the ethical claim on us. It is the specific way this heritage is treated by Harvey through his image that is properly experienced as a moral provocation.

Therefore, it is ultimately a measure of the artistic effectiveness and success of the work that it precipitated the extreme negative reaction it did. This is equivalent to concluding that the work is aesthetically successful only to the extent that it may be experienced as immoral. Although this conclusion may appear commensurate with aesthetic immoralism (which, to recall, holds that morally defective features of a work of art can contribute positively to its aesthetic value), it is subtly, but critically, dissimilar.

Immoralism assumes that the work under discussion *is* immoral without defining what particular aspect of a given work of art actually counts as a moral 'defect' (and whether this moral defect is attributed to the work's content or its form and whether immoralism is always, necessarily, a moral *defect*). As we have seen, although Harvey's work has morally problematic formal aspects, his work, crucially, cannot be assumed to be immoral simply because it does not explicitly condemn Hindley. We could be certain of the immorality of *Myra* only if it in some way explicitly celebrated Hindley's crimes (or otherwise glorified or glamorised her, her crimes or child abuse in general). As argued, however, this is clearly not the case. Harvey's painting is considered by many to be transgressive because it remains tacitly non-judgemental on precisely these issues; ambiguity, silence or even non-condemnation does not automatically entail endorsement. It is simply that the work does not (and perhaps *should* not) provide catharsis;[133] it cannot achieve this, simply because, as Martin Amis explained with reference to the murder of James Bulger in 1993,[134] no explanation (psychological, sociological or even pathological) can reduce the true source of the horror surrounding the incident: it was random, irrational, absurd, radically evil. According to Amis, the story of James Bulger, like the Moors Murders, is 'seminal' for this reason; 'it is', he writes, 'a tragedy that allows no hope of catharsis.' He refers to the crowds that gathered to protest as the story slowly percolated through, as looking 'for purgation where there was none to be had'.[135]

The conclusion I have reached may not be to everyone's satisfaction. Nevertheless it can be parsed in the following hypothetical proposition:

> *If* Harvey's painting is experienced as unethical, *then* it is artistically effective.

Given everything claimed above, we would expect that, if it is effective in its representation of – that is, if it refers effectively to – one of the most disturbing transgressive incidents in recent history, Harvey's painting *should* elicit the extreme reaction it did. If it is effective it should have the potential to source that lesion in the collective consciousness spoken of above. Perhaps unfortunately, the ultimate test of this hypothesis is the reaction of those who were directly affected by – those on the receiving end of – Hindley and Brady's crimes. Just as their response depends on the artistic effectiveness of Harvey's work, so the effectiveness of his grievous yet extraordinary and 'seminal' painting depends (even more so) on their aggrieved responses to it.

It is possible, however, for other (non-victim) audiences of Harvey's *Myra* to react through empathy, in an emotionally extreme way to the work (this, indeed, has occurred). Although, as Jake Chapman points out, 'at first', the painting's cruel form 'seems to eclipse any sense of empathy for its subject matter', nevertheless this is paradoxically responsible for activating an acute sense of compassion for those affected by the crime. For morally interesting art it cannot be a matter of supplementing a representation with an explicit attitude of condemnation. Rather, the transgressive work becomes morally interesting through other, more subtle means (in this case the cold indifference that chills compels us to react in an emotional way to the work, to *feel* something of the trauma of the victims, to imagine the bereavement of the families). Thus the horror that Harvey's image elicits engages us in ethical practice: we have to work it out for ourselves in the absence of being moralistically recommended to adopt a prescribed attitude (which would be, in itself, of dubious moral value). Because of this, I conclude, Harvey's strategy ultimately compels identification with the victims of Hindley and Brady. We react (perhaps I ought to say: we *should* react) to Harvey's work with horror, anger, disgust or, indeed, profound *sadness*. In fact, wound around it like a dark wreath, this negative response has now become a structural – and morally important – part of Marcus Harvey's 'seminal' painting.

Conclusion

It appears self-evident (or at least many believe that it is self-evident) that transgressive art is (and should be) protected by the freedom of expression provision. By way of conclusion, I would like to question very briefly how self-evident this actually is. Returning to the original Millean definition of the provision, Matthew Kieran points out that his formulation protects freedom of expression in cases where the expression in question, although it may seem obscene or offensive to some, actually contributes in some way to knowledge, understanding and truth. Now, while Harvey's *Myra* 'may be artistically interesting', he remarks, 'it doesn't obviously add anything to the debate about how and why someone like that could come to participate in the murder of children or what the right response to Myra Hindley's punishment should be.'[136] Therefore it is not intuitively obvious, according to Kieran, that Harvey's work is in fact protected by the freedom of expression provision. But, as the extended contextualist discussion of Harvey's work above seeks to demonstrate (in opposition to Kieran's classical liberalist reading), the work may indeed be experienced as profoundly immoral (and therefore potentially harmful) by those affected by its codification of Hindley's transgressions (especially given Harvey's oblique reference to the violent sexual dimension of the crimes). This can, though, actually be construed to indicate that the work represents an artistic equivalent of Hindley's transgressions and is, to this extent, an astonishing, sublime and 'seminal' work of art. Perhaps it is not possible for visual art to add anything to political or ethical debates in the way Kieran proposes. However, as argued above, although the work may not add anything to the debate, it assuredly does raise traumatic awareness of the transgressive nature of Hindley's crimes. More importantly, from a moral viewpoint, as proposed, its cold and cruel lack of catharsis, paradoxically allows us to empathise with the victims by making us react in a way that can ultimately be considered to be in solidarity with those harmed by the crime (and subsequently by the painting). My point is that assessments of the work according to the liberalist utilitarian paradigm are ineffectual and limited by assumptions that cannot quite grasp the issues in question (the central issue being the paradoxical relationship between aesthetic value and moral value, as activated brilliantly in Harvey's project).

As Julian Stallabrass has suggested, the reactions of the protestors should have been taken seriously. But not in the way he thinks. Rather, as a thoroughly legitimate aesthetic response to a work of art that engages morality, their extreme reaction could have been demonstrated to indicate, on the contrary, the particular effectiveness of Harvey's painting. Therefore this reaction could be shown to have contributed to establishing the significant artistic value of *Myra*. In this sense, the reception of Marcus Harvey's painting in 1997 demonstrated the important critical power that visual art (even in a traditional mode) still possesses and, although not in any uncontroversial way universally protected by freedom of expression (because it also showed that art could incite violent mass reaction), nevertheless *Myra* is, *for those very reasons*, an extraordinary and culturally important, if morally questionable, work of art.

3 ATROCITY EXHIBITION

Aesthetic Defences of the Work of Jake and Dinos Chapman

> We've always tried to make work that is ambivalent about its surroundings. Or at least tactically active and entirely strategic in that respect.
>
> *Jake Chapman*[1]

Moral qualms about *Myra* may have been exacerbated by the decision to display Jake and Dinos Chapman's *Zygotic Acceleration, Biogenetic, De-sublimated Libidinal Model (enlarged* × *1000)* (1995) adjacent to Harvey's painting in *Sensation*.[2] The curatorial association set up between the two works seemed the ideal fulfilment of Jake Chapman's ambition 'to make work that is ambivalent about its surroundings'.[3] Although admired at the time by Sarah Kent as an 'extremely clever'[4] strategy, for many, it simply rendered the implicit connotations of Harvey's painting explicit by association; and considering the specific nature of the Chapman piece it is not difficult to see why.

Modelled in the signature Chapman shopping-mall style (a style that might be termed 'retail realism') *Zygotic Acceleration* is a life-size tableau of sixteen anthropomorphic fibreglass resin figures fused into a unified amalgam. The result is a composite yet recognisably female humanoid with its conjoined juvenile bodies constituting a single malformed organism – naked, smooth and featureless as a plastic doll. According to the artists, the model represents the offspring of some botched biotechnological experiment.[5] One of the quasi-girls has been inverted by the process; another has developed upside down from her twin's midriff. Wigs and branded sports shoes have been added to the model.

What is controversial about the work is the manner in which the model has been sexualised. The figures have suffered a disturbing interference:

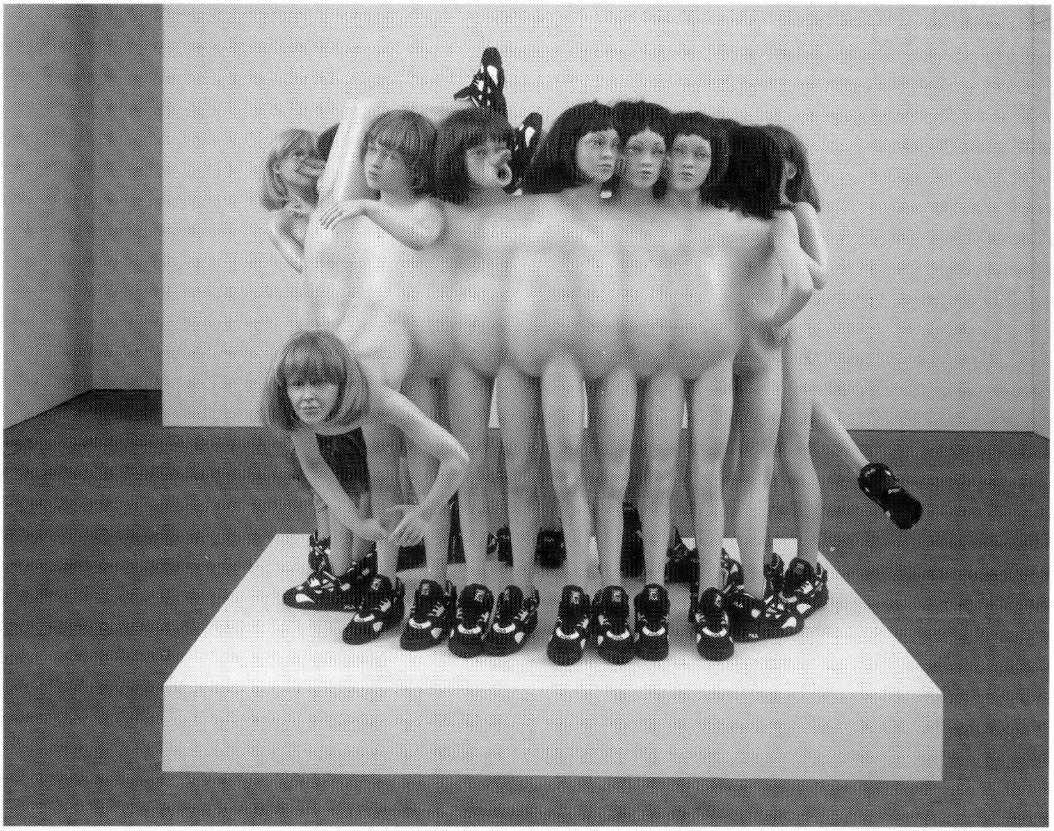

10. Jake and Dinos Chapman, *Zygotic Acceleration, Biogenetic De-sublimated Libidinal Model (enlarged x 1000)*, 1995
Mixed media
58 13/16 x 70 9/16 x 54 14/16 in (150 x 180 x 140 cm)

Courtesy Jay Jopling/ White Cube (London)

anatomically accurate and obviously adult genital organs have been grafted to the faces of the girls. Four have erect penises instead of noses and exaggerated O-shaped anal cavities for mouths; sculpted vaginal labia appear at the seams where the faces of some of the girls have fused together.

Jennifer Ramkalawon describes the unprecedented way in which the Chapmans' sculpture deceives by virtue of its 'least threatening' of forms. At first, the 'mannequins' appear totally innocuous – 'beautiful', she says, and 'beguiling' – 'standing innocently before the viewer'.[6] Suddenly, however, 'with a jolt one sees penises, anuses and vaginas sprouting from some of the children's heads.'[7] In this manner, that is, by way of the deceivingly enticing detour of the Chapman *trompe l'oeil*, she concludes, we are 'immediately put in the unlikely position of the covert pervert'.[8]

So, understandably, especially in the vicinity of Harvey's 'portrait' of a convicted abuser and murderer of children, this work attracted a substantial amount of media condemnation. Any uncertainty regarding the preferred reading of *Myra* was likely to be negatively allayed by association with the Chapman brothers' work; and although *Myra* (perhaps surprisingly, given the explicit character of the Chapmans' work) turned out to be the more denounced in the press reviews, Dalya Alberge did describe *Zygotic Acceleration* as 'the most controversial work ever shown at Burlington House'.[9] Recalling the first public showing of this work at the Victoria Miro gallery in 1995, when the Clubs and Vice Unit of the Metropolitan Police instructed that it be concealed from public view by screening the windows of the gallery, Alberge anticipated intensified controversy at the 'bastion of tradition'[10] that David Norris, writing in the *Daily Mail*, renamed the Royal Academy of Porn in honour of the Chapman brothers' exhibit.[11]

This chapter investigates whether moral misgivings about Jake and Dinos Chapman's art are justified. Clearly, any misgivings associated with *Zygotic Acceleration* owe to the manner in which the brothers have manipulated their model to denote the sexual victimisation of (female) children. However, even though the work's literalness means that the sculpture, as a matter of physical fact, makes an association between adult sexuality and childhood, is there any objective critical means of ascertaining with reference to the work itself whether this association can be construed as ethically justifiable? Is it feasible to aesthetically defend this work in a way that vindicates its ethical status? Or is the Chapman product, like Harvey's *Myra*, worryingly marked by ambivalence towards the moral issues that it provokes?

Does it not therefore become the responsibility of the artists (as well as those who are prepared to vindicate their work) to defend what prima facie appears to be a degrading and sexually victimising violation? But is there, it is also highly tempting to enquire, anything legitimately beyond the prima facie in the Chapman aesthetic?

The strategy used to address the ethical questions provoked by the Chapmans' art will appeal to the criticism that has emerged in review, evaluation or critique in response to their work since the early 1990s. Rather than attempt to expose the attitude manifested by their work, which, as Gaut proposes, 'should be construed in terms of a work's displaying pro or con attitudes toward some state of affairs or things',[12] I am more concerned with how the artists' work has been defended by supportive critics. Because defence strategies are themselves highly defensive, they are also highly revealing. And various theoretical strategies have been employed to defend morally transgressive art on aesthetic grounds.

Through the course of this chapter, these defences will be critically assessed on the basis of how they may be applied to vindicate the controversial aspects of the Chapman aesthetic. Such assessment will make it evident that defences of morally transgressive art have the effect of endorsing the ethical attitude manifested by the work. Critics who defend transgressive art in aesthetic terms implicitly justify its questionable ethical attitude by appearing to eliminate the moral meaning of the work. However, given the extreme literalness of *Zygotic Acceleration*, it is, at the very least, plausible to read the sculpture as an aesthetic expression of the sexual violation of children.

As is the case with transgressive art in general, the disinterested perspective has been disabled by the Chapmans' sculpture. Therefore, is the forced re-adoption of the aesthetic attitude in relation to the artists' work – in the effort to eliminate any moral response to the work – an endorsement of the symbolic violation enacted by the piece? Adopting a disinterested attitude to reprocess the Chapman brothers' sculpture for aesthetic pleasure, I shall argue, effectively represses its troubling moral status. And this has the secondary effect of mitigating its dubious ethical status.

Exposing the specious nature of the aesthetic defence of morally transgressive art, I shall demonstrate that it is not possible to eliminate something as structurally crucial to transgressive art as its moral meaning through the attempt to re-establish the regnant disinterested attitude. (Arguably, every aesthetic defence of transgressive art amounts to such an attempt.) This is especially relevant in relation to *morally* transgressive art that is tacitly considered to *require* an aesthetic argument to defend its value as (good) art and thereby indirectly, yet effectively, indemnify its apparent moral attitude.

The Canonic Defence and the Chapmans' *Disasters of War*

A critical technique typically adopted in defence of transgressive art is to associate the controversial work with a well-established, unanimously respected historical precedent. Identified by Anthony Julius as the *canonic defence*,[13] this highly persuasive procedure involves correlating the 'disturbing new work', by way of a canonical masterpiece, 'to the safe old work'.[14] 'What then appears as radically new and without antecedents is shown to be related, in possibly quite intimate ways, to earlier artworks, and thus is vindicated as art by this lineage.'[15] Unexpectedly perhaps, this critical procedure involves no complications where the Chapmans' work is concerned; many of the salient defences of their work have already been strategically anticipated by the artists themselves. Notoriously sensitive to adverse criticism, their work is revealingly defensive:[16] the link connecting their practice to an institutionally validated art-historical precedent is transparently presented in the work itself.

One of their first projects as an artistic duo was to assemble a modular adaptation of Francisco Goya's (1746–1828) celebrated print cycle *Los desastres de la Guerra* (first edition published posthumously in 1863 from eighty-three plates made in 1810–20[17]) from toy soldiers reshaped according to the scenes depicted in the prints. A text-book example of repetition compulsion, the Chapmans' first engagement with the *Disasters of War* (1993) resulted in eighty-three micro-tableaux set up on round green patches of modelling field-grass and arranged to form a constellation of tiny scenes from Goya's cycle. Exhibited as a unit composed of multiple elements, the resultant effect is a confectionary display of little horror shows or, in the words of James Hall, a 'manicured, "bonsai" version . . . of Goya, almost like greens on a Lilliputian golf course'.[18]

This marked the beginning of an extended engagement with the Spanish painter. In 1994, the artists assembled a life-size version of a scene from the *Desastres*.[19] Three shop-window mannequins were arranged according to the corpses in plate 39 (under which is written on the Ceán Bermudez album proof) *Grande hazaña con meurtos* ('Great deeds with the dead').[20] The artists dismembered and tethered their mannequins to a scaffold-shaped tree-stump upon what one reviewer described as 'an artificial mound of stage-set ground'.[21] The decapitated corpse hanging upside down by the legs from the cross-branch has its arms removed and tied up further down the branch beneath its severed head; another is held upright against the tree by a ligature around its midriff. A third corpse is tied down against the main trunk, arms outstretched, upper-back laid against the ground. All have been subjected to post-mortem rough-cut genital mutilation – the *grande hazaña* referred to in the title. The visceral realism of the scene is at its most intense in the fastidiously rendered wound-sites associated with this mutilation.[22]

Jake and Dinos Chapman have cleverly anticipated aesthetic defences of their work, for the work of Goya is *routinely* applied to in the defence of contemporary transgressive art. For instance, Lucy Lippard defends Andres Serrano's photograph *Piss Christ* by associating it with a Hispanic visual heritage that allows her to link the contemporary American photographer to Goya via Buñuel and Dalí; she claims that the characteristics that enable us to evaluate such difficult, 'violent *and* beautiful' art affirmatively should, if we wish to be consistent, also apply to the problematic works of later artists, and, by extension, to the work of contemporary transgressive artists that might at first appear discontinuous with cultural tradition (and thereby seem artistically dubious).[23] However, Freeland's analysis of Lippard in *But is it Art?* draws attention to certain works by Goya that, in her view, actually 'approach moral

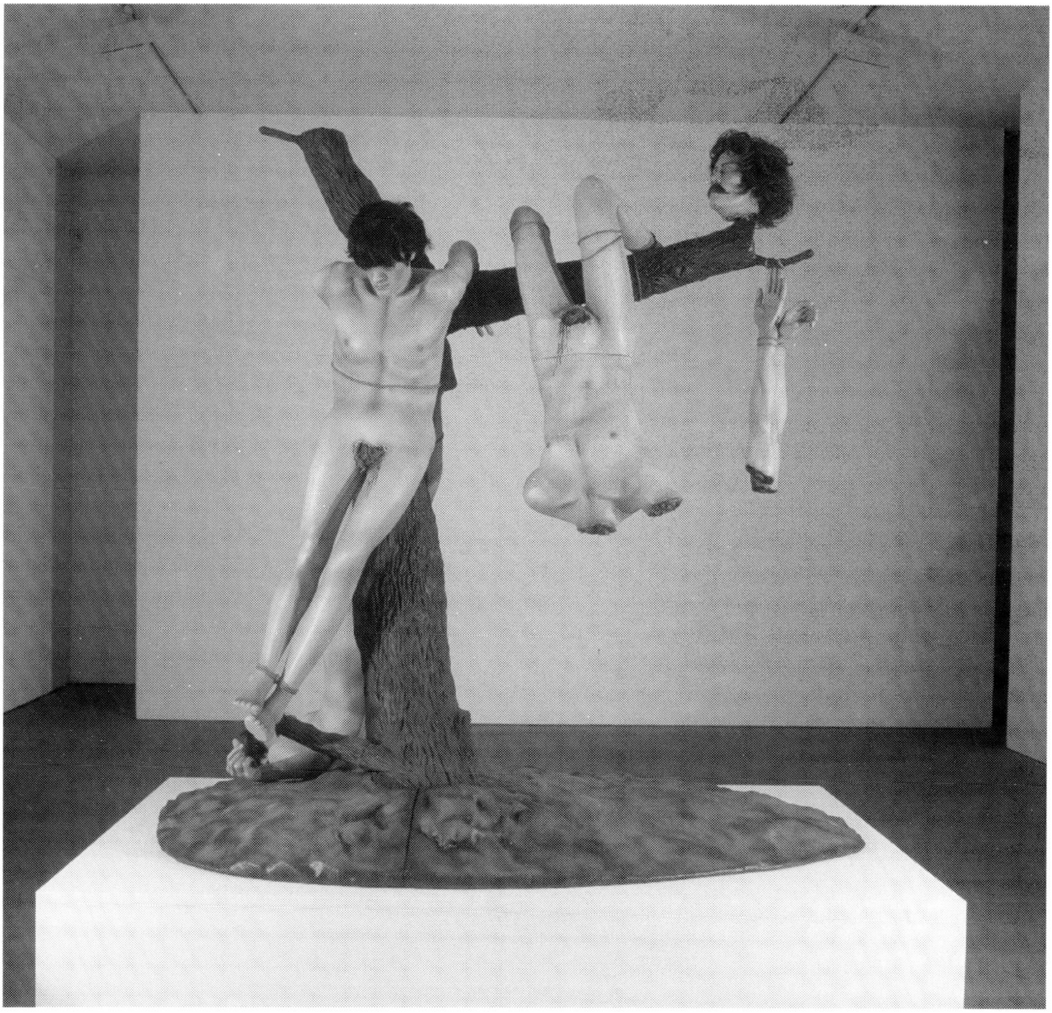

11. Jake and Dinos Chapman, *Great Deeds Against the Dead*, 1994
Mixed media
109 x 96 x 60 in (277 x 244 x 152.5 cm)

Courtesy Jay Jopling/ White Cube (London)

nihilism'[24] (she refers to the *Desastres* and the Black Paintings). 'It is impossible', just as it is with contemporary transgressive art, she persists, 'to view these late works of Goya with aesthetic distance.'[25] They are deeply problematic, indeed traumatic images, with a disturbingly negative morale: 'Are they the product of a diseased mind, a sick imagination, a temporary lapse of sanity?'[26] Yet she ultimately argues that it would be indefensible to claim that Goya is somehow diminished as an artist because these particular works are 'difficult, painful or because their moral point seems obscure'.[27] These problematic works are still *by Goya* after all.

Goya has been employed by defenders of contemporary transgressive art because it is possible to make a case, by deferring to his paradigmatic example, that art has always had a relationship with the shocking, the nihilistic and, most importantly, the morally ambivalent. Ample evidence of this can be gleaned from a basic knowledge of the history of art. The argument that certain works now considered classics of the European tradition were misconstrued by their contemporary audiences as immoral or ugly, and that, only by virtue of our increasing sophistication or the distance afforded by historical hindsight could the cultural imperative of such works finally be appreciated has, at this stage, the interpretative value of a truism. As such, because it explains nothing, the canonic defence cannot really be relied on to argue a case for the defence of contemporary transgressive art with any real conviction. Yet its persuasive power, despite the tenuous or frequently absurd comparisons drawn in its recourse, means that the canonic defence still possesses the rhetorical capacity to convince. Because of this, it remains a standard strategy in the critical defence of contemporary transgressive art.

Charles Booth-Clibborn, for instance, regards the Chapmans' art 'as a debate and dialogue with art history',[28] arguing that their 'connections with art history' should not be 'overlooked'.[29] This, however, is a strange claim as these connections are anything but 'overlooked' in the critical literature. Indeed, it can be counter-argued that it is not possible for something as obvious as the Chapmans' Goya, something, moreover, so transparently present in the work itself, to be overlooked in the way that Booth-Clibborn suggests. Anyway, despite his caveat, practically every critical account of the Chapmans' work has, as a matter of standard, treated their work in some way related to the 'canonic defence', as a dialogue and debate with its perceived art historical precedents.

Mark Holborn's predictable introduction to *Hell*: *Jake and Dinos Chapman*, for instance, begins with the customary Goya allusion. 'The power of [Goya's] work', he claims, is related to the fact that it has, at this stage, 'entered our collective memory'.[30] So, despite the historical specificity of the events depicted in the *Desastres*, the atrocities they depict have arrogated what Holborn calls 'a universal resonance'.[31] Yet, although the prints have been classified as 'masterpieces of Western civilisation', the continuing relevance of Goya's work

– its abiding 'truth' (*sic*) – is located in the 'chilling echoes in such uncivilised acts as took place at Sabra or Chatilla, in Rwanda or Srebrenica'.[32] Hence the foundation for the Goya–Chapman correlation is set up: given the regrettable universality of war, just as in Goya's original prints, the Chapmans' work is a reaction to contemporary military conflict.

Applying the historically specific significance of Goya's work directly to the Chapmans' version, Jennifer Ramkalawon naively construes the artists' work, as Holborn does, as a solemn commentary on the horrors of contemporary war. To this end, she extends the canonic defence by associating the brothers' art with the anti-war work of other, more recent political artists such as John Heartfield and Otto Dix. 'The Chapmans', she writes, 'cannot help but present the viewer with an uncomfortable and disconcerting visual experience of war as seen from a late twentieth century perspective.'[33]

Yet, *pace* Ramkalawon and Holborn, even the most cursory acquaintance with the brothers' art will reveal how critically challenged this interpretation is. Clearly, to connect the Chapmans' Goya-derived work to the horrors of contemporary conflict is laughable. It is obvious that, for the theory-conscious yet defensively autodidactic collaborators, Goya provides a convenient, but ultimately vacuous, means to experiment with the transgressive effects that, from a cynical vantage point, may seem to get all the attention in the contemporary art milieu.

A more carefully considered version of the canonic defence is applied by Stuart Morgan in his complex review of the Chapmans' work.[34] According to Morgan, the Chapmans' de-contextualised repetition of *Grande hazaña con meurtos* distils out the disturbing aspects of Goya's work in isolation from the humanist philosophical framework necessary for them to be construed according to the intellectual and moral programme associated with the European Enlightenment. Goya's predilection for the macabre, his attraction to sinister themes, as well as his fascination with the physiognomy of evil, although long acknowledged, have traditionally been excused in light of the socio-political agenda of the artist and the rational moral standpoint through which his predilections have been sublimated. By alienating these elements of his work from the historical framework that is perceived to imbue them with political cogency, rational value, and, thereby, ethical significance, and by rendering them in a completely schematic way, the Chapmans have subjected Goya's work to a kind of cruel *de-sublimation*. Thus isolating the irrational from Goya and draining it of its satirical alibi (and, importantly, its historical specificity), the Chapmans, according to Morgan, have succeeded in subverting 'the entire framework he had accepted – in other words, by identifying a weakness in the conception of his work – the Chapmans located their own niche'.[35]

Yet this effect is crucial to the transgressive provocation of the Chapmans' art. For, devoid of its supporting framework, Goya's work seems merely *insane*;

and the Chapmans' treatment thus obliges us to acknowledge an 'emotional surfeit' in Goya, a point where 'his powers of objective reporting deserted him and his reactions verged on the manic'.[36]

'The idea of castration, in particular, seems to have resulted in a rush of unbridled emotion as Goya lost control, cancelling the genitals of the murdered men with some of the force that the enemy had already employed.'[37] All that remains of Goya in the Chapmans' relegated repetition is this nakedly perverse spectacle of sexualised violence. The statements made by the brothers lend a degree of accuracy to this interpretation: 'Our interest in Goya', they have claimed, 'is the degree to which he constantly attempts to territorialize transgression to try and somehow represent something which is within the limits of prohibition, within the law, but he constantly exceeds that limit.'[38]

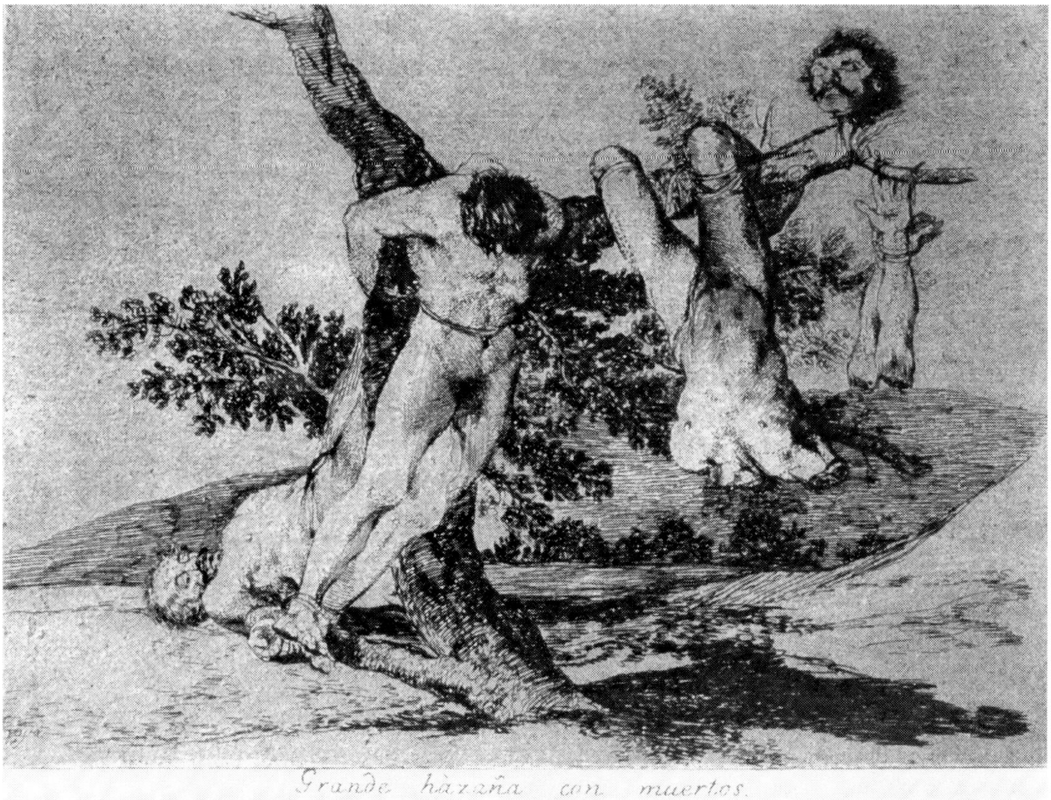

12. Goya, *Grande Hazaña con Meurtos*, 1863
Etching and drypoint

Ultimately, the artist turns out to be an opportunistic alibi for the Chapman brothers' vicarious exploration of the act of violence as activated most intensely in the dismemberment of the mannequins and in the wound sites that punctuate their *disjecta membra*. Perhaps the most generous way of construing the work is as a kind of therapy for the artists, a cathartic acting-out of repressed violent behaviour given safe expression through venting it on passive plastic replicas. But ultimately this means that 'Goya is irrelevant'; but 'there is', Morgan continues, 'an advantage in borrowing from someone, since the work is degraded from the start.'[39] Degraded, Goya is made irrelevant through the transgressive value of the Chapmans' repetition: there is no symbolism here, no metaphorical transfiguration, no satire, and, above all, no irony.

Yet the stark, naked, unadorned literalness of the work's realist and conservative form encourages art critics with savoir-faire to look for cryptic or indirect, sublimated messages. But what Martin Amis says of the fiction of J. G. Ballard can be usefully applied to this aspect of the Chapman aesthetic, for the objective of their art seems similarly 'to actualise' a sensation rather than 'to rationalise' it.[40] According to this distinction, the work is meant to be read as if it has *become* what it depicts; if anything, that constitutes the basic meaning of the Goya prototype in its transgressed version. For, although no representation can be identical to what it represents, nevertheless what has occurred here is that the violence involved in Goya's satire of the insanity of war has not only been isolated for analysis but also acted out in a context deliberately denuded of the possibility of such satirical critique. And, although it is executed with a paranoid awareness of psychoanalytic theory, this awareness leads directly back to the unmediated violence of the vandalising behaviour it enacts.

On a psychoanalytic level, Goya's print might still be construed to constitute an act of sublimation,[41] in that the sexualised violence of the act of genital mutilation is indirectly mediated through a satire on the atrocities of war and therefore rendered socially acceptable. However, what is still merely represented in the prints of Goya – a witnessed event mediated through pictorial form – is in the Chapmans' case given a kind of immediate volumetric presence.[42]

In isolating the act from its context of satirical condemnation and inflicting it on synthetic mannequins, the brothers' efforts with Goya may be considered to represent, in their borrowed terms, a 'de-sublimation' of the sexualised violence involved in the print. The reconstituted work has no purpose other than this – that is to say, it is impossible to discern any motivation in the work that transcends the vacuous use of Goya as an expedient scapegoat for testing 'transgressive effects' – a testing carried out, paradoxically, with a disturbingly 'disinterested' logic. Perhaps the most obvious transgressive act in this case, of course, is that of de-sublimation itself, executed in a more or less formulaic manner, by appropriating an artist's work and removing its satirical, critical function and therefore its 'moral colouring'. As the brothers are well aware, Georges Bataille identified cathartic transgression with de-sublimation, insisting that confronting repressed instincts through the act of exposing latent primal desires from their concealment in aesthetic form is the most effective technique for unblocking the liberating potency of transgression.[43]

More recently, in a comprehensive survey of the Chapmans' engagement with Goya, Christopher Turner explicitly addresses Julius's critique of the canonic defence.[44] Referring to an apocryphal incident when the police, supposedly investigating an allegation of obscenity, paid a visit to the artists' show at the Victoria Miro gallery, Turner quotes Jake Chapman:[45] '"They left with an image of the Goya."' Jake remarked: '"it was historical authenticity that gave us licence."'[46] Given the extent to which the canonic defence has been strategically anticipated by the artists (indeed, it could be argued that it is not Goya's print that their version of *Great Deeds* solidifies but rather Julius's canonic defence itself), what Turner's ingenuous discussion of the Chapmans' Goya fails to address is what this might be taken to imply about the critical technique itself as well as the transgressive aesthetic it is employed to defend.

For the reasons given above, it is critically challenged to take the relationship between the Chapmans' cover-version of *Great Deeds* and Goya's satirical prototype seriously: the connection is a deliberate, disingenuous and premeditated hoax. Enlisting Goya in defence of the Chapman aesthetic is thus entirely naive. Goya (and Booth-Clibborn's strange caveat betrays that he suspects that this is precisely the case) is reduced to a formality or, better, a triviality, in relation to the primary theme of the Chapmans' work. In relation to the Chapman aesthetic, Goya is a chimera not worth pursuing with any serious commitment. A canonic defence of the Chapman brothers' Goya that employs Goya is redundant because it does not add anything to the work that cannot immediately be read there: Goya is irrelevant to the Chapmans' engagement with Goya. So, despite appearances, and, alas for art historians, the work of Goya cannot be solicited in a critical defence of the Chapman aesthetic. So what can?

The Transgressive Defence of Transgressive Art

In 1996, in conjunction with their major exhibition at the Institute of Contemporary Arts in London, important essays were published on the Chapman brothers.[47] Relying on a version of the canonic defence, these texts set a precedent that has since become ubiquitous in the critical literature. This is the evasion and indirect justification of the morally objectionable aspects of the Chapmans' art with reference to a pre-existent discourse of transgression (exhibiting, in parallel with the artists' own claims for the work, a predilection for its literary and philosophical avatars). Critical reception of the Chapmans is replete with obsequious allusions to erotic excess in Bataille, to infantile sexuality in Freud, to Nietzsche's *Beyond Good and Evil*, to sadistic pleasure in de Sade and, less frequently perhaps, to cruelty in the writings of Antonin Artaud.[48] More recent criticism has witnessed a veritable database of references to Jacques Lacan, Julia Kristeva and Gilles Deleuze as well as to the hot new Slovenian philosopher (who must, it seems, be quoted at all costs) Slavoj Žižek, added to the ever-dilating phalanx of canonical figures that have been long-listed to aggrandise the Chapman aesthetic.[49] Sometimes actually reduced to *lists* of names – as if biblical incantation were enough for the canonic defence to achieve its hypnotic effect – the most compelling aspect of this quantitative strategy is that it reveals a telling anxiety on the part of the critics who employ it.

Compulsively cramming as many references as possible into a small vacuum of potential structure, the hope is that some relevant theoretical link will eventually be uncovered that contributes meaning to this work that they fear may be meaningless. To select a recent and typical example of this compulsive stratagem: Christoph Grunenberg, writing in the *Bad Art for Bad People* (2006) catalogue, and explicitly following Douglas Fogle's earlier 'essay' for the *Chapmanworld* catalogue, informs us that 'Nietzsche, Freud, Bataille, Lacan and Deleuze and Guattari are the godfathers of [the Chapmans'] kindergarten of deviation, perversion and science gone wrong.'[50] However, before we have time to digest this *mélange*, the critic is quick to point out that

> the artists not only display an acute historical awareness of psychoanalysis, philosophy and critical theory but [also] continue a productive dialogue with past masters that extends from 'primitive art' and the apocalyptic visions of Goya and Blake via Rodin and the Surrealists to more recent proponents of psychological terror and trauma, such as American West Coast artists Paul McCarthy and Mike Kelley.[51]

Neither the essays in the *Chapmanworld* nor the *Bad Art for Bad People* catalogues make any reference to the sexual abuse of children, paedophilia or child pornography. Far from being critically assessed, therefore, the moral issues raised by the Chapmans' work are never even considered. Given that certain key works in the Chapman oeuvre make reference to paedophilia (and/or child porn) it is extraordinary that, in a context that purportedly serves to evaluate the art under analysis according to theme, content and context, the main provocation associated with their work is cautiously, meticulously avoided. Yet this careful strategy of avoidance is ultimately responsible for the neurotic anxiety we have identified as a constitutive element of the critical responses to the artists' work. It is tempting to postulate that this refusal to confront the morality of the Chapmans' art is comparable to classic Freudian repression.[52] Can the compulsive piling of name upon name be considered a symptom of the neurotic anxiety associated with the repression of the initial ethical response to the unacceptable morality manifested by their sculptures?[53]

As Grunenberg's irritating essay progresses, any hope of fishing some relevant meaning from the bait of names rapidly diminishes. Indeed, by the time the unpredictable conclusion is finally reached, the critic's relief is palpable. Expressed as eloquently as a flatulent exhalation of pent-up breath, Grunenberg's relief vents itself in ecstatic claims made for the Chapman aesthetic: we are breathlessly informed (as if the previous listing of canonical names provided incontrovertible evidence of this) that the art of Jake and Dinos Chapman 'addresses both topical and fundamental questions about human existence and identity, radically challenging orthodox moral parameters and biological truths'.[54] Is this a joke? Does Grunenberg really believe this?

Apart from the ultra-hyperbolic absurdity of such conclusions, what is perhaps most difficult to accept regarding the general strategy under scrutiny here is its uncritical faith in the authority of the canonic defence itself. An apparently reverential credence in the validity of the cited references and their self-evident appropriateness for the art discussed ensures that the relevance of the application itself never comes into question. But is the imperative of criticism not precisely to examine such reverential credibility through investigating the aptness of references and thereby questioning the reliability of the unquestioned authority? Is this imperative not even more insistent when it comes to art manufactured with the canonic defence cynically in mind?

The version of the canonic defence criticised here trades on the presupposition that a work of transgressive art is automatically of aesthetic value. Because the Chapmans' art is taken unquestionably to constitute, according to the authority of the artists and the figures they reference, a work of avant-garde transgression in the Bataillean–Sadean[55] heritage, the suggestion is that it is therefore to be valued, in exactly the same way as Bataille, de Sade et al's texts have been re-evaluated as part of a culturally significant vanguard of artistic expression. The implicit caveat here is that the artists' work should not be misconstrued, as the work of these writers initially perhaps was, as merely obscene or perverse, a dark idiosyncratic deviation from the norm – but rather seen as a courageous and radical form of critical cultural practice, which, precisely because it deviates from aesthetic standards, constitutes a vital artistic expression that ought to be unconditionally celebrated.

Now although he does discuss the contemporary critical tendency to endorse transgressive art unreservedly, this is a defence of transgressive art that Julius does not consider in precisely this way because it would be, given the terms of his analysis, circular. The aesthetic defence of transgressive art on the basis that it is simply *transgressive* relies on the assumption that transgression is an artistic achievement in itself – is, in itself, aesthetically good. According to such endorsement, any associated moral misgivings about transgressive art are overruled as purely epiphenomenal on the basis of the high aesthetic esteem that the concept of transgression *as such* is held in the context of contemporary cultural production. In this context, as we have considered, artistic transgression is valued for its avant-garde (*épater les bourgeois*) ethos of creative taboo-breaking; therefore its sometimes problematic ethical value can be aesthetically elided by indicating transgressive artists' critical prescience in contesting the sclerotic standards of aesthetic ideology as well as their courage in challenging the inured codes of conventional morality. Considered in this sense, transgression, Jenks explains, 'is not an abhorration nor a luxury, it is rather a dynamic force in cultural reproduction – it prevents stagnation by breaking the rule'.[56]

But just how plausible is the transgressive defence of the Chapman brothers' art? As their work constitutes a direct assault on the disinterested attitude – then clearly, according to the definition of transgression developed in this book, their work can be considered eminently transgressive. What is open to being critically contested, however, is the unquestioned critical identification of transgression with artistic value. For, when applied to specific cases, this amounts to the aesthetic justification of the morally problematic aspects of the work.

To elide the ethical problems associated with morally transgressive art successfully, all the critic with an awareness of the contemporary tendency to endorse transgression needs to do is to identify Jake and Dinos Chapman's sculpture as 'transgressive'. Secondly, the fashionable (and predictable) references require to be cited. Should this remain insufficient – that is, should moral questions still remain in the notional reader's mind – this insufficiency can be incrementally diminished with more references to other canonical artists or writers.

Evaluation of the aesthetic defences of the Chapmans' work cannot be considered complete without engaging a revealing lacuna in the critical literature. The prototypically transgressive work of Polish-born German artist Hans Bellmer (1902–75), being both transgressive and canonical, should appear tantalisingly paradigmatic for the kind of aesthetic defence of the Chapman brothers challenged here.

Perhaps not as immediately obvious as Goya, Bellmer seems at least as significant an art historical pretext for the Chapman aesthetic. Yet Bellmer receives only the most subsidiary consideration by critics (usually appearing, if at all, as just one name among others[57]). Why is this? Perhaps it is because the critical pursuit of such a rich artistic precedent might be seen as putting into question the assumption that the brothers' work is *authentically* transgressive and thereby jeopardise the credibility of the transgressive canonic defence itself. Any encounter that may give reason to question how transgressive the Chapmans' art actually is must of necessity be suppressed. Exactly how does Bellmer challenge the authenticity of the Chapmans' work?

Hans Bellmer, Bataille and Authentic Transgression

Epitomising André Breton's (1924) surrealist programme to pursue directions of thought unimpeded by ethical constraints,[58] Bellmer produced a portfolio of extraordinary images in the mid-1930s, featuring a mannequin of his own eccentric design. 'The Doll' (*Die Puppe*) was a juvenile feminoid apparatus with torso, legs and mask moulded of plaster and *papier mâché* over a skeleton of wood and metal; it was completed with ready-made accessories – a wig, eyes of glass, a wooden hand and ball-joints, some fragments of clothing, shoes. Standing approximately 4 feet 8 inches (150 cm approx.) in height, this 'first doll' (1933–4: he made another a year later) was photographed, by Bellmer, in the various developmental phases of its fabrication. (There are several carefully authored *mise en scènes* of the itemised elements of the apparatus that include diaphanous fabrics and frozen flowers and are vaguely reminiscent of Victorian gothic curios.[59]) Ten of these photographs appeared in book form (under the title *Die Puppe*) in 1934 (subsequently translated into French as *La Poupée* in 1936); and also, in 1934, eighteen photographs were famously published as a gatefold spread in Parisian surrealist journal *Minotaure*.[60] Entitled *La Poupée*, this visual narrative included the descriptor: 'Variations sur le montage d'une mineure articulée'.[61]

Unlike the generic mannequin's typical elision of sexual characteristics, Bellmer has given the erogenous zones of his construction a kind of morbid emphasis. Complementing the moulded cleft of the pudenda, the nascent breasts have exaggerated stylised nipples; secondary sexual characteristics are indicated and amplified by the addenda of wig, glass eyes, clothing, fabrics and shoes. In certain photographs, *Die Puppe* is carefully calibrated into postures suggestive of coy flirtation. As Sue Taylor suggests, in these compositions, Bellmer has projected a seductive agency onto the doll.[62] 'The doll is naked, physically exposed, vulnerable, and morose, yet deliberately coquettish.'[63] Yet the state of the doll – her chalky, flaky, crumbling pallor – as well as the complex shadow geometries of the chiaroscuro, suggest a more sinister narrative. Simultaneously pitiable and implacable, the doll appears in these images as both subjugated figure and threatening, ominous, potent presence.

The two dolls were designed to have a specific psychosexual purpose. Codified according to psychoanalytic theory, Bellmer's dolls represent classic fetish-objects, material displacements through which the sexual aim has been redirected. They were explicitly conceived as conduits for his programme of 'erotic liberation',[64] functioning as autoerotic substitutes capable of facilitating the indirect gratification of prohibited perversions. 'It was worth all my obsessive efforts', Bellmer wrote, 'when, amid the smell of glue and wet plaster, the essence of all that is impressive would take shape and become a real object to be possessed.'[65] According to this scenario, the doll-fetish becomes both a manifestation of the perverse eroticism that stimulated Bellmer and an opportune proxy through which safely to discharge its powerful libidinous energy.[66] Yet, in the photographs of forensically dismembered doll elements, or, even more so perhaps, in the hand-tinted images of the contorted *disjecta* of the later doll – all tumescent pinks and *Night of the Living Dead* acid greens – a darker, more hostile and venereal eroticism is suggested, beside which the sadist's desire to inflict sexual 'degradation and humiliation' seems almost sentimental in comparison. (He apparently referred to the dolls as his 'victims'[67].)

These images speak of an effort to master unacceptable desires through their 'convulsive'[68] (Bellmer's word) vicarious expression on artificial surrogates. In acknowledgement of the domination that the fantasy of the eroticised, seductive girl had over him – recognising a challenge to his self-control and moral economy – the weird, muscular constructions lend themselves to being interpreted in terms of the artist's struggle to reassert control over his perverse libido. By exerting a violent destructive intelligence over these inanimate – and absolutely passive – anatomies he would thus symbolically annihilate (and thereby control) the illicit desires stimulated by this fantasy.

What remains morally disquieting about Bellmer's dolls, exactly as in the Chapmans' work, is the manner in which they have been eroticised. *Die Puppe* signifies childhood, *qua* doll, in both form (playthings of children – girls, typically) and content (it is designed to represent a juvenile female); the projection of adult sexuality onto these contorted figures therefore constitutes such a morally threatening juxtaposition that, in the words of one critic, it 'strikes us where we are most vulnerable' – where it may appear indeed 'impossible to appropriate our ethical standards to any effect'.[69] To this extent homologous with the Chapman aesthetic, Bellmer's work may therefore be considered morally threatening due to its problematic corruption of the codes of childhood innocence with a perverse eroticism – bringing the work to the threshold of child pornography. Again, like *Zygotic Acceleration*, although it may not *depict* explicit sexual activity between children and adults, Bellmer's situating of juvenile content in a sexually charged context is sufficient to connote – that is, provoke strong emotional suggestions of – paedophilia. In a manner that also serves to elucidate the modality of the Chapman models, Sue Taylor identifies Bellmer's doll as 'a kind of sex toy' created, she insists, 'to gratify specifically paedophilic desires'.[70]

Jake and Dinos Chapman's work is close, perhaps even *too* close to the canonical Bellmer. It is close enough to engender suspicions that this kind of proximity does not possess the requisite knowing reflexivity that, because not plagiarised or appropriated in the same way as the Chapman–Goya synthesis, and therefore merely repeating the transgressions associated with Bellmer's work, is just an old-fashioned, been-there-before, derivative influence. Secondly, and more significantly from our perspective, is the suggestion that such a *rapprochement* with the 'authentic' transgressive art of Bellmer may also bring the morality of the Chapman sculpture into focus – something that would subsequently require the ethical modality of their work to be confronted. For, despite psychoanalytic efforts to exegete, and thereby aesthetically reappropriate Bellmer's work as an *artistically sublimated* catharsis of sado-masochistic tendencies (in the style of Bataille), it is close, and too close again perhaps, to being construed as self-indulgent fantasies of child rape, murder and post-mortem dismemberment, which, if linked to the Chapman brothers, would simply disambiguate by proxy the moral constitution of their work – the very constitution that critics, as argued, have been most anxious to avoid.

As we have observed apropos the Chapmans, Taylor has noted that 'the pedophilic [*sic*] aspects of Bellmer's project are often elided in the literature';[71] among critics writing on Bellmer she has located an anxiety analogous to that remarked here of the Chapman reviewers. Speaking of a 'nervous need to deny the hostility and aggression everywhere present in [Bellmer's] art',[72] she maintains that the critical writing on Bellmer is 'dominated by poetic adulation of his "daring" treatment of sexual themes and takes at face value his claim to therapeutic intentions – "to help people lose their complexes, to come to terms with their instincts"'.[73] Indeed, his biographer's aim to redeem Bellmer from suspicions of obscenity is accused of relying on canonical figures in the effort to 'secure a noble patrilineage' for the artist and thus, again, as we have suggested regarding the Chapmans, vindicate the problematic aspects of the work by way of the canonic defence.[74]

One of the canonical figures employed in the critical effort to secure a noble patrilineage for the Chapman aesthetic, as we have seen, is Georges Bataille. Despite the brothers' explicit and repetitive allusions to the writer in their work, acknowledgement of the antecedent Bellmer, however, may be considered to cast critical doubt on the credibility of this connection. As has been well documented, Bellmer identified closely with Bataille, regarding the French writer as a kindred spirit – someone with a shared set of preoccupations and mutually validating obsessions.[75] Late in life, looking back at his career, Bellmer remarked: 'I agree with Georges Bataille . . . that eroticism relates to a knowledge of evil and the inevitability of death, it is not simply an expression of joyful passion.'[76]

Awareness of mortality, according to Bataille, gives human sexuality its transgressive dimension – 'its brutally erotic character'.[77] Against the horizon of the ubiquity of death, sexuality becomes, he wrote, emotionally profound, imbued with intense symbolic meaning – a form of life that, in its opposition to the inertness of death, celebrates creative disobedience to natural law.[78] 'When the moment of sexual union first came to be related to conscious desire by human beings,' Bataille suggests, 'the end sought was pleasure.' And there is no desire and no pleasure, he adds, that does not ultimately involve some infraction, some violation. Indeed, he speaks often of 'the violence of pleasure'.[79]

Initially framed by a thaumaturgical semiotic of concealment and revelation – the torah of prohibitions and penetrations that, for Bataille, adumbrates the sacred realm – the zone of the erotic (that is, *human* sexuality) eventually became schematised in the regulative taboos of social morality. But, in that they almost inevitably involve the creative violation of such regulative taboos, the private solipsistic pleasures and intensities of profane erotic recreation constitute for Bataille the 'type of all transgressions'.[80]

The perverse synthesis of sexuality and violence insisted upon in Bataillean eroticism is given corresponding visual expression in the iconography of Hans Bellmer. To the extent that his imagery may be taken to constitute a particularly appropriate profile of this nexus of ideas, his art lends itself to thematisation in the terms of Bataille's theory of transgression. We may be dismayed by Bellmer's fragmented schoolgirls in ankle socks and Mary-Jane shoes, dismayed by encountering childhood presented in erotic circumstances, dismayed by the intimations of child abuse and murder; yet, despite our better judgement, we are nevertheless enticed by the strange images, which draw us in with a kind of excited fascination. 'Taboo and transgression', Bataille writes, 'reflect these two contradictory urges.' Appalled yet fascinated by Bellmer's work, we find ourselves subject to the contradictory emotional responses crucial to the axiological paradox of transgression: 'The taboo would forbid the transgression', Bataille adds, 'but the fascination compels it.'[81]

This explains why merely *looking* at Bellmer's exposure of prohibition *feels* like a violation. The very concept of taboo, according to Bataille, necessarily *includes* violation: the fascination compels it. The significance of the prohibition cannot be conceived without prior experience of the real existence of its violation. Transgression is thus more than a constitutive part of the structure of the prohibition. For Bataille, transgression represents, rather, the *truth* of taboo: the prohibition is not established to deny the reality of what it prohibits, but to generate desire for the reality of what it attempts in vain to deny. 'We can even go so far as the absurd proposition: "The taboo is there in order to be violated".'[82]

A cunning dramatisation of Bataillean transgression, Bellmer's images thus effectively stage the attraction of sin *without actually violating any prohibition*. We may imagine that certain limits of decency have been exceeded, that Bellmer goes too far. But his act of transgression 'like every transgression, conserve[s] or confirm[s] that which it exceeds'; for, as Jacques Derrida notes, 'this is the only way for it to affirm itself as transgression and thereby accede to the sacred which "is presented as the violence of an infraction".'[83] Ultimately, given the manner in which Bellmer's work suggests the taboo of molestation without actually depicting it, we begin to understand Bataille's intractable notion of the 'contradictory experience of prohibition *in* transgression'.[84] We sense the wrong; but Bellmer, because there is no evidence of wrongdoing, no proof of harm, ensures that the fascinated appalling desire that his images evoke in us comes, disturbingly, from ourselves.

Keeping the taboo active, dangerous and fetishised therefore, Bellmer's work can be considered authentically transgressive in the Bataillean sense. His disturbing images are situated at the extreme limit where the taboo and its infringement coincide; they exemplify the 'flashes of lightning' spoken of by Foucault that serve only to intensify the density of the surrounding darkness. Indeed their evocation of the imaginary cancellation of the taboo is the very mechanism that preserves it in its appalling yet fascinating significance. In thus suspending the violation, Bellmer's images evoke the 'profane illumination' that Walter Benjamin[85] associated with the surrealist shock experience, his snapshots intimating or adumbrating – without depicting – the dark zone that shades the nether side of the limit: the zone of the unnameable and inexpressible, the unacceptable and the transcendently transgressive. In this way Bellmer's work fulfils Bataille's proposition that 'transgression does not deny the taboo but transcends and completes it.'[86] According to this interpretation, Bellmer's imagery may be considered to constitute the ethical afterimage of a potentially immoral event: it maintains the prohibition against the transgression it negatively subsumes by crystallising it in an aftershock image, almost as if the artist wanted to remind himself, by accessing the ocular proof, of a line that, although threatened, cannot, and should not, be crossed.

Addressing the influence of Bataille on transgressive art, Jake Chapman elucidates this moral paradox:

> What I mean is that an image of a person being tortured [for instance] comes with the commitment that one has to assume that it's an ethical reading one should have. What's central to Bataille is that the ethical reading is there but it's made manifest by an absolute transgression of ethics.[87]

Bellmer's imagery may be immoral but its transgressive status makes its problematic ethical status much more complex: it is as if the image, in adumbrating the transgression, negatively manifests not the violation but rather the aftershock of its prohibition. In other words, it is only through intimating its violation that the aesthetic form can effectively represent the taboo.

What remains unquestioned by critics who naively take the Bataillean ethos of the Chapman brothers' aesthetic at face value, however, is just how plausible the association with Bataille actually is. Can illustrations of Bataille's ideas *really* be considered transgressive in the spirit of Bataille when this practice is patently opportunistic? Taking advantage of the contemporary cultural zeitgeist (with its assumption that artistic transgression is significant per se), one of the central provocations associated with the Chapmans' work is its imitation of transgression as an artistic *style* instead of socially, culturally or psychologically meaningful practice. Stallabrass's accusation that their work is nihilistic depends on this interpretation: to the Chapmans, transgression is 'transgression', a style open to being effectively, if vacuously, mimicked. But, *pace* Stallabrass, their work is *not* nihilistic, at least not in the interesting or philosophical sense of the concept, as much as cynical. Like Goya, the Bataille connection does not possess significance beyond the brothers' awareness that contemporary artists gain recognition and notoriety through producing work intended to be controversial – on the understanding that art secures celebrity status for its makers, work that, in the words of Jake Chapman himself, 'appears to serve no justifiable purpose other than to mock the public and court controversy'.[88]

Indeed, this is how Martin Maloney interprets their work.[89] However, is this not one of the main reasons why their work is *transgressive*? Although Maloney's analysis of their work is generally accurate, he fails to see that the opportunistic and inauthentic appropriation of an 'authentic' transgressive style is structural to the specific transgression enacted by the Chapmans. Deliberately mannered meaninglessness is essential to the provocation of their work. Therefore, the attempt to legitimate the Chapman brothers' art by adding a canonical, 'authentic transgressive' meaning to it – as the critics attempt in vain to do and as the artists themselves do – fails to appreciate the actual transgressive nature of their work.

It would be fatuous to argue that the Chapmans' work is not genuinely transgressive because it is derivative of Bellmer's prototypical visualisations of Bataillean transgression. For this argument would rely on an entirely dubious conception of 'authentic' (as opposed to inauthentic) transgression. Yet the discussion above is intended to demonstrate that the Chapmans' work *is* derivative of Bellmer (and his aftershock visualisations of Bataille) – I wanted to show that Bataillean transgression has been done better before. On the other hand, I also wanted to establish that this bastardisation of Bellmer–Bataille is precisely the reason why the Chapmans' art *is* transgressive. There is an important *inauthenticity* to the aesthetic of transgression: that is to say, the *inauthentic appropriation* is itself a transgressive gesture. Yes, their work is entirely, cynically inauthentic. And that, in conclusion, is one of the principal reasons why it should be considered paradigmatically transgressive.

The Trivial Pursuit of Psychoanalysis

Next to Bellmer's more disturbing, yet more aesthetically intriguing, indeed more complex work, Jake and Dinos Chapman may appear literal, stylised and obvious. Very little effort is made to aestheticise, that is, formally to mediate or sublimate the 'latent' sexual fantasies directly manifested in their crass and clunky sculptures; indeed, *Zygotic Acceleration* is actually pronounced as a 'de-sublimation'. Yet precisely by virtue of this, their work, unlike Bellmer's, paradoxically *resists* translation via the psychoanalytic method of de-sublimation from manifest to latent content.

There is no latent content to reveal: what is usually subject to concealment in the garb of convention and normally, according to Freud, expressed indirectly in an innocuous form (often unbeknownst to the artist) is, in the Chapmans' work, denuded and cruelly exposed with the full supervisory awareness of the artists. Is the application of Freudian theory to art therefore irrelevant in relation to contemporary transgressive art? A superficial pursuit reduced to mimetic description of the work that tells us nothing we can't already see there, psychoanalysis may be obsolete, but not, as Stallabrass suggests, because the technique is now discredited scientifically. But rather – as Slavoj Žižek has elucidated – as a result of the permissive culture of Western liberalism, it appears that there is no requirement to conceal sadistic, depressingly abject or even illicit repressed human instincts of the most infantile, violent or venereal kind through the socially tolerable mediation of aesthetic form.

Considering how his ideas are being indiscriminately appropriated by the mainstream critical consensus, Žižek's critique of transgressive art is worth quoting at length.

> Freud's 'naïve' reflections on how the artist expresses embarrassing, even disgusting, intimate fantasising in a social context by wrapping it up in a socially acceptable form – by 'sublimating' it, offering the pleasure of the beautiful artistic form as a lure which seduces us into accepting the otherwise repulsive excessive pleasure of intimate fantasising – acquire a new relevance in today's era of permissiveness, when performance and other artists are under pressure to stage the most private fantasies in all their desublimated nakedness.[90]

A cohort of sophisticated artists cognisant of the basic theoretical principles of psychoanalysis has existed for quite some time now. Indeed, Sue Taylor has already put the efficacy of the psychoanalytic method for contemporary art into question. She quotes Jack Spector's prognosis for the analysis of art in a cultural climate of atmospheric Freudianism: 'it will be, in fact, a peculiar problem for future literary historians to distinguish [between] spontaneous and "mannered" examples of the various neurotic syndromes so incisively presented by Freud.'[91]

Conscious of these caveats, we could also enquire: is it feasible to interpret an art object according to psychoanalytic theory if that very theory is consciously deployed by the artist as a knowing creative strategy in the work itself? How ingenuous, to paraphrase Dawn Ades on Salvador Dalí, 'how "automatic" even', are these psychopathological contents? Do such contents consist of symptomatic motifs emerging 'directly from the unconscious, or are they rather images which have already been digested and analysed?'[92] If there is nothing for the psychoanalytic method of de-sublimation to make manifest, then, logically, that method – though ineffectual to clarify any latent content – is not obsolete, perhaps, but trivial.

These general characteristics are nowhere more evident than in the Chapman aesthetic, especially in relation to the artists' reprocessing of Freudian motifs. Critical readings of *Zygotic Acceleration* as a 'manifestation of excess libidinous energy gone awry', or as a 'quite literal translation . . . – or perhaps "embodiment" – of a Freudian preconscious, polymorphously perverse, undifferentiated, noumenal "beyond"'[93] or, again, as a 'literal embodiment of a deterritorialised libidinal desire'[94] in order to validate the work according to a post-Freudian/Lacanian theoretical line are invalidated a priori by the work itself. Such readings appear fatuous in exactly the same way as the critical applications of Goya in relation to *Great Deeds*. This is because, if the works are 'literal translations' of anything, it is of received Freudian concepts[95] and tropes quoted ad lib from the texts of George Bataille or deficient versions of literary transgression.[96] To defend them according to the same conceptual scheme is not just circular but vacuous, reduced to a parlour-game, a charade.

Due to its aggressive juxtaposition of childhood and adult perversity, *Zygotic Acceleration*, despite psychodynamic reductions, remains a disturbing and morally intimidating work. Its extreme literalness ensures that it remains immune to interpretative polyvalence. Therefore the psychoanalytic method of de-sublimation, because pre-digestedly applied as a constructive strategy in the work, can reveal no latent psychopathological significance behind its mediating manifest content. For the work *conceals nothing*: it is all-manifest content. Even according to psychoanalytic exegesis, as Žižek suggests, such 'transgressive' work can thus only signify the manifestation (perhaps forced therapeutically through abreaction) of a once-latent paedophiliac sex fantasy, now successfully out in the open. The marked negative reference to the Freudian theory of sublimation in the title reflexively emphasises the work's resistance to appropriation by the psychoanalytic framework and thus implies that such exegesis has already been dismissed as trivial before it has a chance to be applied.

Evaluation of Aesthetic Defences of Transgressive Art

Aesthetic defences of the Chapman brothers typically have the effect of tacitly denying that there is anything problematic about the work: critics tend implicitly to brand those that believe there is something wrong as conservative or philistine. Or explicitly: '[Given] the shock value of their newest works – a recent portrait of their parents, for example [*Mummy and Daddy Chapman*, 1994] – there is no danger of their lacking philistines to battle against.'[97] Deflecting the issues in terms of some imaginary debate between conservatives and liberals has the effect of cauterising the very debate that the work raises. Avoiding critical examination, such defences amount to the discursive effort to establish a distance from which the work can be safely engaged with, that is: enjoyed with moral impunity. The concept of distance involved in this process is indistinguishable from classical disinterestedness and, because it is invoked to expurgate morally difficult content, ultimately constitutes, I argue, an *ethical* remove.

'The basic strategy is simple,' Mary Devereaux remarks, 'when approaching a work of art that raises moral issues, sever aesthetic evaluation from moral evaluation and evaluate the work in aesthetic (i.e., formal) terms alone.'[98] Julius quotes Steven Dubin as remarking that the art experts in the infamous Robert Mapplethorpe Cincinnati trial, in their ability to 'recast images of extreme sexual acts into figure studies', and, in their capacity to transform 'the arc of urine being directed into a man's mouth into a classical study of symmetry', seemed to him to resemble artistic 'alchemists'.[99] One of the witnesses who testified at the trial, Janet Kardon, claimed that the formal value – the 'aesthetic' configurations and compositions – of Mapplethorpe's work 'purifies, even cancels, the prurient elements'.[100] Abstracting from the problematic subject of the transgressive work by emphasising its formal properties, or the skilfulness of its construction, or applying to the critical distance that ironic disinterestedness allegedly endows us with, in fact, simply 'deflects attention from the difficult subject matter' and avoids having to discuss what images, considered in terms of representations, actually represent.[101]

In the literature on the Chapmans, perhaps the strategy of the critical severance of morality through formalism is nowhere more evident than in the pedantic insistence on referring to the figures as 'mannequins'.[102] For Hall, following Bussel – who had decided, against all evidence to the contrary, that the Chapman figures were 'genderless' – the sculpture represents a 'ring of shop-window mannequins,' he says, 'creatures of undetermined gender';[103] while Maloney, moderating his *Flash Art* excoriation of the sculpture (as a result of some acrimonious riposte from the brothers), identifies them for the *Sensation* exhibition as 'sexually explicit fibreglass mannequins'.[104] Even Stallabrass, in his otherwise relentless critique of the brothers' work in *High Art Lite*, defers to the self-censoring euphemism, 'kiddie-mannequins', when he has to refer directly to the work.

I anticipate the protest: but they *are* mannequins – so what's the problem? The problem is that this insistence on referring to the *actual physical structure* or *substance* of the sculpture deflects from its referential properties: employing the innocuous distancing term *mannequins* avoids what the Chapman mannequins represent. Yet, this critical reluctance is offset by the critics' inconsistent and untroubled identification of the dildos and sex-toy elements incorporated into the sculptures as 'penises', 'vaginas' and 'anuses'. Identifying the physical elements of the work as opposed to what they, as artistic motifs that transmit meaning, represent, inserts itself like a prophylactic screen that has the effect of diverting attention away from (and thus deactivating) the problematic content.

Through the circumlocution 'mannequins', anyone having difficulty with the work is reminded of the obvious: that what we are looking at in *Zygotic Acceleration* is *not* a *real* (that is, present and physically extant) human child but a plastic simulacrum. What is elided in this argument is the truth that no representation can present that which it represents, for the representation and its referent logically exclude each other.[105] Therefore, to repeat insistently the mantra THIS IS A REPRESENTATION and to believe that, through this argument alone, problematic art is excused and its morality justified simply by cancelling its referent, obtusely misconstrues the concept of representation.

Postmodernism, committed, as we have considered, to the absence of the referent dogma, believes it has, if not *completely* collapsed the reality–representation distinction, effectively removed the constraint that reality exerts on the logic of representation. There is now only an iterative process of autonomous cultural information determined by the semiotics of the arbitrary signifier. Sherrie Levine's appropriations of Edward Weston's photographs, as discussed by Douglas Crimp, become particularly relevant to this analysis of the Chapmans' work.[106] In 1980, Levine exhibited six appropriations from a controversial series of photographs by Weston – nude portraits in the Apollonian-classical mode of his young (prepubescent) son Neil, taken in 1925. These images were famously defended in the 1950s (according to the dominant formalist vocabulary associated with high modernism) as autonomous, abstract shapes, emphasising the classically enduring generic Hellenic paradigm still apparently legible in the nude form rather than the boy depicted by this form.[107] According to this formalism, the work was saved for disinterested contemplation through the typical aesthetic alibi that Devereaux criticises. Of course, yet again, this emphasis on form, in abstraction from content, draws attention away from the difficult, potentially discomforting and morally problematic subject matter: Weston's artistic rendition of his son's eugenic body and its photo-erotic codification.[108]

Yet it is precisely the *form* that codifies the image as erotic by drawing on a potent semiotic; this is responsible for the subtle but powerful desire that the image provokes. As the original referent (the boy) can never *actually be present*, but always only absent in relation to his representation, Crimp's anti-realist argument suggests that, only when the work is accepted as a simulacrum, that is, an autonomous aesthetic surface formally divested of its slag of content, can we appreciate that neither the child depicted nor the original author of the work appropriated by Levine can be considered to have been violated in this process.

With the same effect, bizarrely, as the modernism to which it insistently opposes itself, therefore, the perverse formalism of postmodernism assimilates Weston's child nudes to the protective closure of the aesthetic attitude 'by emphasising the status of the photograph as a pure sign, removed from what it represents'.[109] And thus, perhaps unexpectedly, by way of postmodern anti-realism, the transgressive work is again saved for disinterested contemplation[110] and is, by virtue of this process, also cleansed of moral difficulty.[111]

In the effort to cope with its challenges to artistic and moral conventions, aesthetic defences of transgressive art tacitly recuperate the disinterested attitude. But, because of the inured trend to identify aesthetic experience with the disinterested attitude, when used to defend the morally problematic aspects of the Chapman brothers' work – if not completely knowingly, then unconsciously – this strategy has more disturbing and ethically threatening consequences. By expurgating moral meaning through recuperating the disinterested attitude, one of the hidden and disturbing consequences of the aesthetic defence is to render the work available for aesthetic *pleasure*.[112] Indeed, the association of the disinterested attitude and aesthetic pleasure is fundamentally established in the philosophy of art.[113] 'For the aesthetic attitude,' Stolnitz explains, 'things are not to be classified or studied or judged. They are in themselves pleasant or exciting to look at.' He continues: 'When we apprehend an object aesthetically, we do so in order to relish its individual quality, whether the object be charming, stirring, vivid, or all of these. If we are to appreciate it, we must accept the object "on its own terms".' He concludes: 'we must therefore inhibit any responses which are "unsympathetic" to the object, which alienate us from it or are hostile to it.'[114]

Now, of course, this thesis may have currency in relation to complex meta-artistic products with non-picturing and therefore self-referential, reflexive properties; but it seems oddly misplaced in the context of work that employs an *explicitly pictorial* realistic form, a form, indeed, that is paradigmatically transgressive in that it coldly, cruelly and viscerally defies disinterested, distanced contemplation. Such literal, referentially constrained, iconic form inescapably possesses the property of extensional reference. This is precisely why it is so disturbing *and* repulsive – 'convulsive', to use the Chapmans' descriptor. It could be argued that, even if we admit that it is possible to construe such work in meta-artistic, anti-realist fashion, as self-referential, autonomous or reflexive – mere patterned surfaces and moulded substances – the literalism of the work ensures that this reflexivity points nowhere but back to that which the work, equally inescapably, *re*presents.

Consider, for instance, a 1994 prototype of *Zygotic Acceleration*. A toddler wears an outsize T-shirt with a typically and deliberately illiterate Chapman statement printed on it. His face has been distorted by the substitution of an erect adult penis for his nose and a sex-toy anus for his mouth. Now, how are we to interpret such iconography? If it still appears too ambiguous, too cryptic, the meaning of this work is securely anchored by the title: *Fuckface*. This is what I mean by the literalness of their work: there is, in this case, no available scope for connotation, *no room for irony or theoretical distance*, because the message has been thoroughly saturated by its crassly denotative meaning. The naturalistic, retail-realist style of the model ensures that such work is immune to error through misidentification: there is no margin of interpretative play that could allow the viewer to interpret the work in heterogeneous, unpredictable, metaphorical or, indeed, ironic ways. Any metaphorical (or connotative) ironic interpretations of the work *depend on the formulaic process of abstraction* that Martin Maloney has satirised in relation to the Chapman products.[115] In other words, it is only by a defensive effort to be abstract that it is possible to become theoretically (or ironically) distant and disinterestedly circumspect regarding the sculpture.

Zygotic Acceleration is an ultra-literal actualisation. This is indicated expressly in the title: the work is announced as a *de*-sublimation. So therefore, as considered, even the psychodynamic interpretation of art practice as the successful channelling of excess instinctual (and potentially malignant) libidinous energy into socially acceptable forms, has been anticipated by the artists and aggressively, indeed humourlessly, rejected. When confronted with it: 'We do not want to look . . . if we do, it is only by an effort of *abstraction*, looking at part, not whole, or emptying the bodily configurations of meaning. We can only contemplate it if we first abstract from it all representational qualities.'[116] The conceptual mechanism of abstraction thus functions, Julius says, as a 'refuge for the dismayed, assaulted eye',[117] the eye at the opening of a mind that does not want to accept what it sees, that finds what it sees unacceptable. Like an assassin the work sneaks up on us. And we recoil. We are disgusted; it makes us feel like covert perverts.

This may explain why critics are so fastidious about reprocessing transgressive art – art with morally challenging or disturbing content – in the terms associated with aesthetic formalism.[118] For, according to these terms, it becomes possible to ab-*stract*, that is, engage conceptual mechanisms whereby a work of art 'refers [exclusively] to its own conditions of creation' and, by this formal abstraction, screen out its content.[119] However, as Maloney famously put it when confronted with *Zygotic Acceleration*: 'It seemed hard to be abstract when there was a cock staring me straight in the face.'[120]

If the Chapmans' sculpture is experienced, all possible ambiguous metaphorical alternatives disabled by its literalness, as standing precisely for what it depicts, it is fair to say that the artists themselves have acknowledged this. When requested to offer an explanation of the meaning of their work, Jake replies: 'That's for you to work out. I mean the work works. If it didn't work, then we'd need to say what it means.'[121] So accurately referential that its meaning becomes unequivocal, *Zygotic Acceleration* is *obvious*. No further explanation is required. Unfortunately for the critics therefore, the graphic properties of *Zygotic Acceleration*, like those associated with *Great Deeds Against the Dead*, ensure that the work is read as unavoidably literal, entirely transparent. Any aesthetic defence of the work (canonic, abstract, postmodernist-formalist, transgressive, psychodynamic etc.) therefore is thus not just implausible or trivial, but *absurdly* so. As suggested, this is because the Chapmans cynically and shamelessly appropriate morally transgressive material purely for its controversial currency.

However, can this strategy be understood in a less discouraging way? Could this resistance to aesthetic defence be considered a critical interrogation of the capacity of the culture industry to indemnify every artistic transgression according to the implicit moral approbation conferred by the aesthetic attitude – an industry committed, as Jake Chapman has frequently repeated, to the aesthetic recuperation of every moral violation as 'art', and devoted to the ethical sanitisation of immoral content on the basis of artistic status alone? As demonstrated, a work such as *Zygotic Acceleration* forcefully challenges the legacy of aesthetic recuperation; although the artists may be cynically resigned to ultimate aesthetic repossession,[122] with this excessive sculpture they make this process extremely difficult. Close analysis of this work has revealed that the artists have critically targeted, and therefore exposed to view, the ethically cleansing effects we have associated with art-critical discourse. 'In the mind of the ambivalent artist,' Jake Chapman explains, 'the more gratuitous an image, the more its radical potential, since its success is determined by the capacity to resist being adopted by the *very framework* it intends to break.'[123]

The transgressive nature of the Chapman brothers' gratuitously ugly and possibly obscene work, because it fights against being abstracted to the codes of disinterested contemplation and resists psychoanalysis, ultimately involves a concomitant refusal to being morally vindicated according to the typical aesthetic defences of transgressive art. Therefore, even despite the inevitable aesthetic recuperation of the Chapmans' work (to employ the apt words of Lawrence Hyman): 'The ugliness and disgust associated with the images, as well as any disagreement that we may very well have with [the artists'] amoral attitude, resist being [aesthetically] transfigured.'[124] Yet I will conclude that this resistance to aesthetic recuperation, paradoxically, is the very reason why *Zygotic Acceleration* primarily functions at an ethical rather than aesthetic level.

Acknowledging the Immorality of the Chapmans' Work

Aesthetic defences of ethically transgressive art have the effect of exonerating its manifest moral attitude. Even the denominative use of the word 'art' as a value term is often sufficient to connote moral approbation. However, the critical response to any work of art inevitably necessitates engaging with its *salient* aspects. Therefore, if the separation of a particular aspect for primary consideration involves the arbitrary downgrading of any other aspects of the work as aesthetically irrelevant, then it is reasonable to accuse this practice of partiality and misrepresentation. Mary Devereaux uses this argument to establish that engagement with art involves more than a response to form: otherwise the *effort* made to abstract the formal aspect of the work in order to consider it in isolation makes no sense.[125] Isolation from what? we may ask. It is not unreasonable to demand that critical evaluation include everything considered to be artistically relevant to the work under analysis. Devereaux recommends that we should not bracket, screen out, or otherwise consider any artistic element to be marginal to a specific work; this exclusionary practice disregards features that may be artistically intrinsic to the work, features that, in fact, 'make it the work of art it is'.

Any complete critical engagement with *Zygotic Acceleration* must therefore acknowledge that certain aspects, however problematic, objectionable, or depraved they may appear, are nevertheless crucial artistic aspects of this work; they are, that is, inherent to its aesthetic 'vision'. In order to understand fully such morally transgressive art, according to Devereaux, 'we have to engage with its vision. And this means that we have to engage with the moral issues that it raises.'[126] Yet, as observed, the moral issues raised by the Chapmans' work are not engaged with in the critical literature; its principal provocations are deliberately sidetracked, systematically avoided.[127] Bracketing the components that make *Zygotic Acceleration* morally problematic, however, as we have considered, has the effect of diverting attention from the very issue that the artwork raises. Yet aesthetic defences that partition the ethical aspects intrinsic to the work's 'artistic vision' from view *also* preclude any critical appreciation of its artistic significance. 'If we distance ourselves from these features,' she concludes, 'we will not be in a position to understand its artistic value,' for this procedure 'requires us to ignore the essence [of the work]'.[128]

What vision is made manifest in *Zygotic Acceleration*? What, indeed, can be considered 'the essence' of this work? The discussion of *Great Deeds Against the Dead* above concluded that Goya functions as a trivial alibi for the spectacle of sadistic violence – for the Chapmans' exploration of the vicarious expression of acts of (sexualised) violence. The vision manifested in later works (such as *Zygotic Acceleration*) can be seen as a further elaboration of that theme: violence, in this case, as in *Great Deeds*, is *sexualised*. The vision of their work is therefore one of sexual violence. I want to be very clear: even if this means that their work is obscene or immoral, I am not arguing that their work, because of this, does not count as art. Rather, the immorality identified in their work, to use Devereaux's category, is intrinsic to its 'artistic vision'. This is an *artistic immorality*. In fact, it is necessary, I will argue, to accept the immorality of their artistic vision in order to appreciate the aesthetic significance of the Chapmans' work.

Part of the provocation of their work is precisely its derision of the liberal ideology that all art *because it is art* is *ipso facto* moral[129] – that, with the identification 'art', everything is permitted. Iris Murdoch's classical-modernist correlation of aesthetics and ethics, to the point of identification, is perhaps as delusional as this ideology can get: 'art and morals', she has written, 'are . . . one.'[130] However, Valerie Reardon argues that the liberal identification of art and morality is based on the primitive assumption that 'all art is good art and that all art is good for us.'[131] But: 'Enough', she comments, 'has been written about the role art plays in reinforcing ideology to know that this is not true.'[132]

So, although they count as art, *Fuckface*, *Two-faced Cunt*, *Fuckface Twin* – as well as *Zygotic Acceleration* – can only be considered *ipso facto* moral therefore by someone who does not understand, *refuses* to see or *deliberately distances* themselves (through aesthetic disinterestedness and its cognate theoretical positions) from what they are looking at. Such work, it seems, is unconditionally approved of by an art-critical mainstream that, not wanting to appear Victorian, or – anxious that liberal values are threatened by what is erroneously, yet quite generally, seen as a conservative or censorious moral sensibility

– seeks to unconditionally affirm the transgressive impulse associated with the leading edge of contemporary art. But to construe the Chapmans' work as moral simply *because it is art* is to misconstrue its artistic significance. For the visceral Chapman aesthetic is not intended to be moral: 'When our sculptures work they achieve the position of reducing the viewer to a state of absolute moral panic . . . they're completely troublesome objects.'[133]

Although their work counts as art (that is, their work has undeniable art status), that does not automatically entail, as Reardon indicates, that it is morally good. On the contrary, in this case, to repeat, it is necessary to accept *Zygotic Acceleration* as an immoral *work of art* in order to grasp its ethical meaning.

In the concluding section of this chapter, I explicate this proposition by assessing the Chapmans' work in the context of the issues that surround the depiction of children. Some of these have already been tracked obliquely in the discussions of Hans Bellmer and Sherrie Levine. Here, however, I expose the problem with more clarity by drawing on Anne Higonnet's investigative analysis of the cultural representation of children with particular emphasis, in this context, on contemporary art.

Contextualist Ethical Evaluation of *Zygotic Acceleration*

'No subject', Anne Higonnet claims, 'is as publicly dangerous now as the subject of the child's body.'[134] Because *Zygotic Acceleration* hybridises the cultural codes of childhood and 'adult' sexuality, the sculpture can be considered morally disquieting for the same reasons as Robert Mapplethorpe's *Jesse McBride* and *Rosie* (both 1976), or Jock Sturges's portfolio of images published in 1994, *Radiant Identities*, as well as the controversial work of Sally Mann (1985) and Tierney Gearon (2000).[135] These projects can be considered morally problematic for their depiction of children according to an erotic perspective, and transgressive because of the subtle corruption of the conventions of childhood innocence with a self-aware sexualised subject-position that their aesthetic codification involves.[136]

Because their maternal role has been used to legitimise this project, the work of Sally Mann (as published in *Immediate Family*) and the work of Tierney Gearon (holiday snapshots of her children were shown to attendant controversy in the *I Am a Camera* exhibition in the Saatchi Gallery in 2001[137]) have been considered particularly problematic.[138] Mann's portfolio contains photographs of her three (then) prepubescent children (two girls and a boy) according to a perspective that has been described by Emily Apter as conveying 'a raw, impudent sensuality'.[139] Apter is concerned with the 'carnal knowledge' suggested by the 'brazen stares' that interpellate the viewer in these photographs, but she is more unsettled by the particularly subtle, yet inescapable mode in which these images have become eroticised. It is not just that nudity in contemporary society, for better or worse, as Reardon has observed, is inevitably sexualised, but rather that the poses of the children seem to have been contrived to suggest the 'infantile gesture' that covertly recalls the 'standard pin-up or porn shot'.[140] In fact, Apter courageously criticises certain images from the portfolio (including *Virginia at 3*, *Popsicle Drips* and *The Wet Bed*), that, she says, indulge in a damaging game that narrows the gap 'between seduction and violation': she concludes that these images, as a result, are difficult not to interpret 'as paedophilic wish-fulfilments'.[141] Indeed, as Crimp has admitted in a brief self-critique of his former optimistic postmodern anti-realism, Levine–Weston's *Neil*s stimulate *desire for their referent*, namely, the boy they aesthetically inform and render erotic.[142] This occurs because the semiotic codes that they are inspired by and engage (perhaps even unconsciously) – and by engaging, both reinforce and rely on – condition a subject-position that evokes desire not for the signifier but for what it signifies, not for the representation but for what it represents.

Similarly, Mann's photographs, via the semiotic conventions of the erotic, can be considered to evoke this same kind of desire (the morphological similarity of *Popsicle Drips* and Weston's *Neil* reinforces this) for what they represent and render visible. Higonnet has convincingly argued in relation to Mann's photographs, and in blatant opposition to the dominant aesthetic defence of morally problematic art, that it is *not despite* but precisely '*because* everyone agrees that Mann is a superb technician and formalist' that this work can be perceived 'as estheticizations [*sic*] and eroticizations of violence against children'.[143]

The debate in the case of Gearon's pictures focused on the inability of young children to give consent to the taking, exhibition and public display of photographic images of them. Thus it was considered that her 'children's trust had been betrayed' by her public showing and commercialisation of these images.[144] 'The exposure of their most intimate parts to unsought scrutiny is an abuse of the trust that they repose in the maker of the pictures.'[145] In this context, Higonnet relates how Mapplethorpe earnestly emphasised the importance of his subject's consent, saying, 'I would never do that to somebody.'[146] However, she quotes Arthur Danto's caution that, regardless of Mapplethorpe's alleged ethos, it is generally not accepted that children are capable of giving consent in this case, because 'children are inherently powerless in relation to adults.'[147] Her analysis of this caveat is worth quoting at length.

> We hold this to be particularly true in the case of consent to sexual acts because we believe children, by definition, cannot know the adult sexuality to which they might seem to consent. . . . Some would argue that the only person to whom a child can give consent is a parent, while others would retort that a parent is the last person from whom a child would be able to withhold consent.[148]

Yet, the moral issue here relates to the right of adults to photograph the bodies of (in many cases 'their') children for public display. Parents (such as Mann or Gearon) that insist on the right to photograph their children in a state of undress prepared for public display are, according to Reardon, 'expressing an inappropriate assumption of ownership of the child and the child's body'.[149] Children, in this sense, can be irresponsibly misconstrued as 'possessions', she says, and are, to that extent, in danger of being reified as commodities and therefore fetishised to stimulate desire not for what they are but for what they symbolise.

'I have been documenting my family through pictures for over two years, and I take snapshots of everyday life,' Gearon is reported to have said in her defence. 'Some people are describing them as pornographic; others are accusing me of exploiting my children's innocence.' She added: 'I don't understand how you can see anything but the purity of childhood.'[150] Mann, in her defence, says: 'That I photograph my family while we are there is merely documenting what is. Children are graceful sensualists,' she continues 'and what adults perceive to be sexuality is nothing other than an ingenuous openness.'[151]

Now these admissions of perplexity are naive, disingenuous and, indeed, irresponsible for two related reasons. The first concerns the fact that it is precisely the twin eminently violable myths of purity and juvenile innocence that are known to attract the predatory paedophile (as Nabokov's novel *Lolita* brilliantly, if disturbingly, elucidates). Although the concept of childhood innocence (in its opposition to adult perversity) has been critically exposed as an ideological construction, nevertheless, such constructions have powerful, indeed mythical, social and moral influence; and one of the negative consequences of this influence is that the imagery and iconography of childhood, precisely because of its associated ideological 'purity', is 'in danger of becoming erotically appealing'.[152] Such a mythic interplay of purity and innocence, as aesthetically codified in this photographic genre, brings into focus a primordial socio-symbolic taboo, and precisely for that reason – as we have considered – generates a powerful desire for its transgression: 'Photographs of naked children, possibly [even] of children in general [thus] allow adult projections.'[153] Unlike Bellmer's aftershock images, these photographs transgress the taboo by stimulating desire for what they represent.

More problematic perhaps is the second reason. Considering Gearon's photos, despite the widespread (erroneous) assumption that snapshot photos are random and un-authored slices of natural life, these pictures are not born, they are *made*; that is, they are consciously chosen and constructed by a free, decision-making agent. And, indeed, if we look again at the photos, we can discern a similar engagement of and dependence on the semiotic codes of the erotic that, as Crimp has courageously indicated, provoke desire for the boy in Weston's work (as exposed by Levine's appropriations).[154] This latent dependence on (and connotative reference to) these semiotic viewing conventions establishes the interpretative framework – the perspective – from which these images are to be consumed. The distinct similarity between Mann's work and Weston's prototype, as well as the constructed isomorphism of Caravaggio's *Cupid* and Mapplethorpe's *Jessie* renders the artists' claims of unintentional innocent snapshots highly dubious. Even if the dependence on the semiotic codes of the erotic is unconscious, that is to say, even if this structural eroticism is culturally conditioned, in a contemporary climate marked by the critique of (and unmasking of) covert ideologies of vision masked by apparently innocent representational systems, there is no excuse for someone who is involved in the production of images to be unaware of this critical legacy. For anyone with even a rudimentary knowledge of contemporary culture to claim innocence is, in this case, doubly irresponsible.

For better or worse, our own naivety concerning the innocence of images has, by now, been completely eroded. We cannot afford to be anything but cynical when it comes to images, adverts to innocence and admissions of perplexity like those paraded by Sally Mann and Tierney Gearon. They are ultimately responsible, not only for the taking and making of these photos, however, but also for the decision to display them in public. Indeed, once this snapshot documentation of their family life traverses the private–public barrier and becomes the product of display in a gallery (and associated catalogues), their parental responsibility becomes a public issue open to criticism, and not least from the perspective of an ethics of care: 'being a mother, that is, the child's primary carer and nurturer, protecting and deflecting the child from danger, does not necessarily correspond with being an artist, in this case, a "creative" photographer, particularly when your own children are the subject matter.'[155]

However, the eroticism of the photographic images discussed here is ambiguous, because it remains *implicit*. It is a matter of coding, cryptic connotation, covert sexual appeal. Thus the images are *not* obscene; suggestive perhaps, but not obscene. To that extent, they cannot be considered pornographic. Yet, the images are read, according to the (connotative) semiotic codes of the erotic, by a knowing audience as depictions of children from a sexual perspective, and therefore are, to the extent that regarding children from such a perspective may be considered to symbolise the violation of a taboo, transgressive. The reason for this, however, is not due to the explicit sexual representation of the children depicted but rather because of a whole range of other semiotic associations and connotations: the lack of awareness and sexual ignorance of the children, their innocent, uninhibited and unselfconscious attitudes, as well as, of course, the full cognisance of the photographer as to how these erotic images and attitudes are likely to be read by their adult audience.

Needless to say, the issue is very different with regard to the Chapmans, principally because their work is, significantly, *not photographic*;[156] my purpose in making reference to the thematically related images of these other artists is to demonstrate that the ethical issue raised by their work can be clarified and contextualised in relation to, and finally distinguished from, that associated with the Chapman products.

In the work of Jake and Dinos Chapman, unlike the photographic work considered, the children are not indexical depictions of real-life individual children (who will perhaps look back at these images when older); yet also, and conversely, the sexual semiotic of the brothers' work is *not* connotative, implicit or *ambiguous* in any way. As I have indicated: the sexual content of their work is explicit, denotative, plainly evident. Very early in the chapter we drew attention to the way in which the Chapmans have interfered with their model, claiming that this corruption symbolises the sexual violation of children. And, if it is possible to argue that the attitude to this issue as manifested in the photographic work discussed is ambivalent (in that the depictions are implicitly sexualised, that the semiotic codes of the erotic, because connotative, are accessible only to a knowing – but also therefore an ethically sensitive – audience, that the work can perhaps be regarded in various ways), this argument cannot be applied to *Zygotic Acceleration*, an art object so obviously intended to be read as a distorted rendering of female children damaged by a perverse adult imagination.

However, perhaps it *is* possible to argue that the graphic iconicity of the Chapman model discloses – that is, makes *morally* explicit – what remains *latent and connotative* in this photographic genre of eroticised children (*à la* Mapplethorpe, Mann and Gearon). The violation of juveniles represented in iconic mode in *Zygotic Acceleration*, precisely in its crass and extreme literalness, denotes – and thus may be considered to give *moral visibility* to – the connotative, implicit and disingenuously denied projection of adult sexuality onto children associated with the work of these photographers. Thereby the Chapmans' work, I argue, *discredits* this photographic genre by exposing – through a strategy of artistic de-sublimation – *its latent immorality to view*. I will go further.

In one of the marginal notes to his experimental novel, *The Atrocity Exhibition*, J.G. Ballard observes of Hans Bellmer that, although his work hovers 'on the edge of child pornography [nevertheless] it's difficult to imagine any pedophile [*sic*] being excited by his strange dolls and dainty Alice-like little girls with their reversed orifices and paradoxical anatomy'.[157] I believe the same can be remarked, but with even more reason, of the Chapman brothers' work. Of course, it is difficult to be absolutely certain, but the idea of their bizarre configurations being considered conduits of paedophilic desire seems highly unlikely. We cannot imagine someone being aroused or taking any sexual pleasure – however perverse – in the poor Chapman creatures. Why? Because what we're dealing with here, more than likely, will be read – *even* by a paedophile – as a *critical* representation of human damage, that is, a physical manifestation of the psychological consequences of sexual abuse. Bellmer's 'vision', like the Chapmans', Ballard intriguingly adds, 'is far too close for comfort to the truth'.[158]

Such, I imagine, would *Zygotic Acceleration* appear to the paedophile: far too close to the truth. The specific distortions the plastic children have endured at the hands of the Chapman brothers become successful objective analogues of psychological damage caused by sexual abuse. Physical interference, in this instance, is transformed into an effective simulacrum of aggravated psychological harm.

Conclusion

Various theoretical defences of morally problematic art have been considered in this chapter. Critically applied to the Chapman brothers, all share the common purpose of using aesthetic value to vindicate the perceived (and morally threatening) ethics of the work in question. The purpose of such defences is ***not*** to justify the work ***aesthetically*** but rather to excuse its dubious ethics indirectly by way of an 'aesthetic alibi'.[159]

In Chapter 1, we referred to Carroll's argument that *if the moral constitution of the work is relevant to its artistic condition* this will be found potentially to compromise the aesthetic value of the work. It is not plausible, however, to apply this moralist thesis to the work of the Chapmans. Unlike Carroll, yet like Maloney (who reveals that when he looks at their work he feels 'deep embarrassment'), the Chapmans' work has already been compromised – not because of its immorality but rather, he says, because of its deliberate artistic deficiency. Maloney is embarrassed by their work, he concludes, 'not because it is sex or kids or dicks or cunts or arseholes, but because it is second-rate art with a pretense [*sic*] to being something grander, profound and endurable'.[160] The critical *rapprochement* with Bellmer clarified that the brothers employ 'transgression' in a derivative and stylised mode. Yet I also argued that this inauthentic transgression – inauthenticity being central to the provocation of their work – is precisely why their work should be considered properly artistically transgressive. For *Zygotic Acceleration* is both aesthetically *and* morally transgressive: aesthetically transgressive because of a calculated aesthetic deficiency that, as it relates to the banal literalness of its form – to its obviousness – resists being isolated from its content and recast for the purposes of formal (aesthetic) consideration; morally transgressive because it equally calculatedly corrupts the cultural codes of childhood innocence with adult sexual perversity (as Maloney says, it is all sex and kids and dicks and cunts and arseholes).

Because aesthetic defences are exploited to justify or vindicate the ethical status of morally problematic works like *Zygotic Acceleration*, this doubly transgressive art cannot be defended on aesthetic grounds; and because it is iconic, obvious, banal and severe, this sculpture makes a literal, if extreme, moral statement. To that extent, like much transgressive art, the adoption of the disinterested perspective (aesthetic attitude, ironic or formal distance, absence of referent etc.) is disabled: we viscerally withdraw from this aesthetically and morally repulsive work. Confronted with *Zygotic Acceleration*, that is, we feel disgust, and understand implicitly that we are compelled, ethically, to *reject* it. This is the appropriate standpoint to adopt, because *rejecting the work is to condemn what it depicts*.

Therefore I argue strongly that it is important – ethically important – to be disgusted by this work, to accept the disgust that these shocking aesthetic forms have stimulated. For disgusted rejection is an appropriate moral response to this work. But we should remain disgusted and not attempt to rationalise this affective aftershock *ex post facto* (in formalist, ironist, postmodernist, Freudian-anti-moralist protocol) simply because we may be embarrassed by our initial moral response. Indeed, if we accept that the work is both aesthetically and morally *bad* a very interesting transvaluation takes place: we begin to understand that this is precisely the reason why *Zygotic Acceleration* is an ethically significant work.

To defend the work through rehabilitating the aesthetic attitude of disinterested pleasure therefore is to endorse the statement that *Zygotic Acceleration* makes; to repressively screen the moral meaning of the work through formal filters is to affirm, not the work, but the immorality it represents; to repress our ethical response to the work is to become complicit in the violation it symbolically enacts. The aesthetic defences of the work that avoid treating its ethical value are not just critically challenged therefore but morally culpable. This art cannot therefore – but also *should* not – be defended on aesthetic grounds.

4 FEARLESS SPEECH

Tracey Emin's Ethics of the Self

> The vulnerability to shame is part of the exposure of the self that is involved in intimacy.
>
> *Martha C. Nussbaum*[1]

Interviewed for a German exhibition of British art, Tracey Emin addressed a specific if admittedly unrepresentative example of the controversy attached to her work.[2] Despite the celebrated success of her New York shows, she told her interviewer, some work had attracted accusations of obscenity in the US: 'people thought [my drawings]', she explained, 'were paedophile drawings, or that I'd made them for a paedophile audience.'[3]

A distinction suggested inconspicuously in this interview is not only instructive at this early stage of the chapter but crucial to the general endeavour of this book: 'The difference with my drawings', she insisted, 'is that they are of *me* . . . it's me coming to terms with these things in my life, not me trying to turn on some pervert to wank off over.'[4] As Neal Brown (her interviewer at the time) later emphasised, these images come from Emin's 'personal experience of childhood sexual abuse' (she was raped at the age of 13).[5] Best understood as the reconstituted memories of traumatic events that have been aesthetically transmuted into 'something extremely potent',[6] Tracey Emin's work originates in an engagement with her own past experience: her work is awkward, tenuous and troubling, fundamentally so, because it is the result of a difficult yet ultimately affirmative process of retroactive self-investigation. 'I went into the back of my mind', she told Mark Gisbourne, 'and pulled out memories and put them down on paper. [And that is why] They are drawings of young girls.'[7]

Emin's drawings and monoprints are small and childlike, *and* sexually explicit, therefore, not because they make ironic reference to child pornography, but because they document a girlhood interrupted: brought to an untimely

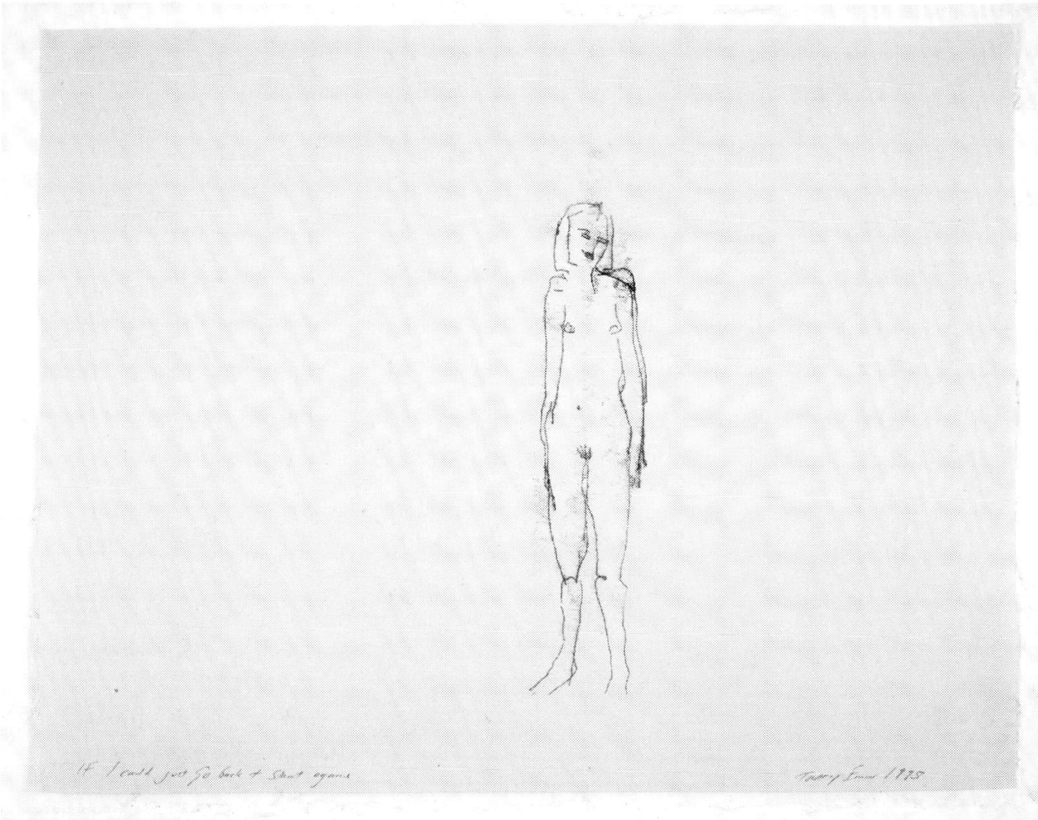

13. Tracey Emin, *If I Could Just Go Back and Start Again*, 1995
Monoprint drawing
25 ½ x 32 in (65 x 81.5 cm) framed
© the artist
Photo: Stephen White
Courtesy Jay Jopling/ White Cube (London)

conclusion by premature sexual experience.[8] Her drawings ... awkward because they represent an engagement with this childhood an... ...ic and fragmentary, yet personality-constitutive, memory-traces.

Like that of Marcus Harvey and the Chapman brothe... ...ork was shown in *Sensation* (in the Royal Academy in 1997 and ... ...a Museum, New York, in 1999), as part of the Saatchi Collection, ... aesthetic may be considered to share many of the characteristics ass... with her contemporaries. This is particularly the case in relation to its fac...

and explicit treatment of sexual themes. However, as this chapter evolves, this mutuality will come to appear increasingly less salient. Unlike Harvey or the Chapmans, the direct engagement with sexuality associated with Emin's project is not affected for provocative purposes to subvert the conventional art/porn antithesis. And, unlike the work of Mapplethorpe, Mann or Tierney Gearon, Emin's art is engendered by an uncompromising self-examination: the effort to confront all aspects of her existence, however distasteful, ugly or painful, in the most daring, fearless and upfront manner possible. This ambition in fact can be considered to constitute the ground of her appeal. The artist appears genuinely confused – fascinated and appalled – about the irreducibly personal and psychologically intense emotional incidents that feature repeatedly in the broken rhymes and blank echoes of her work.

Making art for Emin, perhaps uniquely, has a definite existential and moral purpose: through the creative process she hopes to come to some understanding of her life. In this sense, her project is guided by a kind of 'absolute faith'[9] in the ultimate affirmative power of art – an unconditional belief that art has the potential to transfigure the sordid minutiae of quotidian existence into something fulfilling, life-affirming and beautiful because ultimately *redemptive*. This faith, eclipsing the emphasis on self-harm or dysfunctional sexuality, can be seen to constitute the creative principle behind most of her key pieces. 'People think my work is about sex,' she says, 'but actually a lot of it is about faith.'[10] Yet this admission of faith should not be misconstrued as theological, religious or even spiritual. Despite Neal Brown's recent attempt[11] to contextualise her work in the tradition of sacred art, Emin's faith in art should not be confused with religious fidelity: 'I'm not really talking about religion,' she insists, 'it is something bigger than that.'[12]

It is the unconditional faith in art for Emin that necessitates the uncompromising, uncensored confrontation with all aspects of her life, regardless of the conventions of privacy or socio-symbolic taboo. But the consequent 'unpleasantly assaulting'[13] confrontation 'with the messy reality of female experience', as Liese Spenser[14] puts it, is often perceived as a transgressive disrespect for social and symbolic boundaries (such as, most saliently perhaps, the distinction between public and private – a distinction generally experienced and evaluated in moral terms). This has been responsible for the mistaken critical view that her work [illegible] art than a kind of autodidactic therapy.

Jul[illegible]ss's prominent critical denunciation of her work at the beg[illegible]gh *Art Lite* claims ironically that 'many people [create] co[illegible] self-exploratory work of the kind Emin makes, not for sale and [illegible]e art but as therapy.'[15] Yet this is precisely how the transgressive [illegible] associated with her art manifests itself and which, as this aspect of [illegible]rk relates most immediately to the perceived blatant violation of sexual [illegible]oos, is largely responsible for the controversy it has attracted. Disrespect for socio-cultural conventions (especially those governing the sexual behaviour of women) is generally experienced as moral provocation. The 'strong disregard of opinion' expressed in Emin's art, Brown observes, often 'conflict[s] with the sexual sensibilities and spiritual beliefs of others'.[16] This explains why her work is perceived as a threat to conventional moral values.

There is no doubt that Emin's work is provocative. Like much transgressive art, her work is an *irritant*, intended to elicit an emotive reaction that is deliberately not amenable to the disinterested contemplation associated with establishment aesthetic sensibility. The result of this, as with the work of her contemporaries, is that the viewer, obliged to confront the provocation made by the work, is compelled to stand in a particular manner to her challenging aesthetic. Yet this seems the most difficult and demanding aspect of her work. Uncomfortable with the directness of Emin's confrontation, many art critics have been unable to locate the requisite theoretical categories to discuss, analyse or evaluate her work in any meaningful way.

Martin Maloney, for instance, finds the personal detail in her work 'overwhelming'.[17] Unable to decide whether the 'solipsism' of her work is of any aesthetic value, Paula Smithard proclaims that the 'problem' with Emin's work is its 'immediacy and directness' that, she confidently asserts, is contrived by the artist; as a result, 'she has left little space for any distance to observe and register herself.'[18] Similarly, for Michael Gibbs, Emin's 'messages are too personal'. The same solipsism mars the art: 'If art is to be about life,' he complains, 'it somehow has to become impersonal and transcend the banality of experience.'[19] Finally, Gregor Muir, writing in a special section devoted to the assessment of Emin's work in *Parkett* in 2001, claimed that a nebulous group of certain 'people' were exasperated by her approach to the public exposure of the 'most private emotion'.[20] Clearly documenting his own reservations about her work through the alibi of these 'people', Muir proceeded to indict her work for being 'mawkish, cloying, and [again] solipsistic'.[21] Much of the literature has been similarly marked by a sense of failure to develop a credible understanding of Emin's art.[22] It is with this critical paucity in mind that Stallabrass has invidiously dismissed the writing around her work as 'craven nonsense'.[23] Why is this?

One possible hypothesis is that Emin's practice *cannot* be understood, and therefore must remain ultimately opaque to, traditional aesthetic understanding.[24] Although I do concede that evaluating her work according to standard theoretical attitudes *is* possible, this evaluation, as the brief conspectus of the critical response to her work above strongly suggests, cannot but be negative in orientation. A locus for Emin's art cannot be discovered in its restrictive framework. The least that theories assembled according to such a framework can achieve is to question whether her work counts as 'art', and this, as the most basic appreciation of Emin's case will readily discern, can be eliminated a priori[25] as a pseudo-question by the very existence (not to mention the overwhelming success) of her work.

The reason why critics (and even critics who admire her work) remain uncomfortable with Emin's art, I suggest, is because it demands a certain subjective engagement that is significantly unfamiliar to conventional art-critical intelligence. Many critics have objected to her work on the basis that the kind of engagement that this agent-centred, response-dependent address demands, renders her work somehow immune to the 'objective' procedures of art criticism.[26] Because her practice disobeys the traditional distinction of art and artist, objective criticism of the work may be misdiagnosed as a judgement of the individual responsible for it: the art critic's concern is that engaging with her work will thus embroil them in unsolicited moral evaluation.[27]

Yet this concern is key to Emin's work. What is discerned (and moralistically resisted) in Emin's case is that engaging meaningfully with her art actually *requires* an ethical concern that, in the words of Richard Norman, approaches the work by 'focusing on the needs of the other person and responding to them in their own right'.[28] Presenting emotionally charged, sometimes traumatic events, in a characteristically uncompromising and factually direct manner inspires an irreducibly subjective emotional response in the viewer. Drawing on recent cognitive philosophers who emphasise the importance of emotional life for moral value, I will define the particular response to Emin's work as ethical in nature. It is ethical because, I will suggest, it is characteristically, but not exclusively, linked to shame (or is shame inducing) and is, as philosophers of art would say, *warranted* because it is invoked by characteristics intrinsic to her work. Shame, an ethically rich emotion, is one of the central moral dimensions of Emin's work. Analysis of how it functions in her art will allow us to construe her work as ethically valuable, and yet, precisely because of this, also of artistic significance.

Certain values that may not be considered directly relevant to the artistic dimension may nevertheless become significant to (and indeed inseparable from) the aesthetic evaluation of a particular work of art. Contemporary philosophy of art has come to acknowledge that, in the words of Malcolm Budd, 'artistic value does not exist in a watertight compartment impermeable to other values; on the contrary, other values can be determinants of artistic value.'[29]

This, I conclude, is precisely the case where Emin's art is concerned. The profound (and many-dimensioned) ethical experience of engaging with Tracey Emin's work, although it may appear to eclipse the aesthetic value of her work, yet perhaps *precisely because it does eclipse it*, ultimately becomes the determinant of its aesthetic value. In other words, it is by virtue of its significant moral value, I will argue, that Emin's work becomes aesthetically valuable. The basic motivation of Emin's art practice is determined by the attempt to make something morally valuable that is morally valuable *only as art*. Because of this, engaging with her work not only enriches our emotional repertoire but also has a cognitive effect: by encouraging us to adopt a moral stance in relation to the issues it involves, it deepens our ethical lives.[30]

Almost exclusively, 'attention to history' in Emin's work, Chris Townsend observes, is focused 'upon sexual experience'.[31] This in itself is not unusual – the 'sexual confession' being, as Peter Osborne has accurately observed, routinely understood according to contemporary (post-Freudian) discourse, as a mode of truth-telling aimed towards exposing the authentic self.[32] Osborne cites the work of Michel Foucault as strategic in explaining the current status that the sexual confession enjoys in the now ubiquitous contemporary culture of exposure that promotes the 'liberated' and public expression of private anxieties. Based on a demotic, populist and largely mythopoeic repackaging of psychodynamic therapy, today, the public confession is promoted by the media as a kind of catharsis for the victim of emotional trauma (''fessing up').

As Paula Smithard indicates, however, the other perhaps less salubrious aspect of this liberated culture of exposure is a complementary culture of voyeuristic entertainment that goes hand in glove with it; for this trend of the public exposure of private trauma 'plays upon a form of voyeurism which compels interest in the intimate secrets and lives of other people'.[33] Of course the rich reward of media celebrity outweighs any anxieties that the confessor-victims may still harbour about public humiliation, and encourages the audience to become not only voyeuristic but also, perhaps inconsistently, *envious*; this celebrity-producing exposure is mediated as a highly desirable situation.

It is very tempting to situate Emin's work within the context of this culture of exposure and its celebrity dividends and, admittedly, this practice does reflect the overwhelming critical consensus (both positive and negative) in relation to her work.[34] I do not necessarily wish to dissent from this consensus. Rather, in this chapter I will attempt to approach the problem of confession in the work of Tracey Emin from a different, oblique, but lateral theoretical angle. My approach draws on a series of fascinating lectures that Foucault delivered at the University of California, Berkeley in 1983 (published as *Fearless Speech*), in the final claim that, when it is understood as a form of 'fearless speech' or what Foucault calls, more precisely, 'frankness in speaking the truth' (*parrhesia*),[35] the intrinsic ethical dimension of Emin's work is revealed.

It is clear from these lectures that Foucault placed high moral value on this ancient concept – explaining that focusing the problem of truth on the question of the 'truth-teller' or 'of truth-telling as an activity' rather than on the concept of truth in itself (for instance, in typical philosophical mode, as accurate representation of fact) has not only continuing philosophical relevance but immense normative power in the context of ethical inquiry.

If a certain work of art demands approval, then there is something in that work, some characteristic feature of the work responsible for making the demand that has elicited this particular response. What characteristic feature? Primarily, in Emin's case, what is most admirable about her work, I will argue, is the characteristic fearlessness of its address. It is this feature that is responsible ultimately for the ethical demand that her work makes on us. It is therefore the status of fearless address associated with her work in all its forms that constitutes its high moral value. Yet, it is also, I will conclude, what enables us to consider her project as a kind of Foucauldian 'aesthetics of the self'. Because it elucidates its philosophical and political dimensions as well as its artistic significance, this approach will prove more productive and critically insightful – more attuned, that is, to the features that make her work unique and extraordinary – than the dominant generic interpretations of Emin's work as autobiography or a contemporary incarnation of the confessional impulse.

'With Myself Always Myself Never Forgetting': The Structure of Ethical Subjectivity

Acquired by Charles Saatchi in 1996, attracting controversy when exhibited in *Sensation* in 1997, and subsequently destroyed in a warehouse fire in East London in 2004,[36] *Everyone I Have Ever Slept With 1963–1995*, remains a signature work, a synecdoche of the central thematic concerns of Emin's aesthetic.

A lightweight tent, pitched with its flaps tied back wide open to reveal an empty interior with 102 names spelt out in lettered patches sewn into it, *Everyone I Have Ever Slept With 1963–1995*, along with her slightly earlier work *There's A Lot of Money in Chairs* (1994), were the first episodes of an unprecedented autobiographical project in which 'absorption of a mystic', as Walter Benjamin writes of Proust, 'and the self-consciousness of a monomaniac have combined in [the description of] not a life as it actually was but a life as it was remembered by one who had lived it.'[37] This distinction reveals an ambition that implies, according to Gerhard Richter, the idea of a 'self that can come into its own only in, and as, another, an alterity'.[38] Yet if the self, through externalisation into something other, is altered in this way, should Emin's project be considered autobiographical at all?

Sisyphean searches for the authorial presence responsible for transforming the remembered *disjecta* of her life into the tentative motifs of her art are repeatedly initiated: 'When you look at Tracey Emin's work', Melanie McGrath observes, 'you see the artist struggling to *reach* herself, compelled by her own self-consciousness to fail and condemned by the self-same thing to begin again.'[39] The articulation of the self in Emin thus refuses to be captured by the conventions of autobiography. This is because the mode of address associated with her practice challenges the conception of truth as adequate correspondence that the genre of autobiography remains predicated on.[40] Because her address places a demand on the viewer to respond in a certain way, and because the nature of this response is moral, I suggest that the modality of the self in Emin should be regarded in ethical rather than in autobiographical terms. Constructed as an alterity, exposed in vulnerability, I shall argue that the self in Emin's work is best conceived as an ethical subject in the sense given to this concept by the French philosopher Emmanuel Levinas.

Almost universally construed as a vengeful exposé of her past lovers and exes, *Everyone I Have Ever Slept With* has typically been read 'as an assertion of

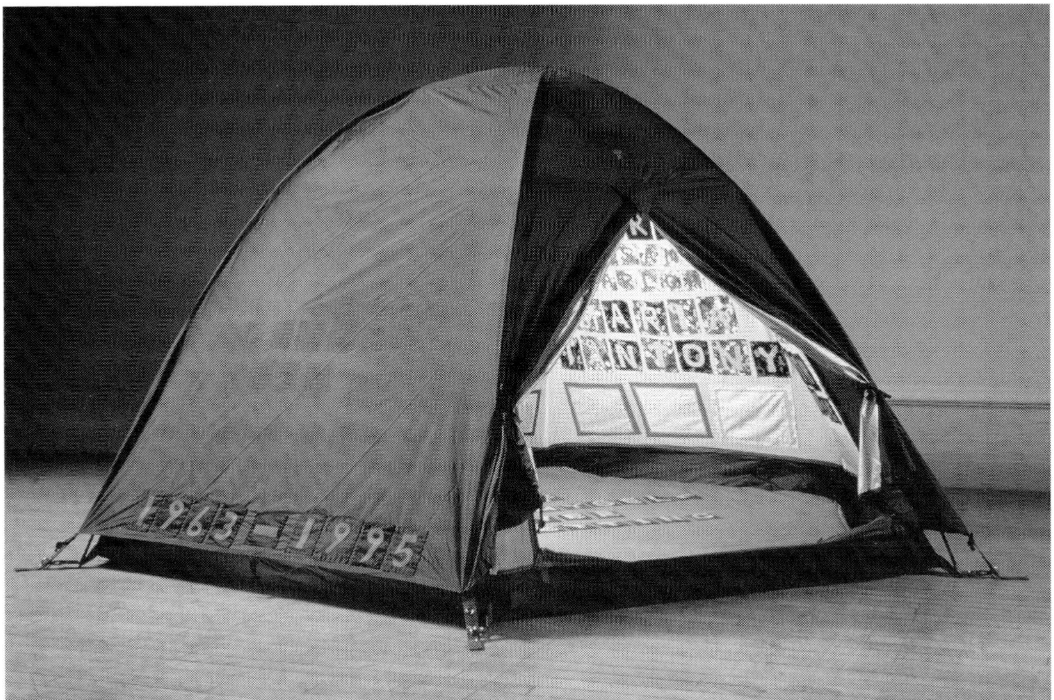

14. Tracey Emin, *Everyone I Have Ever Slept With 1963–1995*, 1995
Appliquéd tent, mattress and light
48 x 96 1/2 x 84 1/2 in. (122 x 245 x 215 cm)

Photo: Stephen White
Courtesy Jay Jopling/ White Cube (London)

"in-yer-face" female sexuality',[41] recalling Kristeva's remark in *Powers of Horror* about the 'confrontation with the feminine'.[42] Emin's tent seems a rebellious and anarchic epitome of female promiscuity. This, however, is a common misconception. In a now famous *Sunday Times* interview,[43] the artist expressed irritation at the way in which the tent had been routinely misconstrued by an obtuse critical fraternity.

> The thing about the tent that really annoys me, when it's in the media, is people just write it's the names of my lovers. But it's not. The tent is everyone I ever slept with 1963–1994. Now, I'm 34, so how could I have had a lover in 1963?[44]

In other words, 'slept with' is intended to signify sleep in a literal sense and is therefore not employed as a euphemism for 'have sex with'. 'It's about conception, sleeping in the womb with my twin brother, up to my last friend or lover that I slept with in 1994. That's what the tent's about. It's about sleep, intimacy, and moments.'[45]

The names sewn into the domed inner membrane of the tent, of family members, friends, platonic as well as sexual co-sleepers, significantly include Emin's grandmother, her twin brother Paul (as she says above) and, movingly, 'Foetus I' and 'Foetus II', whose fates were to be miscarried following a botched termination procedure in 1990, and successfully aborted in 1992, respectively.[46] The former event is described in the twenty-four-minute film *How it Feels* (1996) in upsetting documentary detail: 'I felt something slip,' she says, 'and as it slipped I put my hand there and what I held between my thigh and the palm of my hand was a foetus, kind of mashed-up foetus.'[47] The episode is revisited in her autobiography: 'Amid the London traffic and the summer heat,' she writes, 'I cradled the foetus – my dead baby – between my thigh and the palm of my hand, knowing it had never wanted to leave me.'[48] Also included in the tent is the name 'Ryan' who we learn from *Strangeland* was an eighteen-year-old homeless victim of domestic violence whom Emin comforted when she was twelve: 'She is tiny compared to him, yet she's protecting him.'[49]

Sheath, shelter and sanctuary, the tent represents a safe place, a comfort zone in which such events can quietly, mournfully be contemplated. This is a space which one visits only to be alone. The overwhelming sense of solitude that Emin repeatedly associates with the necessity of developing an independent personal identity is configured precisely in the emptiness of the tent, suggesting that her ultimate fate is to remain alone – completely and profoundly alone.[50] The crypto-hemispherical shape of the tent, glowing from inside, implies the monadic solitude of a metaphysically isolated self, withdrawn from a hostile external environment, sheltered behind vulnerable yet durable walls.

Emin's tent thus identifies intimacy, through linking it with the privacy of the sleeping state, with an ultimate and inescapable solitude. This concern with the solitude of intimacy foreshadows her later controversial work *My Bed* (1998), which, according to Mandy Merck, qualifies as a work of anxiety.[51] 'Hers may be a double bed, the bed for the couple and coupling', Merck writes – but 'that only makes it a more potent figure of longing and abandonment'.[52] Like a pair of parentheses bracketing the main thematic concerns of Emin's project, *Everyone I Have Ever Slept With* and *My Bed* are cognate works, sharing a preoccupation with the privacy of sleep and the ultimate solitude of the self; but, most particularly, I would suggest they share a cognate anxiety that originates in the fear of abandonment. An acute awareness that something has *moved away*, that someone has already departed, augments the atmosphere of *My Bed*; and, exactly like the fate of Emin's unborn foetus, although never wanting to leave, the tent has also been abandoned by its temporary dweller: looking into the tent, seeking the nomadic subject of Emin's art, yields nothing but a deserted, uninhabited and 'deterritorialised' empty shell.[53] Yet it is *in* these nomadic spaces, in the tent and on the bed – in the grounding condition of emptiness and abandonment itself – that the salient forms of Emin's twin self-portraits *without selves* are located.

A cell of somnolent solitude is shelled out in the tent with its mattress-floored cavity surrounded by its sheath of pseudo-walls and domed ceiling; despite the copious indexical evidence of presence in the dishevelled, stained sheets and the bedsit squalor, a profound absence of human agency clings like a smell to the installation *My Bed*. The debris associated with the bed signifies this absence in the most precise way. Something has departed. And this constellation of indigent possessions – leavings, remains – constitutes its final testimony. Emphasising this nomadic absence, two travelling suitcases bound together with chains and padlocks, initially a separate work (*Leaving Home*), was eventually attracted into the orbit of *My Bed*.[54]

What makes the tent and *My Bed* such powerful metaphors for the self is thus the absence intuited in both works – in the glowing heart of the tent, or on the snarl of sheets on the bed. Where we expect to see being and substance we see nothing and no one. Yet this is precisely the condition of personal identity relevant to Emin's project. Here the self is represented as homeless, radically peripatetic, constantly trying to escape from something and always shadowed by the ubiquitous possibility of suicide. Initial installations of *My Bed* included a noose hanging from the ceiling.

Any account of personal identity must acknowledge the fact of suicide. For, as Albert Camus recognised, confronting the problem of suicide brings one face-to-face with existence. It is inescapably *my* existence, and specifically the value of that existence that comes into acute and unflattering focus in the

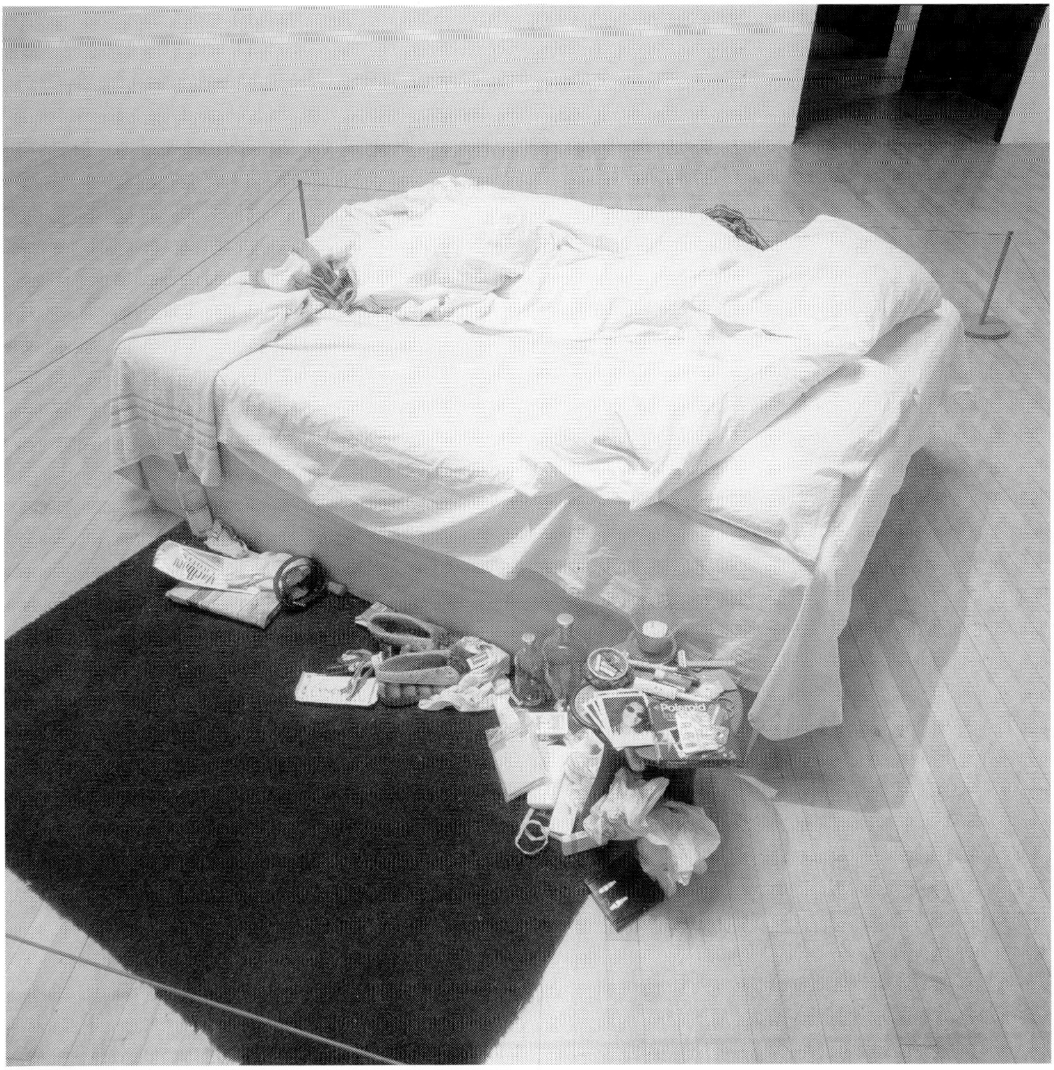

15. Tracey Emin, *My Bed*, 1998
Installation, Turner Prize Exhibition, Tate Gallery, London, 20 October 1999–23 January 2000
© the artist
Photo: Stephen White
Courtesy Jay Jopling/ White Cube (London)

mirror of such a confrontation.[55] 'Judging whether life is or is not worth living amounts to answering the fundamental question of philosophy.'[56]

Now, Emin's entire aesthetic project developed out of such an existentially significant confrontation with suicide. 'At the beginning of 1992,' Emin informs us in *Strangeland*, 'I left art. It was a terrible break-up: all part of my emotional suicide, when I attempted to give up everything I loved that did not love me back.'[57] In the video *Tracey Emin's CV. Cunt Vernacular* (1997), she defines emotional suicide as 'killing yourself without dying. Destroying each friendship and relationship, one by one, till I was alone.'[58] She explains that this was a critical phase in her life, a decisive moment, hence an ethically crucial time. It came about, she says, through the experience of failure. She destroyed her previous work and started again. 'So, by July 1992 I had returned from failure to concentrate on what I believed I was good at. Like a wounded bird, I began to rebuild myself, using the experience of failure as my foundation.'[59]

She told Will Self that following this para-suicidal episode she was unable to 'go on doing art unless it meant something to me emotionally . . . so I began making things out of bits of me'.[60] Since the early 1990s (and up to her solo show in the White Cube Gallery, London, *When I Think About Sex . . .*, in 2005, and her installation for the Venice Biennale in 2007[61]), Emin has used the technique of appliqué (sewing and embroidering) to create a series of intricately worked (and aggressively worded) blankets and fabrics composed from a montage of patterned letters sewn into underlying fabric. Documenting the names on the interior of the tent necessarily involved, for Emin, as in her blankets, a painstaking, time-intensive archival practice of cutting, stitching and patching. Memory fragments emerge only *via* the needlework process, evolving and finally preserved through the work of appliqué: 'Her autobiography is not only the subject matter,' Robert Preece observes, 'but also the process of sewing, with *memories generated* in the *process*.'[62]

The memory theory of personal identity maintains that the sense of self as psychologically continuous through time is established with reference to memories. Interpreted as past subjective experiences, memories are tokens of what was once present in the same way as the immediate present is happening now:[63] 'Memory-experiences must refer to previous occurrences in the history of the same self – and thus memory, as a criterion of personal identity, presupposes a self, or haver of experiences.'[64] Despite the critical objections that have been levelled against the memory theory, it remains a compelling reference for Emin's practice. Memories, as the constellation of 'memorabilia' associated with *My Bed* and the texts sewn into the interior of the tent, become the highly personalised possessions that give the self its private experiential continuity, its distinct identity, its integrity over time.

However, memories, notoriously fickle, fade and depreciate with time, significantly diminishing the reassuring security of self-identity. 'The perpetual activity of forgetting', Milan Kundera writes, 'gives our every act a ghostly, unreal, hazy quality.'[65] Should Emin's archival practice therefore be considered instead an effort to impede the process of forgetting? She sews and stitches 'a counterpart to Penelope's work rather than its likeness',[66] not because she wants to remember but because *she does not want to forget*. The distinction may be subtle but it is crucial. Emin's sewing texts are best understood in terms of a creative resistance to forgetting and a constructive, if compulsive, response to involuntary memories manifested in the process.

The mattress on the floor of the tent is stitched with letter-patches spelling out the words: 'With Myself Always Myself Never Forgetting'. In relation to the memory theory, these words suggest that amnesia is tantamount to a loss of identity. Once it is recognised that 'With Myself Always Myself Never Forgetting' is the key to the tent, far from appearing a tasteless icon to serial promiscuity or a gratuitous violation of public–private taboos, the tent emerges as a work of self-examination in which the salient motif is absent, reduced to an effect generated by a constellation of patched memory fragments. Emin's tent therefore signifies a performative memento that bears witness to the anxiety of loss and separation and the fragility of memories now emphasising – in an inversion of the memory theory – not only the insecurity of the self but also the vulnerability of identity. And yes it *is* a therapeutic work, its physical existence testifying to a period of working through the anxiety of separation, transience and loss, and the claustrophobic continuity of a self that suffers all this social traffic: I suffer the departures and the break-ups, the deaths and the removals, the tent says. Yet I remain behind, solitary, alone. That is why the proper place of the self in Emin's project is identified with the floor of the tent.

According to Emmanuel Levinas, the precise significance of human subjectivity is *subjection*; for the self, above all, is sensitively engaged with existence through structures of sensibility and corporeal feeling. 'It is because the self is sensible, that is to say, vulnerable, passive, open to wounding, outrage and pain, but also open to the movement of the erotic, that it is capable or worthy of ethics.'[67] Therefore, in Levinas, as Simon Critchley observes, the (subjectivity of the) self is best considered in terms of being subject to.[68] Subject to what exactly? Subjectivity is interpreted by Levinas as a kind of subjection to the other person. Drawing on the original Latin in order to emphasise the modality of something that *remains underneath*, a sensitive stratum that things happen to and embed themselves in: 'The self', Levinas writes, 'is a *sub-jectum*.'[69] But, ultimately, the self is sub-ject to the *appeal of the other* who always already disrupts the attitude of self-interest natural to the ego; Levinas identifies such subjection to the other with the very possibility of the ethical relation. This *ethical subject* represents a conception of the self as radically opened up by an otherness that transcends any effort to assimilate it. Subjectivity is marked in its internal make-up by subjection to alterity, a subjection expressed in a 'vulnerability and passivity towards the other'.[70] Edith Wyschogrod clarifies the ethical relevance of this connection in terms that we will later consider crucial for Emin: 'It is the vulnerability of the other', she says, 'that challenges the structure of the self as an egology.'[71]

Subjectivity for Levinas is like a receptive sub-stratum that is gradually filled in with a heterogeneous patchwork of the indelible yet partial traces that the interaction with other people leaves in us: 'the ethical demand is', Critchley confirms, 'a traumatic demand, it is something that comes from outside the subject . . . but which leaves its imprint within the subject.'[72] The names vigilantly stitched into the tent's interior imply an acknowledgement that the named have imprinted Emin's subjectivity, that others *have* had a constitutive part in shaping her sense of self. They have contributed to making her who she has become. The tent therefore implies that the self is less an identity than a heterogeneity, and to this extent cannot be reduced to a coherent identity at all. Citing her past lovers in the context of her family, platonic friends and twin brother suggests such an anti-solipsistic ethic. Meaningful intimacy is possible: intrinsic, experientially rich connections can be formed with other people despite the emphasis on independent self-fulfilment associated with dominant conceptions of human agency.

What I want to emphasise in relation to Emin's work is that, although radically exterior to the self, this irreducible alterity of the other person becomes constitutive of the ethical subject. Levinas believed that ethical experience is made possible only by that which is affected fundamentally, in its very constitution, by the priority of the other person. When this ethical structure of the 'disposition towards alterity'[73] is appreciated, the tent comes to light as a kind of profane tabernacle of scriptures devoted to the other. Far from being a disrespectful violation of behavioural norms or indulgent solipsism, therefore, Emin's *open* tent figuratively intimates the importance of others (and otherness as such) for any meaningful depiction of the self.

Let us sum up with three clarifications.

1. Emin's tent can be considered to signify that the experience of the irreducible otherness that Levinas associated with the other person is crucial to any adequate conception of personal identity.
2. The tent demonstrates (particularly in relation to the words inscribed on its floor) that the condition of possibility for ethical discourse is the subject considered in terms of *sub-jection* to the priority of the other person.
3. Most importantly, perhaps, the tent represents the concept that the self is radically open to the other person without ever adequately comprehending that person's true otherness; this aspect, I think, appears most distinctly in the open state of the tent which, in its exposure, invites

> other people to enter it. It becomes very important in this context of ideas to repeat emphatically that the tent is *not closed*: its open state invites entry, even if this entry is ultimately experienced as a kind of violation of 'personal space'. In fact, Levinas argued that the experience of alterity induces a radical opening in the self, speaking repeatedly of the traumatic breaching of the contours of the subject: the apparently closed monad of selfhood, he believed, was breached a priori by the presence of the other, a state that he believed already presents a distinct challenge to the closure of pure egoism: 'subjectivity as *the other in the same*, as an inspiration is the putting into question of all affirmation for-oneself, all egoism.'[74] And Levinas identifies this condition of openness to the other as the origin of responsibility per se; a state that, for him, further represents an *awakening* to a fundamental responsibility that is 'beyond knowledge', a kind of nocturnal vigilance he associated with the awareness of otherness.[75]

The state of 'insomnia' or wakefulness that Levinas associated with the experience of alterity is not only figured precisely in the openness of Emin's tent but also by the light that, like a plea to stay awake to the approach of the other, glows within its vigilant enclosure.[76] This insomnia, in its association with the vigilance that Levinas identifies with ethical responsibility, is ultimately linked with remembrance and the artist's anxiety about amnesia. For, as amnesia is equivalent to a loss of identity, 'With Myself Always Myself Never Forgetting' expresses a determination to remain wakeful in order to observe a continual commitment to *anamnesia* (rememberance).

It is perhaps possible to concretise Levinas's abstruse notion of ethical subjection as it functions in Emin's art with reference to the concept of anxiety. According to a recent study of the concept, Renata Salecl claims that anxiety always plays an essential part in love relationships because 'the moment we fall in love', she explains, 'we have our subjectivity temporarily suspended in another subject.'[77] This idea of the 'suspension of subjectivity' in the other person corresponds closely to the Levinasian conception of the ethical subject. However, as Salecl explains, this suspension creates an occasion for the return of a more elemental separation anxiety that disrupts 'our previous self-perception' and which retains a close affinity with the fundamental anguish of the child who fears the 'loss of love of the primal caregiver'; this anxiety is fundamental because the originary trauma, repeated in 'future love relationships', actually determines the structure of those later relationships.[78]

Both the originary anguish associated with the child's fear of abandonment and the later anxiety Salecl identifies as a constitutive part of adult relationships are acknowledged in Emin's tent. This is particularly emphatic in that the tent makes a definite association between *in utero* existence and the lovers who later shared Emin's bed. Considering Emin's childhood as represented in *Strangeland*, in the film *Why I Never Became a Dancer* (1995) and in the details disclosed in *Conversation With My Mum* (2001), we can understand why she may have been particularly vulnerable to the separation anxiety Salecl associates with the loss of love of the primary caregiver.

Exposure Without Reserve: Emotional Response and its Moral Significance

In the short film *Why I Never Became a Dancer* (1995) a childhood incident is narrated over a montage of shaky indistinct images that quickly establish the *mise en scène* of Margate, the slightly dilapidated seaside resort on the Kentish coast where Emin grew up. Assuming the innocent monotone of a child, slowly, deliberately reading, the artist's voice[79] speaks of a traumatic rite-of-passage experience while the images of her remembered seatown flicker on the screen.

Shot on Super 8, the margins remain darkly fringed and grainy, lending the imagery a kind of phantasmagorical quality appropriate to the theme. Image fragments are trailed rather than sutured seamlessly together, interrupted by sudden shifts, jolts, weird angles and blanks, while the 'memories' shiver into life on the screen – amusement arcades, wind-blinking lightbulbs, the big wheel of the carousel over the horizon of the town – The Lido, Mario's, The Tivoli – flocks of pigeons, pyramids of soft toys, ice-cream parlours, night-club billboards and, always, the chiaroscuro of the rippled sea breathing on the silver strand.

The narrative recounts an early episode of public humiliation when her participation in a heat of the British Disco Dance Championship 1978 was interrupted by a group of young men loudly abusing her. Following a brief and evocative account of her 'feral'[80] existence as a teenager in Margate, which was, according to this account, alarmingly unregulated by any parental influence ('there were no morals, or rules or judgements. I just did what I wanted to do') she builds up to an auspicious time when she became aware of her self-value and potential.

The voice speaks of leaving school permanently at thirteen, of haunting Margate's 'Golden Mile' in the long headachy afternoons, the empty idylls of truancy: 'The lunchtime discos, drinking cider laying out on the beach.' And, as a young adolescent, the childlike voice informs us: *there was always sex*. She adds, innocently: 'It was something you could just do, and it was for free.'

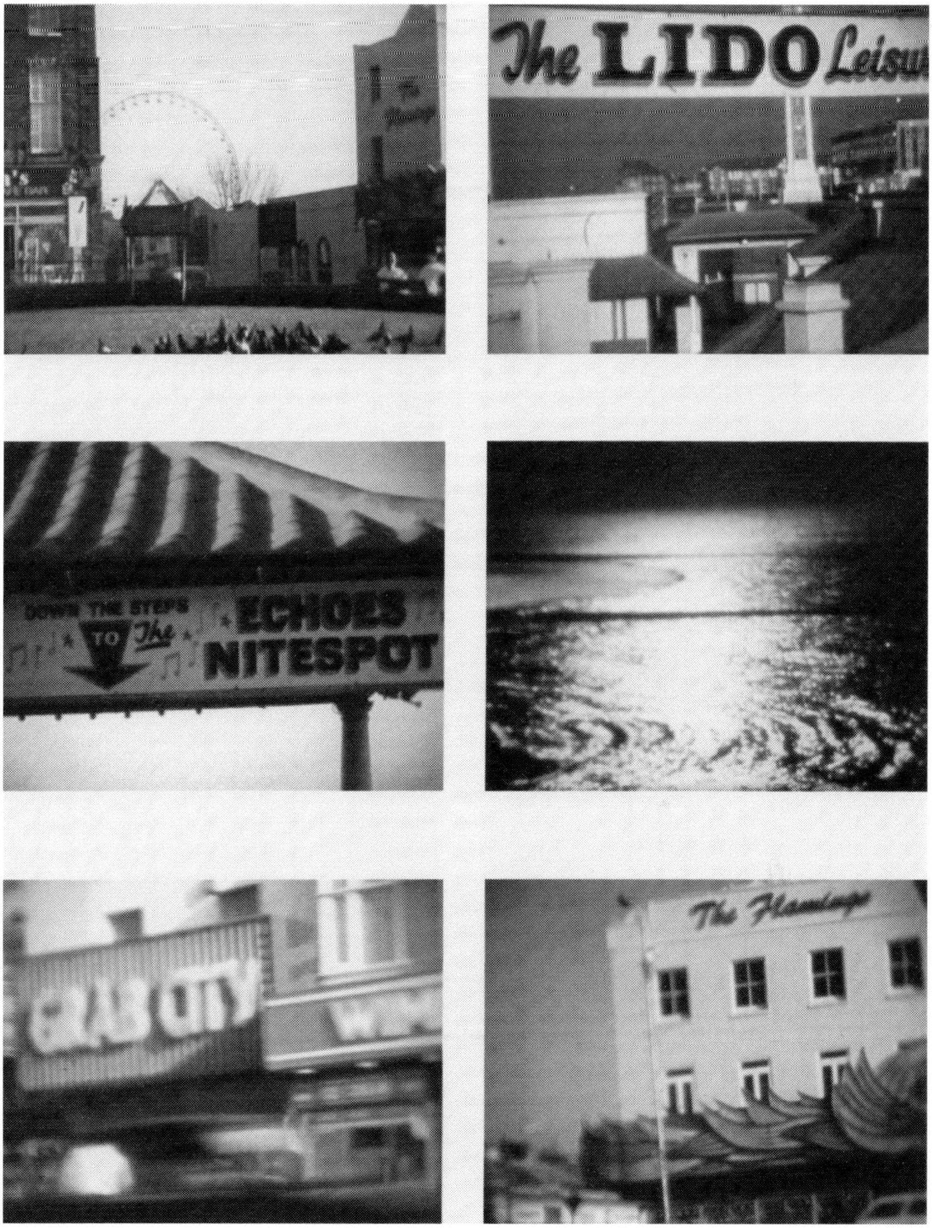

16. Tracey Emin, *Why I Never Became a Dancer (1)*, 1995
Single screen projection and sound shot on Super 8
Duration: 6 minutes 30 seconds
© the artist
Courtesy Jay Jopling/ White Cube (London)

> It didn't matter that I was young: 13, 14. It didn't matter that they were men of 19, 20, 25, 26. By the time I was 15, I'd had them all . . . And I knew the difference between good and bad. The reason these men wanted to fuck me, a girl of 14, was because they weren't men. They were less, less than human.[81]

At a certain point, however, she discovered that she loved dancing: 'That's where I got my real kick, on the dance floor. It felt like I could defy gravity, as though my soul were truly free.'[82]

And she became good at it. She 'stopped shagging'.[83] She entered the championship. And during her dance routine, when people began to applaud her, she felt she had a good chance of winning. But then the group of men, most of whom she had had sex with 'at some time or other were chanting'. They were shouting at her: 'SLAG, SLAG, SLAG!'[84] Finally, completely mortified, she fled the club and ran down to the shore where she vowed to herself that she would leave Margate forever. 'I left those boys,' she says. And then, in a manner that corresponds very closely to the tent's naming protocol, she identifies, by name, the men involved. In fact she dedicates the film to them. In the finale, for the first time in the film, we see Emin dancing to 'You Make Me Feel (Mighty Real)' by Sylvester in a brightly lit empty studio room, with a stereo on the floor, she smiles into the camera, a token of her transformation: 'Shane, Eddy, Tony, Doug, Richard – this one's for you.'[85]

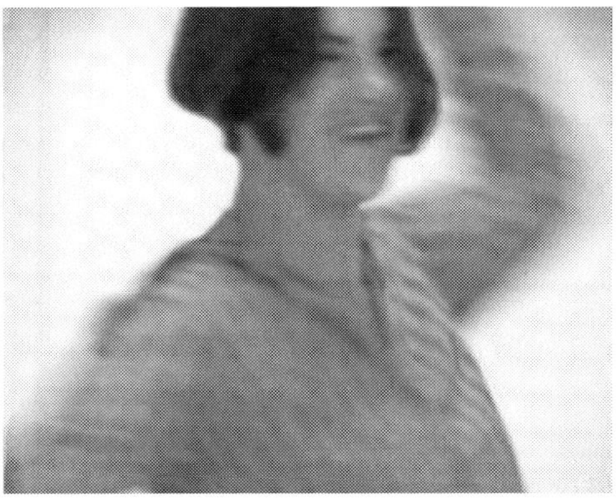

17. Tracey Emin, *Why I Never Became a Dancer (2)*, 1995
Single screen projection and sound shot on Super 8
Duration: 6 minutes 30 seconds
© the artist
Courtesy Jay Jopling/ White Cube (London)

The entire episode is reported in a disengaged and unemotional tone of voice. Emin's work aspires to a forensic, factually descriptive status: *Why I Never Became a Dancer* is almost cruel in the severity of the documentary style used to disclose its confidences. Strangely, therefore, in spite of its irreducibly subjective content, the artist takes great care not to prejudice the episodes exposed in her work by colouring them according to a morally evaluative viewpoint.

Emin's efforts to allow events to emerge by presenting them in as non-judgemental and dispassionate a manner as possible often results in motifs of irreducible specificity. In her first solo show *My Major Retrospective* (1993) she displayed a phial of blood-stained tissue from one of her abortions;[86] *The History of Painting* (1999), which consists of seven mounted wall-pieces (three frames and four cabinets), contains three pregnancy tests, a box of morning-after pills, used tampons and some bloodied tissues.[87] Similarly her memento-piece *Uncle Colin (1963–93)* memorialises her coeval uncle's violent death following a car accident by including a display case containing a crushed box of *Benson & Hedges* allegedly extracted from his post-mortem grasp.[88] And, most representative of this forensic approach, of course *My Bed* dislocates the unmade bed with its stained sheets and wrecked pillows from the bedroom and sites it, complete with satellite detritus, in the incongruous venue of the gallery. Such an out-of-context alienation effect renders the squalid scene devoid of any evaluative perspective. Brown is correct to emphasise that *My Bed* is presented without the 'hygenic exhibition device of a glass vitrine'.[89] The refusal to provide an evaluative framework that would allow the work to be morally mediated is symbolically marked by the refusal to enclose the scene in a display case. This makes Emin's art threatening – its dirty anti-sublime realism giving the impression of something uncontained and morally hazardous, even contagious. This abject externalisation, to borrow Kristeva's motif, *disturbs* because it corrupts the moral limits that define the socio-symbolic regime of hygiene and propriety with discharged somatic materials: 'urine, blood, sperm, excrement'.[90] Emin's alienation of the bed – displacing it into an out-of-context location – re-marks an unremarkable object as an abject *mise en obscène*.

Emin's work, I will argue, ethically involves viewers by eliciting emotionally expressive responses; and, although it may seem paradoxical to maintain this, it is precisely *because* she refuses to prescribe a moral attitude from which the content of her work ought to be viewed (symbolically enacted in the refusal to sanitise her work) that compels emotional involvement with her art. This demand ultimately delivers the moral value associated with it. Why is this? Indeed, why *should* this be the case? Uniquely in the context of transgressive art, Emin's anti-sublime aesthetic genuinely makes the matter of the attitude it manifests into a responsibility for the viewer: the work's mode of address calls upon viewers to become responsible for their attitude towards the behaviour she documents. Therefore, despite how the work may be constructed to have this effect, this is ultimately experienced as an attitude towards *her* as the agent understood as responsible for this behaviour.

What specific connection is hereby implied between emotion and ethics? If Emin's art elicits an emotional response, it also evokes an *ethical* response. Recent cognitive philosophers have suggested that 'by moving us to emotion, [as Emin's work does] and requiring that we makes [*sic*] sense of these emotions as responses . . . art can singularly contribute something like moral understanding.'[91] Indeed, according to cognitive theory, emotions have been re-constituted as ethically significant in that they 'essentially incorporate evaluations'.[92] Increasingly, moral philosophers are conceding the importance of emotional responses for moral intelligence: any 'emphasis on reason' in ethical discourse (such as the dominant utilitarianism or deontological paradigms), as Robert Solomon observes, 'underestimates the power of compassion'.[93] Martha Nussbaum, who has persistently emphasised the informative value of art for ethical theory, has similarly criticised the conservative opposition between reason and the emotions, attacking in the process any absolute distinction between fact and value: 'emotions are not simply blind surges of affect . . . identified by their felt quality alone'; rather, she insists, 'they are intimately related to beliefs or judgments about the world', cognitively significant 'discriminating responses' vital for the process of moral evaluation.[94] And Nel Noddings has also emphasised the evaluative component of emotion, establishing its centrality for the ethics of care: 'What I undergo as I experience emotion is the result of perceiving something that matters to me.'[95]

Transmuting fact into value, the dispassionate disclosure of traumatic experience in *Why I Never Became a Dancer* provokes an affective emotional reaction. What we react to is the *factual* character of her exposure 'without reserve' to the other in 'vulnerability and pain'; and therefore, with our discussion of Levinas in mind, the nature of this response can be identified as ethical. In an important essay addressing Levinas's notorious hostility to aesthetics, Dorota Glowaka characterises the consequence of an art of deliberate exposure to the other as a radical subversion of 'traditional aesthetics'.[96] Glowaka's analysis is highly significant for this interpretation of Emin because it allows us to identify the transgressive aspect of her work with its ethical meaning.

Bernard Williams has also defended the relevance of what he calls 'creative emotional responses' for the development of an engaged 'moral attitude'.[97] And it has been claimed that active sympathy (or *care* that what happens to others matters) constitutes a paradigmatic example of what Williams characterises as the creative emotional response necessary for moral motivation and – to the extent that it corresponds to the concept of the other person 'as [a] self-determining agent', identification with the subject of a life – such sympathy becomes crucial: 'a necessary component in the attitude of respect'.[98] As Edith

Wyschogrod explains in an essay that identifies a relationship between the Levinasian concern for alterity and such ethically significant emotional empathy: 'The vulnerability of the other evokes one's own capacity for experiencing pain, for emptying oneself of egoistic orientation, so that one's corporeality may be at the service of the other.'[99] Engaging with Emin's work means to consent to the particular emotional challenge it sets. This challenge ultimately involves a process of empathy or 'active sympathy' – the identification with the other's subjective life that has been described as 'a matter of feeling oneself into the experience of the other'.[100] To avoid this empathetic engagement or resist the creative emotional response to Emin's work, or to exercise self-control and force oneself to accept that her work counts as art only if it can be assimilated to a rational, objective or *disinterested* mode of access, is to prejudice it. For what elicits the ethically significant emotional responses in Emin's art is precisely *its resistance to traditional aesthetic categories*. Thus the transgressive features of her work – alienation of private experience, refusal to sanitise, non-judgemental attitude and dispassionate mode of address – coincide with its morally significant features.

To the established procedures of institutional art theory Emin's work cannot but appear as a disrespectful contravention of socio-symbolic (and aesthetic) conventions. In opposition to this perspective, whoever engages with and responds to the subjective emotional demands made by Emin's art will, through active sympathy, ultimately experience the ethical value associated with it; and, if the moral value of her art, as claimed above, informs its aesthetic value, the latter will remain necessarily unintelligible to those who resist responding emotionally to her work. What is distinctive about Emin's project, to borrow and modify Lorna Healy's[101] term, is precisely its *ethical effect*. The particular character of the subjective, emotional response to her work differentiates it from that associated with transgressive ambivalence in general because its dispassionate, cold and factual address stimulates a reaction in the viewer that is specifically ethical in code, character and value.

Thus the emotional reactions stimulated by *Why I Never Became a Dancer*, for instance, are determined by the invasive position that the film implicates the viewer in. Engaging with the film entails deep misgivings that are associated with our complicit role in the intrusion into the personal, subjective life of another person that it documents. In this sense, through involving us in the behaviour it documents, her project evokes emotions of self-conscious shame or embarrassment: just *looking* somehow requires an added violation. Preece's claim that the names on Emin's tent are only legible to an inherently prurient consciousness that intrudes 'into [its] space' therefore accurately discerns its crucial ethical character.[102] And we may feel hurt by being coerced into being made to feel unsolicited negative emotions in this way.

Ulrich Lehmann's analysis of the recurrent motifs of Emin's work makes a cognate point: the tent, he says, ought to be seen as a metaphorical representation of the 'open legs' which he identifies as the leitmotif of Emin's art; in the context of the pattern of open legs throughout her work, the tent can be considered a similar kind of public exposure, 'where the viewer is asked to literally enter the artist's creative persona through a central parting in the sculptural object'.[103] However, the point is not that it is necessary to enter the tent *physically* to invade the personal space shelled out by the work: it is already displayed to the invasive gaze that the viewer is compelled to adopt simply by virtue of its splayed form and its public exposure, as well as its gynaecological structure. (This reading is reinforced in the *Saatchi 100* DVD,[104] which shows footage of a spectator who, while squatting down to look inside the tent, becomes aware of a presence behind her and, clearly embarrassed, checks her trousers before quickly exiting.)

Why I Never Became a Dancer, like the open tent, elicits an emotionally expressive response: specifically in this instance, shame. Experiencing shame at the violation involved in witnessing the openness of display, the viewer is compelled to respond emotionally and therefore, as argued, ethically to these works. The result of the emotional response of shame that Emin's work prescribes is, perhaps perversely, a basic sense of responsibility. In the following section, Emin's project of self-examination will be presented as motivated by the experience of shame. Levinas characterised shame as the awareness of an existential exposure (to the other) and was thus, for him, as we would imagine, central to ethics: 'Shame arises each time we are unable to make others forget our basic nudity,' he writes. 'It is related to everything we would like to hide and that we cannot bury or cover up.'[105] Shame means not being in a position to conceal what we need to conceal. In attempting to escape and hide, the ashamed self that needs to be hidden becomes, contrarily, impossible to cover up. When we are in the state of shame, we become 'riveted to' our own factual existence, we cannot evade the self, as we cannot hide within the self; in shame therefore is revealed the 'unalterably binding presence of the I to itself'.[106] Therefore, I believe that shame, provided it is understood in the existential and moral sense, is structural to the overall ethical significance of Emin's aesthetic. These claims will be established by drawing on Jean-Paul Sartre's analysis of the state of shame in *Being and Nothingness.* [107]

Shame: An Existential Analysis

In order to explicate the value-difference between the private and the public registers of reality, Sartre, in *Being and Nothingness*, presents one of the celebrated fictive vignettes unique to his mode of philosophising. He invites us to imagine a man, motivated by jealousy or curiosity, stooping at a keyhole, eavesdropping. He uses this motif to characterise the natural everyday attitude as one of existential solitude. Most of the time, in other words, Sartre explains, we act as unobserved agents, our actions characterised by a kind of unreflective, solipsistic impunity. In such private states, Sartre comments, we are exhaustively identified with our acts; I am wholly involved with the quotidian, absorbed by my act: such acts 'carry in themselves their whole justification'.[108]

However, Sartre, at this point, has us imagine the man absorbed in his private act of voyeurism being disturbed by a footfall behind him. Suddenly he is aware of someone observing *him*. This change results in what Sartre defines as an irruption of the self (that is, an interruption of the solipsist impunity of the natural state) in self-consciousness: 'I see *myself*', Sartre writes, 'because *somebody* sees me' –

> This means that all of a sudden I am conscious of myself as escaping myself . . . as I am a pure reference to the Other. . . . I do not reject it as a strange image, but it is present to me as a self which I *am* without *knowing* it . . .[109]

He identifies conditions where the self is regarded as the object of the other's look with *shame*: 'it is the *recognition* of the fact that *I am* indeed that object which the other is looking at and judging.'[110] Such conditions, Sartre says, define the moral importance of shame in the existential sense.

Commenting on this episode, Mary Warnock observes that Sartre is not requesting our agreement to an abstract hypothesis but rather 'to *experience*, in imagination, a *familiar emotion*'.[111] He then employs this image, she says elsewhere, to argue that solipsism is incoherent: it is impossible to consider oneself in isolation from or as unconnected with other people; part of the self-awareness which each of us has, she claims, 'along with our awareness of the world', originates foundationally in the acknowledgement of others brought to us through shared emotional states.[112] And shame, for Sartre, is a particularly impressive example of this because it is not only emotionally rich but also, for existentialism, ethically basic. Shame, Warnock comments, 'is essentially experienced in a social context, where others are either actually or *potentially* present'.[113] She concludes that the emotion of shame, in the existential sense, is fundamental to the very possibility of the ethical experience; indeed, it is ethically crucial because it is stimulated by coming to terms with and assessing our behaviour *as witnessed* by potential observers. In shame, we see ourselves from the perspective of others and this moderates our behavioural practice, resulting ultimately in our becoming aware of our own otherness.

> The eavesdropper minds being caught in the act not because of the consequences his being caught may have . . . but here and now, without thought of the future, because he does not like to think of himself as mean, dishonourable, *low*. He despises such characteristics in others and now he has to despise himself as well. This is what shame is.[114]

As already considered in relation to the articulation of the ethical subject in Levinas, the claim that the self may be subject to the other person involves the suspension of egoism and the engaging of the ethical subject. Altruistic concern awakens as a consequence of the recognition of the otherness exterior to the self that ultimately undermines the solipsistic ego. We have already identified this structure of alterity in Emin's work generically in relation to the problematic of autobiographical form, and specifically in our analysis of the tent. Sartre, to repeat, acknowledges the moment of this awakening of alterity within the closure of the ego with the concept of the 'irruption of self' in the mood of shame.

Emin publicly presents, by proper name, all the people she spent private intimate moments with in the tent, and those who subjected her to post-coital public humiliation in *Why I Never Became a Dancer*; there is reason to consider these works part of a 'name-and-shame' campaign. In reaction to the tent piece, for instance, one of the named – counter-cultural writer Billy Childish – allegedly took exception to the violation of his privacy, retaliating by selling some private snapshots of Emin.[115] Another angrily questioned Emin's entitlement to name him. 'Then you shouldn't have fucked me, should you?' she unhesitatingly countered.[116] The same can be claimed of the naming strategy associated with *Why I Never Became a Dancer*. Indeed, with respect to this work, Emin has related that one of those named in the film made the effort to contact her in order to apologise personally to her. She was delighted.[117] For this was evidence that the film had the desired effect.

These satellite episodes associated with her work lend credence to the notion that the film – and, indeed perhaps, despite claims to the contrary, the tent – represent nemesis pieces for Emin. As well as exacting retribution for wrongdoing, the intention here seems to occasion shame in those whose names have been archived in this accusatory way. A related effort directly to evoke shame can be seen in Emin's video *Conversation With My Mum*, where she subjects her own mother (who, clearly ashamed, actually becomes quite agitated and upset) to a relentless cross-examination, questioning (for the first time, as she admits to Melvyn Bragg[118]) her mother on her intention to have an abortion when pregnant with her and her twin brother Paul and coldly criticising her subsequent permissiveness and general lack of responsibility for her children.[119]

These constitute what I believe to be relatively superficial instances of shame in Emin's project. But because, as well as occasioning this specific sense of shame in the named individuals, the nemesis works also effect a general feeling of morally fundamental shame, I will argue, *in the viewer*. Some of her neon pieces, for instance, spell out statements such as *My Cunt is Wet with Fear* (1998) or questions such as *Is Anal Sex Legal?* – her candid, apparently, indeed paradoxically, shameless repeated references to urination, defecation, inebriation, menstruation and anal sex in her work also involve viewers emotionally by making them feel ashamed at the forensic invasion of privacy they perceive to be enacted in such disclosures.

We are now in a position to claim that Emin's work presents a visual manifestation of the 'irruption of the ego' spoken of by Sartre in his analysis of shame. The viewer of Emin's work (and this is true not only of the tent but also *My Bed* and *Why I Never Became a Dancer*) is made to feel shame in the way described in Sartre's vignette of the eavesdropper. Approaching *My Bed* (or watching *Why I Never*) we become ashamed for witnessing the exposure, the violation of privacy seen there. Feeling like an intruder invading personal space, we look left, right – perhaps behind – forced into the position of unintentional voyeur by the work. We experience shame because Emin's openness threatens privacy by confronting us with the possible exposure of the secret data of our *own* lives; indeed, I would suggest that the experience of her work forces this confrontation with the shameful secret, which, paradoxically, takes place privately – in the imagination of the viewer.

Shame in the existential sense is a public experience; more accurately perhaps it is the becoming-public of a private state through exposure: it thus occurs in the social order as a trans-subjective phenomenon where the self acknowledges the actual or potential others that can regard me, and *constitutes* that sense of self-aware self-consciousness fundamental to the experience of morality. Ethics originates when we begin to consider ourselves from the perspective of the other and therefore begin to regard ourselves as other – *for* the other.

Because it elucidates further the ethical dimension of Emin's practice, Levinas's phenomenological examination of shame in his early study *De l'evasion* (1935)[120] should be supplemented to Sartre's existential analysis. Levinas observes that the theme of shame prima facie appears to be 'reserved for phenomena of a moral order'. 'One feels ashamed', he writes, 'for having acted badly, for deviating from the norm.'[121] However, his analysis of the condition of shame is motivated by the intention to liberate the analysis of shame from being understood as identified entirely with 'a morally *bad* act'.[122] This is also what we wish to achieve here: to thicken the existential understanding of shame by demonstrating its significance for the relationship between subjectivity and the structure of the ethical experience considered more generally and more positively.

Encouraged to view shame as primarily a social phenomenon, Levinas argues that we tend to forget its *personal* significance. He indicates that the 'intensity' associated with the shame experience is identified with the fact that the subject who feels ashamed has actually been changed in some way. Here shame is defined as engendering the possibility of self-transformation. Given the characteristic features of such transformation, we find it difficult, Levinas says, to identify with an earlier incarnation of the self who now perhaps confronts us as a completely different person; indeed it is sometimes difficult even to comprehend the motivation that stimulated this person's behaviour. Shame, he concludes, despite appearances to the contrary, is morally relevant because it is in fact 'founded upon the solidarity of our being, which obliges us to claim responsibility for ourselves'.[123] However, this claim of responsibility of self-consciousness is determined by what we called above, in the context of the existential analysis of shame, our becoming *other* to ourselves.

Both Sartre's and Levinas's apparently opposed accounts are in fact necessary for a complete analysis of shame. In the structure of shame, the self-awareness that Levinas says obliges us to claim responsibility for ourselves spurs us to radical self-examination. Shame facilitates our becoming ethical witnesses of our own lives and this *is only made possible* through the awareness of others and the subsequent acknowledgement of our own otherness (becoming other to ourselves, we uncannily confront a familiar stranger). This ethical self-evaluation is, in Sartre's view, as we have seen, motivated by the emotion of shame.

The experience of shame in the existential sense – and having to cope retroactively with this shame in order to overcome it – constitutes the motivating experience of Emin's project. Yet she uses the experience of shame in a creative way to precipitate a process of self-transformation. All her most significant work testifies to the role that shame played in this process of transformation and moral development. This ethical dimension of shame has recently been defended by Michael Morgan. In motivating us to act, he argues, the emotion of shame can become the crucial catalyst in the 'process of moral education'. He calls this process 'mobilising shame'.[124]

At this point, I want to bring the two of these positions together by highlighting that the self-awareness caused by the imagined observation of others in self-consciousness ultimately converges with an awareness of the *otherness of the self*, where the self-as-other is revealed. Indeed, this awareness of the self-as-other brought about through shame, as Simon Critchley has also argued,[125] constitutes perhaps the very possibility of the ethical experience. A desire to be something other than what one is (and the glimpse towards future projects intimated by this departure from a previous form of life) manifests itself in moments of failure, Critchley explains, where the discontinuity between what one is (or has become) and what one would like (or feels one ought) to be, is abjectly exposed. 'Anyone, who has tried – and failed – to cure themselves of some sort of addiction', he illustrates, 'will understand what is meant here. The subject that I have chosen to be enters into conflict with the self that I am, producing a divided experience of self as self-failure.'[126]

The self from the past now confronts me, even though it *is* me (or *was* me), as radically other: 'I could not even imagine my past; and when I think of it now, it seems to be showing me the life of some *other person*.' In an extraordinary piece of writing, Milan Kundera quotes E.M. Cioran: 'I seem to be observing the obsessions of a stranger, and I am stupefied to learn that that stranger was myself.'[127] Observed from a quasi-external perspective afforded by temporal distance (and memory), the past self is regarded by Cioran with 'amazement'. Who is this person? Developing a coherent sense of personal identity involves coming to terms with this state of retrospective amazement caused by the process of temporal remoteness at the heart of the dividing subject.

Such a dialectic between incompatible phases of the self (where the self and its otherness come into conflict) is a vital component of all Emin's work, but is perhaps most starkly presented in her short video installation *The Interview* (1999), where she (Emin version one) relentlessly subjects herself (Emin version two) to ruthless cross-examination. Again the self-examining method here involves confrontation. It is important to observe that this confrontation is determined, like all her work, not by the effort to justify her actions retrospectively, but rather by the effort *not to shirk responsibility* for them. Transformative progression beyond past selves takes place through a process of externalisation and subsequent abandonment. Once a stage is transcended, Emin can look back at her past avatars as a series of shed shells, episodic instars that once held vital presence, but now any substantial existence they contain is preserved in memory. A more involved reading of the category of absence crucial to Emin's exploration of personal identity now suggests itself. We argued that her self-portraits without selves involve a kind of nomadic abandonment. However, with the departure of the self, an essential moving-on has occurred. I may suffer the exits and departures that the tent, the bed and *Why I Never* imply, but I *do not* remain behind as claimed above: *I also move on*.

In this context, Neal Brown has emphasised the liberating, transformative function of Emin's art. At the end of *Why I Never Became a Dancer*, she smiles while dancing, gives an 'I'm alright now' gesture, and the film cuts to a gull flying away towards the sun. Her art exists as a kind of testament to this metamorphic effort existentially to transform 'her status, through art, from victim to victor'.[128] Producing art for Tracey Emin is much more than just a matter of artistic production. What is misconstrued by the therapeutic critique of her work therefore is that aesthetic activity for Emin involves a solemn confrontation with trauma-inducing events in her life. Yet it is by exposing these events through her practice that she hopes to transform herself by externalising them and making them into art. As argued above, she believes that art has the potency to transform; her life events are therefore transfigured through reprocessing them as thematic aesthetic motifs. Emin's creative impulse is driven by the conviction that this defiantly courageous confrontation with the shame-inducing episode will result in *aufheben* – a dialectical annulment – ultimately becoming a phase in a kind of emotional life-rebuilding project. 'I began to rebuild myself', she writes, by '*using* the experience of failure as my foundation'.[129]

Through an uncompromising non-judgemental examination of her own existence, Emin has created a unique artistic project that, for the many reasons we have discussed in this chapter, is not only ethically valuable, but also artistically significant precisely because of its *ethical status*: through her work she creates something that is morally valuable *only as art*. Owing to the transformation of vulnerability into a kind of empowerment through an unconditional belief in the metamorphic power of art, her practice seeks to overcome the condition of shame through the fearless and rigorous exposure of (and confrontation with) weakness and, in this manner, to sublimate and transcend her past 'selves' through paradoxically accepting responsibility for them. Traces of these past selves are preserved and annulled in morally transgressive artworks that become vehicles of the sense of shame that engendered them by transferring this shame reflexively and uncomfortably – yet ultimately affirmatively – to the viewer. Emin's art, as we have seen, transforms a shameful, vulnerable, existential nakedness into a project of defiant self-empowerment.

In the final section I conclude that Emin's work can be defended as ethically valuable ultimately by identifying in it the form of discourse that Foucault has analysed under the rubric 'fearless speech'. As we shall see, this concept has the interpretative capacity to bring the disparate aspects we have identified with Emin's art practice to synthesis. For, as Foucault explains at the end of his study, all the truth practices that he associates with fearless speech concern in some way the problem of *memory* (*anamnesia*): 'in the form of an attempt to remind ourselves of what we have done, thought or felt'.[130] And, as he makes very clear, the exercises of self-examination central to the practice of fearless speech share a relationship with aesthetic principles, in particular with what he calls the 'aesthetics of the self',[131] for what is in question with respect to the techniques of *parrhesia* is 'the relation of the self to truth'.[132]

Concluding Ethical Evaluation: Tracey Emin's Fearless Speech

Foucault develops the concept of fearless speech in a short text compiled from cassette recordings of his seminar 'Discourse and Truth' (delivered at Berkeley in 1983). His familiarity with Ancient Greek and Roman thought led Foucault, late in his career, to discern a continuing relevance in the classical ethical principle of *parrhesia* or 'frankness in speaking the truth'. An inquiry into the provenance of this fearless speech, and particularly into its modality – how the principle was used and to *whom* it was applied – is far more than a philological exercise, but actually has the potential to elucidate the basic ethical impulses of 'what we could call the "critical" tradition in the West'.[133] A further ambition associated with his inquiry is the effort to recognise why truth-telling as a value *should* matter; this inquest into knowing why we ought to tell the truth and in what situations it is appropriate gives this project a highly significant normative turn.

People who practise fearless speech, Foucault begins, are those who, through their discourse, express *everything* they have in mind; for in fearless discourse nothing is concealed, the speaker 'opens his [*sic*] heart and mind completely to other people'.[134] Fearless speech is characterised above all therefore by *direct* address, and what is made manifest in the fearless speech act is emphatically and inescapably the opinion of the speaker. Thus fearless discourse is opposed to the techniques and manoeuvring of rhetoric and its schematic techniques, which are carefully designed to be persuasive and to, at all costs, convince an audience, *despite the truth*.

Fearless speech therefore, as practised *par excellence* by Socrates, is fundamentally philosophical in attitude: it is hostile to 'the false teachings of the sophists' and committed to self-knowledge.[135] 'The sophist can give very fine and beautiful discourses on courage, but is not courageous himself.'[136] As opposed to the techniques of rhetoric, where it does not matter whether the sophist *actually believes* in what is said, by contrast, the fearless speaker, according to Foucault, 'acts on other people's minds by showing them as directly as possible what he [*sic*] actually believes'.[137] Thus, in the speech activity of the fearless speaker there is a complete convergence of belief and truth.[138]

As well as the condition of frankness, Foucault's analysis highlights four further attributes of *parrhesia* (namely: truth, danger, criticism and duty). For the purposes of this application I want to focus on certain themes that are brought to light in the course of Foucault's discussion of these attributes. The first of these, *courage*, is particularly apt in the context of Emin's art. For above all, the fearless speech act involves courage, not only in relation to the other people, the socio-symbolic value systems or the moral pressure structures that threaten the disclosure of truth, but also because the effort to face this often difficult and demanding – highly personal – form of truth involves bravery and daring; it may involve, for instance, the self-critical confrontation of previous self-deception or pretension in a way that threatens the complacency associated with the pseudo-self persisting in what Sartre would have called the structures of 'bad faith'. *Parrhesia*, Foucault insists, is therefore 'linked to courage in the face of danger: it demands the courage to speak the truth in spite of some danger'.[139]

Stallabrass's repeated critique that the evaluation of Emin's art depends entirely on whether she is perceived to be sincere can perhaps be tempered according to this connection. Referring to Emin's assertion, 'I'm genuine' – which Stallabrass says sounds more like a plea than a statement – he remarks, in a pronouncement that reveals his doubts about his own criticisms of Emin's work: 'If she is believed, as she is by so many fans whose relationship to her is passionate and adoring (and very far from the cool appreciation of most contemporary art-goers), then Emin courageously displays female, but also more generally human desires, emotions and weaknesses directly.'[140] The implication here is that this 'fan-based' enthusiastic approach is somehow either inappropriate or an entirely illegitimate way of appreciating art. As discussed in Chapter 1, this critical attitude reflects the conventional prejudices (disinterestedness, attitude of distance etc.) associated with traditional aesthetic paradigms. Yet because Emin's work encourages the viewer to react in an emotional way, as argued above, reaction to her work cannot be grounded in a rational, speculative scheme; therefore, the ethical response appropriate to her work is resistant to being assimilated to or otherwise abstracted into the pseudo-objective principles associated with orthodox institutional aesthetics.[141] To answer Stallabrass's critique (if such a progressively flagging critique in fact requires to be answered): if, as Foucault claims, 'there is a kind of "proof" of the sincerity' of the fearless speaker, it is *courage*.[142] Indeed, the very fact that Emin has the courage to say something dangerous, that is, according to Foucault, 'different from what the majority believe', provides the evidence that she is 'speaking' in a fearless mode;[143] and the danger inherent in fearless discourse brings up the second characteristic that I want to draw attention to in relation to Emin's art practice, namely: *risk*.

To be in possession of truth is assured in the classical sources by the attribution of certain moral features to the speaker: 'when someone has certain moral qualities', Foucault teaches, 'then that is proof that he has access to truth.'[144] These moral qualities were established only if the fearless speaker demonstrated courage through expressing the truth, regardless of the danger connected with doing so. Speaking thus was therefore a high-risk activity.[145] However, speech does not always necessitate the risk of *death* in order to be considered fearless. There are countless prosaic everyday situations that demand the application of fearless speech[146] – risk of death being only the most extreme threat associated with it. Indeed, as Foucault qualifies, the danger associated with fearless discourse is its inevitable capacity to *upset* or *offend*. 'So you see,' he says, 'the function of *parrhesia* is not to demonstrate the truth to someone else, but has the function of *criticism*: criticism of the interlocutor or the speaker himself.'[147] The fearless speaker above all is attempting to be *true* to *herself*, that is, to express her beliefs whatever demands this makes of others, regardless of the discomfort it may cause people, and respectful of the challenge it poses for both self and others. Like Emin, the fearless speaker 'prefers himself as a truth-teller rather than as a being who is false to himself'.[148]

Foucault goes on to document carefully how the practice of *parrhesia* becomes *transgressive* with the Greek Cynics – their philosophical practice, in the effort not to shirk the responsibility to confront the truth, to accept its difficult challenges and inherent dangers, as provocative, sensationalist, and sometimes even offensive.[149] Later, under the influence of Stoic philosophy, Foucault says that cynicism, and specifically its provocative discursive practice, was turned *inward* and *applied to the self*. And, according to this paradigm, fearless speech became a 'duty toward the self'. Parrhesiastic bravery now resided in being 'courageous enough to disclose the truth about oneself'.[150] He quotes Seneca, who, in his writings directly characterised his philosophical practice as the 'examination of self' and asked: 'Who dares tell himself the truth?'[151] 'I conceal nothing from myself, I omit nothing. For why should I shrink from any of my mistakes, when I may commune thus with my self?'[152]

Careful to distinguish this practice from the more generally understood Christian confession (and this is why we remain unconvinced concerning religious interpretations of Emin's work), Foucault emphasises that it would be mistaken to interpret Seneca's 'mistakes' here as 'sins'.[153] They are not understood by him in terms of the transgression of external prohibitions; there is nothing comparable to atonement or penance in Seneca's discourse. Rather, 'what is at stake' in the exercises of *parrhesia* 'is not the disclosure of a secret which has to be excavated out of the depths of the soul. What is at stake is the *relation* of the self to the truth.'[154]

As he openly admits, Foucault is not concerned with the problem (or the nature) of truth *as such*: *Fearless Speech* does not attempt to elaborate a philosophical theory of truth. Rather the interests of his investigation lie in a conception of truth considered as an *activity*. In this way, he wishes to make his audience aware of the continuing moral relevance of the practical use of truth in public discourse. Thus Foucault's retrieval of the classical concept of *parrhesia* functions as a kind of scholastic alibi for his own ethical teaching. And therefore he continually emphasises that,

> *Parrhesia* as it appears in the field of philosophical activity in Greco-Roman culture is not primarily a concept or theme, but a *practice* which tries to shape the specific relations individuals have to themselves.[155]

In that it relates to the effort to develop ethical knowledge through self-examination, fearless speech is a basic mechanism of the more general classical philosophical project of 'knowing oneself' and in this sense relates most directly to Emin's art practice. For, as argued above, the artist's self-analytical practices function in a way that not only subverts the adequate simulation of a stable self-identity that persists through time and text; but rather, as indicated, the 'confessional' self-exploratory aspects of her practice are oriented to the attempt to develop self-knowledge through *working* out the problematic and necessarily incomplete theme of the self. Discerning the connection to Foucauldian *parrhesia* in this project finally provides us with a way of explaining the contrarian efforts of our initial attempt to differentiate Emin's practice from the critical consensus that situates it in the autobiographical or confessional tradition.

As indicated, the fragmented texts of her project of self-exploration inherently escape closure in ways that paradoxically challenge the very formula of the autobiographical confession itself. Her project in this sense constitutes an inquest for practices that facilitate the problematic exposure of the self precisely as a continual problem and in a manner that cannot be reduced to the expression of secret contents. And Foucault, adamant to differentiate the practice of *parrhesia* from modern or contemporary conceptions of confession (especially of the Christian or Roman Catholic type), insists that the discursive reckonings associated with fearless speech have nothing to do with the notion of 'confessional autobiography'.

Rather, as is the case with Emin's art practice, the project of self-examination associated with *parrhesia* is aimed towards the *creative* reconstruction of the self and this means coming to an understanding of how truth informs one's identity, and thus influences one's entire comportment to life:

> Here, giving an account of your life, your *bios*, is also not to give a narrative of the historical events that have taken place in your life, but rather to demonstrate whether you are able to show that there is a relation between the rational discourse, the *logos*, you are able to use and the way you live your life.[156]

Central to this practice of self-examination through discourse is the motivation to change (not just passively accept) one's life we have associated with the 'mobilisation of shame'. The practice of truth in this sense becomes a means of inspiring life change, and administering a complete or partial process of self-*aufheben* or preservative transformation: 'it is no longer just a matter of altering one's belief or opinion,' he writes, 'but of changing one's style of life, one's relation to others, and one's relation to oneself.'[157] When the self I have chosen to be conflicts with the self that I have discovered that I am, a discrepancy opens between character and value. Such an ethos of personal evaluation relates to the Greek care of self (*epimeleia heautou*)[158] celebrated in Foucault's late work; I want to briefly demonstrate the connection between Foucauldian care of the self and the analysis of shame (as presented above).

Desire to be something other that manifests itself in failure, as we have seen, is the central ethical significance of the emotion of shame, where the discontinuity between what one is and what one would like to be is exposed. In a recent defence of the significance of emotion for legal judgement, Martha Nussbaum presents a philosophical investigation of shame that differs in important respects to the phenomenological analysis of Sartre and Levinas.[159]

Shame is characterised alternatively as a 'ubiquitous' emotion, and a particularly 'painful' emotional response to the revelation of weakness. According to Nussbaum, when a person experiences weakness as a result of a perceived failure to realise certain norms dictated by an introjected social value system, the result is shame – shame thus haunts the horizon of our lives, she says, because 'we all have weaknesses that if revealed would mark us off as in some ways "abnormal".'[160] Shame is the sister of the fear that keeps us from exposing our perceived 'weaknesses'.[161] Thus, despite her ultimately negative conclusions regarding the emotion of shame (at least in the context of critical jurisprudence), Nussbaum does admit that shame can be a creative emotion, one that, in crucial existential situations actually contributes to the articulation of the self.[162] Indeed, it often 'tells us the truth', she writes. 'In that sense, shame should not be thought of as a nonmoral emotion, connected only with social approval or disapproval.'[163] Shame, she continues, therefore ought to be construed as an ethically valuable emotion that, because it can become actively responsible for motivating moral action, plays a crucial and creative role in the transformation of the self.[164]

As an emotional response that encourages us to examine our character therefore, shame represents a crucial ethical motivator in the care-of-the-self and is thus also associated with the ethics of care more generally; for, in ways critical for moral development, shame is one existential modality that enables lived truth to give form to the practice of life. Emin's project of self-examination or care-for-the-self is above all inspired and motivated by the experience of alterity induced by the emotion of shame. Foucault understood the moral dimension of the care-of-the-self as a life-practice oriented to the articulation of a form of ethical subjectivity. In Emin's situation, the emotion of shame is the catalyst for this process of morally relevant self-formation.[165]

In Nussbaum's definition, however, shame is also characterised as a 'painful' emotional response to the revelation of vulnerability that the condition of nakedness always strongly suggests. Yet Emin insists on fearlessly exposing her own weaknesses. She invades her own privacy, denuding her character again and again, exposing her life to public scrutiny – the details of which seem more damaging to herself than to anyone else. Such a conception of shameful vulnerability is nowhere more directly conveyed than in Emin's film fragment *Homage to Edvard Munch and All My Dead Children* (1998). In this Super 8 film, Emin crouches naked, curled tightly foetus-like at the end of a wooden promenade on the edge of a lake accompanied by a non-diegetic one-minute shriek.

Nussbaum's analysis concludes, echoing Levinas and Foucault, that the emotion of shame, at least in its creative aspect is morally constructive because it provokes self-examination, a 'search into ourselves' that initiates us to 'reexamine our habits and . . . character'.[166] Therefore, it is possible to argue that shame not only plays a role in moral development but actually represents, according to this interpretation (and perhaps even despite Nussbaum's intentions), *the* crucial moral motivator. For shame encourages us to examine our character in the ways discussed by Foucault in relation to *parrhesia* and *feel* ashamed for what we discover there: if what we discover there is a discrepancy between our present character and the moral values we profess, the philosophical ideals we aspire towards or the past self we have come into conflict with. Shame therefore, according to Nussbaum, is a creative and productive, but above all, self-caring emotion that challenges us to have the courage to examine our character and personality fearlessly. Emin's art practice is a testament – a touchstone – to the ethics of care-for-the-self. Yet, by getting us to experience the emotion of shame involved in witnessing displays of vulnerability, nakedness and exposure, the artist compels us to respond emotionally, and therefore ethically, to her art. The emotion of shame, Nussbaum concludes, simultaneously facilitates the acknowledgement of a 'common vulnerability that all human beings share'.[167] In a manner that brings all these ideas to convergence, Morgan's discussion of shame concludes that the emotion of shame ultimately has the capacity to transcend the self-formative mode and become 'a motivation to care for others'.[168] Arguing that shame is a 'permanent feature of our social and moral lives', Morgan suggests that it is that transitive emotion where care-of-the-self, in the Foucauldian sense, fuses with care for others. Being '*of* ourselves, our character or identity as a whole . . . it is [also] *before* others, either real or imagined'.[169] He concludes: 'Given such a structure, shame as an emotion is uniquely capable of calling attention to personal inadequacies and so doing by calling us to self-reflection and to a sensitivity to how others view us simultaneously.'[170]

Eliciting *shame*, the ethical purpose of Emin's transgressive aesthetic is finally disclosed: she transgresses social prohibitions to provoke a subjective, emotional and, as argued, *moral* reaction; in this way therefore the ethical response to her work is achieved precisely through techniques of fearless, that is, *parrhesiastic* transgression.

Through re-evaluating failure and transforming weakness into strength, Tracey Emin has rediscovered real *parrhesia* – fearless speech in its positive, critical aspect. She has struggled and succeeded, developing a unique, fearless and unremittingly critical voice that is uncompromising in its expression of subjectivity. In her art practice this voice appears in the form of an argument for her right to explore the self without censure. Her courageous exposure of vulnerability, as Nussbaum has pointed out, speaks a human concern that ultimately transcends 'women's issues' not only because it concerns the status of damaged subjectivity in general but also because it draws on the powerful legacy of care (for self and other) to redress damaged status through original and inspiring cultural production.

Perhaps the most general way of understanding the ethical implications of Emin's art practice therefore is according to Foucault's interpretation of the ancient practice of *parrhesia*. For it is clear that her art practice makes an issue of exhibiting all the characteristics (directness, courage, risk and critical, including self-critical, discourse) that Foucault associated with the concept. And it is particularly relevant and appropriate therefore in relation to this chapter's objective. The idea of fearless discourse is, I conclude, what makes her project ethically *admirable* and her work morally good; indeed, as it runs right through Emin's project, through all the various shapes and forms this project has assumed, we could say that her work perhaps constitutes a paradigm of fearless speech in the contemporary context. Ultimately it is the fearless characteristic of her work that elicits our emotional response and thus finally, as we have argued above, produces the ethical effect connected with it. Thus to identify her work with the practice of fearless speech is to respond ethically to its demand and thereby reveal its general ethical – and ultimately aesthetic – significance.

5 HORRORSHOW

The Transvaluation of Morality in the Work of Damien Hirst

I don't want to talk about Damien.

Tracey Emin[1]

With these words Tracey Emin deprived the art world of her estimation of her nearest contemporary and perhaps the most notorious artist associated with the young British art phenomenon. Frustrating her interviewer's attempt to discuss Damien Hirst is of course entirely Emin's prerogative; why should she be under any obligation to discuss the work of a rival artist in interview? Given the theme of this book, however, no such discursive dispensation can be entertained. Why Damien Hirst? What exactly is problematic about Hirst's art? It is time to talk about Damien.

An early installation *When Logics Die* (1991) provides a useful starting point for identifying the features of the Hirstean aesthetic. High-definition, post-mortem forensic photographs of a suicide victim, a road accident fatality and a head blown out by a point-blank shotgun discharge are mounted on aluminium above a clinical bench strewn with medical paraphernalia and biohazard material. Speaking to Gordon Burn in 1992, the artist explained that what intrigued him about these images was the incongruity they involve: an obscene content yet amenable to disinterested contemplation in the aesthetic mode as a 'beautiful' abstract form. 'I think that's what the interest is in. Not in actual corpses. I mean, they're completely delicious, desirable images of completely undesirable, unacceptable things. They're like cookery books.'[2] Now remember what he's talking about here.

Sustained, speculative and clinically detached, Hirst's preoccupation with the stigmata of decomposition, disease and mortal suffering may be considered to violate instinctive taboos forbidding pleasurable engagement with the spectacle of death. Fascination with autopsy and industrial slaughter, vivisection and

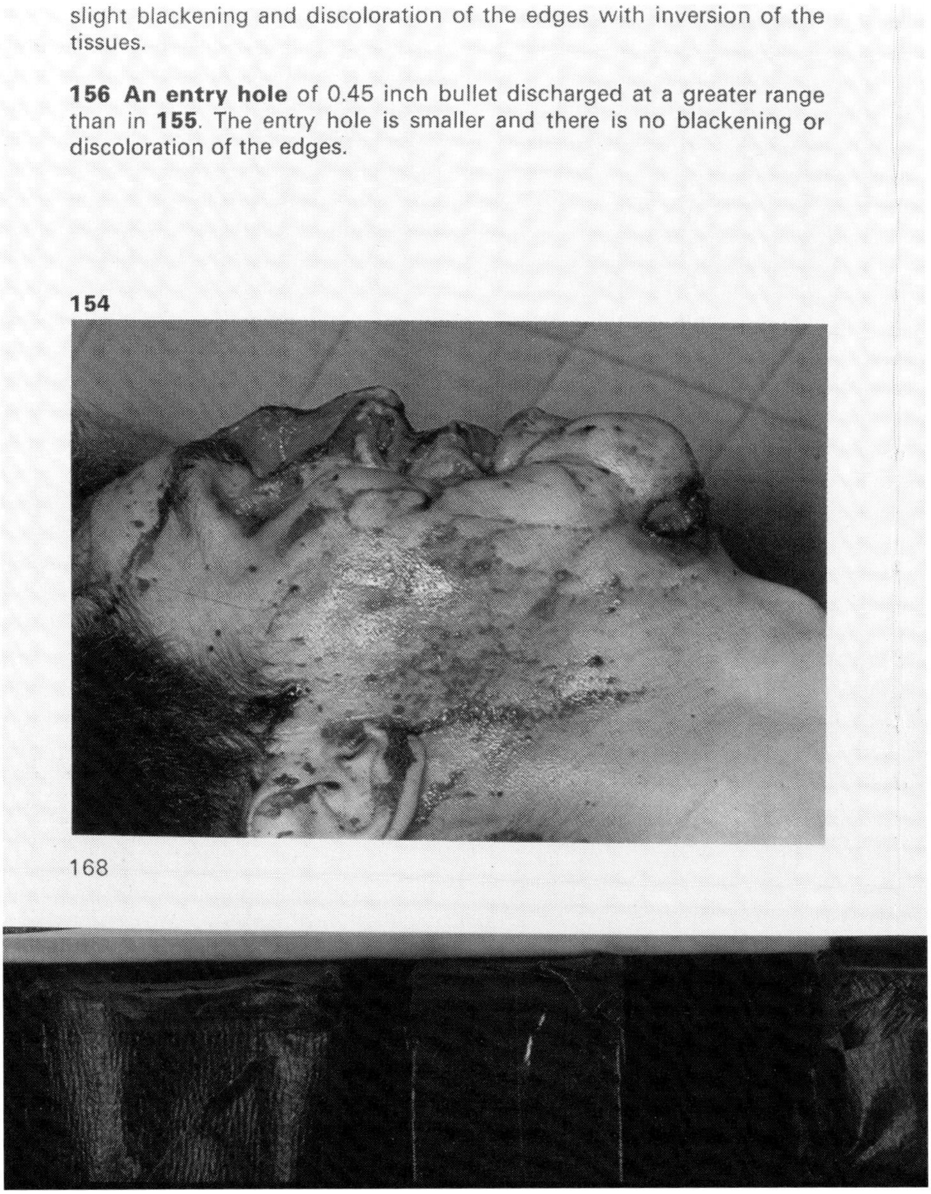

18. Damien Hirst, *When Logics Die*, 1991
Photograph on aluminium and medical equipment
Dimensions variable
© the artist
Courtesy Jay Jopling/ White Cube (London)

serial murder – repeated excursions from the abattoir to the pathology lab – is guaranteed to disturb for related reasons. As we are morally threatened by those who take pleasure in decay and death, so we are intimidated by Hirst's morbid *modus operandi*. Even the ironic scientific alibi under which the artist presents his prurient curiosities seems cynically perverse in an aesthetic context and may act to serve up a supplementary chill to a long travelogue of transgressions. Yet his work also plays on the deep curiosity that draws us irresistibly to the horror of the morgue and the MO of the serial murderer. There appears to be no other way to perceive the artworks of this cruel and perverse intelligence other than as the obscene objects of pleasurable fascination.

Disturbing: certainly. Yet aestheticised cruelty and morbid curiosity are not necessarily morally problematic. Nevertheless, some works by the 1995 Turner Prize winner can be considered, if not indisputably immoral, certainly more uncontroversially dubious from an ethical standpoint. Hirst's on-going series of sculptures that incorporate animals into the pathological context identified above are understood to be problematic, not primarily because they transgress social taboos, but because they can be considered to violate the ethically significant interests of the non-human animals involved in their production. As a result of convincingly argued recent work in the area of applied moral philosophy, it is becoming increasingly unjustifiable to exclude non-human animals from ethical consideration. The work of Peter Singer, Tom Regan and Mark Rowlands, which argues for the extension of our moral horizons to acknowledge the ethical entitlements of other species, in particular, makes it difficult not to consider art practices that use animals in such a cynically instrumental fashion as anything other than morally wrong.

With a chronically reduced capacity to articulate our moral objections, however, Hirst's obscene yet fascinating objects may result in the inability to register our scepticism in moral terms. This may be because we also view such work, despite its obscenity, with astonishment. Hirst's work, in other words, renders us speechless. But the question posed in this final chapter is precisely this: is it justifiable to accuse Damien Hirst of moral trespass in his animal works? Does Hirst's work with non-human animals constitute an ethical violation? Can we enquire if he has harmed, demoralised or otherwise disrespected the animals he 'ignominiously'[3] uses to make his work? If he hasn't harmed 'his' animals, do these things matter? As considered in the previous chapters of this book, when transgressive art practices are accepted as *art* (defended or even identified as art) this is in effect to claim that they *ipso facto* possess an unqualified aesthetic or cultural value. However, identification as art implicitly and often without argument has the indirect effect of justifying any cultural production, no matter what dubious moral features or ethical difficulties it may involve. This, as considered, also has the effect of defending, by tacit acceptance of its artistic value, the moral value of the same work.

Far from denying that the Hirstean aesthetic is (at the very least) morally problematic, this chapter will argue that, *despite its immorality*, it is possible to vindicate morally indefensible works of art. Although this position may appear to contravene our objections to the widespread institutional aesthetic defence of ethically problematic art, our position differs substantially from uncritical aesthetic autonomism in its acceptance that the morality of the work of (morally transgressive) art is crucial to its adequate aesthetic evaluation. This position also differs from moralism by accepting that a work of art can be immoral and not necessarily suffer a diminished aesthetic value as a consequence. The ethical vindication of Hirst's work is conditional upon acceptance of its immorality. In elaborating this argument I draw on recent work undertaken by analytic philosophers of art on the complex and vexed relationship between aesthetic value and moral value. Counter-intuitive though it might now appear, I will conclude that the immorality of Hirst's work, in the most vivid and unique (but not unprecedented) way, actually contributes positively to its artistic value.

Obscene Objects of Pleasurable Fascination

Hirst's work with animals began in 1991 with what is indubitably his most celebrated work: a fourteen-foot (420 cm) Australian tiger shark (*Galeocerdo cuvier*) suspended in perfect equilibrium in a gigantic aquarium of liquid preservative (5% formaldehyde solution).[4] *The Physical Impossibility of Death in the Mind of Someone Living* (1991) is an extraordinary aesthetic object. Like most of the work discussed in this book, it was exhibited in *Sensation* (1997) and again in the New York show two years later. Two other 'natural history' pieces, *A Thousand Years* (1990) and *This Little Piggy Went to Market, This Little Piggy Stayed at Home* (1996) were also exhibited. The shark, however, quickly became the signature-piece of the young British artist phenomenon.

Strictly speaking, for the sake of accuracy, the shark may not have been the very first piece associated with this continuing series: *A Thousand Years* (1990), a double-chambered vitrine with a severed cow's head, maggots, flies and an electric insect killer, pre-dated it; but the tiger shark was certainly (and arguably remains) the most complete and accomplished instance of Hirst's on-going practice of preserving large-scale animals of various species in display tanks of liquid preservative.[5]

Since the shark piece, Hirst has, with a dispassion usually reserved for scientific research, consistently pursued this practice in a single-minded and methodical manner.[6] In *Mother and Child Divided* (1993) two animals, an

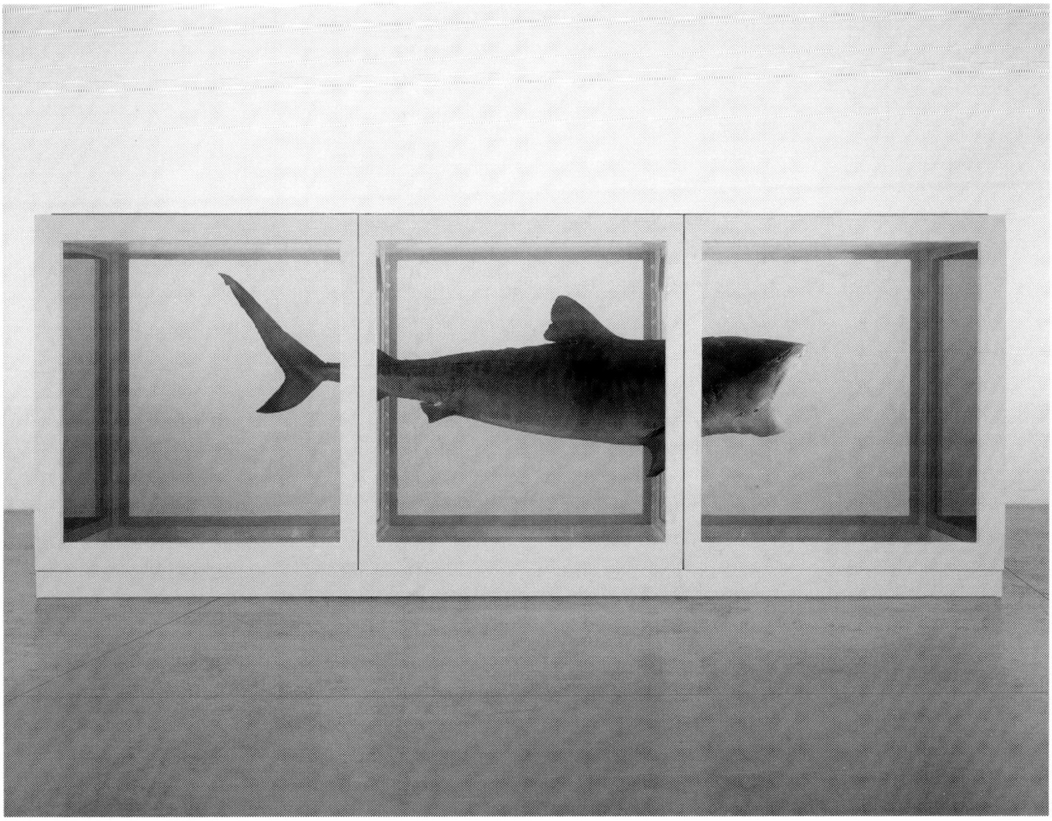

19. Damien Hirst, *The Physical Impossibility of Death in the Mind of Someone Living (1)*, 1991
Glass, steel, silicone, shark and 5% formaldehyde solution
84 x 252 x 84 in (213.4 x 640.1 x 213.4 cm)
© the artist
Photo: Antony Oliver
Courtesy Jay Jopling/ White Cube (London)

adult cow and calf, are displayed in distinctive glass-and-steel tanks (or in Hirst parlance, 'vitrines') of formaldehyde solution. For this installation, each animal was sectioned in the saggital dimension, each half then arranged inside its tank so that the open side of the animal is pressed up against the glass interior (thereby ensuring the clear display of internal organs). Filled with preservative and sealed, the tanks are carefully arranged so that each animal's separate half matches up with its other half. (A small distance is allowed to remain between the tanks.) To underscore the statement, the mother's halves

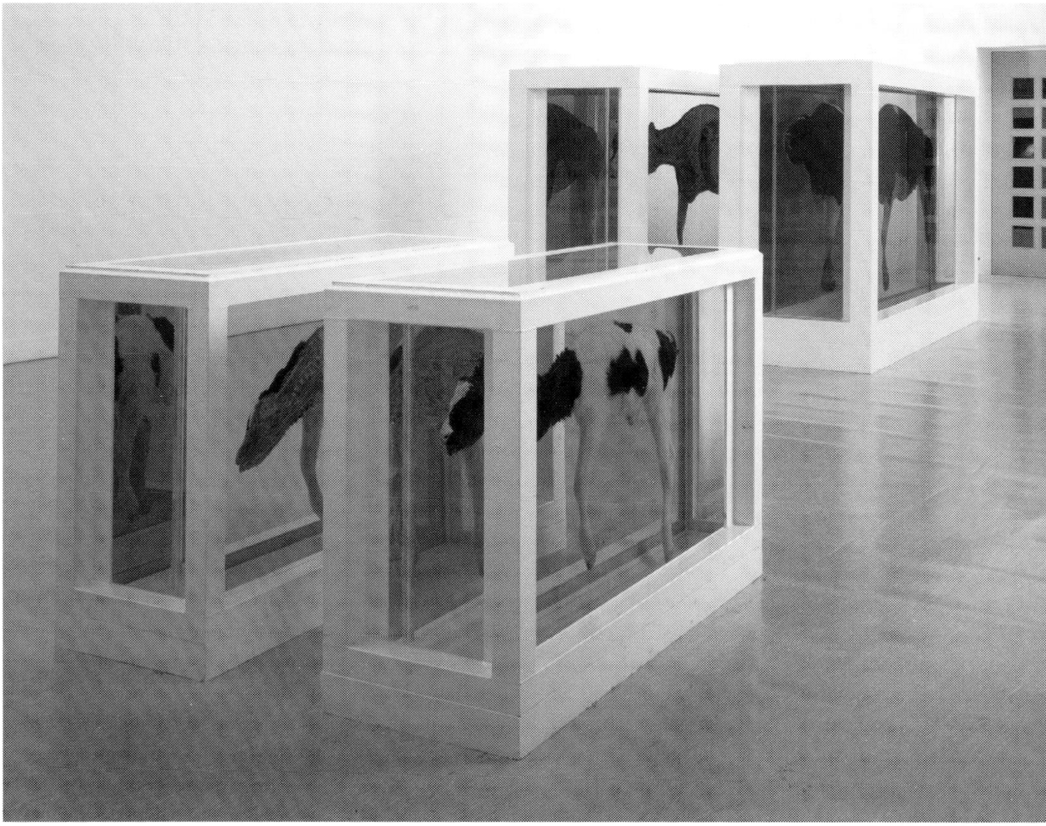

20. Damien Hirst, *Mother and Child Divided*, 1993
Steel, GRP composites, glass, silicone sealant, cow, calf and formaldehyde solution
2 tanks: 190 x 322.5 x 109 cm / 2 tanks: 102.9 x 168.9 x 62.3 cm
© the artist
Photo: Stephen White
Courtesy Jay Jopling/ White Cube (London)

are positioned some little distance away from, and behind, her similarly divided 'child'.

A whole sheep suspended in a vitrine of formaldehyde and entitled *Away From the Flock*[7] was created for the 1994 group exhibition *Some Went Mad . . . Some Ran Away*.[8] And for his 1995 exhibition in the New York Gagosian Gallery *No Sense of Absolute Corruption*,[9] two Friesian cattle were sectioned for sequential display in twelve separate tanks. In this work, *Some Comfort Gained from the Inherent Lies in Everything*, the sectioned animals are compressed against the transparent interior as before. This time, however, they have each been cross-sectioned vertically into six separate parts. The high, narrow tanks are rearranged so that every alternative tank contains the body-part of a different animal. The two tanked carcases are then interleaved sequentially top-to-tail with each other.

Heads of cattle severed, peeled and preserved in sealed glass containers have also featured prominently in his work. In *Romance in the Age of Uncertainty*,[10] his 2003 show at the White Cube Gallery in London, Hirst allegorised each of Christ's disciples using (*inter alia*) the heads of cattle. Eyes bound, the head representing Judas is immersed in a black-framed container (all the other container-frames are white). Christ's container, rather obviously, is empty. This exhibition also featured *Adam and Eve*, a glass container with two heads multiply skewered with broken pieces of mirrored glass.

Hirst's 2006 show in Mexico, *The Death of God*, featured two excoriated sheep manipulated into distorted anthropomorphic postures, their limbs broken to emulate attitudes of reading and praying. This exhibition also included *In the Name of the Father*: a trio of skinned, drawn-and-quartered sheep with necks broken and heads hanging – arranged in simulation of the crucifixion scene. His 2007 exhibition *Beyond Belief* (at the White Cube Gallery, London) featured a thirteen-foot female tiger shark, bisected and preserved in 7% formaldehyde solution (*Death Explained*, 2007), a black sheep, an upright cow transfixed with several crossbow bolts and manipulated into a grotesque parody of St Sebastian (*Exquisite Pain*, 2007), three lambs manipulated into obscene and tragicomic mimesis of devout supplicants, and a triptych of stripped cruciform sheep arranged in mirror-backed vitrines (*God Alone Knows*, 2007).[11]

Finally, to end this brief bestiary, Hirst has also worked extensively with insects. One of several prepared environments, the extraordinarily imaginative installation *In and Out of Love* (1991) featured newly hatched butterflies alighting on a series of canvases stretched above flowering plants. Also, his on-going series of entomological, polychromatic 'paintings', created by embedding dead tropical butterflies into specially prepared surfaces is offset by a dark sequence of 'fly paintings' – black surfaces of seemingly impenetrable density layered over with a crust of innumerable dead flies.

Hirst's work has attracted significant negative attention from various animal rights organisations. Among those protesting against the 1999 *Sensation* exhibition in the Brooklyn Museum of Art, the animal rights contingent specifically objected to the use of 'dead and dismembered animals by artist Damien Hirst'.[12] Part of their protest was to display images of animal slaughter that had, ironically, a similar didactic status to the Hirstean aesthetic. Prior to his show at the New York Gagosian Gallery in 1995, animal rights collectives organised a letter-writing campaign to condemn officially the artist's 'cruelty to animals'.[13]

Oddly, considering that the show featured the severed heads of cattle, the focus of protest at the *Romance in the Age of Uncertainty* exhibition was its billed 'centrepiece': a trigonometric plane layered with a complex chromatography of countless butterfly wings. Describing Hirst as a 'sadist', the European director of People for the Ethical Treatment of Animals (PETA) commented: 'One has to wonder if Hirst was the sort of child who would pull the wings off flies for fun. He certainly has become that kind of an adult. Butterfly wings are beautiful on a butterfly but tearing small creatures into bits is not art, it's sadism.'[14] And at an exhibition in Germany, activists challenged a zoologist that Hirst had contracted to breed butterflies and supervise the installation. 'So they got to him and thought he was the artist, and just said "look this is really cruel, what are you doing to these butterflies?" And he just said, "I'm the butterfly breeder, I'm the guy that he's got in to do them".'[15]

Where the mammals are concerned, things are more difficult and more complex. Hirst excuses himself by claiming that he acquires his specimens from what he refers to as a 'knacker's yard' in Guildford. Although he denies that this is for ethical reasons, he does claim that the animals he uses are already dead and were destined to be destroyed or rendered for pet food. '[I get my animals] from a guy, they just get, how does he describe it? He says "the animals that fell down". But they get all the dead ones and have to chop them up for dog food.'[16]

On another occasion, when asked to comment on the various and extensive animal rights protests against his work, he replied: 'I . . . try and cover my ass before they start. I'll talk to the RSPCA . . . I'll talk to those kind of people and find out about it first. I will invite them down to look at the butterfly exhibition and say, "Is everything okay?"' He continued, referring to his work with live fish (*Love Lost* and *Lost Love*, 2000):

> You try and give the animals everything they need so if someone comes up to me and says 'The fish are unhappy', I go, 'Well there is the fish guy talk to him. He says they have never been happier in their lives; they have never been in a bigger tank. They are really happy.' People don't like it when there are animals in art. I think that's the problem using animals for art. It doesn't matter if they are happy, people just don't like it. I just really wanted it to be real. It's just a way of making art real. . . . It is not a representation it is actually a real thing . . .[17]

Animal rights protestors, Hirst concludes, often 'get the facts wrong so they have to go away looking a bit stupid'.[18] Originally intending to use a great white shark for *The Physical Impossibility of Death*, he discovered that it had been registered as a protected species just prior to his initial enquiries so he used the tiger shark as a substitute: 'we had something with the shark, somebody came in and said: "It's a great white and it's a protected species, what are you doing?" And we said it's not, it's a tiger shark. I think they smeared dog shit in the gallery, or something.'[19]

Is it possible to establish *why* such art practice is morally problematic rather than presuppose, with the animal rights protestors, that it is? Specifically what kind of *philosophically relevant* ethical issues are raised by Hirst's work with animals? And what precisely makes these issues specifically philosophical and specifically ethical? Is there any occasion in which it might be warranted or defensible to use animals for the purposes of art? In the context of recent applications of ethical rights to non-human animals, it might in fact appear indisputably unethical to render animals for art and, at least to this extent, make it appear entirely reasonable to critique Hirst's work as an ethically significant contravention of the moral rights of animals.

Non-Human Animals and Ethical Inclusion

In a popular but not uncontroversial book on ethics written in 1998,[20] Mary Warnock expresses the view that the philosophical vindication of animal rights is incoherent. This is because, she explains, the concept of rights only applies to civil agents capable of recognising and therefore acknowledging the significance of the concept of justice associated with claiming or respecting a right. In other words, the concept of rights applies crucially only to the *human* case. Therefore, for Warnock, it makes no sense to speak of rights in relation to the moral claims that non-human animals may justifiably, or otherwise, make on us. 'It is humans', she remarks, 'and they alone who can form a civil society within which the concepts of rights and duties arise.'[21] This is reinforced by the following analysis: 'To speak of the rights of animals, then, is necessarily inappropriate, simply because "animal" here means "animal other than human." And to use the language of rights in this context is dangerously to debase the currency of rights.'[22]

With this proposition, Warnock articulates an intuitively humanistic disposition to treat non-human animals as different in some fundamental way to humans. Such views forget that there exists biogenetic and neurological evidence of the continuity of human with other animal life. She thereby expresses what has increasingly come to be seen by moral philosophers as an unjustifiable anthropocentric prejudice. However, it is not this belief in itself (unwarranted as it may be) that is ethically objectionable but rather the corollary implication it is often considered tacitly to entail: that non-human species are therefore excluded from 'our' *moral consideration*.

Has Warnock misconceived the concept of rights as applied to the non-human situation? Neo-utilitarian philosopher Peter Singer has demonstrated[23] that the concept of rights in this context involves expanding the fundamental principle of equality to include the non-human. This should not be taken to entail that cattle have a right to vote, that goats have the right to freedom of speech or whatever. Just as it is senseless to speak of a man's right to have an abortion, so it is nonsensical to refer to a pig's right to vote. 'Since a pig can't vote, it is meaningless to talk of its right to vote.'[24] This is not what is meant by the concept of rights as applied to the non-human situation. Voting (or freedom of speech) is simply not relevant to the animal's life because it does not count among its interests. The basic idea of rights for non-human animals is the morally fundamental *principle of equality*, according to which the interests of all sentient life-forms (those capable of expressing an interest) that may be affected by human decisions are given equal consideration.[25]

With the principle of equality as a moral benchmark, the idea of ethical (as opposed to legal) rights comes into view. Ethical rights are possessed by any being that can be said to have interests (capable of communicating specific, if simple, preferences, and is known to possess the capacity to suffer or experience desire and satisfaction). Such rights differ from *legal* rights (and this is crucial) in that they, according to Tom Regan, 'belong to all subjects-of-a-life [that is, those who possess sentience: the ability to perceive, experience pain and pleasure, feel emotion] regardless of their colour, nationality, sex, and . . . species'.[26] Thus Mary Warnock's view can be considered the result of a failure to appreciate the philosophical difference between legal and ethical rights in this sense; the reference to animal *rights* pertains to ethical as opposed to legal rights and indicates that a member of a non-human species, just like any human, should be protected by the basic right 'to be treated with respect as an individual with inherent value'.[27] According to Regan, therefore, the function of ethical rights is simply to protect others from harm. 'Those who possess these rights have a kind of protective moral shield, an invisible "No Trespassing" sign, so to speak, that prohibits others from injuring their bodies, taking their life, or putting them at risk of serious harm, including death.'[28]

What is required, according to Singer, is that the principle of equality that constitutes our ethical standard should compel us to the moral consideration of *all* sentient beings likely to be affected by us.[29] All Singer is proposing here is that the ethically basic principle of the equal consideration of interests be extended to apply 'to members of other species as well as our own'.[30] Therefore, apart from the xenophobic interest to protect and maintain the privileges of an arbitrarily dominant group, there is no compelling reason not to expand 'the basic principle of equality' to include the interests of species other than human.[31] Drawing comparisons with racism and sexism, Singer shows that there is no justification for excluding members of another species (in the same way as we cannot discriminate against members of another race or gender) from moral consideration *just because they are different*. As the racist denigrates the entitlements of other races, and the sexist discriminates in favour of the interests of his own gender, so 'the speciesist allows the interests of his own species to override the greater interests of members of other species.'[32]

For Singer, the problem of moral rights comes into focus with the issue of pain. Following Jeremy Bentham's celebrated framing of the morality of the problem in terms of whether animals are capable of suffering[33] (and not arbitrary anthropocentric differences like language ability or reasoning), Singer argues that there is convincing evidence that all mammals and most vertebrates share the capacity to experience pain and that this is ethically sufficient evidence to expand moral consideration to include harms perpetrated on other species if these harms involve the infliction of pain. The capacity to suffer pain, therefore, gives us our moral benchmark: inflicting pain on those capable of suffering it is morally wrong. And, for Singer, no defensible reason to exclude non-human animals from morality can, according to this benchmark, be *rationally* defended. Therefore, the principle of equality ought to be extended and our ethical responsibility expanded to accommodate the interests of other species.

> No matter what the nature of the being, the principle of equality requires that its suffering be counted equally with the like suffering – in so far as rough comparisons can be made – of any other being. If a being is not capable of suffering, or of experiencing enjoyment or happiness, there is nothing to be taken into account.[34]

On the basis of this analysis, the conclusion seems compelling that non-human animals are deserving of the basic *ethical* entitlements of respect and moral consideration as accorded by law to members of the human species. If these premises are accepted, disregarding the interests of members of other species in the realisation of the satisfactions of humans should logically appear unjust and therefore judged to be unethical.

Is it plausible, in light of this critical discourse, to defend the art practices of Damien Hirst that involve the damage and display of dead animals? Because it gives legitimacy to his openly discriminatory behaviour, any defence of Hirst's art practice involving animals (including his own ass-covering defences) would seem, in some way, to reinforce the unjustifiable prejudice against members of non-human species that, as we have seen, Singer et al. term 'speciesism'. In relation to the exploitations to which non-human animals are routinely subjected in order to satisfy the interests of humans, rendering animals for art may appear one of the most indefensibly trivial. Using animals in such an instrumental way may seem manifestly unjust because it 'is not consistent with treating them as beings with inherent worth'[35] and thus can be considered a serious infringement of the basic moral entitlement that protects sentient others from exploitation. For a defender of the philosophy of rights, according to Gruen, 'using an animal as a means to an end' – in this case as an object of display in an art gallery or (as appears to be the case increasingly with Hirst) to attract collectors for reasons of commercial return – 'is a violation of that being's right to be treated with respect'.[36] This categorical respect, if we are to continue to regard ourselves as morally responsible beings, represents a minimal ethical demand that the members of other (non-human) species place on us and that it is morally right to respond to.

Of the sometimes gratuitous and cynical exploitation of animals in postmodern art practice, Julius has remarked that this art often 'fail[s] to respect the dignity of the animals, suitors for our moral concern, but instead treat[s] them instrumentally, as mere things'. But such art practice also fails to respect human dignity 'because it debase[s] its spectators'.[37] Julius is commenting here on a proposed installation by the Chinese artist Huang Yong Ping, *Le Théâtre du monde*, which would have involved introducing diverse (and incompatible) insect species into a closed environment, but it was cancelled for reasons of cruelty 'to those species put at risk by having to share an environment with their natural predators'.[38]

Steve Baker reports another disturbing exhibit by Marco Evaristti involving food liquidisers containing goldfish with visitors invited to activate the machines.[39] As a consequence of objections from parties concerned for the welfare of the animals, this work was removed by police during its presentation in a Danish art gallery. In an attempt to monitor the artist's responsibility to other species as a result of this kind of work, a Minnesota-based art collective established the Justice for Animals Arts Guild (JAAG) in 2000, which proposes to control 'cruel or degrading' art practices that involve living animals. The Guild recommends that, as sentient creatures, non-human animals should not be reduced to concepts or used as raw material in the production of art. The artist's interests should be ethically circumscribed relative to the interests of the animals being reprocessed as art objects.[40]

Of the several further examples of the use of animals in art surveyed in Baker's book *The Postmodern Animal* (2000), not all of them are negative or harmful.[41] The eco-art of collaborative duo Olly and Suzi, to instance just one example of ethically good art practice involving animals, is committed to the careful artistic documentation of predators in their natural habitats.[42] Their work interestingly includes *Shark Bite* (1997), an extraordinary interface with a great white shark off the coast of South Africa. 'The fearful proximity this other involves', Baker comments, 'could not be further from Damien Hirst's detachment from his animal subjects, exemplified in his claim that "you kill things to look at them".'[43]

Yet despite what may appear to be evidence to the contrary, it is anything but definitive that Hirst's work involves harming the animals he works with. With the exception of his entomological projects (and his work incorporating live fish), his animal work is insistently post-mortem: the animals are dead on arrival in his studios. This would appear to indemnify him from the JAAG ethical provisions (which apply only to *living* animals) but does it exonerate Hirst of all moral blame? Perhaps not, but it does allow us to confirm that the animals are not subjected to any undue pain by the artist. Except perhaps for the sharks that are hooked (but obviously not by Hirst) in their natural habitats, they do not undergo unnecessary suffering for the sake of the art they end up as. For the utilitarian, *pain is bad*; and therefore inflicting suffering in the absence of clear benefits that justify this pain is morally wrong. 'Pain and suffering are in themselves [morally] bad . . . and should be prevented or minimised, irrespective of the race, sex or species of the being that suffers.'[44]

It is far from empirically or scientifically established that invertebrates suffer pain as we feel, experience and understand it; can Hirst's treatment of these creatures plausibly be accused of moral trespass? Hirst claims, as mentioned above, that he acquires his specimens from a reputable entomologist. So, although his work with insects can perhaps be accused of gratuitous destruction and, to the extent that some ethical philosophers have associated destructive behaviour per se with immorality, be condemned as morally wrong, this would be misconceived: however destructive his work, it is also indisputably creative,[45] it cannot be considered unethical according to the utilitarian paradigm.

Although it is disturbing, Hirst's work cannot be accused of causing any direct harm to, or inflicting any suffering on, the animals involved in its production. If the animals have had 'happy, stress-free, natural lives' prior to their being put to a humane, as-painless-as-possible death, the utilitarian, 'may not object to their use' even in such an ultimately non-functional or non-beneficial context.[46] Indeed, Singer is committed to endorse this preference-utilitarian view, admitting that he can envisage such circumstances in which farm animals, having had a high quality of life, are humanely killed: 'I would still prefer not to do that, nor would I want to eat the products of such farms,' he said in interview (betraying a personal, 'irrational' preference), 'but I wouldn't campaign against them – such a life would seem a reasonable deal from the animal's point of view.'[47] If Hirst cannot be accused of causing any direct suffering, because he does not inflict any harm on the animals he uses, his work cannot, according to this utilitarian framework, be morally impugned.

On the other hand, the only ethical defence of the human behaviour that adversely affects animal welfare is that, despite harms caused, these injuries are excusable relative to the important benefits they deliver. For such a benefit to count morally it must be so important as to outweigh our ethical responsibility to the animal that suffers or is harmed in the process. The benefits argument states that 'at least the majority of the most important improvements in human health and longevity are indebted to vivisection.'[48] The relatively extreme harms suffered by animals subject to experimentation in the name of progress are regrettable but necessary: they are compensated for by the benefits to humanity afforded by the ethical exemptions granted under the alibi of scientific investigation.

Evaluated according to this standard, however, Hirst's animal works read as insane experiments undertaken without hypotheses or findings.[49] Rejecting from the outset any benefit that might result, such purposeless investigations assume the aspect of purely malevolent acts undertaken for some inscrutable curiosity or perverse pleasure. 'I wanted to be stopped,' Hirst declares, 'and no one stopped me. I just wanted to find out where the boundaries were. So far I've found there aren't any.'[50] Is there an ethical problem here?

Incorporating two separate halves of a bisected pig in containers of preservative with one half attached to motorised tracks so that it repeatedly but temporarily reconnects with its other half[51] for display as art cannot be accommodated to the benefits argument as outlined here. Such an objectionable apparatus may remain significantly outside any calculation of benefits. What benefits accrue from the practice of attaching and embedding hundreds of rare butterflies or houseflies into the surfaces of paintings other than that which may result from perceiving a pretty or mildly interesting picture? Who benefits from these depressingly distasteful and morbid art exhibits? Yet this lack of benefit is *precisely the provocation of this transgressive art*. Who benefits? No one: that is the point. What are the benefits? There are none: that, yet again, is the point, for the moral problem with his work does not lie directly with the artist but rather with the industrial process that preceded his involvement with the animals and the ethical amnesty that facilitates his relatively minimal contributions to it.

Attending to the Other of the Animal: Art and the Ethics of Care

Damien Hirst, anticipating recriminations from animal rights pressure groups, prepares himself accordingly: he 'covers his ass'. Any protestation, as a result, looks 'a bit stupid'. But because it functions to expose Hirst's awareness that his actions are (or may justifiably be understood to be) morally wrong, this paranoid preparedness may be considered to make his animal work even more problematic. His avoidance of the issue of speciesism by abrogating responsibility for the harm and/or putative pain the animals he acquires may suffer by outwitting utilitarian reasoning and making animal rights protestors appear foolish only serves to increase our moral suspicion. Why? Because it indicates that there is something wrong with the entire system that facilitates this abrogation; it also indicates that there is something wrong with the utilitarian arguments that actually contribute to this moral abrogation. Yet even if certain weaknesses can be identified in the positions of Regan and Singer, these can be associated with the rational framework that these moralists have committed to – as well as their emphasis on universality of judgement and impartial application. The logically rigorous application of their theoretical paradigms often leads to absurd (and indeed, some believe, unethical) inevitabilities.[52] There may be no rational method by which it can definitively be concluded that Hirst's treatment of animals is objectively unethical. Is there another method?

His treatment of animals remains deliberately cruel and disrespectful; no efforts to justify this from an ethical perspective can effectively counteract this fact because it expresses an officially acceptable yet unethical contempt for the dignity of animals. Is it possible to consider the problem under the aegis of categorical 'respect'? The relevant moral principle here is the respectful concern to treat the animal always as an end and never as a means. Such an extension of the categorical imperative would involve replacing the concept of 'person' in the Kantian ethical semiotic with the more inclusive concept of the 'sentient'. As it ultimately acknowledges the otherness of the animal, this kind of categorical respect can be (and has been) identified, not uncontroversially, with Levinasian alterity.[53] And it is in this modality that Derrida's reference to a 'fundamental compassion',[54] which completely changes 'the philosophical problem of the animal,' should be thematised. Our compassionate response to the 'victims' of Hirst's practice reveals that there is something wrong here but perhaps only to the extent that it insouciantly reflects a widespread but unethical instrumental human attitude – our own attitude – toward the *other* of the animal.

Although I remain convinced by the impressive ethical defence of animal rights undertaken by Singer, Regan and (most particularly) by Mark Rowlands, there is still, I believe, no application based on exclusively rationalist, consequentialist or right-based natural justice paradigms that can objectively prove that it is morally wrong for one species to live at the expense of another – especially in cases where no harm or pain is caused to the animals in question. Despite our desire to imitate nature, as Nietzsche presciently observed, it 'does not by any means strive to imitate man'. His conclusion is deeply troubling: 'None of our aesthetic and moral judgments apply to it.'[55] Nature, to widespread *human* horror, remains stubbornly callous, cruel and capricious. Refusing to conform to human ought, it just is.

Depressing as it may be to admit, therefore, Sarah Kent's assertion that, because nature is not 'benign', living morally (as determined by all-too-human concepts) may not even be possible, constitutes a serious difficulty for the extension of ethical responsibility argued for by Singer et al. However, I would challenge Kent's received Nietzschean postmodernism by countering, against utilitarianism, that it is precisely the so-called 'marginal cases' that constitute the significant instances that demand our moral consideration. These marginal cases, far from indicating exceptions to our responsibility, are rather the very instances that stimulate an acute sense of that excessive non-calculable responsibility referred to by Derrida, and that therefore make an ethically relevant demand on us.

Now, in opposition both to utilitarianism's blind faith in rational calculus[56] and the irrationality of Levinas-inspired non-calculable excess, the ethics of care prioritises the marginal cases, the vulnerable and precisely *not* those of equal status or privilege. Ethical responsibility is therefore not defined by the 'principle of equality' but actually pertains most intensely to the vulnerable, the dispossessed and damaged status, the defenceless and unprotected: in other words, to those very marginal cases whose manifest, asymmetrical, specific alterity makes an urgent moral demand on us. And, in our present social reality, this marginal status includes non-human animals.

It does not follow, however, as Nel Noddings correctly points out, that this makes me 'obligated to the entire class of animals'.[57] She cogently argues that 'we cannot preserve animal life in general by refusing to kill and eat animals.'[58] Choosing to be a vegetarian or a carnivore is, therefore, Noddings suggests, just not an ethical issue: 'What I must prevent, having made either decision, is pain to consciousness.'[59] Responsibility to non-human animals becomes an ethical issue when those animals in my care are at risk of suffering through neglect and when my concern for them is the attitude required to prevent this. Yet this does not mean that it is necessary to have a relationship with non-human animals to live morally exemplary lives. 'Our ethical domain [can nevertheless be] complicated and enriched' by forming such relationships, Nodding adds.[60] Ultimately, the moral injunction associated with the ethics of care is that 'to behave uncaringly toward one of its members diminishes it and diminishes us'.[61] For the ethics of care, moral emphasis falls not on equality (or objectivity) but rather on the ethically significant asymmetric difference in status between those endowed with social autonomy and the disenfranchised (or, in Nodding's terms, the one-caring and the cared-for). The reason why (and this may not, I am aware, constitute a reason in the rationalist sense that Singer would demand) we *care* for the so-called 'marginal cases' is precisely *because* they are vulnerable, and we recognise that they require our ethical attention. We subjectively empathise with their subjected condition, the recognition of our own potential weakness in them constituting a particularly intense manifestation of the inclusive categorical imperative spoken of above. And, despite what Noddings claims, such ethical care should not be confused with sentimentality in its rightful trans-species extension to include non-human animals.

I suggest that it is according to the morally significant empathy associated with the ethics of care (a moral paradigm not restricted by the promotion of reason to absolute arbiter) that we intuitively sense that there remains something morally wrong with Hirst's practice, even if this intuition ultimately refuses to be reparsed in a rational, objective theorem. The previous chapter highlighted the ethical importance of 'active sympathy'. Evaluated in the context of Emin's art practice, we argued that a creative emotional response was necessary for the development of a complex, subtle and engaged ethical attitude. Sympathy, we concluded, is crucial for experiencing the ethos of respect and the concept of responsibility. And I believe that the intuitive experience of moral wrong in relation to Hirst's work comes about according to this engagement of active sympathy – or 'fundamental compassion' that has been, in this context, associated with the caring obligation.

Because it involves the disrespectful deployment and gratuitous manipulation of non-human animals (damaging their post-mortem remains for display as art objects) Hirst's art, despite standing up impressively to the moralist philosophical arguments presented above, *remains* morally wrong therefore from the viewpoint of the ethics of care. Should his practices be condemned? Yes: but only to the extent that the instrumental or commercial treatment of animals that disregards ethical considerations should be condemned. According to the active sympathy and 'fundamental compassion' we intuitively feel in the presence of a Hirst exhibit, it may be conceded that it can never be ethically warranted or defensible to abuse animals instrumentally for the sake of art. Yet, as a mode of fundamental unconcealment, *art* reveals this appalling, yet profound reality to us; therefore, as Baker accurately claims, it remains 'one of the few contemporary forms that can claim properly and respectfully to attend to the other of the animal'.[62] Hirst evokes an emotional response that activates the 'sympathy' associated with the ethics of care to provoke our fundamental compassion for the animal-as-other. His work may as a result compel us to feel acute shame, humiliation and guilt for the instrumental and systematic abuse of those that deserve our care.

Exquisite Corpse: Death and the Sublime

Hirst's work presents considerable complications for the ethical analysis of art. Paradox made vivid, his work is a visual scandal: an unjustifiable and demonstrably unethical practice is metamorphosed through an unprecedented aesthetic intelligence into what is undeniably one of the most fascinating manifestations of contemporary art. How is this achieved? This section argues that the exceptional artistic value of Hirst's work ultimately involves a transvaluation of its problematic morality. This will involve establishing, however, that his work *is* of exceptional artistic value despite its associated unethical practices. No easy task.

Yet this can be achieved, I believe, by characterising his art as *sublime*, in spite (and yet perhaps ultimately *because*) of its unethical content. I have argued elsewhere[63] that the sublime can be identified in the Hirstean aesthetic – provided this concept is understood as defined by the Irish philosopher Edmund Burke (1729–97) in *A Philosophical Enquiry into the Origin of our Ideas of the Sublime and Beautiful* (1757)[64] and not in the more familiar Kantian version. Application of this hypothesis here will enable us to conclude that the specific immorality associated with Hirst's practice undergoes a process of transvaluation that ultimately compels a deeper ethical structure to manifest itself in his work.

Anticipating certain undercurrents in postmodern thought by recognising that art, as well as beautiful objects, also includes much dark, pessimistic and even horrific works, Burke's discussion of the sublime acknowledges, in a way that the Kantian analysis fails to do, the satisfaction of indulging our morbid curiosity. Yet the originality of Burke's analysis is that it offers an explanation for why certain dark and perverse objects of art can also remain, in exceptional cases, aesthetically compelling. Sometimes, indeed, the darkness and perversity are precisely the aspects responsible for delivering the most intense aesthetic experiences.

Burke argues that because anticipation of pain is more intensely experienced than pleasure, *terror*[65] is the true source of the most powerful – indeed *compulsive* – human emotion.[66] 'Whatever is fitted in any sort to excite the ideas of pain, and danger, that is to say, whatever is in any sort terrible . . . is a source of the *sublime*; that is, it is productive of the strongest emotion which the mind is capable of feeling.'[67] Yet terror is experienced as sublime, according to Burke, when its associated anticipation of danger is mediated in such a manner that its harm is rendered innocuous.[68] When it is realised that the threat of real pain or fatality is not immediately harmful and when the danger has been neutralised and can be witnessed from a safe vantage, the visceral shock initially stimulated is rationalised into *astonishment*: a state of radical amazement that is

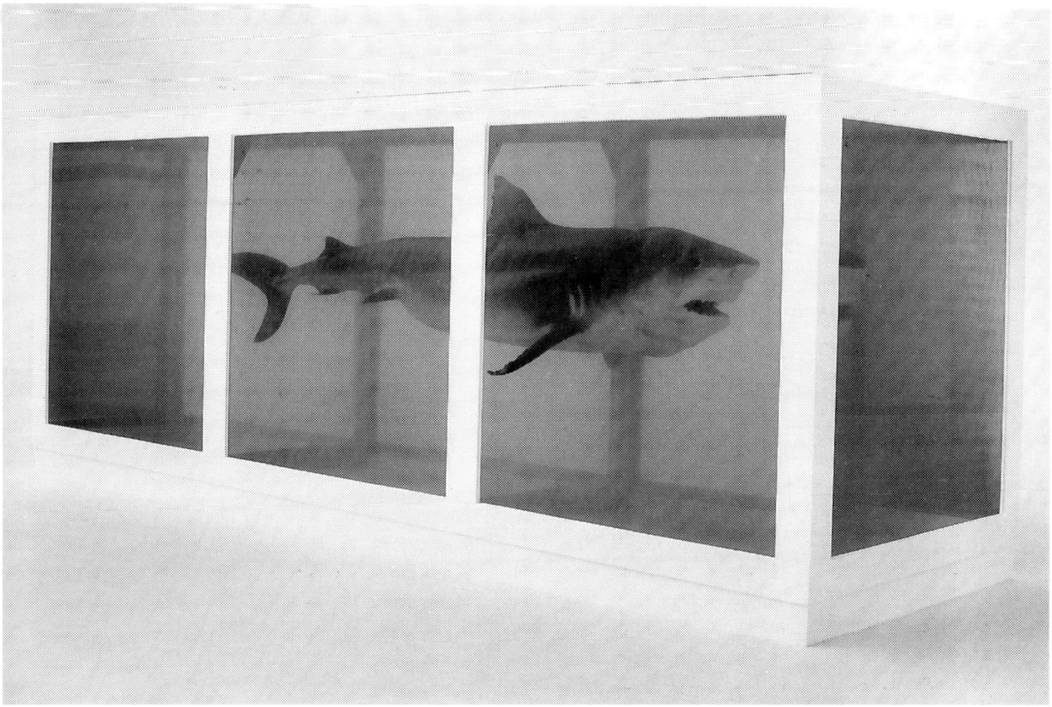

21. Damien Hirst, *The Physical Impossibility of Death in the Mind of Someone Living (2)*, 1991
Glass, steel, silicone, shark and 5% formaldehyde solution
84 x 252 x 84 in (213.4 x 640.1 x 213.4 cm)
© the artist
Photo: Antony Oliver
Courtesy Jay Jopling/ White Cube (London)

experienced, in the idiom of the *Enquiry*, as 'delightful'. In particular, however, it is the fear of death, being the most intensely felt and powerful of human emotions, immediately relegating any non-fatal pain innocuous by contrast, that, when successfully yet safely evoked, precipitates the sublime.

Invoking death while keeping it in abeyance, Hirst's *The Physical Impossibility of Death* induces the sublime experience by providing us with a safe means of mediating the terror of confrontation with a hostile predator. The attraction–repulsion conflict produced by the appearance of the dark figure motionless in its death-tank is finally reconciled in astonishment. And this completes the sublime experience. 'Astonishment', Burke concludes, 'is the effect of the sublime in its highest degree.'[69] Yet, the aesthetic power of Hirst's sculpture can be attributed to the fact that it circumvents any patent picture of human demise. Rather, precisely by virtue of its fundamental refusal, *The Physical Impossibility of Death* more profoundly evokes a pregnant – and I hesitate to qualify *human* – fear of death. How does it achieve this?

It can be attributed to the fact that the sculpture *concedes* death to be absolute zero, the impossible, the ruination of representation. Making something manifest by acknowledging its impossibility, its status as one of those 'ideas' that, in the words of Burke, 'present no distinct image to the mind', this is the remarkable effect of Hirst's shark. In the living mind, death is impossible. Yet *with* this very concession, Hirst gives palpable presence instead to the horribly amorphous, pathogenic, *horror of death*. This experience may not be pleasurable – but it is, in Burke's terms, more profound than pleasure.

> I've always looked at pictures and read stories about sharks. They've got this really kind of powerful horror. And then I worked out if I could get a shark into a gallery . . . because I didn't want to paint one, and I didn't want to have, like, a really beautiful *Cibachrome* light box or a photograph. And then I thought, well, if I can get one big enough to frighten you, that you feel you're in there with it, feel it could eat you, it would work.[70]

With this statement Hirst acknowledges the true modality of his sculpture. Taking advantage of the fear that he knows the shark has the power to invoke, the abstract horror[71] of death is thereby more effectively accessed. 'The intellect is still engaged, but it is an intellect involved in an anxious body, viscerally conscious.'[72] Going for the real thing, Hirst rejects the process of representation. Refusing to depict is hardly disturbing in itself; but precisely because there is *no representation* here, Hirst's shark shocks more effectively because it insidiously *stimulates* the phobia of death (what *is not* there) by producing a compulsive emotional reaction to what *is* there.[73] The somatic reaction to the external stimulus of the shark is powerful enough to generate an equally powerful, but more subtle, internal cognitive aftershock: the idea of death – precisely what the work itself concedes to be impossible. We are in fact made to *feel* the anxiety spoken of by Heidegger when confronted with this dark being-towards-death.[74]

To the extent that the organism remains postponed at the moment of death, Hirst's shark does more than provoke an intense involuntary visceral reaction to the immediate threat of danger. Rather, because the creature is *embalmed* in this liminal phase, a deeper, more abstract metaphysical fear is thereby suggested. 'Through the formalism,' Hirst comments, 'you can make people think about things they don't want to.'[75]

Less a *memento mori*, the formal invitation to contemplate mortality, than an intention to *produce* a profound fear adequate to the fundamental anxiety of death therefore, Hirst's shark invokes that emotion that Burke identifies as 'the king of terrors'.[76] Finding the perfect method to induce terror by forcing us to confront an instinctively feared object, the artist stimulates the human phobia of death by accessing the innate fear of a natural predator. Identifying a displacement phobic object onto which thanatophobia can be projected, Hirst reaches down into the *id* and locates 'people's worst fears'.[77] Contemplating this shark-in-a-vat we are divested of rationality in the way Burke describes, through our visceral anxious encounter with this very powerful avatar of death. From this moment we are inescapably involved: 'It is almost impossible', Hirst comments, 'to avoid mentally inhabiting it.'[78]

Looking into the darkness of the black mouth spiked with teeth, a darkness merely made more visible by the scientific *clarité* of Hirst's sculpture, Hirst's exquisite corpse inspires a terrified awe, evoking that condition of astonishment that Burke associates with the sublime experience. Hirst's sculpture effectively, if insidiously, evokes the existential anxiety of death (we are brought face-to-face with the horror of 'nothing') by providing a phobic object adequate to threaten our sense of self-preservation. Because it achieves this in a safe environment, however (that yet makes it even more disturbing), *The Physical Impossibility of Death* should be considered paradigmatically sublime in the Burkean sense.

Therefore the problematic morality of this work (it involves the destruction of a sentient, but dangerous, highly efficient, exquisite predator) does nothing to undermine its exceptional artistic value. Despite its dubious ethics, Hirst's shark is one of those exceptional cases of dark yet aesthetically fascinating art spoken of by Burke in the *Enquiry*. A non-reconcilable conflict of aesthetic and moral values remains fundamental to this corrupt yet sublime art. Yet, even characterising this art as sublime cannot ignore or excuse the immorality that remains fundamental to its metaphysical vision.

Cognitive Immoralism

Analysis of the work of Damien Hirst has established that a significant aesthetic value may be attributed to a particular artwork that nevertheless manifests an attitude of questionable morality. Such artistic problem cases are discussed in Daniel Jacobson's important article 'In Praise of Immoral Art',[79] which demonstrates that it is plausible to reject moralism without commitment to autonomism (or any theory that identifies aesthetic value with form).

Violations enacted by transgressive practices can be understood as subversions of the isolation of art from its allegedly extra-aesthetic features.

One of the most effective methods of achieving this subversion, as argued, is to engage the morality of the audience by stimulating a negative emotional reaction. Confronted with such artistic provocations, it becomes absurd (if not strictly impossible) to attend *exclusively* to the aesthetic formal properties of a transgressive work of art. To continue dogmatically to be abstract in relation to whatever is 'fucking up' the formal structure of such art is to adopt the position of a neurotic censor, in denial of its intrinsic moral content.

However, Jacobson's defence of immoral art has cautioned us to be circumspect when applying ethical analysis to art that is considered, for whatever reasons, to be immoral. In relation to ethically problematic cases of artistic production, Jacobson claims that moralism is forced into a double bind: in order to account for the artistic quality of certain artworks considered unethical, moralists are compelled *either* to counterfactually deny that the immoral work has any aesthetic value whatsoever (by eccentrically relinquishing it of artistic status) *or* to continue to accept that it qualifies as art while remaining distanced from its unethical status.[80] Compelled to assume the disinterested attitude to the immorality of the work, the moralist is forced, paradoxically, to identify the artistic value of ethically problematic art with its formal or putatively 'aesthetic' qualities (and thus adopts a position identical with autonomism, the very theory that moralism defines itself against).

Both autonomism and moralism are rejected for proving inadequate in application to the analysis of contemporary transgressive art practices. In this discussion, the specific difficulties associated with both theoretical directions (and with alleged, yet precipitous, 'solutions' such as 'cognitive immoralism') shall be made evident in application to ethically problematic, yet nevertheless manifestly consummate, art – art that, although highly significant artistically remains morally questionable (if not manifestly unethical), and therefore, like Hirst's, provokes moral shock with the very gesture with which it engages sublime aesthetic responses. Careful consideration of such art brings to light works that are problematic because they appear (like Hirst's) to involve an intrinsic conflict of aesthetic and moral values; indeed, such works are judged transgressive principally *because* they violate the conceptual partition of the aesthetic and the moral.

Although endorsing the anti-autonomist intuition that moral value in certain cases *is* allied inextricably with aesthetic value, Jacobson remains unconvinced by the more prescriptive tendencies of the Humean moralists.[81] If moral value becomes the standard of evaluation, Jacobson cautions, if, that is, it comes to dominate criteria of aesthetic judgement, then 'some very great works will have to be condemned'.[82] The problem with moralism is the willingness of its proponents to 'praise art that is insipid but virtuous, and to condemn the wicked but sublime':[83] in its obstinate refusal to acknowledge that 'good art *can* express false ideas and evil perspectives', moralism mistakenly identifies aesthetic value with moral value.[84] *Good art can be bad*: recognition of the non-contradictory structure of this admission leads to Jacobson's endorsement of what he calls immoral art. Immoral art? He defines a work of art as immoral if it promotes 'or is complicitous with, a morally suspect point of view' (whatever in the context may be considered to be 'morally suspect').[85]

Is the work of Damien Hirst *immoral* in the sense defined by Jacobson? It was concluded above that Hirst's work with animals is unjustifiable from an ethical perspective. To this extent, it may be taken to manifest a 'morally suspect' ethical perspective (at least to those who consider the post-mortem dismemberment and display of non-human animals to be ethically wrong – and whoever doesn't, fails to appreciate Hirst's aesthetic). Does this allow us to say that his work is complicit with a morally suspect point of view?

To the extent that Hirst does not mark his animal work with the necessary characteristics of 'disapprobation or blame', to the moralist, his work will remain frustratingly ambivalent about the very ethical issues it so vividly engages. It is much easier therefore *either* to condemn it outright as unethical (moralism) *or* to aesthetically defend it by denying it has any moral relevance whatsoever (autonomism); both responses are equally inadequate because they fail to appreciate that the moral transgression involved in Hirst's work is intrinsic to its aesthetic value. I propose that the morality of Hirst's work – even if it is accepted as unjustifiable – is crucial to whatever aesthetic value it possesses. Yet this intrinsic morality cannot be absolved by direct conversion to aesthetic value. Therefore, it seems unwarranted to assert, according to the moralist perspective, that the aesthetically relevant moral defect, *because it is defective*, necessarily diminishes the artistic significance of Hirst's work. On the contrary, the immorality of his work is both aesthetically and ethically structural to it.

Does that which constitutes, in the particular case of Hirst's work, a properly 'moral defect' (the instrumental and therefore unethical use of non-human animals for a relatively trivial human end) contribute 'positively and ineliminably to its aesthetic value'?[86] Not only does Hirst's work provide a good example of the kind of exceptional art spoken of by Jacobson that is actually 'better for its immorality' but also, highly significantly, it is precisely the manifest immorality of Hirst's work that fulfils, perhaps circularly, viciously and paradoxically, an 'important ethical function'. How can this be?

Recent cognitive theoretic[87] followers of Jacobson's 'immoralism'[88] have defended the view that certain works of art 'which are morally problematic because of the ways in which they are morally defective' can indeed 'enhance our understanding'.[89] According to this approach, as one of the few mediums capable of making immoral experience 'accessible and intelligible', art is alleged to enrich ethical knowledge – despite its apparent moral transgressions.[90] Works of exceptional art exist that, although being morally 'defective', nevertheless possess an inalienable aesthetic value. In certain special cases, the artistic value of the work appears in fact to be amplified by its immoral nature.[91] Cognitive immoralism exonerates any ethically problematic aspects of transgressive art in the name of *knowledge*. The epistemic value of the work according to this theory[92] eclipses its moral value by way of its exceptional artistic quality, thereby redeeming the moral value of the work in respect of a broader-spectrum conception of ethical value that – as considered in Chapter 4 in relation to Tracey Emin's ethically significant *fearless speech* – transcends specific immoralities for the sake of a meta-ethical *truth*.

The work of Damien Hirst provides a unique opportunity to explore the cognitive immoralist's radical approach to the epistemology of values. What requires to be emphasised in this case is that the transgression of specific conventional moralities in the service of a transcendent meta-ethical significance takes place through the sublime artistic effect of the work, an effect that, because it transcends the conflict of aesthetic value and moral value, paradoxically includes and reinforces both.

The Artistic Transvaluation of Morality

Moralism, it seems, is condemned to be *moralistic*. If an artwork conflicts with one's own moral convictions, it is likely to be condemned; if not – if it corresponds to those convictions – it is likely to be applauded. Can we therefore, as Jacobson admits, 'expect no more agreement about immoral art than there is about morality'?[93] Back to square one? Perhaps.

Yet I will conclude that the sublime artistic value of Hirst's work *compels* a suspension and ultimate re-evaluation of its negative moral status; but this does not render its immorality irrelevant or redundant. Quite the contrary: this phenomenon is perhaps best characterised by employing a key concept of speculative dialectics, *aufheben*, a word privileged by Hegel[94] – and developed as *Aufhebung* in the writings of Derrida[95] – because it carries the double semiotic capacity to mean both *cancelled* and *preserved*. (The conventional English translation 'sublated' is inadequate to capture the irreducible double modality of the term). I want to be as clear as I can about this: the unethical condition of Hirst's work is *not eliminated* but rather *aufgehoben*, that is, preserved yet simultaneously cancelled in the work. According to the dialectical concept therefore, we could say, more accurately, that the immorality of Hirst's art is *embalmed* in the work, because, ultimately, the morality of the work refuses to be extricated from, or sanitised in opposition to, the aesthetic dimension of the work. Absolutely resistant to elimination, preserved in the work yet nevertheless transmuted by the work, the immoral condition of Hirst's aesthetic remains suspended, yet raised beyond ('re-lifted', in the Derridean[96] idiom) the work, into a sublime state. This is not an unprecedented phenomenon.

In a recent analysis of the art-morality paradox that follows Jacobson's critique, Matthew Kieran[97] argues that because moralism has led some critics to counterfactual solecisms it is manifestly 'false'. He cites Peter Fuller's animadversion of the work of Francis Bacon as such an error of judgement.[98] Fuller argued that the conception of human existence expressed by Bacon necessitates 'a moral refusal'. Because it is not ethically right for us to accept the uncompromising nihilism manifested in Bacon's work, the critic concluded that we ought not to praise his work as great art.[99] Now clearly, in this instance, Fuller's 'moral concerns', Kieran concludes, 'are clouding his critical judgment'.[100]

So, demonstrating the spuriousness of moralism requires the identification of two kinds of artistic phenomena:

1. An instance where aesthetic value is diminished because of a 'morally admirable character.'[101]
2. An instance where aesthetic value is 'enhanced' because of immorality.

Kieran's example of work with good moral value and yet poor aesthetic value is instructive. American artist Norman Rockwell's schmaltzy scenes of mythical Americana, in that they advocate family values, the happy work ethic and other socially admirable virtues may indeed be considered morally good. However, lamentably perhaps, his work is also of pitiably low aesthetic value (even by virtue of its 'good' moralistic characteristics). This example demonstrates, according to Kieran, that 'moral character, appropriate as it may be, [can] count against rather than for its value as art.'[102]

The work of British artists Olly and Suzi provides a controversial yet more apposite example in the present context. Their project to depict animals in their natural environment, as described at length by Steve Baker,[103] is highly sensitive to the ethical issues involved in human interaction with other species. Yet, although respectful of non-human alterity, ethically responsible, ecologically undamaging and zoologically interesting, the resultant art is, relatively speaking, aesthetically anodyne.

Consisting of drawings and impressionistic paintings accomplished *en plein air* in the presence of the predators, their work – even though it is documented as 'a performance' by a photographer 'who travels with them' – is, Baker admits, 'unusually straightforward in the context of contemporary art'.[104] Offering their blood-and-paint shark drawing to a great white and photographing the subsequent action, and finally retrieving the resultant scarred and masticated work from the sea for exhibition, while morally inoffensive, does nothing to increase the aesthetic value of the work. Artistically, the artists' work remains stubbornly what it is: a badly drawn shark.

Kieran's example of work with distinguished aesthetic value yet ignoble moral value is also instructive. He considers the work of Francis Bacon as paradigmatic of art in which aesthetic value is enhanced by virtue of what he believes to be its negative moral meaning. The nihilistic vision conveyed in the paintings of Bacon ought to be rejected as unethical, Kieran suggests, because, as 'a general conception of humanity, it is not only false but morally pernicious'.[105] The British painter's work articulates an attitude that 'morally speaking, many of us do not share and none of us should accept'.[106] Yet the ex-moralist[107] Kieran, strangely, finds that, although he cannot bring himself to condone the view of existence integral to Bacon's aesthetic vision, he equally recognises that his morally questionable attitude *does* nothing to diminish its considerable artistic value. On the contrary: it seems that the moral status of Bacon's vision somehow *actively contributes* to its aesthetic appeal. For the artistic integrity and consistency of this vision – the frankly incredible manner in which this vision has been realised in material form – ensure that Bacon facilitates a response that is entirely commensurate with his nihilism: 'there is something important about ourselves we can come to recognise in Bacon's work . . . we can and should respond to Bacon's work as solicited.'[108] This recognition brings Kieran to agree with Jacobson's conclusion that good art can be bad,[109] a conclusion he admits to be completely antithetical to his own earlier held position.

It is perhaps inevitable that certain works of art will offend because they convey attitudes that conflict with conventional morality. Such works of art may strive to bring a moral ethos to depiction that cannot be ethically justified; such works may indeed also be artistically substandard in that their meaning is marred as a consequence of this immorality. However, certain exceptional artists possess the capacity to induce a subjective response that conflicts with our moral beliefs and yet, because such works may simultaneously manifest a degree of artistic value (whatever this value may ultimately consist of), and because both conflictual aspects of the work are recognised by the viewer, this results in our being compelled to suspend customary ethical prejudice. However, is this, as Kieran concludes, 'because of the potentially insightful rewards engaging with a morally problematic work might bring'?[110]

For Kieran, Bacon's artistic vision constitutes an axiological paradox where moral value and aesthetic value come into non-reconcilable conflict. Indeed, it even appears to Kieran as if the artist's work is aesthetically valuable precisely 'due to its morally defective aspect'.[111] He rationalises the conflict by insisting that the aesthetic value of a work of art consists in the enrichment of experience and thereby the contribution it makes to knowledge and understanding. In other words, because engaging with Bacon's work can bring us to a novel metaphysical conception of human existence snarled up inexorably in the physical process of an indifferent, or worse, a cruel reality – but with the Nietzschean injunction not to mourn but to *exult* in this visceral knowledge – Bacon succeeds admirably in the creative transmission of truth for Kieran. This demonstrates, he concludes, that moralism is mistaken: for what the analysis of the conflict between our moral and aesthetic responses to the work ultimately demonstrates is that it is not *despite* but rather *because* of its 'morally defective' nature that Bacon's work (for him) ultimately possesses aesthetic value. 'Immoral works, where they deepen our understanding, can be better rather than worse works of art for so doing.'[112]

Kieran finally admits that the aesthetic value of certain works of supreme art may compel us to parenthesise our immediate ethical judgement. Bacon's work, he says, rewards long-term engagement with the recognition that his 'general conception does rest on a truth about particular aspects of our human nature – something from which we often shrink or self-deceivedly push to the back of our minds'.[113] His reluctant 'cognitive' acceptance of what he believes to be the immorality of the Baconian aesthetic with reference to the knowledge that the artist's exceptional vision makes accessible, however, only makes sense against a moralistic background. Kieran has responded *morally* to Bacon: something in the art conflicts with his moral convictions and therefore, according to his moralist leanings, ought to be condemned. Yet, as his example of the confused Fuller illustrates, a critic willing to condemn the work of one of the most celebrated artists of the twentieth century on moralistic grounds will quickly be discredited.

However, despite his moralist conditioning (his concern for the effect immoral art may have on his 'higher nature'[114]) Kieran's tortuous experience with Bacon has helped articulate the crucial discovery of our evaluation of Hirst: *the artistic transvaluation of morality*. This outcome can be attributed to certain exceptional artistic phenomena in which the paradoxical relationship (the non-reconcilable conflict) between moral and aesthetic value is recognised as relevant to the general artistic significance of the work. With regard to the art of Damien Hirst, the phenomenal artistic significance of such a creative programme obliges us to suspend and re-evaluate our initial (prima facie) negative moral judgement. What happens is that the specific immorality of the work undergoes a process of transvaluation (it is *aufgehoben*, as described) through acknowledgement of its exceptional status (for, as argued, it is evocative of the sublime experience) for the sake of a general meta-ethic that transcends the immediate negative moral value of the phenomenon and compels re-evaluation at another, higher, level. Recognition of the general artistic vision of Hirst's work necessitates the *acceptance of the immorality involved in its production*. Indeed, in this chapter I have tried to demonstrate that his work can be considered of sublime artistic significance only if its immorality is acknowledged – or, to put this in another way: only if the non-dialectical conflict of its aesthetic value and moral value is allowed to remain in an unsynthesised state.

In that it includes an unethical practice as an integral element, Hirst's art counts as immoral in Jacobson's sense; yet, equally unavoidably, as we have seen, his work is of sublime artistic value and therefore essentially admirable. As complete a metaphysical vision as recognised in the work of Bacon (by Kieran) is articulated by the Hirstean sublime. This vision has crystallised around several works of supreme artistic status that demonstrate the hallmark of consummate art: commitment to the (unprecedented, sublime and astonishing) artistic materialisation of a philosophical vision. Yet his work, as demonstrated, is also *appalling*: it is convulsive, it is terrible, it engages negative emotional responses and provokes moral shock, and yet is artistically significant despite (more accurately because of) these characteristics since, as Burke acknowledged, convulsion, terror and shock are precisely the elements responsible for evoking the sublime experience.

In an important paper on tragedy largely neglected by contemporary philosophical aesthetics, Lawrence Hyman elaborates an account of the relationship between aesthetic value and moral value in art that is capable of offering an explanation of the phenomenon of artistic transvaluation discussed here.[115] The paradox of axiology when it occurs, Hyman argues, should *not* be reconciled under duress, for this conflict of value may be fundamental to the artistic significance of certain art. For instance, the specific artistic achievement of tragedy, he explains, is often due precisely to the irreconcilable tension – or unsynthesisable conflict – that is allowed to remain active, troubled and raw between the aesthetic and the moral dimensions.[116] 'We need the conflict between our ethical and our aesthetic feelings to create the poetry,' we require it to experience the *art*.[117] Hyman insists, indeed, that the 'dramatic power' of tragedy actually depends upon its capacity to 'subvert' moral judgements.[118] Abject cruelty, evil and ugliness, aspects that in *King Lear*, for instance, provoke the most trenchant moral responses, are crucial and irreducible aspects of the tragedy. However, Hyman also maintains that these moral elements *resist* being converted directly to aesthetic value. Yet the artistic significance of the drama somehow actually *depends* on this resistance. Its artistic value, in other words, must be considered to encapsulate moral shock – outrage, disgust, shame – that experience of *King Lear* so importantly includes. So the elements that provoke negative moral responses must be maintained as fundamental artistic motifs of Shakespeare's play. In fact (and Hyman adverts to Rosalie Colie's fascinating analysis of *King Lear* to help him conclude this), the artistic 'effect requires our moral disapproval'.[119]

The artistic significance of Hirst's paradoxical work, in a cognate manner, similarly requires our moral disapproval. However, and this is the point I wish to emphasise here, just as indicated by Hyman and Colie, although our moral principles are subverted by *King Lear* they are actually re-signified and consolidated on a higher level by the very artistic transgression that threatens them in the play. In other words, as our moral attitudes are threatened or actually subverted by *Lear*, an equal and opposite resistance to this subversion also takes place, a resistance that keeps the immorality associated with the play (and its threat to our moral principles) embalmed within the sublime framework of the drama, which results in the preservation or sublation (*aufheben*) – or ultimately, in the transvaluation of those moral principles – at a meta level.

The experience of what I have termed the transvaluation of morality is crucial to the aesthetic value afforded by the tragic vision of Damien Hirst. But I want to add here that, following the initial shock of the threat to morality, this ultimately results in the real shock associated with the work: the 'reassertion of the values of life with all of its limitations even in the teeth of adverse experience' (to employ Colie's terms).[120] We finally accept this subversion, this transgression of moral values as essential to the artistic integrity of the work, as we accept the moral shock, paradoxically, as fundamental to the meta-ethical framework of tragedy that finally supports the work's dramatic action and is essential to the artistic experience of the kind of artwork it is. 'We are *supposed* to be shocked by Lear's callous treatment of Gloucester's blindness,' as we are *supposed* to be shocked by Hirst's treatment of animals.[121] In other words we are encouraged to evaluate the treatment in such cases as morally wrong. The more uncompromising – the more visceral and incorrigible – the moral shock provoked by the art, the more the art strives towards the sublime experience of transvaluation. But *that does not mean that the moral wrong is made right by the work*.

Hyman concludes that 'this power to take and to give delight in what shocks the virtuous philosopher requires [both the simultaneous] *presence*, and the *suspension*, of our moral attitudes.'[122] And this is exactly my point. It is not that Hirst's work is aesthetically valuable *because* of its negative moral value (as Jacobson would argue) but rather that the sublimity of the work is due precisely to the irreconcilable conflict that remains in our judgement of its moral and aesthetic dimensions. Our final judgement is that, because the work has made us experience this non-dialectical conflict of its aesthetic and moral values in such a visceral and emotionally involved manner, the work is sublime: irreducibly both aesthetically excellent *and* morally problematic – and yet, strangely, precisely because of this, finally, *ethically* important.

As Hirst's artistic programme involves a severe and uncompromising confrontation with the 'terrible side of life' that Schopenhauer was appalled to discover in classic tragedy,[123] I conclude, following Hyman's analysis, that Hirst's work with animals ought to be understood as a contemporary and creative, artistically original, recapitulation of tragedy. It is the meta-ethical structure of tragedy that is ultimately responsible for the phenomenon of transvaluation that the immorality associated with Hirst's practice undergoes in his work. Indeed, there exists evidence that this is precisely how he himself understands his work with animals: 'I never really thought of them as violent,' he remarked in interview. 'I always thought of them as sad. There is a kind of tragedy with all those pieces.'[124] If it can be argued that the artistic function of tragedy is to sublimate the same 'unspeakable pain, the wretchedness and misery of mankind . . . and the irretrievable fall of the just and the innocent'[125] that we find in Hirst and thereby raise it, or *re-lift* it (to use the Derridean translation of the Hegelian *Aufhebung*) to arrogate a morally significant ethical meaning, then it is possible to argue that Hirst's work compels us to re-evaluate, by sublimation (literally by cancelling and yet preserving) his speciesist – and therefore ethically unjustifiable – ultimately *immoral* use of non-human animals for art through the metaphysical, meta-ethical vision associated paradigmatically with classical tragedy. And this, finally, is no trivial end.

Aftershock: Tragic Sympathy and Meta-Ethical Significance

Oh my God! What have I done?

Damien Hirst

In one of the cells of a twin-chambered steel-framed glass container, in a pool of blood darkened by the ultraviolet glow of an electronic insect-killer, the severed head of a cow is left to decay. In the other cell, a smaller cubic container with jars of sugar-water has been spiked with the larvae of the flesh-fly. Quickly, one gets the picture: this is a controlled mini-environment, a simulated bio-cycle, an experiment. Watch and wait. In this simulation of what physicists term a *closed system*, the law of the random is played out: as maggot develops into fly and finds its way (through holes cut in the glass partition between the cells) to the decomposing head, eggs are laid and new larvae form, facilitating the process of decay; or shiny blue neonate is zapped and its spent shell collected in the angled trays underneath the live panels of the insect executor. In the beginning, the environment appears clean, almost hygienic; but as time passes, more and more flies – buzzing, feeding, reproducing, dying – fill the container like black zits, until it is swarming with them and the trays of the insect executor overflowing with their dead. In the fullness of time, of course, the environment will be still again. Except now it will no longer be the clinical

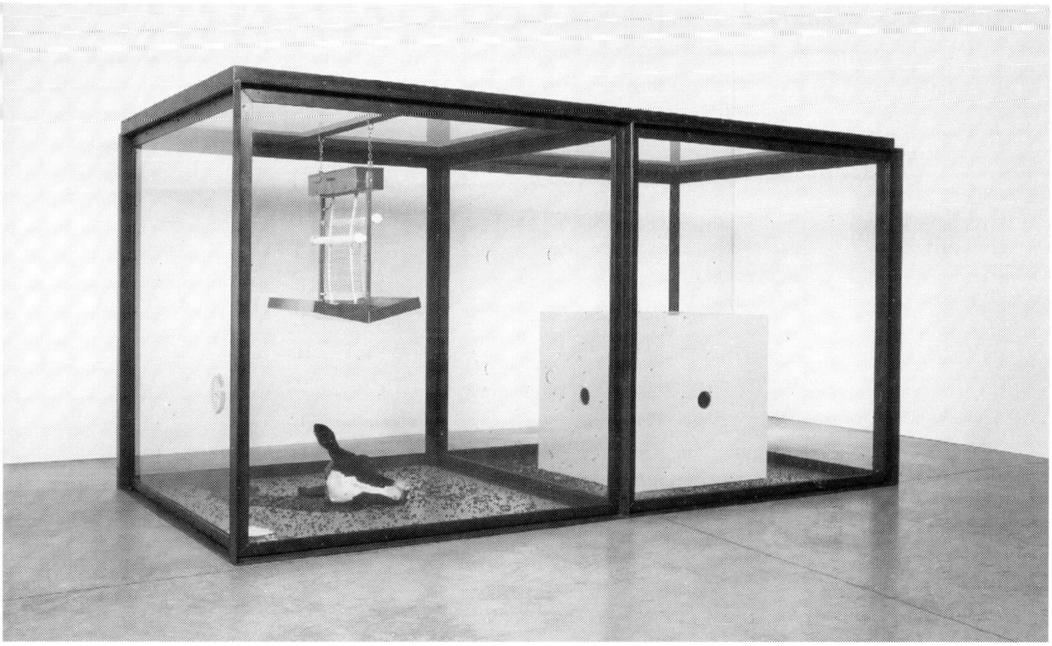

22. Damien Hirst, *A Thousand Years*, 1990
Steel, glass, flies, maggots, mdf, insect-o-cutor, cow's head, sugar, water
84 x 168 x 84 in. (213.4 x 426.7 x 213.4 cm)
© the artist
Courtesy Jay Jopling/ White Cube (London)

space it started out as: it will be thoroughly contaminated with piles of dead flies. Until someone decides to plug it out, the insect-o-cutor will continue to cast the final scene in its pale blue light.

Dating to 1990, this grim spectacle was one of the first 'sculptures' conceived by Damien Hirst following his graduation from Goldsmiths' College (the preparatory drawings for the piece date back to 1989). Called *A Thousand Years*[126] and, although nothing less than satanic in its speculative experimental cruelty,[127] it is, nevertheless, a profound and deeply compelling work of art. Hirst in fact considers it to be his most successful work.[128] Synoptically paradigmatic of the main thematic concerns of his entire artistic project, *A Thousand Years* can be characterised as a metaphysic of life reduced to 'Birth, and copulation, and death'.[129] In this concluding section I will argue that in the dark cosmological fatalism manifested by Hirst's entomological experiments (and natural history works, especially his work involving livestock), the distinctive lineaments of what Peter Lamarque has termed the *tragic vision* can be recognised. What is the tragic vision?

'Characteristically,' Lamarque explains, 'the tragic vision can be defined as a metaphysical picture of a world governed by fate or natural law which is depicted as blindly indifferent to human suffering and the human conception of fairness and benevolence.'[130] The unremitting anti-humanist conception of reality that this scheme of life involves constitutes the paradigmatic tragic sensibility. In fact, the speculative cruelty associated with Hirst's aesthetic at the very outset of this chapter can now be seen to be determined by the tragic vision as defined by Lamarque. In *A Thousand Years*, for instance, the abundant life inside the system is inhibited, contained in precise confinement, by the clinical parameters of its necessarily unintelligible (at least from the perspective of those subject to its regime), and ultimately fatal, architectonic.

Certainly, therefore, Stallabrass's identification of horror in Hirst is analytically accurate; he fails, though, to recognise the *tragic* nature of this horror and thus commits the critical error of attempting to domesticate its sublimity – its most disturbing (and artistically significant) feature. In light of the comparative analysis presented here, Stallabrass's satirical critique of Hirst's work as *schlock* ('the stuff of horror movies'), although quaint and attractive ('it's all so Peter Cushing') appears fatuous and, to employ his own bromide, 'lite'.[131] Perhaps such a resolutely indifferent critic will ultimately remain unconvinced by any argument for the profound artistic significance of Hirst's work. However, a convincing case shall be made for its tragic status that may also explain why Stallabrass might have misconstrued it so unfortunately.

In a very early review, Richard Cork succinctly identified the work's crucial effects. 'Mesmerised and nauseated in equal measure' – mesmerised by the geometric elegance of the experiment, nauseated by the foul content housed by its sleek parameters – Cork writes that *A Thousand Years* 'shocks the viewer into confronting the unacceptable brevity of existence'.[132] His review concludes that Hirst is the 'most uncomfortable of artists, and the fact that he presents his murky findings with calm, surgical exactitude only adds to the disquiet'.[133]

In conversation with Mirta d'Argenzio, Hirst quoted Hobbes's fatalist nominalism as the philosophic provenance of the work: 'He said that thing about life being "nasty, brutish and short".'[134] This is what Hobbes in fact said: 'No arts; no letters; no society; and which is worst of all, continual fear, and danger of violent death: and the life of man, solitary, poor, nasty, brutish and short.'[135] Interestingly, at this point Hirst went on to misattribute the image of mortal humanity as so much 'flies brushed off a wall' to Hobbes when in actual fact this image derives from Francis Bacon, who claimed to have in his youth become distressed by the idea of life rendered absurd by the inescapability of mortality, 'till I came to, as it were, accept that here you are, existing for a second, brushed off like flies on a wall'.[136] Of course Bacon, thoroughly familiar with the works of Aeschylus and Shakespeare, was more than likely playing his interviewer here for melodramatic effect, but nevertheless he claimed (on several occasions) to have employed tragic imagery to inspire his paintings.[137]

Here therefore, in Hobbes and Bacon, lies the provenance of *A Thousand Years*: like flies brushed off a wall. 'I like that metaphorically,' Hirst says. 'Your whole life could be like points in space, like nearly nothing. Also if you stand back far enough,' he adds, 'people are just like flies, like the cycle of a fly is like your own life.' He concludes (with reference to his later black monochrome fly paintings): 'That amount of death is pretty black.'[138] Apparently, shortly before he died, Bacon visited the Saatchi Gallery to see *A Thousand Years*. 'When he was there I got a call,' Hirst claims, '"I don't know if this is interesting to you, but Francis Bacon's here, and he's been in front of your piece for an hour" . . . I didn't know what the fuck to say. I dismissed it, but I understand why he could have liked it – dead fucking flies.'[139]

Life patterns that change and alter shape, coming into random constellations and dissolving again, are inhibited in *A Thousand Years* by the physical framework that contains and temporarily supports them before killing them. A thought experiment given physical form, Hirst has elucidated the structural ambitions of the work in terms of 'an empty space with moving points within it, moving like stars . . . constantly changing pattern in space'.[140] My argument here is that this objective, coupled with the proposition contained in one of Hirst's *aperçu* to the effect that the irrepressible desire to live is 'fucked up' by the inescapable certainty of death,[141] is efficiently embodied in the morphological schematic environment of *A Thousand Years* with its burgeoning yet confined black mass of pure decompositional energy. Entrenched by principles that lack any coherent aim or direction and are therefore denied any metaphysical meaning, existence in this ecosystem – although highly regulated by the parameters of the experiment – becomes subject ultimately to the caprice of chance. Reminiscent of the tragic-ludic cosmology Nietzsche identified in the thought of the pre-Socratic philosopher Heraclitus, here the 'eternal joke of world destruction and world creation'[142] vividly appears. Precisely, in this sense, *A Thousand Years* provides a micro-dramatic model of the cosmological outlook expressed *par excellence* in tragedy. The line that most synoptically characterises the dark metaphysics, the cosmic cruelty of the tragic vision is perhaps most precisely, elaborated:

> As flies to wanton boys are we to the gods;
> They kill us for their sport.[143]

All existence, but human existence in particular (because the sick joke is that humanity is given some sense, some awareness of it), is subject to the whims of chance, an administrative intelligence not so much capricious as sadistic. Thus *King Lear* constitutes, according to the analysis of G. Wilson Knight, 'the most fearless artistic facing of the ultimate cruelty of things'.[144] The tragedy, however, is all the more affecting, trenchant, Knight insists, for its depiction of 'a scene of wraithlike unreason'.[145] He continues: 'We watch humanity grotesquely tormented, cruelly and with mockery impaled: nearly all the persons suffer some sort of crude indignity in the course of the play.'[146]

Although the bitter pessimism of the tragic philosophy of life represented here is already disturbing, it is admittedly brought to another level in Hirst through his soliciting of the motifs of corruption and decay (as well as the meaningless preservation of death in life, a perfect simulacrum, and therefore a critical comment on, the meaningless medical preservation of life in the shadow of death) to epitomise the aimless procedure of existence. It is not that the presence of death is, not without horror, acknowledged in life, but rather that death is brought into existence through the processes of life; living life produces its own nemesis: death. Challenging Burke's argument that images are unable to present the sublime, this is a micro-universe of death.[147]

A Thousand Years is 'starkly tragic'[148] therefore not because it articulates that life is meaningless but rather precisely because it suggests that *death* is meaningless, a far more disturbing thought. 'Mankind is, as it were, deliberately and comically tormented by "the gods". He is not even allowed to die tragically.'[149]

Later iterations of *A Thousand Years* incorporate a simulated head (a cow skin face stuffed by taxidermist Emily Mayer): 'if you have a real cow's head, no one goes and looks at it.'[150] Yet, because it does not stimulate a visceral reaction (no decomposition, uninterested flies, no maggot activity, etc.), this work is not conducive to the sublime experience. Burke, in fact, identifies 'intolerable stenches' with the sublime.[151] But Hirst says: 'So long as they think it's real . . . I don't fucking care.'[152] Many critics have been deceived. Townsend, for one, naively accepts the allegations of the Gagosian Gallery staff that the 2006 head had to be replaced every week.[153]

Strangely, however, the cruelty portrayed in *Lear* frequently assumes an absurd or, more accurately, a ludic form. Shakespeare's play is infused with 'a cruel, ugly sense of humour'.[154] Yet Knight's argument is that the black comedy in *Lear* is in fact 'intrinsic to the texture of the whole play';[155] indeed, he claims that the tragic intensity of the cruelty would be diminished were it not for the grinning streaks of 'ghoulish humour'[156] running through the drama: 'we are [made] continually aware of the humour of cruelty and the cruelty of humour.'[157]

Such a tragicomic duality has been repeatedly identified in Hirst's work with animals, most obviously perhaps in the work already referred to, *This Little Piggy*

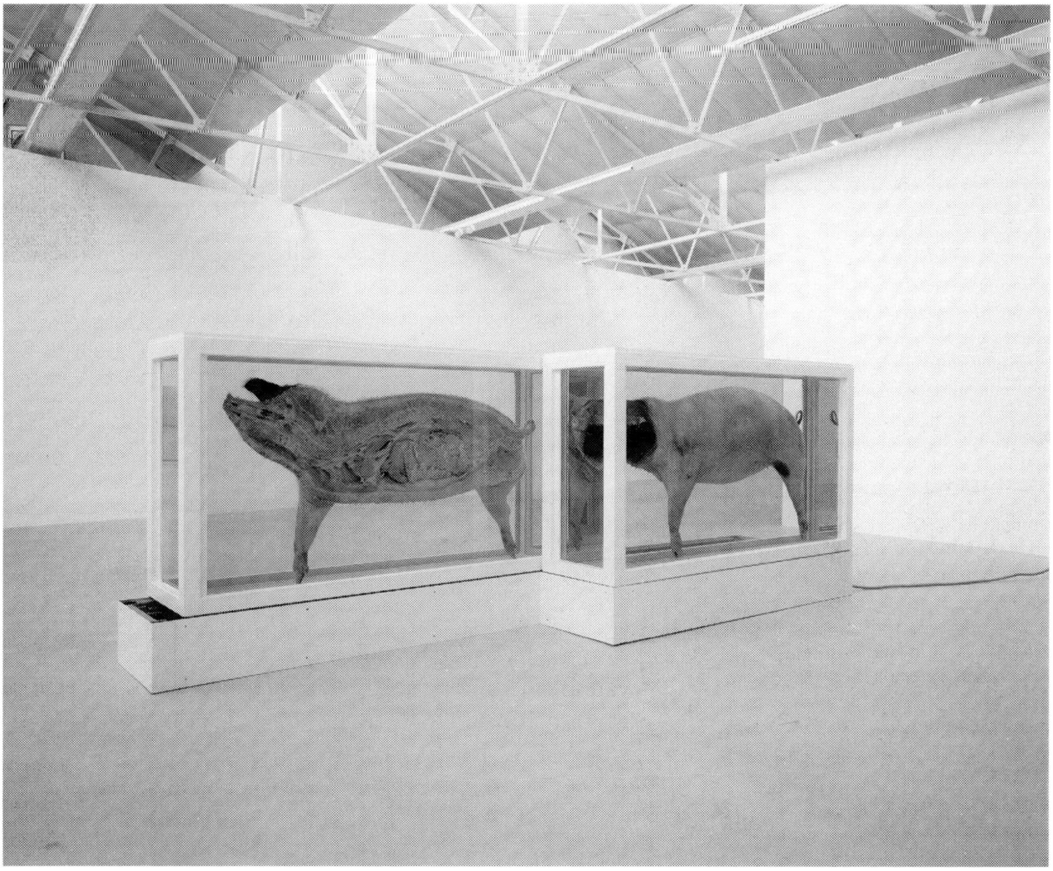

23. Damien Hirst, *This Little Piggy Went to Market, This Little Piggy Stayed at Home*, 1996
Steel, glass, pig and formaldehyde solution
2 tanks: each tank 120 x 210 x 60 cm
© the artist
Courtesy Jay Jopling/ White Cube (London)

Went to Market, This Little Piggy Stayed at Home, a pig bisected in the saggital dimension, the halves displayed in two separate steel-and-glass containers facing each other with one of them on a motorised track that continually grinds[158] back and forth in front of its other half, the halves onanistically alternating between the states of quasi-togetherness and separation. 'It looks like a bacon slicer and it is a pig slicing itself,' Hirst coldly comments.[159] Not only horror: there is also something satanically comic embedded in Hirst's tragic vision.

'We are clearly pointed to this grim fun, this hideous sense of humour, at the back of tragedy . . . the humour a boy – even a kind boy – may see in the wriggles of an impaled insect.'[160]

However, it still remains unclear why tragedy in general, and therefore Hirst's work in particular, is morally valuable. What evidence can be adduced that tragedy is of significant moral value? Why should such a nihilistic world-view involving the sometimes gratuitous (or ludic) presentation of suffering and cruelty raised to aesthetic form have any value (let alone a moral value)? Does it transcend good and evil?

In a significant essay (already referred to), Peter Lamarque enquires why tragedy should be thought of as ethically valuable. One obvious way of addressing the doubts raised here is to indicate the transcendent aesthetic purpose of tragedy: it has a long-recognised capacity to develop and sustain themes of universal human concern. Part of the value of tragic art then will be discovered in its aesthetic ability to 'express' what Lamarque calls a 'metaphysical picture' that he says itself possesses an 'independent moral significance'.[161]

What kind of metaphysical picture? Paradigmatically for Lamarque, this metaphysical picture may be epitomised by the fatalistic cosmology envisioned in *King Lear* where a world indifferent to human conceptions of good and evil is elaborated: a cold and cruel zone determined by inscrutable natural laws where good is unlikely to prevail and nothingness rewards endeavour. Tragic art *par excellence* therefore – through focusing on motifs with conventionally negative value such as moral failure and, in the case of Hirst, nihilistic, ludic and meaningless cruelty – nevertheless possesses the potential to elaborate, through *sublimation* in the tragic, themes of universal or meta-ethical validity. Many of the connections made here come to a surprising convergence in Jacques Lacan's writings. The *Ethics of Psychoanalysis* suggests that the ethical significance of tragic art (epitomised for him in the motif of Antigone) is to effect an *aufheben* of the moral within the aesthetic. In this way the essential excess of the ethical *over* the aesthetic is revealed by way of the sublime art object.[162] According to Critchley, the Lacanian term for this dynamic is *até* or *transgression*.[163] Tragic art, precisely through transgressing the conventions of the symbolic moral order therefore succeeds in demonstrating the excess of the ethical above the aesthetic – but only as *aufgehoben* through the sublime power of the aesthetic. Exactly.

Finally, however, in order to demonstrate how the aesthetic transvaluation of morality is effected through tragedy, Lamarque, possibly influenced by Wittgenstein's discussion of aspect seeing in the *Philosophical Investigations*, makes an important distinction between the internal and the external aspects of the artwork. And although this distinction is characterised as 'absolutely fundamental',[164] it is a little simplistic: it would perhaps be more genial to reparse Lamarque's internal–external register in temporal terms as immediate reaction and post-reflective response. Lamarque does though, in fact, elucidate the ethical benefits of morally problematic transgressive art that is nevertheless, like Hirst's, of sublime artistic, and therefore, as we have argued, of meta-ethical, significance.

Distinguishing between the internal and external aspects of the work, Lamarque draws attention to the temporality of response. As intimated above: the emotional reaction to a work of art takes place at a level of immediate affective reaction; thus the internal aspect of the work is determined by contemporary reaction to the work *as it is being experienced*. And this almost involuntary (visceral) response may be registered in relation, for example, to transgressive art, as moral outrage, disgust, shame, guilt, pity, compassion etc. – all now considered to be morally significant emotions.[165] In terms of the initial experience, it is determined by complete absorption in – or indeed, paradoxically, in visceral repulsion from – the work in question.

In the instance of the original (1990) *A Thousand Years*, one may have been so overwhelmed by coming into the presence of putrefaction that it was impossible to even make the approach across the gallery to observe the work.[166] Similarly, one may be overwhelmed by visceral horror when confronted with a fourteen-foot monster shark, or so morally repulsed at the spectacle of dead pigs, sheep and cattle, that one cannot, again, even bring oneself to engage with these works *as art*. Yet this immediate visceral dimension is complemented (particularly in tragic art), according to Lamarque, by the external aspect of the work – this being a later consequential, and considered post-response to the work that temporally follows, and yet depends upon, the earlier initial reaction.

According to the 'external' aspect, we come to appreciate, after time (considerable time, in some cases) that the same work that provoked this initial visceral reaction is a work of sublime artistic significance, that is, a work representative of the kind of 'metaphysical' vision elaborated by Lamarque. The work appears *ex post facto*, according to its 'external' perspective, as expressive of a meta-ethical vision that transcends (and perhaps also ultimately justifies) the specific local immoralities responsible for the immediate moral shock. The significant theme of the work is later revealed by gradual release; it comes to light through the 'external' aspect that cancels and transcends the immediate immorality associated with the work for the sake of a (perhaps ultimately equally disturbing) meta-ethical significance. This results in a re-evaluation of the immorality of the work (it may be seen as having been necessary and essential to the ethical meaning of the piece); for, according to Lamarque, the principal characteristic of the 'external' aspect is precisely the questioning of the emotional or visceral response associated with the 'internal' immediate reaction. This questioning of the initial reaction to the work fulfils itself in a 'meta-response' (an astonished response to our own initial visceral reaction) through which the visceral presentation associated with the 'internal' aspect is overruled (is *now* seen to have been aesthetically necessary) for the sake of a wider conception of ethical value – a larger meaning thus emerges that, through the transgressive aesthetic, encompasses and transcends, and finally suspends (*aufheben*) the immorality initially discerned in the work. This process corresponds exactly to what was termed above the transgressive 'transvaluation of morality'; for in this instance, the immediate apparent immorality of the artwork is again transformed into something not only morally defensible but ethically admirable and we are reminded again that 'Certain techniques of shock are embedded in the way we determine right from wrong.'

Likewise, the moral value of tragedy consists in immediate affective, visceral moral shock – shame, revulsion, horror, fear, disgust, nausea – to the tragic spectacle undraped before us, providing an aesthetically controlled, architectonically mediated 'imaginative access'[167] to deeply disturbing themes of suffering, violence, meaningless death, absurd cruelty, horror and abjection. Aristotelian catharsis, Lamarque concludes, is not merely the pleasurable release of vicarious experience as canvassed by vulgar tragedians, but rather a form of 'self-knowledge, one involving a clarification or "working through" of the emotions, revealing their proper [ethical] objects'.[168] It does not matter therefore if it can be rationally established that the work is in fact unethical: what matters in this context is the effect of considering the situation that the work invariably refers to as tragically immoral. Tragedy 'elicits a sympathetic response'[169] to immediate scenes that are sublimated through architectonic structures: the 'moral themes' are paradoxically rendered more abrupt, urgent and intensely *felt* through evaluation of our emotive reactions to the transgressive work *posterior* to the immediate reaction to it. Following the experience of moral shock, given time in which to develop a reflective meta-response to this initial shock, the ethical aftershock arrives.

Conclusion

Sympathy sensitises us to the emotional life of others. Feeling as another feels is a form of trans-subjective ethical substitution: self for other. This process, as we have seen, is now considered fundamental to the ethical experience: 'moral conduct requires that we see the world as others see it . . . And this requires that we must not strive for emotional distance, but rather emotional connectedness.'[170] Tragic sympathy sensitises us to the suffering of others: Hirst's 'specimens', although dead and displayed in a cold and dispassionate aesthetic (which mimics scientific detachment in order to subvert aesthetic disinterestedness more effectively and thereby challenge the ideology of science), solicit a trans-species form of moral sympathy. 'I hope', he says, that people 'feel sorry for the cows'.[171] Sympathetic sensitivity to the animal preserved in its death by a cruel yet sublime architectonic: this is what gives his work that meta-ethical significance discovered here.

Indeed, it is no arbitrary decision of Aristotelian scholar Martha Nussbaum to characterise the condition of animal existence in human society as tragic.[172] 'We should admit, then, that there will be an ineliminable residue of tragedy in the relationships between humans and animals.'[173] This suggests very strongly that we should feel the guilty pathos of sympathy for this tragic condition. We care about these animals; and therefore, the moral issue raised by Hirst's work, in a way bizarrely compatible with Nussbaum's ethical conclusions, is to acknowledge 'the dignity of animals and our own culpability toward them'.[174] Moreover, if Hirst's specimens were displayed in a scientific context as opposed to an artistic one, the animals would be an-aesthetised and we, as a result of cognitive conditioning, would become morally desensitised to the condition of animal existence in human society – desensitised, that is, to their tragic universe of suffering. 'I want the viewer to do a lot of work and feel uncomfortable, they should be made to feel responsible for their own view of the world rather than look at an artist's view and be critical of it.'[175]

Cognitivist Matthew Kieran believes that the benefits of art can be calculated according to what is contributed to knowledge as a result of the experience it affords; how art enhances understanding or enriches experience constitutes the beneficial value of art. 'The value of a work depends', he writes, 'on the quality of the experience the work affords and the insight and understanding it conveys to us.'[176] Immoral works of art, when demonstrated that they make a contribution to knowledge, can be considered, despite their dubious moral value, to be cognitively valuable nevertheless. But what contribution to knowledge does a work like Hirst's *A Thousand Years* make? Well, in answering this, we can defer to William Golding's novel *The Lord of the Flies*: 'At last Simon gave up and looked back, saw the white teeth and dim eyes, the blood – and his gaze was held by that ancient, inescapable recognition.'[177]

Thus it is with Hirst's work. Such re-igniting of an ancient, dark recognition in the heart of a technologically advanced, medically antiseptic, pharmacologically desensitised, scientifically self-progressive and reinforcing global zeitgeist gives us pause. His project thus qualifies as a *Zeitdiagnose* in the spirit of Dominique Janicaud.[178] Yes, perhaps it is true that, as Sarah Kent suggests, flies don't matter. But *neither do we*. And that, of course, is precisely the point.

And this finally brings the wider ethical value of Hirst's entire aesthetic project to light: his work presents a visual challenge to civilised advanced society to account for its random and multiple acts of anonymous barbarism. Likewise, it demonstrates how technological advancement and corporate control – the 'deeply anti-philosophical conception of progress'[179] – involve their own, more subtly administered, more speculative forms of pure palpable horror (see, for instance, *The Acquired Inability to Escape*, 1992).

One of the perennial concerns of his practice is the contemporary meaning of human mortality, specifically, what significance death possesses when reduced to a technological process and determined by the termination of care. As Shuster says, contemporary death can be defined as 'the exhaustion and failure of medical procedure'.[180]

Finally, because his transgressive autopsies eliminate any benefit that might conceivably result, as a consequence they question the entire notion of potential benefits; his work problematises our unconditional faith in science and represents an ethical critique of 'disinterested' scientific research and experimentation that remains somehow outside all moral accountability (and protects, for instance, the morally dubious practices of artist-pathologist Gunther von Hagens).

Similarly, Hirst's work engaged particular ethical concerns about our instrumental treatment of animals that began to emerge in the early 1990s: the Bovine Spongiform Encephalopathy (BSE) scare was a particularly troubling consequence of 'treating animals as commodities, subject only to commercial constraints ignoring all . . . moral considerations', especially when the human variant of this disease (Creutzfeldt-Jacob Disease, CJD) was discovered and its link to the consumption of diseased animals established.[181] Hirst's work may, indeed, oblige us to view the history of our instrumental treatment of animals as a kind of holocaust.

And yet the aftershock of the Hirstean aesthetic ultimately compels us to read his work 'metaphorically' (or, perhaps, 'allegorically'), not as pertaining directly to animals but indirectly to *human* existence: to what Janicaud terms the 'human condition'. Then, experiencing the aftershock associated with his work would involve, in the words of Critchley, attending 'to the finally enigmatic character of the human condition, and to the utterly fragile and un-heroic nature of that condition. The human being is not something to be overcome, but *undergone*.'[182] Janicaud asks a question that may offer an adequate propositional translation of the aftershock associated with the Hirstean tragic:

> if the specificity of man is more and more difficult to define in purely biological terms, if this specificity also diminishes from a cognitive point of view, if the notion of 'human nature' is obsolete, are the boundaries between human beings and animals, between what man is now and potential humanoid mutants, not very fragile?[183]

In the period of the aftershock, it will be seen that, through a consummate tragic art, Hirst's work involving non-human animals transforms a specific immoral practice into a meta-ethical artistic phenomenon that finally, having shocked us to its moral wrongs, causes us reflexively to re-evaluate prevailing human attitudes to animals by displaying these wrongs clearly to investigation. Because of its tragic transgressive sublime, I conclude, we are compelled to recognise seriously – even despite ourselves – the ancient importance, the inescapable significance and, finally, the really shocking ethical value of Hirst's work.

NOTES

0 Introduction

1 See Cohen's definition of abjection in the work of Paul McCarthy: 'Abjection is disgust, horror, pleasure, and disorientation beyond all thinkable limits'. Cohen, Michael, 'Leap into the Void: Abjection and Survival in the Work of Paul McCarthy', *Flash Art* 26:170 (1993), pp. 60–2; p. 60. All characterisations of abject art practices rely on the *locus classicus* of the philosophy of the abject: Kristeva's *Powers of Horror*: *An Essay on Abjection* (trans. L.S. Roudiez) (Columbia University Press, New York, 1982).

2 Julius, Anthony, *Transgressions: The Offences of Art* (Thames & Hudson, London, 2002), p. 177.

3 Taylor, Simon, 'The Phobic Object: Abjection in Contemporary Art', *Abject Art: Repulsion and Desire in American Art*, ISP papers no. 3 (Whitney Museum of American Art, New York, 1993), pp. 59–84; p. 59.

4 Julius, *Transgressions*, p. 104.

5 Ibid., p. 111.

6 Ibid., p. 107.

7 Bataille, Georges, *Erotism: Death and Sensuality* (trans. M. Dalwood) (City Lights, London and San Francisco, 1986), p. 63.

8 Julius, *Transgressions*, p. 151; on Nietzsche's 'discrediting of morality', see Foot, Philippa, 'Nietzsche's Immoralism', in R. Schacht (ed.), *Nietzsche, Genealogy, Morality: Essays on Nietzsche's* On the Genealogy of Morals (University of California, Berkeley and Los Angeles, 1994), pp. 3–14.

9 Holert, Tom, 'Schooled for Scandal: Paul McCarthy', *Artforum* November (2000), pp. 134–40; p. 136.

10 Jenks, Chris, *Transgression* (Routledge, London and New York, 2003).

11 Julius, *Transgressions*, pp. 19–21.

12 Nitsch in Morgan, Stuart, 'Hermann Nitsch, Exhibition Review, 30 Underwood St London', *Art Monthly* 212, December–January (1997–8), p. 30.

13 Julius, *Transgressions*, p. 147.

14 Ibid.

15 'I think my work deals with trauma, my experience of trauma, physical/mental trauma/abuse'. McCarthy in Stiles, Kristine, 'In Conversation', in Ralph Rugoff, Kristine Stiles and Giacinto Di Pietrantonio, *Paul McCarthy* (Phaidon, London, 1996), p. 26.

16 Freeland, Cynthia, *But is it Art? An Introduction to Art Theory* (Oxford University Press, Oxford, 2001).
17 Critchton, Fenella, 'Blood and Soil', *Art Monthly* 220, October (1998), pp. 8–10; p. 10.
18 Freeland, *But is it Art?*, p. 4.
19 Ibid.
20 Chapman, Jake, *Artshock: Is Bad Art for Bad People?* TV programme, Channel 4 (2006).
21 Ibid.
22 Ibid.
23 Chapman in ibid.
24 Julius, *Transgressions*, p. 191; but see also p. 262: 'Lumping together the Viennese Actionists and McCarthy, as I do, risks eliding differences to which McCarthy himself is very much alive.' On this point, see also Malbert, Roger, 'Exaggeration and Degradation: Grotesque Humour in Contemporary Art', in T. Hyman and R. Malbert (eds), *Carnivalesque* (University of California Press, CA, 2000), pp. 74–97. Indeed, against critical attempts to contextualise, McCarthy himself has repeatedly insisted on the differences between his programme and that of the Viennese Actionists: 'I didn't go through Catholicism and World War II as a teenager, I didn't live in a European environment. People make reference to Viennese art without really questioning the fact that there's a big difference between ketchup and blood.' Paul McCarthy in Selwyn, Marc, 'Paul McCarthy: There's a Big Difference Between Ketchup and Blood', *Flash Art* 26:170 (1993), pp. 63–4; p. 64.
25 This argument is developed more completely in my '"Everybody Hates a Tourist . . ." The Incompatibility of Aesthetics and Contemporary Art', in A.F. Mathew (ed.), *Some Essays on Post-Modernism, Globalization and the Media* (MICA Publications, Ahmedabad, 2008), pp. 77–89.
26 For a short account of the pre-Kantian origins of the concept in eighteenth-century (British empirical) philosophy see Gasché, Rodolphe, 'Linking Onto Disinterestedness, or the Moral Law in Kant's *Critique of Judgment*', in D. Glowacka and S. Boos (eds), *Between Ethics and Aesthetics: Crossing the Boundaries* (State University of New York Press, New York, 2002), pp. 49–71; p. 70. See also Berleant, Arnold, 'Beyond Disinterestedness', *British Journal of Aesthetics* 34:3 (1994), pp. 242–54; esp. p. 244; and his 'The Historicity of Aesthetics – I', *British Journal of Aesthetics* 26:2, Spring (1986), pp. 101–11.
27 Kant, Immanuel, *The Critique of Judgment* (trans. W.S. Pluhar) (Hackett, Indianapolis, 1987).
28 Kant, *Critique of Judgement*, §2.
29 Ibid. Michael Podro has associated the Kantian definition of disinterest with the concept of *independence*. Podro, Michael, 'Kant and the Aesthetic Imagination', in D. Arnold and M. Iversen (eds), *Art and Thought: New Interventions in Art History* (Blackwell, Oxford, 2003), pp. 51–70; p. 59.
30 Kant, *Critique of Judgment*, §5.
31 'Everyone must allow', Kant's analysis concludes, 'that a judgment on the beautiful which is tinged with the slightest interest, is very partial and not a pure judgment of taste.' Ibid., §2.
32 Mothersill in Lorand, Ruth, 'Beauty and Its Opposites', *Journal of Aesthetics and Art Criticism* 52:4 (1994), pp. 399–406; p. 399.

33 Recycled by psychologist Edward Bullough in his celebrated 1912 essay, it was later reincarnated by Jerome Stolnitz as the 'aesthetic attitude'. See Bullough, Edward, '"Psychical Distance" As a Factor in Art and As an Aesthetic Principle', *British Journal of Psychology* 5 (1912), pp. 87–117, and Stolnitz, Jerome, 'On the Origins of "Aesthetic Disinterestedness"', *Journal of Aesthetics and Art Criticism* 20:2 (1961), pp. 131–43. For analysis see Kieran, Matthew, *Revealing Art* (Routledge, London and New York, 2005), p. 65.
34 Because moral concerns are considered to be corruptive of the pure, emotionally detached modality of the aesthetic attitude, if we begin to feel uncomfortable because the nude model is cold or is humiliated by a compromising pose, then we have broken the spell and destroyed the effect of disinterestedness.
35 Cohen, 'Leap into the Void', p. 62.
36 Berleant, 'Beyond Disinterestedness', p. 246.
37 Lorand, 'Beauty and Its Opposites', p. 399.
38 Ibid., p. 400.
39 'Because to have commodity foodstuffs begin to assume that kind of horrific thing has to do with what you do with them how you use them and not what they are intrinsically', Storr, in Chapman, *Artshock*.
40 See McCarthy: 'The props of ketchup and mayonnaise are the right consistency for the action to be visceral. They cover the objects in a kind of body lubricant.' McCarthy in Rugoff et al., *Paul McCarthy*, p. 26.
41 Rugoff, Ralph, 'Survey', in ibid., p. 71.
42 Storr, in Chapman, *Artshock*.
43 Kieran, *Revealing Art*, p. 75.
44 Ibid., p. 76.
45 Ibid.
46 Ibid.
47 Ibid.
48 Freeland, *But is it Art?*, pp. 25–6.
49 Ibid., pp. 28–9.
50 For another related feminist-inspired critique of disinterestedness and its attendant concepts, see Deutsch, Rosalyn, 'Boys Town', *Environment and Planning D: Society and Space* 9 (1991), pp. 5–30.
51 Brand, Peggy Zeglin, 'Disinterestedness and Political Art', in Carolyn Korsmeyer (ed.), *Aesthetics: The Big Questions* (Blackwell, Oxford, 1998), pp. 155–70; p. 155.
52 Apparently, Orlan's idea of the body as a site of change and alteration in the manner of a work in progress or 'readymade' came to her when she underwent a local anaesthetic operation for an ectopic pregnancy. See Rose, Barbara, 'Is it Art? Orlan and the Transgressive Act', *Art in America* February (1993), pp. 82–7, 125; p. 84.
53 Mahon, Alyce, *Eroticism and Art* (Oxford University Press, Oxford, 2005), p. 277. See also Rose, 'Is it Art?', p. 84: 'Recalling that the Ancient Greek artist Zeuxis made a practice of choosing the best parts from different models and combining them to produce the ideal woman, Orlan selected features from famous Renaissance and post-Renaissance representations of idealised feminine beauty.'
54 Brand, 'Disinterestedness and Political Art', p. 162.

55 Rose, 'Is it Art?', p. 125.
56 Ibid.
57 Brand, 'Disinterestedness and Political Art', p. 162.
58 Indeed, Rose had already suggested that this was possible; at the end of her article she makes the extraordinary claim that 'The visceral effect and sensory overload of her imagery . . . are sufficiently alienating to afford the detachment required for judgment and interpretation. She creates aesthetic distance through a Brechtian *Verfremsdungseffekt* or alienation effect . . .' (p. 125). This, as well as Brand's argument, demonstrate very clearly the kind of inescapable captivating magnetism that the motif of disinterestedness has for aesthetics and art criticism generally.
59 Wittgenstein, Ludwig, *Philosophical Investigations* (trans. G.E.M. Anscombe) (Blackwell, Oxford, 1953), p. 194.
60 Brand, 'Disinterestedness and Political Art', p. 163.
61 Self, Will, 'A Steady Iron-hard Jet', *Modern Painters* Summer (1994), pp. 50–2; p. 52.
62 Laura Cottingham in her review of Orlan's *Seventh Surgery Performance*, *Omnipresence*, at the Sandra Gering Gallery New York in 1993, criticises her work on a moral level as 'collusion with the traditional cultural hatred meted out against the female body, and its stated goal of an idealised female form drawn from the conventional canon of art historical representations, Orlan's *Reincarnation* . . ., if it means anything,' she concludes, 'shows that misogyny is so engrained in our social ideology that we don't call violence in its name, barbarism – we call it art.' Cottingham, Laura, 'Orlan's *Seventh Surgery Performance*, *Omnipresence*, at the Sandra Gering Gallery New York', *Frieze* (1993), p. 60.
63 Parveen Adams, quoted in Mahon, *Eroticism and Art*, p. 278.
64 Julius, *Transgressions*, p. 165.
65 See Furrow, Dwight, *Ethics: Key Concepts in Philosophy* (Continuum, New York and London, 2005), pp. 56–60, for a clear accessible account of the non-objective status of moral value.
66 Nussbaum, Martha C., 'Flawed Crystals: James's *The Golden Bowl* and Literature as Moral Philosophy', *New Literary History* 15 (1983), pp. 25–50; p. 43.
67 Whatever ethical theory we advert to must necessarily recognise the 'genuinely perplexing' phenomenon of value plurality and consent to the consequent inability to definitively settle some moral disputes. Baghramian, Maria, *Relativism*, (Routledge, London, 2006), p. 293.
68 It is possible to contest the distinction between taboo and moral principle that Julius tries to sustain in order to keep the problematic (and itself, indeed, in its own way, transgressive) ethical dimension out of the assessment of transgressive art.
69 Baghramian, *Relativism*, p. 288.
70 Disagreement over moral issues does not arise through inadequacy of ethical theory therefore. Rather, according to the pluralist, disagreement may be the result of 'genuine indeterminacy about what morally ought to be done in the case of certain moral problems, such as the permissibility of abortion.' Gaut, Berys, 'Moral Pluralism', *Philosophical Papers* 22:1 (1993), pp. 17–45; p. 45.
71 Ibid., p. 18.
72 Gaut, Berys, 'Rag-bags, Disputes and Moral Pluralism', *Utilitas* 11:1 (1999), pp. 37–48; p. 42.

73 Ibid., p. 46.
74 Ibid., p. 42
75 See in particular Noddings, Nel, *Caring: A Feminine Approach to Ethics and Moral Education* (University of California Press, Berkeley and Los Angeles, London, 1984).
76 Furrow, *Ethics*, pp. 62–3.
77 Interestingly, and paradoxically perhaps, in a critique of Peter Singer's preference utilitarianism, see Solomon, Robert C., 'Peter Singer's Expanding Circle: Compassion and the Liberation of Ethics', in Dale Jamieson (ed.), *Singer and his Critics* (Blackwell, Oxford, 1999), pp. 64–84; p. 75.
78 Singer, Peter, *Practical Ethics* (Cambridge University Press, Cambridge, 1993), pp. 12–13.
79 Sedofsky, Lauren, 'Being by Numbers: Lauren Sedofsky Talks with Alain Badiou', *Artforum* October (1994), pp. 84–124. Badiou's original formulation of the generic set appears in his *Being and Event* (trans. O. Feltham) (Continuum, London, 2005).
80 Chapman, *Artshock*.

1 Everybody Hates a Tourist

1 Hauser, Kitty, 'Sensation: Young British Artists from the Saatchi Collection', *New Left Review* 227, January–February (1998), pp. 154–60. The track appears on Pulp's 1995 recording *Different Class* (Island Records).
2 Harris, John, *The Last Party: Britpop, Blair and the Demise of English Rock* (Harper Perennial, London, 2004), p. 218. Alex James and Graham Coxon (both of Blur) attended Goldsmiths (Hirst et al.'s *alma mater*), Justine Frischmann (Elastica) and Brett Anderson (Suede) attended UCL.
3 Ibid.
4 Ibid., p. 219.
5 Stolnitz, 'On the Origins of "Aesthetic Disinterestedness"', pp. 131–43.
6 Moran, Dermot, *Introduction to Phenomenology* (Routledge, London and New York, 2000), p. 124.
7 The *epoche*, he hoped, would render existence pure and unadulterated. Ibid., p. 147.
8 Stolnitz, 'On the Origins of "Aesthetic Disinterestedness"', pp. 132–3 and *passim*.
9 Harris, *The Last Party*, p. 219.
10 Kitchen-sink dramas, popular in the 1960s, are characterised by a working-class, predominantly Northern, British realism, emphasising the values of honesty and a sense of community: Karel Reisz's *Saturday Night and Sunday Morning* (1960), Tony Richardson's films of John Osborne's *Look Back in Anger* (1959), Shelagh Delaney's *A Taste of Honey* (1961), Alan Sillitoe's *The Loneliness of the Long-Distance Runner* (1962) and Bryan Forbes's film of Lynn Reid Banks's *The L-Shaped Room* (1963).
11 Devereaux, Eoin, *Understanding the Media*, (Sage, London, 2003), pp. 118–20.
12 Fiske, John and John Hartley, *Reading Television* (Routledge, London and New York, 1978).

13 Ibid., p. 81.
14 The pleasure associated with the genre is delivered by the generally repeated narrative pattern of equilibrium–disruption–equilibrium (EDE). See Neale, Steve, *Genre* (BFI, London, 1981). The ideological function of the narrative triad EDE has been exposed by Robert Hodge and Gunther Kress. They show how the moment of narrative closure (considered in terms of the resolution of oppositions) is a method of establishing a preferred interpretation and thus reinforcing conditioned ideological beliefs. See Hodge, Robert and Gunther Kress, *Social Semiotics* (Polity, Cambridge, 1988). For commentary see Chandler, Daniel, *Semiotics: The Basics* (Routledge, London, 2002) and Nelmes, Jill (ed.), *An Introduction to Film Studies* (Routledge, London, 1999), p. 117.
15 Thomas, S. and B.P. Callanan, 'Allocating Happiness: TV Families and Social Class', *Journal of Communication* 32:3 (1982), pp. 184–90.
16 Fiske and Hartley, *Reading Television*, p. 82.
17 Ibid., p. 83.
18 Mulvey, Laura, 'Visual Pleasure and Narrative Cinema', in L. Braudy and M. Cohen (eds), *Film Theory and Criticism* (Oxford University Press, Oxford, 1999), pp. 833–44.
19 'As the spectator identifies with the main male protagonist, he projects his look onto that of his like, his screen surrogate, so that the power of the male protagonist as he controls events coincides with the active power of the erotic look, both giving a satisfying sense of omnipotence.' Ibid., p. 838.
20 One notable exception to this is the reality television series *The Family* (1974), which filmed the Wilkins's family home in Reading. *The Family* was the focus of recent work by Gillian Wearing. *Family History* (2006) is a video installation that features a twin reconstruction of Wearing's own childhood family living room in Birmingham with a girl watching Heather Wilkins of *The Family* on the TV and, beside this, a fully reconstructed day-time chat show set with Trisha Goddard interviewing the present-day Heather Wilkins. Wearing's comments apropos *The Family* are relevant to our argument: 'There had been nothing like it on British TV. There was *Coronation Street*, but that was too acted, too nostalgic to be real . . . [and] There was no frame of reference for [the Wilkins] nothing for them to copy' (Jeffries, Stuart, 'Get Real', *Guardian*, 6 July 2006).
21 Stallabrass, Julian, *High Art Lite: British Art in the 1990s* (Verso, London, 1999), p. 246.
22 Lewis, Jim, 'No Place Like Home', *Artforum International*, January (1997), pp. 62–7.
23 Ibid., p. 67.
24 Stallabrass, *High Art Lite*, pp. 251–2.
25 Lewis, 'No Place Like Home', p. 62.
26 Ibid.
27 Ibid., p. 65.
28 Ibid.
29 Ibid.
30 Sontag, Susan, *On Photography* (Penguin, London, 1979), p. 34. This is Arbus's own term for those she photographed. See Greer, Germaine, 'Wrestling with Diane Arbus', *Guardian*, 8 October 2005.

31 Sontag, *On Photography*, p. 34.
32 Ibid.
33 Ibid., p. 41.
34 Budd, Malcolm, *Values of Art* (Penguin, London, 1995).
35 Carroll, Noël, 'Moderate Moralism', *British Journal of Aesthetics* 36:3 (1996), pp. 223–37; p. 226.
36 For a conspectus of the different lines of debate and theories developed in attempted solution see Carroll, Noël, 'Art and Ethical Criticism: An Overview of Recent Directions of Research', *Ethics* 100 (2000), pp. 350–87. See also Carroll's follow-up to his moderate moralism theory, 'Moderate Moralism Versus Moderate Automatism', *British Journal of Aesthetics* 38 (1998), pp. 419–24.
37 Beardsmore, R.W., *Art and Morality* (Macmillan, London, 1971).
38 Wilde, Oscar, 'The Critic as Artist', in *The Collected Works of Oscar Wilde* (Wordsworth Editions, Hertfordshire, 1997), pp. 963–1016. See also the 'Preface' to *The Picture of Dorian Gray* (first published 1891) (Penguin, London, 1994), p. 5: 'There is no such thing as a moral or an immoral book. Books are well written or badly written. That is all.' The irony of this statement in the context of the novel that follows seems lost on many commentators.
39 Gass, William, 'Goodness Knows Nothing of Beauty: On the Distance Between Morality and Art', *Harper's Magazine* 274 (1987), pp. 37–44.
40 Ibid., p. 42.
41 Brown, Curtis, 'Art, Oppression, and the Autonomy of Aesthetics', in A. Neill and A. Ridley (eds), *Arguing About Art: Contemporary Philosophical Debates* (Routledge, London and New York, 2002), pp. 399–421; p. 400 (my emphasis).
42 Carroll, 'Moderate Moralism', p. 231.
43 Hume, David, 'Of the Standard of Taste' (1757), in C. Korsmeyer (ed.) *Aesthetics: The Big Questions* (Blackwell, Oxford, 1998), pp. 137–49.
44 Ibid., p. 148.
45 Jacobson, Daniel, 'In Praise of Immoral Art', *Philosophical Topics* 25:1 (1997), pp. 155–99; p. 158.
46 Ibid., p. 159.
47 Besides Berys Gaut, Jacobson's paradigmatic modern Humean moralists are Noël Carroll and Kendall Walton (he also mentions Matthew Kieran and Richard Moran).
48 Gaut, Berys, 'The Ethical Criticism of Art', in P. Lamarque and S.H. Olsen (eds), *Aesthetics and the Philosophy of Art: The Analytic Tradition* (Blackwell, Oxford, 2004), pp. 283–94.
49 McGinn, Colin, *Evil, Ethics, and Fiction* (Clarendon Press, Oxford, 1997).
50 Ibid.
51 Carroll, 'Moderate Moralism', p. 233.
52 Ibid.
53 Ibid.
54 The fourth plinth was designed by Charles Barry and installed in Trafalgar Square in 1841. The original intention was to erect an equestrian statue of King William IV on the plinth; however, due to diminished funds, the project was aborted. See Rogers, Richard, *Marc Quinn Fourth Plinth* (Steidlmack, Göttingen, 2006), unpaginated.

55 The series was first exhibited in 2000 at the Prada Foundation, Milan and subsequently at the Victoria and Albert Museum, London in 2001. The sculpture of Lapper was shown in the company of another portrait of her with her child on her knee in the White Cube Gallery, London in 2000.
56 It was replaced in November 2007 by Thomas Schütte's 'Model for a Hotel 2007'.
57 Yentob, Alan, *Imagine: The Plinth, the Model, the Artist and his Sculpture*, TV documentary (BBC, 2006).
58 Ibid.
59 It was previously shown at the Grob Gallery, London in 1991 and at *Young British Artists II* at the Saatchi Gallery in 1993. On Quinn, see Bussel, *Sensation* (RA, London, 1997), p. 205; Mulholland, Neil, 'Sensation', *Burlington Magazine* 139:1137, December (1997), pp. 886–8; Sanders, Marc, 'Invasion of the Body Sculptures', *Dazed and Confused* 13 (1995), pp. 42–5; see also Quinn, Marc, *Incarnate* (Booth-Clibborn, London, 1998).
60 See the review of *Young British Artists II* by Julian Stallabrass where he memorably describes Quinn's work as 'high-tech horror', *Art Monthly* 164, March (1993), p. 19. See also Stallabrass, *High Art Lite*, p. 157.
61 Yentob, *Imagine*.
62 Kristeva, *Powers of Horror*, *passim*.
63 Ibid., p. 11.
64 Ibid.
65 Ibid., p. 53.
66 Ibid., p. 54.
67 The final sculpture is 3.5 metres in height and weighs 12 tonnes, it is hand-carved from white marble and called *Alison Lapper Pregnant* (2005).
68 Nussbaum, Martha C., *Hiding From Humanity: Disgust, Shame and the Law* (Princeton University Press, Princeton and Oxford, 2004), p. 305.
69 Ibid.
70 Ibid., p. 306.
71 Ibid., p. 311.
72 Quoted in ibid., p. 307.
73 Ibid.
74 Yentob, *Imagine*.
75 Kant's single 'categorical imperative' states: 'Act only on that maxim through which you can at the same time will that it should become a universal law.' Kant, Immanuel, 'Foundation for the Metaphysic of Morals', in *Groundwork of the Metaphysics of Morals* (trans. H.J. Paton) (Random House, London, 1948), II, §421; reprinted in Pojman, Louis P., (ed.), *Classics of Philosophy* (Oxford University Press, Oxford, 1998), p. 836.
76 Ibid., p. 840.
77 Kant, *Critique of Practical Reason* (trans. L.W. Beck) (Bobbs-Merrill, Indianapolis, 1977).
78 Furrow, *Ethics*, p. 50.
79 Downie, R.S. and Elizabeth Telfer, *Respect for Persons* (Allen and Unwin, London, 1969), p. 14.
80 Ibid. Incidentally, this is the authors' recommended definition of 'end' in the Kantian sense.

81 Ibid., p. 17.
82 Kant, 'Foundation for the Metaphysic of Morals', p. 842.
83 Norman, Richard, *The Moral Philosophers: An Introduction to Ethics*, (Oxford University Press, Oxford, 1998), p. 89.
84 Downie and Telfer, *Respect for Persons*, p. 14.
85 Norman, *The Moral Philosophers*, p. 89.
86 Both Arbus's and Witkin's images are transgressive precisely because they encode a frame of reference that defines a superior, i.e. 'normal', subject position.
87 For examples of her work see Yentob, *Imagine*.
88 Ibid.
89 Lapper in ibid.
90 Rogers, *Marc Quinn Fourth Plinth*.
91 In the context of this argument, Rogers's remarks are revealing when he insists that *Alison Lapper Pregnant* 'is not a sculpture of a disabled person, but of a proud Helenic [*sic*] warrior. The very absence of limbs', he continues, 'allows us to focus on the beauty of her head and torso.' See ibid.
92 Yentob, *Imagine*.
93 She makes her living by painting Christmas cards for the mouth and foot painters' association, ibid.
94 Grob was Quinn's dealer and the Eyestorm Gallery was where Quinn first showed *Self*.
95 Yentob, *Imagine*.
96 Ibid.
97 Ibid.
98 Ibid.
99 Note that this concession by advocates of so-called sophisticated aestheticism (or moderate autonomism, see Kieran, Matthew, 'Art and Morality', in J. Levinson (ed.), *The Oxford Handbook of Aesthetics* (Oxford University Press, Oxford, 2005), pp. 451–70; p. 453) leaves everything as it is. It is readily seen that a work with low moral value and equally low aesthetic value is not a problem: it's just a bad work; neither is a work with high aesthetic value and correspondingly high moral value: it's just a good work. The problem arises with paradoxical art, morally transgressive works, problematic because they are considered to have a questionable moral value and yet a *very* significant aesthetic value.
100 See Bullough, '"Psychical Distance"', for the classical formulation of this prescription. Also Gass, 'Goodness Knows Nothing of Beauty'. Alan Yentob's *Imagine* documentary included footage of a debate between David Lee, an art critic and editor of *The Jackdaw*, and Lapper about Quinn's work; Lee's views can be taken to be an extreme form of autonomism (aestheticism) when he tries to argue that the sculpture is 'ghastly' and 'not art', maintaining it had 'nothing to do with art' and defining the sculpture, because it raises social issues, as 'agitprop'. See also the contemporary reactions of art critics like Brian Sewell ('I dislike the Quinn intensely') and Robin Simon who described himself as 'infinitely [!] depressed' when he heard about the committee's decision to award Quinn.
101 Gaut identifies autonomism with aestheticism. See Gaut, Berys, 'Art and Ethics', in B. Gaut and D. McIver Lopes (eds), *The Routledge Companion to Aesthetics* (Routledge, London, 2001), pp. 431–44; p. 432. Also p. 434: 'The main support for autonomism', he writes, 'has come from formalists such as Beardsley and Clive

Bell; and formalists generally have held there to be an aesthetic attitude, an attitude we adopt when we assess artworks aesthetically.'

102 Hanson, Karen, 'How Bad Can Good Art Be?', in J. Levinson (ed.), *Aesthetics and Ethics: Essays at the Intersection* (Cambridge University Press, Cambridge, 1998), pp. 204–26.

103 Ibid., pp. 218–19.

104 Walton, Kendall L., 'Morals in Fiction and Fictional Morality', in ibid., pp. 339–57.

105 Ibid., p. 341.

106 Jacobson, 'In Praise of Immoral Art', p. 190.

107 Ibid., p. 192.

108 Ibid., p. 192.

109 Jacobson, Daniel, 'Ethical Criticism and the Vice of Moderation', in M. Kieran (ed.), *Aesthetics and the Philosophy of Art* (Blackwell, Oxford, 2006), pp. 342–55; p. 342.

110 Gaut, 'Art and Ethics', p. 435; Kieran, Matthew, 'Forbidden Knowledge: The Challenge of Immoralism', in J. Bermudez and S. Gardner (eds), *Art and Morality* (Routledge, London, 2003), pp. 56–73.

111 Jacobson, 'Ethical Criticism', p. 342.

112 Gaut, 'Art and Ethics', p. 435.

113 Kieran, 'Forbidden Knowledge'; see also John, Eileen, 'Artistic Value and Opportunistic Moralism', in Kieran (ed.), *Aesthetics and the Philosophy of Art*, pp. 332–41; p. 336.

114 Some, however, have questioned whether people with disabilities would have counted as 'persons' for Kant; but clearly whatever difficulties the empirical individual Immanuel Kant had doesn't affect the general ethical status of the categorical imperative; whatever counts as a person for *us* in whatever context is the issue. See Nussbaum, *Hiding From Humanity* and her later study, *Frontiers of Justice: Disability, Nationality, Species Membership* (Belknap Press, Cambridge, MA, 2006), which presents an argument for extending the social contract to include equal rights of citizenship to people with physical and mental disabilities.

115 Nussbaum, *Hiding From Humanity*, p. 312.

116 Orr in Rogers, *Marc Quinn Fourth Plinth*. 'The great thing about Marc Quinn's sculpture is that it says something about the human condition, in just the same way as Lapper herself does.'

117 Benjamin, Walter, 'Theses on the Philosophy of History' (trans. H. Zohn), in H. Arendt (ed.), *lluminations* (Fontana, London, 1973), p. 248, translation adjusted.

118 Felman, Shoshana, 'Benjamin's Silence', *Critical Inquiry* 25:2 (1999), pp. 201–34; p. 209.

119 Ibid., p. 210.

120 Löwy, Michael, *Fire Alarm: Reading Walter Benjamin's 'On the Concept of History'* (trans. Chris Turner) (Verso, London and New York, 2005), p. 54.

121 Ibid., p. 51.

122 Ibid., p. 82.

123 Quinn says: 'The other sculptures commemorate an event that has happened, they commemorate the past, but Alison is pregnant in the sculpture, and for me, she commemorates the future potential of humanity, possibility and hope. I also felt that motherhood was an ignored achievement in general, in terms of public art.' See Rogers, *Marc Quinn Fourth Plinth*.

124 Devereaux, Mary, 'Beauty and Evil: The Case of Leni Riefenstahl's *Triumph of the Will*', in J. Levinson (ed.), *Aesthetics and Ethics: Essays at the Intersection* (Cambridge University Press, Cambridge, 1998), pp. 227–56; p. 243.
125 Ibid.
126 'Riefenstahl's film portrays National Socialism (something morally evil) as beautiful. To view the film in the way in which it was intended to be seen is to see and be moved by (what Riefenstahl presents as) the beauty of National Socialism.' Ibid., p. 241.
127 Sontag, Susan, 'Fascinating Fascism', in *A Susan Sontag Reader* (Farrar, Straus and Giroux, New York, 1982), pp. 305–25.
128 See her autobiography, Lapper, Alison, and Guy Feldman, *My Life in My Hands* (Simon & Schuster, London, 2005), p. 250.

2 Carte Blanche

1 Wilde, *The Picture of Dorian Gray*.
2 Which makes the imperial dimensions, 13' × 10.5'; however these dimensions conflict slightly with those provided in contemporary press reviews (which give the dimensions as 11' × 9').
3 Robertson, Bryan, 'Something is Rotten in the State of Art', *Modern Painters* Winter (1997), pp. 15–16. See also contemporary newspaper reviews by Kay, John, 'It's an Artrage', *Sun*, 26 July 1997; Burn, Gordon, 'The Hand that Rocked the Academy', *Guardian*, 6 September 1997; Mouland, Bill, 'Invitation to an Outrage', *Daily Mail*, 17 September 1997; Daniels, Anthony, 'The Royal Academy is Degrading Us All . . .' *Daily Mail*, 17 September 1997; Anon., 'How Can this Pile of Shit be Worth £250,000?', *Daily Sport*, 19 September 1997 (reprinted in *Young British Art: The Saatchi Decade* (Booth-Clibborn Editions, London, 1999)).
4 Delgado, Martin, 'Outrage at "Children's" Portrait of Hindley', *Evening Standard*, 12 March 1996.
5 Weathers, Helen, 'The Master Manipulator', *Daily Mail*, 28 January 2006.
6 Kay, 'It's an Artrage'. See also Stallabrass, *High Art Lite*, p. 207.
7 Julius, *Transgressions*, p. 165.
8 Harvey in Delgado, 'Outrage at "Children's" Portrait'. Harvey's attempt to depict the victims' perspective in the work may have been influenced by the controversial song, 'Suffer Little Children' by British band The Smiths (first released as a track on their album *The Smiths*, in 1984, and subsequently as the B-side of 'Heaven Knows I'm Miserable Now', also in 1984). In the song, the voice of a dead child is imagined calling across the moors: 'find me . . . find me.' As Simon Goddard observes, this line assumes extra poignancy in the wake of Brady and Hindley's confession to the murders of Pauline Reade and Keith Bennett in 1987. Identifying with the victims, Morrissey ends the song by imagining the children, through him and using his voice as a medium to address their killer directly, reminding Hindley that they will haunt her until she dies. Although clearly sympathetic to the victims and condemnatory of the perpetrators (especially Hindley), the song nevertheless caused offence. For historical commentary, see Goddard, Simon, *The Smiths: The Songs That Saved Your Life* (Reynolds and Hearn, London, 2002), pp. 79–83.

9 Ibid. Harvey in Delgado, 'Outrage at "Children's" Portrait'.
10 Ibid.
11 See Naomi Siderfin's review of *Sensation*, where she argues that the show represented the contradictory taste of Charles Saatchi: for her, the contradiction is structural to the art that is characterised for her in general by a radical content expressed through a conservative form. Siderfin, Naomin, 'The Title Gives Nothing Away', *Make* 78, December–February (1998), p. 25. It was also exhibited in the Brooklyn Museum *Sensation* in 1999 to no comparable controversy.
12 Reuters, 18 October 1997, www.museum-security.org/97/october181997.html#4; Jury, Louise, '"Sensation" Proves Shockingly Popular', *Independent*, 30 December 1997.
13 See Sandle, Michael, 'The RA is Rotten at the Top', *Daily Telegraph*, 23 September 1997; also quoted in Stallabrass, *High Art Lite*, p. 207; Sutcliffe, Thomas, 'Those Who Take Offence: A Portrait in Tyranny', *Independent*, 29 October 1997; also Robertson, 'Something is Rotten in the State of Art', p. 16.
14 Molyneaux, John, 'State of the Art: A Review of the "Sensation" Exhibition at the Royal Academy of Arts, September–December 1997', *International Socialism: Quarterly Journal of the Socialist Workers Party (Britain)* July (1998), online at http://pubs.socialistreviewindex.org.uk/isj79/molyneaux.htm.
15 Siderfin, 'The Title Gives Nothing Away', p. 25.
16 Stallabrass, *High Art Lite*, pp. 206–7.
17 Wallinger, Mark, 'The Pygmalion Paradox', *Art Monthly* 218, July/August (1998), pp. 1–4; p. 3.
18 Kay, 'It's an Artrage'; Thomas, Alwyn, 'Paint Attack on Hindley's Picture', *Daily Sport*, 19 September 1997; Harrison, Tracey, Mark Oliver and Emily Wilson, 'You're All Idiots', *Mirror*, 19 September 1997; see *Young British Art: The Saatchi Decade*.
19 Sawer, Patrick, '2,800 a Day Visit RA's Myra Show', *Evening Standard*, 30 December 1997; Jury, '"Sensation" Proves Shockingly Popular'; Anon., 'Royal Academy's Shock Art Show Proves a Sensational Success', *Yorkshire Post*, 30 December 1997; see *Young British Art: The Saatchi Decade*.
20 *Mirror*, 19 September 1997, p. 7; Thomas, 'Paint Attack on Hindley's picture'; Anon., 'Ink and Eggs Hurled at Myra Picture', *Express*, 19 September 1997; Harrison, Oliver and Wilson, 'You're All Idiots'; Deeley, Tony, 'I Should Have Wrecked it for Good', *Birmingham Evening Mail*, 18 October 1997. See also: *Art Crime*, 18 September 1997, www.artcrimes.net/pages/harvey.html.
21 Ibid.; also Landesman, Cosmo, 'Are Contemporary Artists Asking for it?, *Sydney Morning Herald*, 18 October 1997, www. museum-security.org97/october181997.html#11.
22 Stallabrass, *High Art Lite*, p. 208.
23 *Lubbock Avalanche-Journal* in association with Associated Press, 18 September 1997.
24 Bowker, Hillary, *World News Story Page*, 26 October 1997.
25 Exceptions to this include Matthew Kieran who, in *Revealing Art*, attempts to provide a brief Millean reading; Julius in *Transgressions*, who, drawing silently on Gaut's ethicist thesis, talks about the attitude it manifests but eventually concedes that it is impossible to conclude that the work is immoral; and, finally, Stallabrass's

critique counts as ethical because it takes seriously those who were wronged by Hindley as crucial to the overall assessment of the work.

26 Stallabrass, *High Art Lite*, p. 206.
27 Gaut, 'The Ethical Criticism of Art', pp. 283–94.
28 Ibid., p. 284.
29 Ibid.
30 Julius, *Transgressions,* p. 167.
31 Stallabrass, *High Art Lite*, p. 206.
32 Julius, *Transgressions*, p. 167.
33 Stallabrass, *High Art Lite*, p. 209.
34 Mulholland, Neil, 'London: "Sensation"', *Burlington Magazine* 89:1137, December (1997), pp. 887–9; p. 888.
35 Stallabrass, *High Art Lite*, p. 64.
36 Stallabrass, *Young British Artists II*, p. 20.
37 Stallabrass, *High Art Lite*, p. 205.
38 Archer, Michael, 'No Politics Please We're British?', *Art Monthly* 194 (1996), pp. 11–14; p. 13.
39 In Stallabrass, *High Art Lite*, p. 206.
40 Molyneux, 'State of the Art', p. 9.
41 Ibid.
42 Ibid.
43 Mulholland, 'London: "Sensation"', p. 887.
44 Hanson, Karen, 'How Bad Can Good Art Be?', pp. 204–26; p. 219.
45 Hall, Allan, *Partners in Crime* (Bookmart, Leicester, 1993), pp. 70–1.
46 Williams, Emlyn, *Beyond Belief, The Moors Murderers: The Story of Ian Brady and Myra Hindley* (Hamish Hamilton, London, 1967). See also the Channel Five production, *Myra: The Making of a Monster*, Five, 3 September 2003; and the Bafta Award-winning ITV1 dramatisation *See No Evil* (2006) and Channel 4's *Longford* (2006).
47 Williams, *Beyond Belief*; see also Hall, *Partners in Crime*, p. 69, for reproductions of the photographs.
48 Hall, *Partners in Crime*, p. 66.
49 Castleden, Rodney, *Serial Killers: They Live to Kill* (Time Warner, London, 2005), p. 178.
50 Stanford, Peter, 'Myra Hindley', *Guardian*, 15 November 2002.
51 According to Davis, during his interviews with Hindley and Brady in 1986, Peter Topping found Hindley, unlike Brady, to be sincerely concerned: she 'genuinely wanted to help find the bodies'. Davis, Carol Anne, *Women Who Kill: Profiles of Female Serial Killers* (Allison & Busby, London, 2002), p. 69.
52 Davis, *Women Who Kill*, pp. 64, 66, 68. Although Brady initially claimed that Hindley had no part in the murders, he has since maintained (in an open letter to the press in 1990) that she played an equal part (notably that she strangled Lesley Ann Downey).
53 Jenks, *Transgression*, p. 184.
54 Ibid., p. 185.
55 Ibid.
56 Ibid.

57 Davis, *Women Who Kill*, p. 58.
58 Millar, Stuart, 'With Release in Sight and After 36 Years in Jail, Myra Hindley Dies', *Guardian*, 16 November 2002.
59 Slyce, John, 'Sensation', *Flash Art* 30:197 (1997), pp. 106–7; Stallabrass, *High Art Lite*, p. 204; Cohen, David, '"In and Around December 1997": *Sensation* at The Royal Academy' DC's Dozen, http://www.artcritical.com/dc'sdozen/sensation.htm.
60 Cited in Burchill, Julie, 'The Death of Innocence', *Guardian*, 12 November 1997.
61 Julius, *Transgressions*, p. 165; Hall, *Partners in Crime*, p. 63; Stallabrass, *High Art Lite*, p. 204.
62 Davis, *Women Who Kill*, p. 67.
63 Julius, *Transgressions*, p. 19.
64 Ibid., p. 20.
65 Ibid., p. 150.
66 For this reason, the transgressive aesthetic, for Julius, cannot be considered 'an aesthetic of immorality'. See Bataille, *Erotism*, also *The Accursed Share* (trans. R. Hurley), vols 1–3 (Urzone Books, New York, 1988–93), quoted in ibid., p. 21.
67 Jenks, *Transgression*, p. 3.
68 Ibid., p. 2.
69 Julius, *Transgressions*, p. 167.
70 Jenks, *Transgression*, p. 183.
71 Ibid.
72 Ibid.
73 Ibid., p. 185.
74 Cohen, Stan, *Folk Devils and Moral Panics: The Creation of Mods and Rockers* (Mac Gibbon & Kee, London, 1972).
75 Stallabrass, *High Art Lite*, p. 204.
76 Jenks, *Transgression*, p. 185.
77 Badiou, Alain, *Ethics: an Essay on the Understanding of Evil* (trans. P. Hallward) (Verso, London and New York, 2001), p. 62.
78 Ibid., p. 63.
79 Ibid., pp. 62–3.
80 Jenks, *Transgression*, p. 184.
81 This is the word Marx uses to describe the phenomenon he calls 'commodity fetishism' (that which uncannily conceals the social structure of the commodity, investing Capital with a super-human power it does not independently possess) at the beginning of *Das Kapital*: thus, Marx writes, in the commodity structure '. . . a definite social relation assumes the *phantasmagorical* form of a relationship between things'. Marx, Karl, *Capital: A Critique of Political Economy* (ed. F. Engels, trans. S. Moore and E. Aveling) (International Publishers, New York, 1967). See also Benjamin, Walter, *The Arcades Project* (trans. H. Eiland and K. McLaughlin) (Belknap Press of Harvard University Press, Cambridge, MA, and London, 1999), pp. 669–70.
82 Chapman, *Artshock*.
83 See Derrida, Jacques, *Specters of Marx: The State of the Debt, the Work of Mourning and the New International* (trans. P. Kamuf) (Routledge, London and New York, 1994).

84 Jenks, *Transgression*, p. 183.
85 Stallabrass, *High Art Lite*, p. 205.
86 As well as the work of Douglas Crimp, see for instance the writings of Hal Foster, Rosalind Krauss, Craig Owens and Benjamin Buchloh; see also the theoretical writings of the Belgian art historian, Thierry de Duve.
87 Crimp, Douglas, 'The Photographic Activity of Postmodernism' (originally published as 'Pictures' in *October* 8 (1979)), in Douglas Crimp, *On the Museum's Ruins* (MIT Press, Cambridge, MA, and London, 1993), pp. 108–25. See also Crimp, Douglas, 'On the Museum's Ruins', in Hal Foster (ed.), *Postmodern Culture* (Pluto Press, London, 1983), pp. 43–57; and Crimp, Douglas, 'Appropriating Appropriation' (originally published in *Image Scavengers: Photography*, exhibition (Institute of Contemporary Art, University of Pennsylvania, 1983), republished in Crimp, *On the Museum's Ruins*, pp. 126–37.
88 On the nature and definition of indexical signs see Peirce, Charles S., 'Logic as Semiotic: the Theory of Signs', in J. Buchler (ed.), *Philosophical Writings of Peirce* (Dover, New York, 1955); and P.P. Wiener (ed.), *Charles S. Peirce: Selected Writings* (Dover, New York, 1958). See also Cashell, Kieran, '*Ex Post Facto*: Peirce and the Living Signs of the Dead', *Transactions of the Charles S. Peirce Society* 43:2, Spring (2007), pp. 320–45; Atkin, Albert, 'Peirce on the Index and Indexical Reference', *Transactions of the Charles S. Peirce Society* 41:1, Winter (2005), pp. 162–88.
89 This point is made most cogently in Higonnet, Anne, *Pictures of Innocence: The History and Crisis of Ideal Childhood* (Thames & Hudson, London, 1998), p. 135 (for details see below Chapter 3).
90 Tozer, John, 'From Today, Painting is Dead', *Contemporary Visual Arts* 21 (1999), pp. 60–5; p. 62.
91 Even Harvey's statements indicate an awareness of this: Stallabrass quotes him as saying that he wanted to suffuse the image with a child's innocence.
92 Packer, William, 'Artists with Irritating Attitudes', *Financial Times*, 11 April 1995.
93 Kent, Sarah, *Shark Infested Waters: The Saatchi Collection of British Art in the 90s* (Philip Wilson Publishers, London, 1994), p. 33.
94 Ibid., p. 33.
95 Ibid.
96 Ibid., p. 35.
97 Berger, John, *Ways of Seeing* (Penguin, London, 1972); Pollock, Griselda, *Vision and Difference: Femininity, Feminism and the Histories of Art* (Routledge, London and New York, 1988).
98 Kieran, *Revealing Art*, p. 162.
99 Ibid., p. 161.
100 Ibid., p. 160.
101 Commensurate with *Myra*, his painterly technique in this instance is employed in a knowing way to indicate that the intended subject of his work is the photograph: in this case, more accurately, the photographic conditions of the generic sex-industry porno image.
102 Foucault, Michel, 'A Preface to Transgression' (trans. R. Hurley and others), in J. Faubion (ed.), *Aesthetics, Method and Epistemology: Essential Works of Foucault 1954–1984*, vol. 2 (Penguin, London, 1998) pp. 69–87.

103 Ibid., p. 73.
104 Ibid., p. 69.
105 Ibid., p. 74.
106 Ibid.
107 Mulholland, 'London: "Sensation"', p. 887.
108 Kieran, *Revealing Art*, p. 155. See also his 'Pornographic Art', *Philosophy and Literature* 25:1 (2001), pp. 31–45.
109 Tirrell, Lynne, 'Aesthetic Derogation: Hate Speech, Pornography, and Aesthetic Contexts', in Levinson (ed.) *Aesthetics and Ethics*, pp. 283–314; p. 299.
110 Kent, Sarah, 'YBA Woman', in *World of Art Magazine* (Thames & Hudson, London, 2000), pp. 22–3; p. 23. Kent writes of Sarah Lucas's work *Human Toilet*, 'If women are sardonically equated with faulty plumbing, Lucas portrays men as sex-obessed [*sic*] wankers.'
111 I appropriate this phrase (which I invert) from Darryl Jones's discussion of Frankenstein in *Horror: A Thematic History in Fiction and Film* (Arnold, London, 2002), p. 63.
112 Ibid.
113 Harvey claimed that his painting treated Hindley as nothing more than 'a piece of cultural ornamentation, like a bowl of fruit'. Delgado, 'Outrage at "Children's" Portrait'.
114 Julius, *Transgressions*, p. 165.
115 Chapman, *Artshock*.
116 Ibid.
117 Norris, David, 'The Royal Academy of Porn', *Daily Mail*, 16 September 1997.
118 See Stallabrass, *High Art Lite*, pp. 207–8. He quotes Julie Burchill's controversial piece 'The Death of Innocence'.
119 Harvey in Kent, *Shark Infested Waters*, p. 33; Stallabrass, *High Art Lite*, p. 137.
120 Harvey in *About Vision: New British Painting in the 1990s*, exhibition catalogue (Museum of Modern Art, Oxford, 1996). Quoted in Stallabrass, *High Art Lite*, p. 137.
121 Freud, Sigmund, 'Three Essays on Sexuality' (trans. J. Strachey), in A. Freud (ed.), *The Essentials of Psycho-Analysis: The Definitive Collection of Freud's Writings* (Penguin, London, 1886), p. 298.
122 Ibid.
123 Tozer, 'From Today, Painting is Dead', p. 65.
124 Julius, *Transgressions*, p. 165.
125 Chapman, *Artshock*.
126 Gaut, 'The Ethical Criticism of Art', p. 288.
127 Kieran, 'Art and Morality', p. 457.
128 Ibid.
129 Ibid., pp. 457–8.
130 Ibid., p. 457.
131 Burke, Edmund, *A Philosophical Enquiry into the Origin of our Ideas of the Sublime and Beautiful* (Oxford University Press, Oxford, 1990). See Chapter 5 below.
132 Julius, *Transgressions*, p. 163.
133 Chapman, *Artshock*.
134 Amis, Martin, 'The Fuck-it Generation', *Esquire*, November 1993.

135 Ibid.
136 Kieran, *Revealing Art*, p. 202.

3 Atrocity Exhibition

1 Chapman cited in Ramkalawon, Jennifer, 'Jake and Dinos Chapman's *Disasters of War*', *Print Quarterly* 18:1, March (2001), pp. 64–77; p. 73.
2 As with Harvey's piece, the Chapmans' work caused much less controversy in the New York *Sensation* (1999). The focus of controversy in New York was Chris Ofili's *Holy Virgin Mary*, which incorporated elephant dung and collages from porno magazines.
3 Chapman in Ramkalawon, 'Jake and Dinos Chapman's *Disasters of War*', p. 73.
4 Kent, Sarah, 'Rogue's Gallery', *Time Out*, 24 September 1997; also cited in Stallabrass, *High Art Lite*, pp. 205 and 314.
5 Chapman, in Alberge, Dalya, 'Shocking? Not Us, Say Artists as Academy Issues a Taste Warning', *The Times*, 20 August 1997; see also Hall, James, 'Collaborating with Catastrophe', in M. Archer (ed.), *Apocalypse: Beauty and Horror in Contemporary Art* (Royal Academy of Arts, London, 2000), p. 213.
6 Ramkalawon, 'Jake and Dinos Chapman's *Disasters of War*', p. 67.
7 Ibid.
8 Ibid.
9 Alberge, 'Shocking? Not Us'.
10 Ibid. See also Stringer, Robin, 'Vice Squad Gives the All Clear to Sensation Show', *Evening Standard*, 18 September 1997.
11 Norris, 'The Royal Academy of Porn'.
12 Gaut, 'The Ethical Criticism of Art', p. 284.
13 Julius, *Transgressions*, p. 28.
14 Ibid., p. 31.
15 Ibid., p. 43.
16 When Franco Toselli, director of a gallery in Milan, refused to show the brothers' work, in retaliation the Chapmans made a porno film: *Bring me the Head of Franco Toselli!* which featured two (female) models employing a decapitated mannequin head (originally from *Mummy and Daddy Chapman*, 1994) with a sex-toy grafted onto its nose. 'It stands as a kind of warning': Chapman in Pouncey, Edwin, *Loaded Magazine*, December 1997. See also Collings, Matthew, *Blimey! From Bohemia to Britpop: The London Artworld from Francis Bacon to Damien Hirst* (21 Publishing, London, 1997), pp. 41–2. Regarding the Freudian notion of defence, see: Freud, Sigmund, 'The Neuroses of Defence', 'Instincts and their Vicissitudes (1915)' and 'Repression (1915)', in P. Gay (ed.), *The Freud Reader* (Vintage, London, 1995), pp. 562–8, 568–71 (later elaborated by Anna Freud into the notion of the defence mechanism): see Freud, Anna, *The Ego and Mechanisms of Defence* (Chatto & Windus, London, 1936).
17 However, Goya made a set of proofs with the printer Ceán Bermudez.
18 Hall, 'Collaborating with Catastrophe', p. 212.
19 This was not their first engagement with plate 39; they had earlier recycled the

image in 'multiple miniature model form'. See Ramkalawon, 'Jake and Dinos Chapman's *Disasters of War*', p. 68.

20 It is alternatively inscribed: 'Grande hazaña! Con meurtos!' (Great deeds! With the dead!), see Turner, Christopher, 'Great Deeds Against Dead Artists: How the Chapman Brothers Nearly Changed their Name to Goya', in C. Grunenberg and T. Barson (eds), *Jake and Dinos Chapman: Bad Art for Bad People* (Tate Publishing, London, 2006), p. 43.

21 Worsdale, Godfrey, 'Dinos and Jake Chapman: Victoria Miro Gallery, London', *Art Monthly* 180, October (1994), pp. 36–7; p. 37.

22 This engagement is on-going. In 1999, they published an edition of eighty-three mixed intaglio prints again based on the *Desastres* (see Ramkalawon, 'Jake and Dinos Chapman's *Disasters of War*', pp. 64–77). They have since acquired a set of Goya's original prints and 'defaced-completed' them with their own additions. It is interesting to note that shop-window mannequins do not possess genitals and therefore the wounds indicate an addition that refers to an absence of something that was never there in the first place.

23 Lippard, Lucy R., 'The Spirit and the Letter', *Art in America* 80 (1990), pp. 238–45.

24 Freeland, *But is it Art?*, p. 24.

25 Ibid.

26 Ibid.

27 Ibid., p. 26.

28 Cited in Ramkalawon, 'Jake and Dinos Chapman's *Disasters of War*', pp. 68, 75.

29 Cited in ibid., p. 68.

30 Holborn, Mark, 'Introduction', in *Jake and Dinos Chapman: Hell* (Jonathan Cape and the Saatchi Gallery, London, 2003), pp. 11–14; p. 11.

31 Ibid.

32 Ibid., p. 12.

33 Ramkalawon, 'Jake and Dinos Chapman's *Disasters of War*', p. 77.

34 Morgan, Stuart, 'Rude Awakening', *Frieze: Contemporary Art and Culture* 19, November–December (1994), pp. 30–3.

35 Ibid., p. 32.

36 Ibid.

37 Ibid.

38 Chapman, in Ramkalawon, 'Jake and Dinos Chapman's *Disasters of War*', pp. 76–7.

39 Morgan, 'Rude Awakening', p. 33.

40 Amis, Martin, *The War Against Cliché: Essays and Reviews, 1971–2000* (Jonathan Cape, London, 2001), p. 95.

41 Sublimation is a form of displacement whereby unacceptable instincts are mediated through an acceptable substitute and thereby given indirect cathartic expression. See Freud, *Civilization and its Discontents* (1930), in Gay (ed.), *The Freud Reader*, pp. 722–72 and *Three Essays on the Theory of Sexuality* (1905), in A. Freud (ed.), *The Essentials of Psycho-Analysis* (Penguin, London, 1991), pp. 277–375. For analysis see Singh, Kalu, *Sublimation* (Icon, Cambridge, 2001); in a specific art context: Emerling, Jae, *Theory for Art History* (Routledge, London and New York, 2005), p. 8.

42 In one of the earliest critical evaluations of their work, Wolford interprets *Great Deeds* along similar lines, observing that the Chapmans' 're-appropriation' restores to Goya's image 'the scale and physicality from which it was originally reduced'. Worsdale, 'Dinos and Jake Chapman', p. 37.
43 See Emerling, *Theory for Art History*, pp. 80–1.
44 Turner, 'Great Deeds Against Dead Artists', p. 49.
45 Ibid.
46 Ibid.
47 See Falconer, David, 'Doctorin' the Retardis', Fogle, Douglas, 'A Scatological Aesthetics for the Tired of Seeing', both in Dinos and Jake Chapman, D. Falconer, D. Fogle and N. Land, *Chapmanworld* (Institute of Contemporary Arts Publications, London, 1996), np.
48 Fogle, 'A Scatological Aesthetics'.
49 For an example of this tendency, see the essays by Christoph Grunenberg, Christopher Turner and Tanya Barson in Grunenberg and Barson (eds), *Bad Art for Bad People*.
50 Compare this with Neal Brown's statement: 'It does not seem a coincidence that the great Chapman patriarchs in Unholy Libel are libertines: Freud, de Sade, Nietzsche and, especially, Bataille who – lapsed aspirant priest and pornographer that he was – particularly informs the background theory of the Chapman moral index.' Brown, Neal, 'Burger Fetish', *Modern Painters* Spring (2003), pp. 94–7; p. 96.
51 Grunenberg, 'Attraction–Repulsion Machines: The Art of Jake and Dinos Chapman', in *Bad Art for Bad People*, p. 13. See also *passim*, and his description of *Hell* as 'a gigantic vision of Dante's inferno and apocalyptic orgy of pain in the spirit of Jacques Callot, Hogarth, Goya and Pasolini', p. 23.
52 An exception to this is Alyce Mahon, who admits that the Chapmans' *Tragic Anatomies* 'picks at a very real sore in society, paedophilia, given its blatant conflation of childhood innocence and sexual perversion', *Eroticism and Art*, p. 232. On neurotic anxiety see Freud, 'The Aetiology of the Neuroses', in Gay (ed.) *The Freud Reader*, pp. 58–9. Also, 'Anxiety and Instinctual Life: Lecture XXXII', in ibid., pp. 773–83.
53 See Salecl, Renata, *On Anxiety* (Routledge, London and New York, 2004).
54 Grunenberg, 'Attraction–Repulsion Machines', p. 28.
55 On Bataille and de Sade in relation to the concept of transgression, see Jenks, *Transgression*, pp. 107–10.
56 Ibid., p. 7.
57 Grunenberg, 'Attraction–Repulsion Machines', pp. 14 and 16 (where the difference between the artists is emphasised); Turner, 'Great Deeds Against Dead Artists', p. 49.
58 In the first issue of *La Révolution surréaliste*, Breton's manifesto defined Surrealism as 'Psychic autonomism in its pure state . . . Dictated by thought, in the absence of any control exercised by reason, exempt from any aesthetic or moral concern'. Quoted in Foster, Hal, R. Krauss, Y. Bois and B. Buchloh, *Art Since 1900: Modernism, Antimodernism, Postmodernism* (Thames & Hudson, London, 2005), p. 190.
59 See Lichtenstein, Therese, *Behind Closed Doors: The Art of Hans Bellmer* (University of California Press, Berkeley and Los Angeles, 2001); Taylor, Sue, *Hans Bellmer:*

The Anatomy of Anxiety (MIT Press, Cambridge, MA, 2000); Webb, Peter and R. Short, *Hans Bellmer* (Quartet, New York, 1985).

60 Edited by Albert Skira and André Tériade.
61 Lichtenstein, *Behind Closed Doors*, pp. 42–3.
62 Taylor, *Anatomy of Anxiety*, p. 8.
63 Lichtenstein, *Behind Closed Doors*, p. 35.
64 Bellmer in Taylor, *Anatomy of Anxiety*, p. 23.
65 Bellmer in ibid., p. 32.
66 Ibid., p. 29.
67 Broughton, Linda, 'The Work of Hans Bellmer; Reading Bataille, Lacan and Kristeva', in H. O'Kelly (ed.), *Thought Lines 5: An Anthology of Research* (NCAD, Dublin, 2001), pp. 17–27; p. 19.
68 Bellmer in Taylor, *Anatomy of Anxiety*, p. 23.
69 Broughton, 'Reading Bataille, Lacan and Kristeva', p. 24.
70 Taylor, *Anatomy of Anxiety*, p. 32.
71 Ibid., p. 29.
72 Ibid., p. 3
73 Ibid.
74 Ibid.
75 Broughton, 'Reading Bataille, Lacan and Kristeva', pp. 17–18.
76 Taylor, *Anatomy of Anxiety*, p. 137.
77 Bataille, *The Accursed Share*, Vol. 1, p. 159; also M. Richardson (ed.), *Bataille: Essential Writings* (Sage, London, 1998), pp. 96–7; Bataille, Georges, *The Tears of Eros* (trans. J. Connor) (City Lights, San Francisco, 1989), p. 33.
78 Bataille, *Tears of Eros*.
79 Ibid., p. 42.
80 Julius, *Transgressions*, p. 22.
81 Bataille, *Erotism*, p. 68.
82 Ibid., p. 64.
83 Derrida, Jacques, 'From Restricted to General Economy: A Hegelianism without Reserve', in *Writing and Difference* (trans. A Bass) (Routledge, London and New York, 1978), pp. 251–78; p 274.
84 Ibid.
85 Benjamin, Walter, 'Surrealism: The Last Snapshot of the European Intelligentsia' (trans. E. Jephcott), in M.W. Jennings, H. Eiland and G. Smith (eds), *Selected Writings 2, 1927–1934* (Belknap Press, Cambridge, MA, and London, 1999), pp. 207–21; p. 209.
86 Bataille, *Erotism*, p. 63.
87 Chapman in Baker, Simon, 'Jake Chapman on Georges Bataille: An Interview with Simon Baker', *Papers of Surrealism* 1, Winter (2003), pp. 1–17; p. 3. www.surrealismcentre.ac.uk/publications/papers/journal1/.
88 Chapman, *Artshock*.
89 Maloney, Martin, 'The Chapman Bros. When Will I be Famous', *Flash Art* 29:186, February (1996), pp. 64–7; p. 67.
90 Žižek, Slavoj, *The Parallax View* (MIT Press, Cambridge, MA, and London, 2006), p. 311.
91 Spector in Taylor, *Anatomy of Anxiety*, p. 7.

92 Ades in ibid., p. 8.
93 See Falconer, 'Doctorin' the Retardis'.
94 Fogle, Douglas, 'A Scatological Aesthetics'.
95 This is admitted in the Foreword to the *Chapmanworld* catalogue, where their work is described as 'hybrids between myth, a basic household knowledge of psychoanalysis and some other sciences . . .' (Biesenbach and Dexter, in *Chapmanworld*).
96 On the Chapman brothers' response to Bataille, see Ramkalawon, 'Jake and Dinos Chapman's *Disasters of War*', p. 72, and Morgan, 'Rude Awakening', p. 33. For Bataille's theory of transgression see Bataille, *Erotism*; also, Bataille, Georges, *Visions of Excess: Selected Writings, 1927–1939* (ed. A. Stoekl) (University of Minnesota Press, (Minneapolis, 1985); M. Richardson (ed.), *Bataille: Essential Writings*. See also Bataille, *The Accursed Share*, vols 1–3.
97 Morgan, 'Rude Awakening', p. 33.
98 Devereaux, 'Beauty and Evil', p. 242.
99 Julius, *Transgressions*, p. 50.
100 Hughes, Robert, *The Culture of Complaint: The Fraying of America* (Harvill Press. London, 1993), pp. 155–6.
101 Ibid.
102 Hall, 'Collaborating with Catastrophe'; Maloney, Martin, 'Everyone's a Winner! Selected British Art from the Saatchi Collection 1987–97', in *Sensation: Young British Art from the Saatchi Collection*, pp. 26–34, *passim*.
103 Bussel, 'Jake and Dinos Chapman', in ibid., p. 195; Hall, 'Collaborating with Catastrophe', p. 213.
104 Maloney, 'Everyone's a Winner!', p. 32.
105 Otherwise the representation would actually *be* the thing it represents and we would not have the critical capacity to distinguish between a representation and what it represents.
106 Crimp, 'The Photographic Activity', pp. 108–12; and Crimp, 'Appropriating Appropriation', pp. 126–37.
107 Newhall, Nancy, 'Edward Weston and the Nude' (1952), in B. Newhall and A. Conger (eds), *Edward Weston Omnibus: A Critical Anthology* (Gibbs Smith, Salt Lake City, 1984), p. 103.
108 Crimp, 'The Photographic Activity', p. 119.
109 Ibid.
110 Crimp, by the 1990s, had become aware of this. Higonnet cites an article published in *Art in America* (1990) where Crimp 'recanted his position on Weston's and Levine's *Neil*s, writing of a 'blindness' and 'a failure of theory, generally'. He had decided that the content of the *Neil*s did matter after all. Ibid., p. 137. See Crimp, 'The Boys in my Bedroom', *Art in America* 78:2, February (1990), pp. 47–9. The blind spot of postmodernism that Crimp indicates relates to the incapacity of post-structuralist theory to account for how images provoke desire, not for themselves, but for what they *represent*.
111 From the critical viewpoint of 1990s visual culture, as Anne Higonnet has noted, it had become possible to appreciate that both modernism and the postmodernist position ostensibly opposed to it 'insisted on the formal autonomy of Weston's

photographs by making a categorical distinction between reality and representation'. Higonnet, Anne, *Pictures of Innocence*, p. 135.

112 I consider defences of the Chapmans' work that propose *laughter* as a means of coping with its (morally) disturbing aspects a version of this strategy. For a recent example, see Tanya Barson's essay in the *Bad Art for Bad People* catalogue, 'Powers of Laughter', in Chapman, *Bad Art for Bad People*, pp. 67–85.

113 The classic treatment is Kant, *The Critique of Judgment*, §5, §11; see also Bullough, 'Psychical Distance' and Stolnitz, 'The Aesthetic Attitude'; for commentary see Guyer, Paul, 'Kant's Conception of Fine Art', *Journal of Aesthetics and Art Criticism*, 52:3 (1994), pp. 275–85; p. 277; Podro, 'Kant and the Aesthetic Imagination', pp. 51–70; Freeland, *But is it Art?*, p. 12. See also Carroll, Nöel, 'Aesthetic Experience: A Question of Content', in Kieran (ed.), *Aesthetics and the Philosophy of Art*, pp. 69–97; p. 71; and Korsmeyer, Carolyn, 'Terrible Beauties', in ibid., pp. 51–63; pp. 59–60.

114 Stolnitz, 'The Aesthetic Attitude', pp. 80–1.

115 Maloney, 'The Chapman Bros.', pp. 64–7 (see below).

116 Julius, *Transgressions*, p. 132.

117 Ibid.

118 In a recent art-obscenity case that has been the subject of detailed documentary, the director of the Cincinnati Contemporary Arts Centre, Dennis Barrie, was charged for 'pandering obscenity and showing minors in a state of nudity' during the centre's 1990 Robert Mapplethorpe exhibition *The Perfect Moment*. During the subsequent trial, expert witnesses testified for the defence that Mapplethorpe's work could not be considered obscene because it was *Art*. The burden therefore rested upon witnesses for the defence to prove that these images could be appreciated *aesthetically*. Then the work could be defined as art and its problematic aspects excused (on the basis of the identification of art and moral edification). It was possible, the expert witnesses argued, to screen out the content of the photographs by making a conceptual distinction between the content and the form of Mapplethorpe's work. If the form is then focused on in isolation from – and in opposition to – the content, the artistically significant elements will become evident: 'careful lighting, classical composition, and elegant sculptural shapes' will immediately come to the fore and the content (however disturbing) will seem secondary, irrelevant, artistically inferior (Freeland, *But is it Art?* p. 17). On the 1990 Cincinnati trial see Merkel, Jayne, 'Report from Cincinnati: Art on Trial', *Art in America* December (1990), pp. 41–52; see also Bolton, Richard (ed.), *Culture Wars: Documents for the Recent Controversies in the Arts* (New Press, New York, 1992), and Hughes, *The Culture of Complaint*, pp. 133–73.

119 Freeland, *But is it Art?*, p. 16.

120 Maloney, 'The Chapman Bros.', p. 66.

121 Chapman, in Norris, 'The Royal Academy of Porn.'

122 'One of the things that is central to the production of our art', Jake Chapman explains, 'is the cynical, pessimistic, fatalistic view that the work will always be a part of, recuperated to, the very discourse that it has distaste for.' Chapman in Baker, 'On Georges Bataille', np.

123 Chapman, *Artshock*.

124 Hyman, Lawrence W., 'Morality and Literature – The Necessary Conflict', *British Journal of Aesthetics* 24:2, Spring (1984), pp. 149–55; p. 150.
125 Devereaux, 'Beauty and Evil', p. 246.
126 Ibid., p. 247.
127 Falconer, 'Doctorin' the Retardis'; and Fogle, 'A Scatological Aesthetics'.
128 Devereaux, 'Beauty and Evil', p. 243.
129 If something 'counts as art', according to Norman Rosenthal, the co-organiser of the *Sensation* exhibition, 'it is *ipso facto* moral'. Rosenthal in Daniels, 'The Royal Academy is Degrading Us'.
130 Murdoch, Iris, *Existentialists and Mystics: Writings on Philosophy and Literature* (Chatto, London, 1997).
131 Reardon, Valerie, 'Whose Image is it Anyway?', *Art Monthly* 195, April (1996), p. 45.
132 Ibid.
133 Chapman, in Fogle, 'A Scatological Aesthetics'.
134 Higonnet, *Pictures of Innocence*, p. 133.
135 Sturges, Jock, *Radiant Identities* (Aperture, New York, 1994); Mann, Sally, *Immediate Family* (Phaidon Press, London and New York, 1993); Gearon, Tierney, *I Am a Camera* (for details see below).
136 Higonnet, *Pictures of Innocence*, p. 195.
137 Tierney Gearon showed fifteen photos at the *I Am a Camera* exhibition at the Saatchi Gallery in 2001. The series included pictures of her children Michael and Emilee (aged six and four) naked or partially clothed (sometimes wearing masks). Officers from Scotland Yard's obscene publications unit visited the gallery, in response, they claimed, to complaints via the newspaper, *News of the World*. A police inspector ordered the removal of two of the photos and threatened prosecution for failure to comply. The Director for Public Prosecutions announced on 16 March 2001 that there would be no further action and no prosecution of the gallery or its director. See Lydiate, Henry, 'I Am a Camera: An Inspector Calls', *Art Monthly* 245, April (2001), pp. 48–9; Toynbee, Polly, 'For Shame! The Arts Versus the Plod', *Modern Painters*, Summer (2001), pp. 18–20; Trevis, Di, 'Working the Mask: Why Tierney Gearon Was Playing with Fire', *Modern Painters*, Summer (2001), pp. 21–3; Grant, Simon, 'Saatchi Gallery Spared Child-Porn Case', *Art News* May (2001), p. 108.
138 Ibid. See also: Codd, Maria, 'Representing Children: The Maternal Photographer. *The Immediate Family* Project by Sally Mann', in O'Kelly (ed.), *Thought Lines 5*, pp. 39–49.
139 Apter, Emily, 'Just Because You're a Man', *Make* 75, April–May (1997), pp. 3–8; p. 7.
140 Ibid.
141 Ibid., pp. 7–8.
142 Crimp, 'The Boys in my Bedroom', pp. 47–9.
143 Higonnet, *Pictures of Innocence*, p. 195.
144 Lydiate, 'I Am a Camera: An Inspector Calls', p. 48.
145 Julius, *Transgressions*, p. 141.
146 Mapplethorpe, in Higonnet, *Pictures of Innocence*, p. 168.
147 Danto, in ibid.

148 Ibid., pp. 168–9.
149 Ibid.
150 Gearon, in Grant, 'Saatchi Gallery Spared', p. 108.
151 Mann in Codd, 'Representing Children', p. 43.
152 Ibid., p. 40.
153 Ibid.
154 Crimp, 'The Boys in my Bedroom'.
155 Codd, 'Representing Children', p. 44.
156 A photograph is never merely an image, 'it is also a trace, something directly stencilled off the real, like a footprint or a death mask'. Sontag, *On Photography*, p. 154. The form of the photograph ensures that its content is indexical, that its referent is a *real existent*. However, in 1995, US senator Orrin Hatch proposed an amendment to the then current federal law that can prosecute only on the basis of visual representations that depict real children (i.e. photographic material). He proposed that the law be amended to include any sexually explicit image that involves reference to minors. As Higonnet remarks, this specifically targeted computer-generated pornographic imagery. See Congressional Record, US Senate 13 September 1995 in Higonnet, www.ipce.info/library _3/files/higonnet.htm.
157 Ballard, J.G., *The Atrocity Exhibition* (Flamingo, London, 1993), p. 58.
158 Ibid.
159 Julius, *Transgressions*, p. 142.
160 Maloney, 'Chapman Bros.', p. 67.

4 Fearless Speech

1 Nussbaum, *Hiding from Humanity*, p. 216.
2 Brown, Neal, 'I Need Art Like I Need God: Interview with Tracey Emin', in Brown et al. *Art From the UK* (Sammlung Goetz, Munich, 1997) pp. 63–71.
3 Ibid. p. 68; see also Brown, Neal, *Tracey Emin* (Tate Publishing, London, 2006), p. 28; also Gisbourne, Mark, 'Life into Art', *Contemporary Visual Arts* 20 (1998), pp. 31–2.
4 Emin in Brown, 'I Need Art Like I Need God', p. 68.
5 'January 1977 – I was raped down an alley.' Emin, Tracey, 'CV Part I, Curriculum Vitae November 1962 to December 1995', in Tracey Emin, *Works 1963–2006* (Rizzoli, New York, 2006), p. 146; see also *Exploration of the Soul* (1994), Counter Gallery (London, 2003) and Emin, Tracey, *Strangeland* (Hodder & Stoughton, London, 2005), pp. 23–4. In the latter, she also suggests that she was sexually abused by her mother's lover Chris when she was very young (aged nine or ten), ibid., pp. 14–15. See also the monoprint *Fucking Down an Ally – 16-5-95*.
6 Brown, *Tracey Emin*, p. 28.
7 Gisbourne, 'Life into Art', p. 31.
8 Emin, *Strangeland*, p. 16: 'I'm going to get you / You cunt you / FUCKING BASTARD / And when I do – The / Whole world will know / That you destroyed part / Of my childhood.' See also: *Top Spot*, Tartan Films (2004). 'When I was 14–15 / There was nothing to my life / but dancing and sex . . . like a bird / I thought I was free – Tracey Emin 1978.' (In Emin, *Strangeland*, p. 37.)

9 Emin in Appleyard, Bryan, 'The Girl Most Likely to . . .', *Sunday Times*, 16 October 2005, p. 8.
10 Emin in Wright, Karen, 'Maid of Margate', *Arts Books & Culture Magazine, Independent on Sunday*, 28 May 2005, p. 6.
11 Brown, *Tracey Emin*, pp. 111–21.
12 Emin in Wright, 'Maid of Margate', p. 6.
13 Brown, *Tracey Emin*, p. 10.
14 Spencer, Liese, notes for *Top Spot*. *Top Spot*, Tartan Films (2004).
15 Stallabrass, *High Art Lite*, p. 41.
16 Brown, *Tracey Emin*, p. 10.
17 Maloney, 'Everyone's a Winner!', p. 31.
18 Smithard, Paula, 'It's a Tenuous Line Between Sincerity and Sensationalism', *Make* 76, June–July (1997), pp. 27–9; p. 29.
19 Gibbs, Michael, 'Tracey Emin: Stedelijk Museum, Amsterdam', *Art Monthly* 262 (2003), pp. 32–3; p. 33.
20 Muir, Gregor, 'Like a Hole in the Head', *Parkett* 63 (2001), pp. 36–42.
21 Ibid. p. 42.
22 Neal Brown's writing is a prominent and welcome exception to this generalisation.
23 Stallabrass, *High Art Lite*, p. 42. We could perhaps instance Deborah Cherry's solecism as an example of this: 'The title of *My Bed* suggests ownership, someone to whom the bed belongs.' Cherry, Deborah, 'On the Move: *My Bed*, 1998–1999', in M. Merck and C. Townsend (eds), *The Art of Tracey Emin* (Thames & Hudson, London, 2002), pp. 134–54.
24 Summed up most succinctly in another of Stallabrass's aphorisms, 'It's so unmediated, I wonder if it's art,' this critical attitude can be shown to be a direct legacy of conventional aesthetic theory and its dogma of disinterested contemplation.
25 Just as it was in the infamous Mapplethorpe 1990 obscenity trial in Cincinnati (see Chapter 3).
26 Paula Smithard's proposition is representative of this objection: 'So personal is some of the work,' she writes, 'that to criticise it is somehow to violate the artist' (Smithard, 'It's a Tenuous Line', p. 29).
27 One of Stallabrass's main criticisms of Emin's work is that it is very difficult if not impossible to clearly distinguish between the art and the artist: 'to reject the art', he argues, entails 'heartlessly' rejecting the artist, who, he adds, in the same ironic tone, is presented as 'a vulnerable-tough fighter-victim' (Stallabrass, *High Art Lite*, p. 42).
28 Norman, *The Moral Philosophers*, p. 45.
29 Budd, Malcolm, 'Artistic Value', in P. Lamarque and S.H. Olsen (eds), *Aesthetics and the Philosophy of Art: The Analytic Tradition* (Blackwell, Oxford, 2004), pp. 262–73; p. 266.
30 'Art can teach us about what is ethically correct', Gaut, 'The Ethical Criticism of Art', p. 290; the cognitive value of art according to Carroll is considered to be 'the opportunity it affords for deepening our moral understanding', Carroll, 'Moderate Moralism', p. 236. See also Jacobson, 'In Praise of Immoral Art', p. 193.
31 Townsend, Chris, 'Heart of Glass: Reflection, Reprise and Riposte in Self-

Representation', in Merck and Townsend (eds), *The Art of Tracey Emin*, pp. 79–101; p. 90.

32 Osborne, Peter, 'Greedy *Kunst*', in ibid., pp. 40–59; p. 50.

33 Smithard, 'It's a Tenuous Line', p. 29.

34 See Brown, *Tracey Emin*, pp. 8–9, for brief analysis of this consensus.

35 Foucault, Michel, *Fearless Speech* (ed. J. Pearson) (Semiotext(e), Los Angeles, 2001).

36 See Demetriou, Danielle, 'Fire Destroys Saatchi Art', *Independent*, 26 May 2004; also, Johnson, Andrew, 'Fears for Saatchi's Collection After Fire Guts Art Warehouse', ibid. 'Reports last night suggested that Emin's *Everyone I Have Ever Slept With, 1963–1994* [*sic*] – a tent on the inside of which are embroidered 102 names, including those of her family – and *Hell* by Jake and Dinos Chapman may have been lost . . . .' See also, Sears, Neal, 'Warehouse Fire Destroys Saatchi's Art Collection; "Devastated" tycoon loses his multimillion-pound works and Shirly Conran's set of paintings goes up in flames', *Daily Mail*, 26 May 2004.

37 See Benjamin, Walter, 'On the Image of Proust' (trans. H. Zohn), in Benjamin, *Selected Writings Volume* 2, pp. 237–8.

38 Richter, Gerhard, 'Acts of Self-Portraiture: Benjamin's Confessional and Literary Writings', in D.S. Ferris (ed.), *The Cambridge Companion to Walter Benjamin* (Cambridge University Press, Cambridge, 2004), pp. 221–37; p. 221.

39 McGrath, Melanie, 'Something's Wrong', *Tate Magazine* 1 (1998), available online at www.tate.org.uk/magazine/issue1/something.htm.

40 See de Man, Paul, 'Autobiography as De-facement', in M. McQuillan (ed.), *Deconstruction: A Reader* (Edinburgh University Press, Edinburgh, 2000), pp. 171–4.

41 Betterton, Rosemary, 'Why is My Art Not as Good as Me?', in Merck and Townsend (eds), *The Art of Tracey Emin*, pp. 22–39; p. 33.

42 Kristeva, *Powers of Horror*, p. 58.

43 Januszczak, Waldemar, 'Eminism', *Sunday Times Magazine*, 12 July (1998), pp. 28–35.

44 Emin in ibid., p. 34.

45 Ibid.

46 Emin, 'Tracey Emin CV Part I' (1997), in Emin, *Works 1963–2006*, pp. 148–9. For details see *Strangeland* (*passim*) and video, *How it Feels* (1996).

47 Emin, *Works 1963–2006*, p. 280.

48 Emin, *Strangeland*, p. 158.

49 Ibid., p. 22.

50 See Brown, *Tracey Emin*, p. 83: 'Emin's presence was located and defined by other people, but remained isolated and alone, somewhere between solitude and loneliness.'

51 Emin describes the background of *My Bed* as follows: 'I woke up after four days of complete abuse and total despair. I got up to get some water and came back and just looked at this room and thought Ugh – fuck! I closed my eyes and thought "I could have died in there and people would have just found my body." But I didn't, so this room actually saved me. There was something beautiful about it, something enchanting, something charming, like a damsel in distress saying "help me".' Emin, in Wright, 'Maid of Margate', pp. 5–6. See also Bragg, Melvyn, 'Tracey Emin', *The South Bank Show*, LWT, 2001.

52 Merck, Mandy, 'Bedtime', in Merck and Townsend (eds), *The Art of Tracey Emin*, pp. 119–33; p. 128.
53 See Deleuze, Gilles and Felix Guattari, *Nomadology: The War Machine* (trans. B. Massumi) (Semiotext(e), Columbia University, New York, 1986), p. 52.
54 First shown in Sagacho Exhibition Space, Tokyo in 1998, *My Bed* was part of an installation titled *Sobasex* (*My Cunt is Wet With Fear*) which included (*inter alia*) the noose, neon pieces, two suitcases bound together, and a video piece: *Homage to Edvard Munch and All My Dead Children*. The noose was removed for later installations, including the Tate's 1999 Turner Prize showing. See Emin in 'Break on Through to the Other Side', in Emin, *Works 1963–2006*, p. 251. Her solo show at the Lehmann Maupin Gallery, New York, in 1999 (*Every Part of Me's Bleeding*) also included the noose. Deborah Cherry's essay 'On the Move', in Merck and Townsend (eds), *The Art of Tracey Emin,* pp. 134–54, tracks the nomadic peregrinations of *My Bed*.
55 See Cashell, Kieran, 'Sing Me to Sleep: Suicide, Philosophy, and The Smiths', in S. Campbell and C. Coulter (eds), *Why Pamper Life's Complexities* (Manchester University Press, Manchester, 2009).
56 Camus, Albert, *The Myth of Sisyphus* (Penguin, London, 2000), p. 11.
57 Emin, *Strangeland*, p. 167. See also Emin in Bragg, where she explains that to paint following her abortion seemed to her an utterly false response.
58 As transcribed in Emin, *Works 1963–2006*, p. 149; see also Emin in Brown, *Tracey Emin*, p. 30.
59 Emin, *Strangeland*, p. 168.
60 Emin and Self in Vara, Renée, 'Another Dimension', in Merck and Townsend (eds), *The Art of Tracey Emin*, pp. 172–94; p. 190.
61 Wright, Karen, 'Letters and Luggage: Tracey Emin Unpacks her Thoughts on Love, God and Needlework', *Modern Painters* (2006) pp. 34–7.
62 Preece, Robert, 'Artist Over – and In – the Broadsheets', *Parkett*, 63 (2001), p. 53, my emphasis.
63 See Locke, John, *An Essay Concerning Human Understanding* (Penguin, Harmondsworth, 1997).
64 Hospers, John, *An Introduction to Philosophical Analysis* (Routledge, London and New York, 1956), p. 415.
65 Kundera, Milan, *The Curtain: An Essay in Seven Parts* (Faber & Faber, London, 2007), p. 149.
66 Benjamin, 'On the Image of Proust', p. 238.
67 Critchley, Simon, 'Post-Deconstructive Subjectivity?' in Simon Critchley, *Ethics, Politics, Subjectivity* (Verso, London and New York, 1999), p. 64.
68 Critchley, Simon, 'The Original Traumatism: Levinas and Psychoanalysis', in R. Kearney and M. Dooley (eds), *Questioning Ethics* (Routledge, London and New York, 1999), pp. 230–42; p. 235.
69 Levinas, Emmanuel, *Otherwise than Being or Beyond Essence* (trans. A. Lingis) (Martinus Nijhoff, The Hague, 1981); see also Levinas, Emmanuel, 'Substitution', in S. Hand (ed.), *The Levinas Reader* (Blackwell, Oxford, 1989), pp. 88–125; p. 105.
70 Critchley, 'The Original Traumatism', p. 235.
71 Wyschogrod, Edith, 'Towards a Postmodern Ethics: Corporeality and Alterity', in

E. Wyschogrod and G.P. McKenny (eds), *The Ethical* (Blackwell, Oxford, 2003), pp. 54–65; p. 63.

72 Critchley, Simon, *Infinitely Demanding: Ethics of Commitment, Politics of Resistance* (Verso, London and New York, 2007), p. 51.

73 Ibid., p. 62.

74 Levinas, 'Substitution', p. 101.

75 Levinas, Emmanuel 'Philosophy and Awakening (1977)', (trans. R.A. Cohen and M.B. Smith), in Emmanuel Levinas, *Discovering Existence with Husserl* (Northwestern University Press, Evanston, IL, 1998), pp. 169–80; pp. 177–8.

76 Indeed, with reference to Levinas's hypothesis of the openness of the self to otherness, the tent becomes less about sleep than about *wakefulness*: Levinas believed that the self is stirred to a profound wakeful state by the presence of the other.

77 Salecl, Renata, *On Anxiety* (Routledge, London and New York, 2004), p. 72.

78 Ibid.

79 Brown describes the blank verse of the voice as 'Analogous to the line of her monoprints in its diction', *Tracey Emin*, p. 78.

80 Brown, 'I Need Art Like I Need God', p. 63.

81 See Emin, Tracey, *Why I Never Became a Dancer* (1995); transcribed in Emin, *Works 1963–2006*, pp. 194–9; see also *Strangeland*, pp. 42–6 for a slightly different version of the text.

82 Emin, *Works 1963–2006*, p. 196.

83 Ibid.

84 Ibid. p. 198.

85 Ibid. See also Brown, *Tracey Emin*, p. 79.

86 Grieve, Lara, 'Tracey Emin', *Artists in Profile*, 2003, Grieve, Lara, 'Tracey Emin', BBC *Artists in Profile*, 2003, www.bbc.co.uk/arts/news_comment/artistsinprofile/emin.shtml (site since disabled: article partially available at http://talentdevelop.com/visualarts2.html).

87 Vara, 'Another Dimension', p. 190.

88 'It looked like real gold.' Morgan, Stuart, 'A History of I', *Frieze* 34 (1997), pp. 56–61; p. 59. Townsend, Chris, *Art and Death* (I.B.Tauris, London and New York, 2008).

89 Brown, *Tracey Emin*, p. 100. See also interview with Emin in *Saatchi Gallery 100: The Work That Changed British Art,* DVD (Illuminations, London, 2004).

90 Kristeva, *Powers of Horror*, p. 53.

91 Jacobson, 'In Praise of Immoral Art', p. 158.

92 Gaut, Berys, 'The Paradox of Horror', in Neill and Ridley (eds), *Arguing About Art*, pp. 295–307; p. 302.

93 Solomon, 'Peter Singer's Expanding Circle', pp. 64–84; p. 75.

94 Nussbaum, Martha C., *Love's Knowledge* (Oxford University Press, Oxford and New York, 1990), pp. 291, 41. See also Nussbaum, 'Flawed Crystals', pp. 25–50.

95 Noddings, *Caring*, p. 137.

96 Institutional aesthetics, with its emphases on symbolic pictorial form, iconic representation and mediation, facilitates, she argues, 'contemplative distance', thus traducing and disrespecting 'the [ethical] encounter with the Other'. Glowacka,

Dorota, 'Disappearing Traces: Emmanuel Levinas, Ida Fink's Literary Testimony, and Holocaust Art', in D. Glowacka and S. Boos (eds), *Between Ethics and Aesthetics: Crossing the Boundaries* (State University of New York Press, New York, 2002), pp. 97–116; p. 112.

97 Williams, Bernard, 'Morality and the Emotions', in Downie and Telfer, *Respect for Persons*, p. 27. See also, Williams, Bernard, *Shame and Necessity* (University of California Press, Berkeley and Los Angeles, 1993).

98 Ibid.

99 Wyschogrod, 'Towards a Postmodern Ethics', p. 63.

100 Maclagan, W.G., 'Respect for Persons as a Moral Principle', in Downie and Telfer, *Respect for Persons*, p. 24.

101 Healy, Lorna, 'We Love You Tracey: Pop-Cultural Strategies in Tracey Emin's Videos', in Merck and Townsend (eds), *The Art of Tracey Emin*, p. 166.

102 Preece, 'Artist Over – and In – the Broadsheets', p. 52.

103 Lehmann, Ulrich, 'The Trademark Tracey Emin', in Merck and Townsend (eds), *The Art of Tracey Emin*, p. 213n.

104 *Saatchi Gallery 100* DVD.

105 Levinas, Emmanuel, *On Escape* (trans. B. Bergo) (Stanford University Press, Stanford, 2003), p. 64.

106 Ibid.

107 Sartre, Jean-Paul, *Being and Nothingness: An Essay on Phenomenological Ontology* (trans. Hazel E. Barnes) (Methuen, London, 1958).

108 Ibid., p. 259.

109 Ibid., p. 260.

110 Ibid., p. 261.

111 Warnock, Mary in ibid., p. xi.

112 Warnock, Mary, *Existentialist Ethics* (Macmillan, London, 1967), p. 27; see also Warnock, Mary, *An Intelligent Person's Guide to Ethics* (Duckworth, London, 1998), p. 84.

113 Ibid., (my emphasis).

114 Ibid.

115 McGrath, 'Something's Wrong', p. 4.

116 Bragg, 'Tracey Emin'.

117 Emin, in Morgan, 'The Story of I', p. 60.

118 Emin, in Bragg, 'Tracey Emin'.

119 'I mean I know when you were pregnant with Paul and I, that you didn't want to have us to [hmm.] to the point where you actually booked into a clinic to have an abortion [hmm.]. And it was at the stroke of 12 you got out of the bed and changed your mind and left the abortion clinic.' *Conversation With my Mum* (2001) as transcribed in Emin, *Works 1963–2006*, pp. 302–15.

120 Levinas, *On Escape*.

121 Ibid., p. 63.

122 Ibid., my emphasis.

123 Ibid.

124 Morgan, Michael L., *On Shame*, (Routledge, London and New York, 2008), pp. 91–5.

125 Critchley, Simon, 'Demanding Approval: On the Ethics of Alain Badiou', *Radical*

Philosophy 100, (April 2000), pp. 3–10, available online at www.radicalphilosophy.com/default.asp?channel_id=2188&editorial_id=10066.

126 Critchley, *Infinitely Demanding*, p. 22.
127 Kundera, *The Curtain*, pp. 139–40.
128 Brown, *Tracey Emin*, p. 79.
129 Emin, *Strangeland*, p. 168.
130 Foucault, *Fearless Speech*, p. 166.
131 Ibid.
132 Ibid., p. 165.
133 Ibid., p. 170.
134 Ibid., p. 12.
135 Ibid., p. 102.
136 Ibid., p. 100.
137 Ibid., p. 12.
138 Ibid., p. 14.
139 Ibid., p. 16.
140 Stallabrass, Julian, 'Making a Show of Herself', *Evening Standard*, 13 November 2002.
141 The traditional aesthetic paradigm, it can be shown, is a paradigm that requires art to be re-presentational, that needs its art to be fictitious and constructed, that prescribes and idealises the condition of mendacity for art and, finally, that prohibits any claim to truth as audacious.
142 Foucault, *Fearless Speech*, p. 15.
143 Ibid.
144 Ibid.
145 Expressing the truth in this sense involves risk (involves, in the extreme case, a risk to the speaker's life). Ibid., p. 17.
146 Ibid., p. 16.
147 Ibid., p. 17.
148 Ibid.
149 Diogenes famously put his life at risk by publicly insulting Alexander the Great. Ibid.
150 Ibid., p. 164.
151 Ibid., p. 146.
152 Ibid.
153 Ibid., pp. 148, 149.
154 Ibid., p. 165.
155 Ibid., p. 106.
156 Ibid., p. 97.
157 Ibid., p. 106.
158 See Foucault, Michel, *The Care of the Self* (Random House, New York, 1986).
159 Nussbaum, *Hiding From Humanity*.
160 Ibid., p. 173.
161 Ideological pressures positively value concepts of perfection, functional stability and, above all, *rationality* as virtues. The valorisation of these concepts involves the downgrading of emotional responses; social competence is considered to depend on this active repression of emotions. As a consequence, emotions have been

stigmatised as weak, destructive and irrational. As a result, 'need and vulnerability are viewed as shameful' (ibid., p. 199).

162 Ibid., pp. 206–7.
163 Ibid., p. 207.
164 Nussbaum acknowledges that emotion is 'always moral in a broad sense of that term' (ibid., p. 204).
165 See Critchley's discussion of this process in *Infinitely Demanding*, pp. 41–2.
166 Nussbaum, *Hiding From Humanity*, p. 212.
167 Ibid., p. 213.
168 Morgan, *On Shame*, p. 91.
169 Ibid., pp. 96–7
170 Ibid., p. 97.

5 Horrorshow

1 Emin, in Brown, 'I Need Art Like I Need God', p. 67.
2 Hirst, in Burn, Gordon and Damien Hirst, *On the Way to Work* (Faber & Faber, London, 2000), p. 35.
3 Julius, *Transgressions*, p. 142.
4 For a brief history of the shark, its gradual decomposition and eventual replacement, see the report by Carol Vogel, 'Damien Bites Back', *Observer*, 19 November 2006, pp. 8–10.
5 The assemblage of fish in smaller-scale containers, *Isolated Elements Swimming in the Same Direction for the Purposes of Understanding* (1991) also pre-dated the shark.
6 Recent reports suggest that Hirst is seeking to capitalise on his early success by cannibalising his most celebrated pieces; he is currently organising to have smaller-scale replicas of his work made. The *Sunday Times* reported that Hirst recently acquired another shark from Australia; however, this specimen, measuring 'only' five feet (150 cm) is much smaller than the 'original'. *The Wrath of God* has been sold for £2.28m to Leeum Samsung Museum of Art in Seoul. Dunphy in Brooks, Richard, 'Hirst Earns 3m for Second Shark', *Sunday Times*, 19 March 2006, p. 12.
7 There are at least three versions of this work.
8 See review: Self, Will, 'A Steady Iron-Hard Jet', *Modern Painters* Summer (1994), pp. 50–2.
9 See interview: Bowie, David, '(s)Now', *Modern Painters* Summer (1996), pp. 36–9.
10 See review: Searle, Adrian, 'So What's New?', *G2*, *Guardian*, 9 September 2003, pp. 12–15.
11 *Beyond Belief* was at the White Cube Gallery in Hoxton Square and at Mason's Yard in central London from 3 June to 7 July 2007. The animal works in this instance were eclipsed by the media mania surrounding the *memento mori* of bling: *For the Love of God*, a human skull cast in platinum and encrusted with 8,601 'VVS to flawless' D-coloured diamonds with the real teeth re-inserted back into the mandible. For the record, the most necessary definition of this work, despite the

mundus vult decipi of 'distinguished' art historians willing to describe the piece as 'celestial', is that of Will Self: 'the skull', he writes, 'is a tangible exclamation mark at the end of this era of excess.' Self, Will, 'To Die For', *Sunday Telegraph Magazine*, 2 June 2007, p. 28; see also Damien Hirst, *Beyond Belief*, press release, White Cube, 2007; also Januszczak, Waldemar, 'On Sparkling Form', *Sunday Times Culture*, 3 June 2007, pp. 18–19.

12 Volpe, Nicole, 'Catholics, Animal Rights Activists Protest Art', Reuters, 3 October 1999.

13 The work he intended to exhibit, *Two Fucking, Two Watching* (a quartet of peeled cattle, one on top of another simulating intercourse by means of a hydraulic apparatus, two more on either side – all in a vitrine *without formaldehyde*) was vetoed by New York sanitation officials; this delayed the show for six months. Lyall, Sarah, 'Is it Art, or Just Dead Meat', *New York Times*, 12 November 1995.

14 Gibbons, Fiachra, 'Hirst Accused of Sadism Over Butterfly Collage', *Guardian*, 15 August 2003.

15 Hirst, in *Furball* interview: www.artfact.com/artist/hirst-damien-t9wpclihrn; www.intute.ac.uk/artsandhumanities/?id=2028.

16 Ibid.

17 He continues: '. . . if you're reading it metaphorically that's just you. . . . You know, like with the shark, I did think of doing a light box or a painting, a big painting of a shark. But it was like no one is going to believe that because we are so used to images. So I just wanted to make something real. Real enough to frighten you.' Cicelyn, Eduardo, Mario Codognato and Mirta D'Argenzio, *Damien Hirst, Napolia Museo Acheologico Nazionale* (Electa, Naples, 2004), p. 116.

18 Hirst, *Furball* interview.

19 Ibid. See also Kent, *Shark Infested Waters*, p. 37.

20 Warnock, *An Intelligent Person's Guide to Ethics*.

21 Ibid., p. 69.

22 Ibid.

23 Singer, Peter, 'All Animals are Equal', in P. Singer (ed.), *Applied Ethics* (Oxford University Press, Oxford, 1986), pp. 215–28; p. 223.

24 Ibid., p. 217.

25 Ibid., p. 220.

26 Regan, Tom, *The Case for Animal Rights* (University of California Press, Berkeley, 1983), cited in Gruen, Lori, 'Animals', in P. Singer (ed.), *A Companion to Ethics* (Blackwell, Oxford, 1991), p. 346.

27 Ibid.

28 Regan, Tom, 'Empty Cages: Animal Rights and Vivisection', in T. Gilland (ed.), *Animal Experimentation: Good or Bad?* (Hodder & Stoughton, London, 2002), pp. 19–36; p. 25.

29 Singer, Peter, *Writings on an Ethical Life* (Fourth Estate, London, 2000), p. xvii.

30 Singer, 'All Animals are Equal', p. 221.

31 Singer, Peter, 'From *Animal Liberation*', in Singer, *Writings on an Ethical Life*, p. 24.

32 Singer, 'All Animals are Equal', p. 222.

33 Bentham, Jeremy, *An Introduction to the Principles of Morals and Legislation* (1789)

(Methuen, London, 1996), ch. XVII; cited in Singer, *Writings on an Ethical Life*, p. 33.

34 Singer, 'All Animals are Equal', p. 222.
35 Gruen, 'Animals', p. 349.
36 Ibid.
37 Julius, *Transgressions*, p. 145.
38 Ibid., p. 140. The installation was intended for the *Hors limites* exhibition at the Pompidou Centre, Paris in 1994. 'A scandal ensued,' Julius reports, and a 'compromise reached: in place of the insects themselves, there was a note explaining the artist's conception, together with various documents that the controversy had generated', ibid., p. 140.
39 Baker, Steve, 'Haunted by the Animal', *Tate Magazine 26*, September (2001), pp. 42–7. www.ekac.org/haunted.html.
40 Ibid.
41 Baker, Steve, *The Postmodern Animal* (Reaktion Books, London, 2000).
42 Ibid., pp. 11–12
43 Baker, 'Haunted by the Animal'.
44 Singer, 'From *Animal Liberation*', p. 42.
45 See Nietzsche: 'in creation, however, destruction is included.' *The Will to Power* (trans. W. Kaufmann), in R. Grimm and C.M. y Vedia (eds), *Philosophical Writings* (Continuum, New York, 1995), pp. 79–80.
46 Gruen, 'Animals', p. 349.
47 Singer in Iggers, Jeremy, 'Peter Singer: Interview', *Philosophy Now* 31, March/April (2001), pp. 16–17; p. 17.
48 Regan, 'Empty Cages', p. 20.
49 On the mad science genre of horror see Jones, *Horror*, pp. 50–69; and Freeland, Cynthia, *The Naked and the Undead: Evil and the Appeal of Horror* (Westview, Boulder, CO, 2000).
50 Hirst in Bonami, Francesco, 'Damien Hirst: The Exploded View of the Artist', *Flash Art* 29:189 (1996), pp. 112–16; p. 113.
51 *This Little Piggy Went to Market, This Little Piggy Stayed at Home* (1996) also exhibited in *Sensation*.
52 See Jamieson (ed.), *Singer and his Critics*; and, in particular, McBryde Johnson, Harriet, 'Unspeakable Conversations', *New York Times Magazine*, 16 February 2003. McBryde Johnson was a lawyer and disability rights activist in Charleston SC (she died on 4 June 2008) and this article documented her meeting and subsequent philosophical discussion with Peter Singer (and his students) at Princeton in 2002. Full text at www.utilitarian.net/singer/about/20030216.htm. Coffey, Mark, 'Ten Reasons Why I Love/Hate Peter Singer', *Philosophy Now* 59, January/February (2007), pp. 28–32.
53 And has been – see Llewelyn, John, 'Am I Obsessed by Bobby? (Humanism of the Other Animal)', in R. Bernasconi and S. Critchley (eds), *Re-Reading Levinas* (Athlone, London, 1991), pp. 234–45. He enquires 'whether Levinas's concept of the neighbour includes the nonhuman animal'. His solution is reluctantly negative: 'In the metaphysical ethics of Levinas I can have direct responsibilities only toward beings that can speak, and this means beings that have a rationality that is presupposed by the universalising reason fundamental in the metaphysical ethics

of Kant' (p. 241). See also Derrida, Jacques, '"Eating Well", or the Calculation of the Subject: an Interview With Jacques Derrida', in E. Cadava, P. Connor and J.L. Nancy (eds), *Who Comes After the Subject?* (Routledge, London and New York, 1991), pp. 96-119; also Derrida, Jacques, *The Animal That Therefore I Am*, (trans. D. Wills), (Fordham University Press, New York, 2008), pp. 369–418.

54 Derrida, *The Animal That Therefore I Am*, p. 27.

55 Nietzsche, Friedrich, *The Gay Science* [*Die fröliche Wissenschaft*, 1887] (trans. W. Kaufmann) (Vintage Books, New York, 1974), p. 168.

56 Noddings, *Caring*, p. 154.

57 Ibid.

58 Ibid.

59 Ibid.

60 Noddings's analysis concludes: 'an ethics of caring is perceptive and creative rather than judgemental. I may, as an individual, be willing to enrich and complicate my ethical life by including some members of the animal kingdom in it but, aside from demanding justification for the infliction of pain, I cannot judge you if you do not decide to complicate your life in a similar fashion.' Ibid., p. 159.

61 Ibid., p. 157.

62 Baker, 'Haunted by the Animal'.

63 Cashell, Kieran, 'Sublimated Horror: Locating the Burkean Sublime in Late 20th Century Aesthetics', paper presented at the *Edmund Burke and Irish Literary Criticism, 1757 to 2007* Conference, Royal Irish Academy, 25 April 2007. (publication forthcoming).

64 Burke, Edmund, *A Philosophical Enquiry into the Origin of our Ideas of the Sublime and Beautiful* (Oxford University Press, Oxford, 1990).

65 'Whatever therefore is terrible, with regard to sight, is sublime too' (Burke, *Enquiry*, Part 2, Section II, p. 53); Terror 'is in all cases whatsoever, either openly or latently the ruling principle of the sublime' (Ibid., Part 2, Section II, p. 54).

66 Ibid., Part 2, Section V, p. 59.

67 Ibid., Part 1, Section VII, p. 36.

68 For an application of this aspect of the Burkean sublime to Barnett Newman's 'avant-garde' paintings, see Lyotard, Jean-François, *The Inhuman* (Polity, Cambridge, 1991), p. 99.

69 Burke, *Enquiry*, Part 2, Section I, p. 53.

70 Hirst and Burn, *On the Way to Work*, p. 19.

71 Burke, *Enquiry*, Part 2, Section II, p. 53.

72 Hirst, in interview, on Damien Hirst website: www.artfact.com/artist/hirst-damien-t9wpclihrn.

73 We are not forced to confront death in an obvious sense, in the way, for instance, Bill Viola forces us to 'see' death happening in the *Nantes Triptych*. What cannot be shown, what must be passed over in silence, can be more subtly, and therefore more powerfully, suggested by obscure means.

74 'Being-towards-death is essentially anxiety,' Heidegger writes. Death is the privation of all possibility, that is to say, it can be defined as the possibility of the impossibility of my own existence (and the termination of the ground of existence as such). Heidegger, Martin, *Being and Time*, (trans. J. Macquarrie and E. Robinson) (Blackwell, Oxford, 1962) § 53 p. 310; see also p. 263.

75 Hirst in Kent, *Shark Infested Waters*, p. 36.
76 Burke, *Enquiry*, Part 1, Section VII, p. 36.
77 Hirst, in Kent, *Shark Infested Waters*, p. 37.
78 Hirst, www.artfact.com/artist/hirst-damien-t9wpclihrn.
79 Jacobson, 'In Praise of Immoral Art'.
80 Ibid.
81 Ibid., p. 181.
82 Isenberg, Arnold, 'The Aesthetic Function of Language', in Isenberg, *Aesthetics and the Theory of Criticism* (Chicago University Press, Chicago, 1973), quoted in ibid., p. 180.
83 Ibid.
84 Ibid., p. 181, my emphasis.
85 Ibid., p. 162.
86 Ibid.
87 The cognitive theory of artistic value can be defined as the conception that art can facilitate the development of non-trivial knowledge; that the experience of art contributes positively to 'our' knowledge. See Gaut, Berys, 'Art and Cognition', in Kieran (ed.), *Aesthetics and the Philosophy of Art*, pp. 115–26: 'art can nontrivially teach us; . . . [and] this capacity to teach partly determines art's aesthetic value.' He cites as proponents of this theory (among many others) Beardsmore, Carroll, Nussbaum and Nelson Goodman (p. 115).
88 See John, Eileen, 'Artistic Value and Opportunistic Moralism', in M. Kieran (ed.), *Contemporary Debates in Aesthetics and the Philosophy of Art* (Blackwell, Oxford, 2006), pp. 332–41; and Kieran, Matthew, 'Art and Morality', in J. Levinson (ed.), *The Oxford Handbook of Aesthetics* (Oxford University Press, Oxford, 2005) pp. 451–70; and Kieran, Matthew, 'Forbidden Knowledge: the Challenge of Immoralism', in J. Bermudez and S. Gardner (eds), *Art and Morality* (Routledge, London and New York, 2003), pp. 56–73.
89 Kieran, 'Forbidden Knowledge', p. 72.
90 John, 'Artistic Value and Opportunistic Moralism', p. 336.
91 Kieran, 'Forbidden Knowledge', p. 72.
92 Jacobson claims that his defence of immoral art does not constitute a general theory of the relationship between moral and aesthetic value (despite the fact that in the wake of his article many have dubbed his defence 'immoralism'). Baker also defends the unethical practices of artists who (ab)use animals with reference to a cognitive alibi: 'Regardless of ethical stances, it is still materials that count here, creating knowledge and encouraging open and imaginative thought . . .' Baker, 'Haunted by the Animal'.
93 Jacobson, 'In Praise of Immoral Art', p. 167.
94 Hegel, G.W.F., *Science of Logic* (Allen & Unwin, London, 1929), p. 119.
95 Derrida, Jacques, 'The Pit and the Pyramid', in *Margins of Philosophy* (trans. A. Bass) (Harvester Press, Brighton, 1982), pp. 69–108; and Derrida, Jacques, 'Violence and Metaphysics', in *Writing and Difference*, p. 114.
96 *La relève*, Derrida, 'The Pit and the Pyramid', p. 71.
97 Kieran, *Revealing Art*, p. 261.
98 Fuller tried to argue that Graham Sutherland was a 'better artist' than Bacon simply because it was impossible for the critic to accept the moral message that he

received from paintings such as *Three Studies for Figures at the Base of a Crucifixion* (1944). See ibid., p. 177.

99 Ibid.

100 Ibid., p. 178.

101 Ibid., p. 183.

102 Ibid., p. 184.

103 'Since 1993 the artists have sought to make pieces that reflect their immediate encounters and interactions with animals in the wild. The *Raw* exhibition, of work made since 1995, included paintings of lions, zebra, wild dogs and rhinoceros in the African bush, polar bears in the Arctic tundra, tigers and elephants in Nepal, leopards and tigers in India, white sharks in the ocean off South Africa, and ravens, wolves and deer in Minnesota'. Baker, *The Postmodern Animal*, p. 11.

104 Ibid., p. 11–12 (the photographer is Greg Williams).

105 Kieran, *Revealing Art*, p. 193.

106 Ibid., p. 179.

107 By way of a footnote he informs the reader that he 'used to' be a moralist: he 'used to think' that a moral 'defect' in a work of art constituted an artistic flaw. Kieran, *Revealing Art*, p. 261.

108 Ibid., p. 179.

109 Ibid., p. 180.

110 Ibid., p. 191.

111 Ibid., p. 191.

112 Ibid., p. 194.

113 Ibid., p. 193.

114 '. . . part of us does remain revolted and fascinated by the way our brutish animal natures can flatten our higher nature, thus leading us to be appalled at the horror of existence.' Ibid., p. 193.

115 Hyman, Lawrence W., 'Morality and Literature – The Necessary Conflict', *British Journal of Aesthetics* 24:2, Spring (1984), pp. 149–55.

116 Ibid., p. 150.

117 Ibid., p. 155.

118 Ibid., p. 153.

119 Ibid., p. 154.

120 Colie, Rosalie, 'The Energies of Endurance: Biblical Echo in *King Lear*', in R. Colie and F.T. Flahiff, *Some Facets of King Lear: Essays in Prismatic Criticism* (Tornoto University Press, Toronto, 1974), pp. 117–44; p. 119, quoted in ibid., p. 153.

121 Ibid., p. 155.

122 Ibid.

123 Schopenhauer, Arthur, *The World as Will and Representation* (trans. E.F.J. Payne, Vol. I), (Dover, New York, 1958) p. 253 (cited in Lamarque, Peter, 'Tragedy and Moral Value', in P. Lamarque and S.H. Olson (eds), *Aesthetics and the Philosophy of Art: The Analytic Tradition* (Blackwell, Oxford, 2004), pp. 274–82; p. 275).

124 Hirst in Eduardo et al., *Damien Hirst, Napolia Museo Acheologico Nazionale*, p. 134.

125 Lamarque, 'Tragedy and Moral Value', p. 275.

126 See review by Michael Corris, 'Openings', *Artforum* January (1992), p. 36. As well

as its almost identical twin, *One Hundred Years*, *A Thousand Years* was the first of several works Hirst has made involving flies. In 1993 he installed *Bad Environment for White Monochrome Paintings* in the Mattress Factory in Sampsonia Way. See *Parkett*, 40/41 (1994), pp. 59–75. For *Romance in the Age of Uncertainty* (2003) he produced a series of black monochrome 'paintings' composed entirely of dead flies. Thus the rich surfaces of these 'Plague Pictures' are encrusted with the tiny black shells of thousands of dead flies. The titles of these identical works are *Typhoid*, *Genocide*, *Holocaust*, *AIDS*, *Cancer* etc. See G2 section, *Guardian,* 9 September 2003.

127 Julian Stallabrass refers to a contemporary review where the writer calculated that 'sixty generations' of flies had come into being and passed away in Hirst's environment. (Stallabrass, *High Art Lite*, p. 24).

128 Speaking on the occasion of the opening of *Sensation* in New York (1999), Hirst told Gordon Burn: 'I just said, "What if I had a life-cycle in a box? And what if it was a rotting fucking head, and if it was real, and if it had flies on it . . ." I swear I don't know where it came from. Which is why I think it's the best piece I ever made. The best piece I made to date' (Hirst in Burn and Hirst, *On the Way to Work*, p. 128).

129 Eliot, T.S., 'Sweeney Agonistes', in T.S. Eliot, *Collected Poems 1909–1962* (Faber & Faber, London, 1974), p. 131.

130 Lamarque, 'Tragedy and Moral Value', p. 275.

131 Stallabrass, *High Art Lite*, p. 26.

132 Cork, Richard, 'Tanks for the Memories', *The Times*, 3 April 1992.

133 Ibid.

134 Hirst in Eduardo et al., *Damien Hirst, Museo Archeologico Nazionale*, p. 94.

135 Hobbes, Thomas, *Leviathan or the Matter, Form and Power of a Commonwealth Ecclesiastical and Civil*, in L. P. Pojman (ed.) *Classics of Philosophy* (Oxford University Press, Oxford and New York, 1998), §12.

136 Bacon in Gayford, Martin, 'The Brutality of Fact', *Modern Painters* Autumn (1996), p. 44.

137 'I'll tell you what I really read,' he told David Sylvester, 'things which bring up images for me. And I find that this happens very much with the translations of Aeschylus.' Bacon in Sylvester, David, *Looking Back at Francis Bacon* (Thames & Hudson, London, 2000), p. 236. On the relationship of the Baconian aesthetic and the work of Hirst, see the recent book by Townsend, *Art and Death*, pp. 37–52. Townsend also recognises the tragic as a key component of the work of both artists.

138 Hirst in Eduardo et al., *Damien Hirst, Museo Archeologico Nazionale*, p. 94.

139 Hirst in Burn and Hirst, *On the Way to Work*, p. 177. Hirst has spoken in interview of the importance of the Baconian aesthetic for his own artistic programme (see ibid., pp. 68–9, 180). In official recognition of the Bacon–Hirst affinity, the Gagosian Gallery in London hosted a joint exhibition of their work in 2006, which featured Hirst's reworking of Bacon's triptych *In Memory of George Dyer* (1971) adjacent to the original. *Francis Bacon: Triptychs* and *Damien Hirst: A Thousand Years and Triptychs*, Gagosian Gallery, Britannia Street London, June–August 2006. See review, Crompton, Sarah, 'Long Live Mortality', *Daily Telegraph*, 11 July 2006.

Hirst also showed two pharmacological cabinet triptychs called *No Arts; No Letters; No Society* and *Like Flies Brushed Off a Wall We Fall* (2006) respectively.

140 Hirst, Damien, *I Want to Spend the Rest of My Life Everywhere, With Everyone, One to One, Always, Forever, Now* (Booth-Clibborn Editions, London, 1997), np.

141 'I'm going to die and I want to live forever. I can't escape the fact and I can't let go of the desire.' Hirst, ibid., np.

142 Nietzsche, 'On the Pathos of Truth (1872)', in *Philosophical Writings*, p. 85. He is referring to Heraclitean fragment B52: 'The Eternal is a child at play . . . the kingdom belongs to a child.' See Wright, M.R., *The Presocratics* (Bristol Classical Press, Bristol, 1985), p. 10.

143 Shakespeare, *King Lear*, IV, i, 36–7. See also Townsend, *Art and Death*, p. 49.

144 Knight, G. Wilson, *The Wheel of Fire: Interpretations of Shakespearean Tragedy* (Methuen, London, 1930), p. 174.

145 Ibid., p. 166.

146 Ibid., p. 173.

147 See Burke, *Enquiry*, Part 4, Section VII, p. 159, where he quotes as an example of the sublime 'without images', Milton's 'universe of death' from *Paradise Lost*, II, 618–22.

148 Knight, *The Wheel of Fire*, p. 160.

149 Ibid., p. 174.

150 Hirst in Burn, *On the Way to Work*, p. 181.

151 Burke, *Enquiry*, Part 2, Section XXI, p. 78.

152 Hirst in Burn, *On the Way to Work*, p. 181.

153 Townsend, *Art and Death*, p. 49.

154 Knight, *The Wheel of Fire*, p. 165.

155 Ibid., p. 174.

156 Ibid., p. 169.

157 Ibid., p. 165.

158 Baker correctly emphasises the noise of the grinding machinery as essential to the impact of the sculpture. See Baker, *The Postmodern Animal*, p. 85: 'in that darkened room the inescapable grinding noise *was* the experience'.

159 Hirst in Eduardo et al., *Damien Hirst, Museo Archeologico Nazionale*, p. 138. See also Bonami, 'Damien Hirst: The Exploded View of the Artist', p. 112. 'I like the stupid idea of the pig moving like a bacon slicer, which is logical, but twisted.'

160 Knight, *The Wheel of Fire*, p. 170.

161 Lamarque, 'Tragedy and Moral Value', p. 275.

162 Lacan, Jacques, *The Ethics of Psychoanalysis* (trans. D. Potter), in J.A. Miller (ed.), (Routledge, London and New York, 1992).

163 Critchley, *Infinitely Demanding*, p. 72.

164 Lamarque, 'Tragedy and Moral Value', p. 279.

165 Furrow, *Ethics*, p. 80.

166 Burke, *Enquiry*, Part 2, Section XXI, p. 78.

167 Hirst and Burn, *On the Way to Work*, p. 281.

168 Lamarque, 'Tragedy and Moral Value', p. 280.

169 Ibid.

170 Furrow, *Ethics*, p. 79.

171 Hirst, www.artfact.com/artist/hirst-damien-t9wpclihrn.

172 Nussbaum, *Frontiers of Justice*, pp. 402–4.
173 Ibid., p. 404.
174 Ibid., p. 405.
175 Hirst, *I Want to Spend the Rest of my Life Everywhere*, np.
176 Kieran, *Revealing Art*, p. 191.
177 Golding, William, *The Lord of the Flies* (Faber & Faber, London, 1954), p. 152.
178 *Zeitdiagnose*: 'diagnosis of the times'. See Janicaud, Dominique, *On the Human Condition* (trans. E. Brennan) (Routledge, Oxford and New York, 2005), p. xix.
179 Critchley, in ibid.
180 Schuster, 'Death Reckoning', np.
181 Rowlands, *Animals Like Us* (cover material).
182 Critchley, in Janicaud, *On the Human Condition*, p. xvii.
183 Ibid., p. 3.

FURTHER READING

Apter, Emily, 'Just Because You're a Man', *Make* 75, April–May (1997), pp. 3–8.

Badiou, Alain, *Ethics: An Essay on the Understanding of Evil* (trans. P. Hallward) (Verso, London and New York, 2001).

Baker, Simon, 'Jake Chapman on Georges Bataille: an Interview With Simon Baker', *Papers of Surrealism* 1, Winter (2003), pp. 1–17. www.surrealismcentre.ac.uk/publications/papers/jpournal1/acrobat_files/chapman_12.pdf.

Baker, Steve, *The Postmodern Animal* (Reaktion Books, London, 2000).

Barrett, David, 'Tracey Emin: South London Gallery, April 16–May 18', *Art Monthly* 207, June (1997), pp. 36–7.

Bataille, Georges, *The Accursed Share* (trans. R. Hurley) volumes 1–3 (Urzone Books, New York, 1988–93).

—— *Erotism: Death and Sexuality* (trans. M. Dalwood) (City Lights, London and San Francisco, 1986).

Beardsmore, R.W., *Art and Morality* (Macmillan, London, 1971).

Benjamin, Walter, *Selected Writings*, 4 vols (Belknap Press of Harvard University Press, Cambridge, MA, and London, 1999–2003).

Bentham, Jeremy, *An Introduction to the Principles of Morals and Legislation* (Methuen, London, 1996).

Berleant, Arnold, 'Beyond Disinterestedness', *British Journal of Aesthetics* 34/3 (1994), pp. 242–54.

Bermudez, J. and S. Gardner (eds), *Art and Morality* (Routledge, London and New York, 2003).

Billingham, Richard, *Ray's a Laugh* (Scalo, Germany, 1993).

Bolton, Richard (ed.), *Culture Wars: Documents for the Recent Controversies in the Arts* (New Press, New York, 1992).

Bonami, Francesco, 'Damien Hirst: The Exploded View of the Artist', *Flash Art* 29:189, Summer (1996), pp. 112–16.

Brown, Neal, 'I Need Art Like I Need God: Interview with Tracey Emin', *Art From the UK* (Sammlung Goetz, Munich, 1997), pp. 63–71.

—— 'Burger Fetish', *Modern Painters*, Spring (2003), pp. 94–7.

—— *Tracey Emin* (Tate Publishing, London, 2006).

Budd, Malcolm, *Values of Art* (Penguin, London, 1995).

Bullough, Edward, '"Psychical Distance" as a Factor in Art and as an Aesthetic Principle', *British Journal of Psychology* 5 (1912), pp. 87–117.

Burke, Edmund, *A Philosophical Enquiry into the Origin of our Ideas of the Sublime and Beautiful* (Oxford University Press, Oxford, 1990).
Burn, Gordon and Damien Hirst, *On the Way to Work* (Faber & Faber, London, 2000).
Carroll, Nöel, 'Moderate Moralism', *British Journal of Aesthetics* 36:3 (1996), pp. 223–37.
—— 'Moderate Moralism Versus Moderate Automatism', *British Journal of Aesthetics* 38 (1998), pp. 419–24.
—— 'Art and Ethical Criticism: An Overview of Recent Directions of Research', *Ethics* 100, (2000), pp. 350–87.
Chapman, Dinos and Jake, D. Falconer, D. Fogle, N. Land, *Chapmanworld* (Institute of Contemporary Arts Publications, London, 1996).
Cicelyn, Eduardo, Mario Codognato and Mirta D'Argenzio, *Damien Hirst, Napolia Museo Acheologico Nazionale* (Electa, Naples, 2004).
Cohen, Michael, 'Leap into the Void: Abjection and Survival in the Work of Paul McCarthy', *Flash Art* 26:170 (1993), pp. 60–2.
Collings, Matthew, *Blimey! From Bohemia to Britpop: The London Artworld from Francis Bacon to Damien Hirst* (21 Publishing, London, 1997).
Corris, Michael, 'Openings', *Artforum*, January (1992), p. 36.
Cotter, Suzanne (ed.), *Jake & Dinos Chapman: The Rape of Creativity* (Modern Art Oxford, Oxford, 2003).
Cottingham, Laura, 'Orlan's *Seventh Surgery Performance*, *Omnipresence*, at the Sandra Gering Gallery New York', *Frieze Magazine* (1993), p. 60.
Crimp, Douglas, 'The Boys in my Bedroom', *Art in America* 78:2, February (1990), pp. 47–9.
—— *On the Museum's Ruins* (MIT Press, Cambridge, MA, and London, 1993), pp. 108–25.
Critchley, Simon, *Ethics, Politics, Subjectivity* (Verso, London and New York, 1999).
—— *Infinitely Demanding* (Verso, London and New York, 2007).
Derrida, Jacques, *The Animal That Therefore I Am* (trans. D. Wills), (Fordham University Press, New York, 2008)
——'"Eating Well", or the Calculation of the Subject: an Interview With Jacques Derrida', in E. Cadava, P. Connor and J.L. Nancy (eds), *Who Comes After the Subject?* (Routledge, London and New York, 1991), pp. 96-119.
Dickie, George, *Evaluating Art* (Temple University Press, Philadelphia, 1988).
Downie, R.S. and Elizabeth Telfer, *Respect for Persons* (Allen and Unwin, London, 1969).
Emin, Tracey, *Exploration of the Soul* (1994) (Counter Gallery, London, 2003).
—— *Strangeland* (Hodder & Stoughton, London, 2005).
—— *Works 1963–2006* (Rizzoli, New York, 2006).
Foot, Philippa, 'Nietzsche's Immoralism', in R. Schacht (ed.), *Nietzsche, Genealogy, Morality: Essays on Nietzsche's* On the Genealogy of Morals (University of California, Berkeley and Los Angeles, 1994), pp. 3–14.
Foucault, Michel, *The Care of the Self* (Random House, New York, 1986).
—— 'A Preface to Transgression' (trans. R. Hurley and others), in J. Faubion (ed.), *Aesthetics, Method and Epistemology: Essential Works of Foucault 1954–1984* (Penguin, London, 1998), pp. 69–87.
—— *Fearless Speech* (ed. J. Pearson) (Semiotext(e), Los Angeles, 2001).

Freeland, Cynthia, *But is it Art? An Introduction to Art Theory* (Oxford University Press, Oxford, 2001).
Furrow, Dwight, *Ethics: Key Concepts in Philosophy* (Continuum, New York and London, 2005).
Gass, William, 'Goodness Knows Nothing of Beauty: On the Distance Between Morality and Art', *Harper's Magazine* 274 (1987), pp. 37–44.
Gaut, Berys, 'Moral Pluralism', *Philosophical Papers* 22:1 (1993), pp. 17–40.
—— and D. McIver Lopes (eds), *The Routledge Companion to Aesthetics* (Routledge, London, 2001).
Gibbs, Michael, 'Tracey Emin: Stedelijk Museum, Amsterdam', *Art Monthly* 262, (2003), p. 32–3.
Gilland, T. (ed.), *Animal Experimentation: Good or Bad?* (Hodder & Stoughton, London, 2002).
Gisbourne, Mark, 'Life into Art', *Contemporary Visual Arts* 20 (1998), pp. 28–34.
Glowacka, Dorota and S. Boos (eds), *Between Ethics and Aesthetics: Crossing the Boundaries* (State University of New York Press, New York, 2002).
Grieve, Lara, 'Tracey Emin', BBC *Artists in Profile*, 2003, www.bbc.co.uk/arts/news_comment/artistsinprofile/emin.shtml (site since disabled: article partially available at http://talentdevelop.com/visualarts2.html).
Grunenberg, Christoph and Tanya Barson (eds), *Jake and Dinos Chapman: Bad Art For Bad People* (Tate Publishing, London, 2006).
Guyer, Paul, 'Kant's Conception of Fine Art', *Journal of Aesthetics and Art Criticism* 52:3 (1994), pp. 275–85.
Hall, James, 'Jake & Dinos Chapman: Collaborating with Catastrophe', in M. Archer (ed.) *Apocalypse: Beauty and Horror in Contemporary Art* (Royal Academy of Arts, London, 2000), pp. 210–25.
Hand, Sean (ed.), *The Levinas Reader* (Blackwell, Oxford, 1989).
Hauser, Kitty, 'Sensation: Young British Artists from the Saatchi Collection', *New Left Review* 227, January–February (1998), pp. 154–60.
Higonnet, Anne, *Pictures of Innocence: The History and Crisis of Ideal Childhood* (Thames & Hudson, London, 1998).
Hirst, Damien, *I Want to Spend the Rest of My Life Everywhere, With Everyone, One to One, Always, Forever, Now* (Booth-Clibborn Editions, London, 1997).
Holborn, Mark, 'Introduction', in A. Lutgens (ed.), *Jake and Dinos Chapman: Hell* (Jonathan Cape and the Saatchi Gallery, London, 2003), pp. 11–14.
Holert, Tom, 'Schooled for Scandal: Paul McCarthy', *Artforum*, November (2000), pp. 134–40.
Hughes, Robert, *The Culture of Complaint: The Fraying of America* (Harvill Press, London, 1993).
Hume, David, *Essays, Moral, Political, and Literary* (Liberty Classics, Indianapolis, 1987).
Hyman, Lawrence W., 'Morality and Literature – The Necessary Conflict', *British Journal of Aesthetics* 24:2, Spring (1984), pp. 149–55.
Isenberg, Arnold, *Aesthetics and the Theory of Criticism* (Chicago University Press, Chicago, 1973).
Jacobson, Daniel, 'In Praise of Immoral Art', *Philosophical Topics*, 25:1 (1997), pp. 155–99.

Jamieson, Dale (ed.), *Singer and his Critics* (Blackwell, Oxford, 1999).
Januszczak, Waldemar, 'Eminism', *Sunday Times Magazine*, 12 July 1998.
—— 'On Sparkling Form', *Sunday Times Culture*, 3 June 2007.
Jenks, Chris, *Transgression* (Routledge, London and New York, 2003).
Julius, Anthony, *Transgressions: The Offences of Art* (Thames & Hudson, London, 2002).
Kant, Immanuel, *Critique of Practical Reason* (trans. L.W. Beck) (Bobbs-Merrill, Indianapolis, 1977).
—— *Critique of Judgment* (trans. W.S. Pluhar) (Hackett, Indianapolis, 1987).
Kearney, Richard and M. Dooley (eds), *Questioning Ethics* (Routledge, London and New York, 1999).
Kent, Sarah, *Shark Infested Waters: The Saatchi Collection of British Art in the 90s* (Philip Wilson Publishers, London, 1994).
—— 'YBA Woman', *World of Art Magazine* (Thames & Hudson, London, 2000), pp. 22–3.
Kieran, Matthew, *Revealing Art* (Routledge, Oxford and New York, 2005).
—— (ed.), *Aesthetics and the Philosophy of Art* (Blackwell, Oxford, 2006).
—— (ed.), *Contemporary Debates in Aesthetics and the Philosophy of Art* (Blackwell, Oxford, 2006).
Korsmeyer, Carolyn (ed.), *Aesthetics: The Big Questions* (Blackwell, Oxford, 1998).
Krauss, R., Y. Bois and B. Buchloh, *Art Since 1900: Modernism, Antimodernism, Postmodernism* (Thames & Hudson, London, 2005).
Kristeva, Julia, *Powers of Horror: An Essay on Abjection* (trans. L.S. Roudiez) (Columbia University Press, New York, 1982).
Lamarque, Peter and S.H. Olsen (eds) *Aesthetics and the Philosophy of Art: The Analytic Tradition* (Blackwell, Oxford, 2004).
Levinas, Emmanuel, *Otherwise than Being or Beyond Essence* (trans. A. Lingis) (Martinus Nijhoff, The Hague, 1981).
—— *Discovering Existence with Husserl* (Northwestern University Press, Evanston, IL, 1998).
—— *On Escape* (trans. B. Bergo) (Stanford University Press, Stanford, CA, 2003).
Levinson, Jerrold (ed.), *Aesthetics and Ethics: Essays at the Intersection* (Blackwell, Oxford, 1998).
—— (ed.), *The Oxford Handbook of Aesthetics* (Oxford University Press, Oxford, 2005).
Lewis, Jim, 'No Place Like Home', *Artforum International*, January (1997), pp. 62–7.
Lichtenstein, Therese, *Behind Closed Doors: The Art of Hans Bellmer* (University of California Press, Berkeley and Los Angeles, 2001).
Lippard, Lucy R., 'The Spirit and the Letter', *Art in America* 80 (1990), pp. 238–45.
Locke, John, *An Essay Concerning Human Understanding* (Penguin, London, 1997).
Lorand, Ruth, 'Beauty and its Opposites', *Journal of Aesthetics and Art Criticism* 52:4 (1994), pp. 399–406.
Mahon, Alyce, *Eroticism and Art* (Oxford University Press, Oxford, 2005).
Maloney, Martin, 'Chapman Bros. When Will I be Famous?' *Flash Art* 29:186, January–February (1996), pp. 64–7.
McGinn, Colin, *Evil, Ethics, and Fiction* (Clarendon Press, Oxford, 1997).
McGrath, Melanie, 'Something's Wrong', *Tate Magazine* 1 (1998), available online at www.tate.org.uk/magazine/issue1/something.htm.
McLeish, Kenneth, *Aristotle: Poetics* (Phoenix, London, 1998).

McKinnon, Catriona, *Toleration: A Critical Introduction* (Routledge, London and New York, 2006).

Merck, Mandy and C. Townsend (eds), *The Art of Tracey Emin* (Thames & Hudson, London, 2002).

Merkel, Jayne, 'Report from Cincinnati: Art on Trial,' *Art in America*, December (1990), pp. 41–52.

Mill, J.S., 'Utilitarianism', in A. Ryan (ed.), *Utilitarianism and Other Essays* (Penguin, London, 1987), pp. 272–340.

Morgan, Stuart, 'Rude awakening', *Frieze: Contemporary Art and Culture* 19, November–December (1994), pp. 30–3.

—— 'Hermann Nitsch, 30 Underwood St London', *Art Monthly* 212, December–January (1997–8), p. 30.

——'The Story of I', *Frieze: Contemporary Art and Culture* 34, May (1997), pp. 56–61.

Mulholland, Neil, 'London: "Sensation"', *Burlington Magazine*, 89:1137 December (1997), pp. 887–9.

Neill, Alex and A. Ridley (eds), *Arguing About Art: Contemporary Philosophical Debates* (Routledge, London and New York, 2002).

Nietzsche, Friedrich, *Philosophical Writings* (ed. R. Grimm and C. Molina y Vedia) (Continuum, New York, 1995).

Noddings, Nel, *Caring: A Feminine Approach to Ethics and Moral Education* (University of California Press, Berkeley, Los Angeles and London, 1984).

Norman, Richard, *The Moral Philosophers* (Oxford University Press, Oxford, 1998).

Nussbaum, Martha C., *Love's Knowledge: Essays on Philosophy and Literature* (Oxford University Press, Oxford and New York, 1990).

—— *Hiding from Humanity: Disgust, Shame and the Law* (Princeton University Press, Princeton and Oxford, 2004).

—— *Frontiers of Justice: Disability, Nationality, Species Membership,* (Belknap Press, Cambridge, MA, 2006).

Parkett, 63 (2001).

Pierini, Esther, 'Tracey Emin', *Flash Art* 30:97, November–December (1997), pp. 102–3.

Pojman, L.P. (ed.), *Classics of Philosophy* (Oxford University Press, Oxford and New York, 1998).

Quinn, Marc, *Incarnate* (Booth-Clibborn, London, 1998).

Ramkalawon, Jennifer, 'Jake and Dinos Chapman's *Disasters of War*', *Print Quarterly* 18:1, March (2001), pp. 64–77.

Reardon, Valerie, 'Whose Image is it Anyway?' *Art Monthly* 195, April (1996), p. 45.

Regan, Tom, *The Case for Animal Rights* (University of California Press, Berkeley, 1983).

Richardson, M. (ed.), *Bataille: Essential Writings* (Sage, London, 1988).

Robertson, Bryan, 'Something is Rotten in the State of Art', *Modern Painters*, Winter (1997), pp. 15–16.

Rogers, Richard, *Marc Quinn Fourth Plinth* (Steidlmack, Göttingen, 2006).

Rose, Barbara, 'Is it Art? Orlan and the Transgressive Act', *Art in America*, February (1993), pp. 82–7.

Rosenthal, Norman et al., *Sensation: Young British Artists from the Saatchi Collection* (Royal Academy of Arts and Thames & Hudson, London, 1997).

Rowlands, Mark, *Animals Like Us* (Verso, London and New York, 2002).

Rugoff, Ralph, Kristine Stiles and Giacinto Di Pietrantonio, *Paul McCarthy* (Phaidon, London, 1996).
Salecl, Renata, *On Anxiety* (Routledge, London and New York, 2004).
Sartre, Jean-Paul, *Being and Nothingness: An Essay on Phenomenological Ontology* (trans. Hazel E. Barnes) (Methuen, London, 1958).
Self, Will, *Junk Mail* (Bloomsbury, London, 1995).
—— 'To Die For', *Sunday Telegraph Magazine*, 2 June 2007.
Selwyn, Marc, 'Paul McCarthy: There's a Big Difference Between Ketchup and Blood', *Flash Art* 26:170, (1993), pp. 63–4.
Siderfin, Naomi, 'The Title Gives Nothing Away', *Make* 78, December–February (1998), p. 25.
Singer, Peter *Applied Ethics* (Oxford University Press, Oxford, 1986).
—— (ed.), *A Companion to Ethics* (Blackwell, Oxford, 1991).
—— *Writings on an Ethical Life* (Fourth Estate, London, 2000).
Slyce, John, 'Sensation', *Flash Art* 30:197 (1997), pp. 106–7.
Smithard, Paula, 'It's a Tenuous Line Between Sincerity and Sensationalism', *Make* 76, June–July (1997), pp. 27–9.
Stallabrass, Julian, 'Young British Artists II', *Art Monthly* 164 (1993), pp. 19–20.
—— *High Art Lite: British Art in the 1990s* (Verso, London, 1999).
Stolnitz, Jerome, 'On the Origins of "Aesthetic Disinterestedness"', *Journal of Aesthetics and Art Criticism* 20:2, (1961), pp. 131–43.
Taylor, Simon, 'The Phobic Object: Abjection in Contemporary Art', *Abject Art: Repulsion and Desire in American Art* (Whitney Museum of American Art, New York, 1993), pp. 59–84.
Taylor, Sue, *Hans Bellmer: The Anatomy of Anxiety* (MIT Press, Cambridge, MA, 2000).
Toynbee, Polly, 'For Shame! The Arts Versus the Plod', *Modern Painters*, Summer (2001), pp. 18–20.
Townsend, Chris, *Art and Death*, (I.B.Tauris, London and New York, 2008).
Wallinger, Mark, 'The Pygmalion Paradox', *Art Monthly* 218, July/August (1998), pp. 1–4.
Warnock, G.J., *Contemporary Moral Philosophy* (Macmillan, London, 1967).
Warnock, Mary, *Existentialist Ethics* (Macmillan, London, 1967).
—— *An Intelligent Person's Guide to Ethics* (Duckworth, London, 1998).
Webb, Peter and R. Short, *Hans Bellmer* (Quartet, New York, 1985).
Wilde, Oscar, *The Collected Works of Oscar Wilde* (Wordsworth Editions, Hertfordshire, 1997).
Williams, Bernard, *Ethics and the Limits of Philosophy* (Fontana, London, 1993).
—— *Shame and Necessity* (University of California Press, Berkeley and Los Angeles, 1993).
Worsdale, Godfrey, 'Dinos and Jake Chapman: Victoria Miro Gallery, London', *Art Monthly* 180, October (1994), pp. 36–7.
Wright, Karen, 'An Overwhelming Sensation?', *Modern Painters*, Autumn (1997), p. 23.
—— 'Letters and Luggage: Tracey Emin Unpacks her Thoughts on Love, God and Needlework', *Modern Painters*, June (2005), pp. 34–7.
—— 'Maid of Margate', *ABC: The Arts Books & Culture Magazine from the Independent on Sunday*, 28 May 2005.
Wyschogrod, Edith and G.P. McKenny (eds), *The Ethical* (Blackwell, Oxford, 2003).

Young British Art: The Saatchi Decade (Booth-Clibborn Editions, London, 1999).
Žižek, Slavoj, *The Parallax View* (MIT Press, Cambridge, MA, and London, 2006).

Others

Bragg, Melvyn, 'Tracey Emin', *South Bank Show*, LWT, 2001.
Chapman, Jake, *Artshock: Is Bad Art for Bad People?* Channel 4, 2006.
Emin, Tracey, *Top Spot*, Tartan Films, 2004.
Myra: The Making of a Monster, Channel Five production, 3 September 2003.
Pulp, *Different Class*, Island Records, 1995.
The Saatchi Gallery 100: The Work that Changed British Art, Illuminations, 2004.
Yentob, Alan, *Imagine: The Plinth, the Model, the Artist and his Sculpture*, BBC, 2006.

INDEX

abject art 1, 8, 36, 75, 141
absence of the referent 66–7
Abramović, Marina 2
abstract expressionism 68
Acconci, Vito 2
Adams, Parveen 11
Ades, Dawn 108
Aeschylus 191
aftershock 12, 66, 105, 106, 188–99
Alberge, Dalya 89
Amis, Martin 83, 96
amnesia 137
Antigone 194
Antoni, Janine 2
anxiety 137
Apter, Emily 116–17
Arbus, Diane 26, 40
Archer, Michael 57
Artaud, Antonin 98
aufheben/Aufhebung 150, 155, 182, 185, 187–8, 196; *see also* Hegel
autonomism 27–31, 42–5, 67, 180–1, *passim*

B., Franko 2
Bacon, Francis 183, 184–5, 190, 191
Badiou, Alain 15, 64
Baker, Steve 170, 175, 183; *The Postmodern Animal* 170
Ballard, J.G. 96, 120, 121; *The Atrocity Exhibition* 120
Bataille, Georges 2, 63, 71, 73, 97, 98, 99, 101–6, 108
Beardsmore, R.W. 28
Bellmer, Hans 74, 100, 101–7, 116, 18, 120, 121; *Die Puppe/La Poupée* 101
Benjamin, Walter 47–8, 105, 129
Bennett, Keith 51, 58, 79,
Bentham, Jeremy 169
Bermudez, Ceán 91
Billingham, Richard 14, 19, 22–7, 29, 40, 46, 49, 57
Blake, William 98
Booth-Clibborn, Charles 93, 97
Brady, Ian 51, 53, 54, 58–9, 61, 63–4, 83, 84
Bragg, Melvyn 147
Brand, Peggy Zeglin 9–11
Breton, André 101
Brown, Curtis 28
Brown, Neal 123, 125, 126, 141, 149
Brus, Gunther 2, 4
Budd, Malcolm 27, 127
Bulger, James 83
Buñuel, Luis 91
Burke, Edmund 82, 176–9, 186
Burn, Gordon 159
Bussel 110

canonic defence 90
Camus, Albert 132
Caravaggio, Merisi 119
Carroll, Noël 27, 29, 30–1, 121
Chapman brothers 14, 87–122, 125; *Zygotic Acceleration* 87–9, 107–22; *Disasters of War* 91–7; *Bad Art for Bad People* 98; *Chapmanworld* 98; *Fuckface* 112; *Fuckface Twin* 115; *Two-Faced Cunt* 115

Chapman, Jake 1, 3, 14, 15, 65, 76, 79, 83; *Artshock: Is Bad Art for Bad People* 3, 76; *see also* Chapman brothers
Childish, Billy 146
Close, Chuck 62
Cocker, Jarvis 17–19, 21
Cohen, Stan 64
Colie, Rosalie 186–7
contextualism 45, 46–8, 68
Cork, Richard 190
Courbet, Gustav 74
Crimp, Douglas 110, 111, 117, 119
Critchley, Simon 135, 136, 148–9, 194, 198
Critchton, Fenella 3

Dalí, Salvador 91, 108
Danto, Arthur 117
Davis, Carol Anne 60, 62
Degas, Edgar 74
Deleuze, Gilles 98; *Nomadology: The War Machine* 132
Derrida, Jacques 105, 173, 174, 182
Devereaux, Mary 49, 109, 111, 114–15
disinterestedness 5–12, 18–19, 46–8, 49–50, 90, 109, 111–12, 115, 126, *passim*
Dix, Otto 94
Downey, Lesley Ann 54, 58, 59
Downie, R.S. 39

Ellis, Bret Easton 31
Emin, Tracey 14, 18, 123–57, 159, 182; *If I Could Just Go Back and Start Again* 124; *Everyone I Have Ever Slept With 1963–95* 129–37, 141, 149; *How It Feels* 131; *Strangeland* 131, 134, 138; *My Bed* 132–7, 141, 147, 149; *Tracey Emin's CV. Cunt Vernacular* 134; *When I think about sex . . .* 134; *Conversation with my mum* 138, 147; *The History of Painting* 141; *Uncle Colin 1963–93* 141; *My Major Retrospective* 141; *Homage to Edvard Munch and all my dead children* 156
ethics of care 14–15, 49; care-of-self 155–7

Evans, Edward, 58, 63
Evaristti, Marco 170

Felman Shoshana, 47
feminist critique 9, 71, 72,
fetishism 65, 78, 102, 105
Fisher, Peter 54, 81
Fiske, John 20
Flanagan, Bob 2
Fogle, Douglas 98
Foucault, Michel 73, 74, 105, 128, 150, 151–7
Freeland, Cynthia 3, 9, 91
Freud, Sigmund 2, 78, 98, 107–9, 122, 218n, 219n.
Fuller, Peter 183
Furrow, Dwight 14

Gaut, Berys 13, 30, 31, 45, 55, 80–1, 89
Gearon, Tierney 116–20, 125
Gibbs, Michael 126
Gisbourne, Mark 123
Glowaka, Dorota 142, 228ff.
Golding, William 197
Goya, Francisco 91–7, 100, 108; *Los desatres de la Guerra* 91, 93–4; *Grande hazaña con meurtos* 91, 94; *Black Paintings* 93
Grob, David 41
Gruen, Lori 170
Grunenberg, Christoph 98, 99
Guattari, Felix 98, 132

Hall, Allan 62
Hall, James 91, 110
Hanson, Karen 44
Hartley, John 20,
Harvey, Marcus 14, 51–85, 87, 89, 124, 125; *Myra* 51–85, 87; *Doggy* 68; *Dudley Like What You See? Then Call Me* 68, 76; *Julie From Hull* 68; *My Arse Is Yours* 68; *Proud of his Wife* 68
Hauser, Kitty 17
Healy, Lorna 143
Heartfield, John 94
Hegel, G.W.F. 182
Heidegger, Martin 178

Heraclitus of Ephesus 191
Higonnet, Anne 116–17
Hindley, Myra 51, 53–4, 56, 58–66, 81–4
Hirst, Damien 14, 18, 159–99; *When Logics Die* 159; *Mother and Child (Divided)* 162; *The Physical Impossibility of Death in the Mind of Someone Living* 162, 166, 177–9; *This Little Piggy Went to Market, This Little Piggy Stayed at Home* 162, 192–3; *A Thousand Years* 162, 188–92; *Away From the Flock* 164; *No Sense of Absolute Corruption* 164; *Some Went Mad . . . Some Ran Away* 164; *Adam and Eve* 165; *Beyond Belief* 165; *Death Explained* 165; *The Death of God* 165; *Exquisite Pain* 165; *God Alone Knows* 165; *In the Name of the Father* 165; *In and Out of Love* 165; *Romance in the Age of Uncertainty* 165–6; *Some Comfort Gained from the Inherent Lies in Everything* 165; *Lost Love, Love Lost* 166; *The Acquired Inability to Escape* 198
Hobbes, Thomas 190–1
Holborn, Mark 93–4
Hume, David, 29, 30
Husserl, Edmund 18
Hyman, Lawrence 114, 186, 187

immoralism 44–5, 179–82
insomnia 137

JAAG (Justice for Animals Arts Guild) 170
Jacobson, Daniel 29, 30, 44, 45, 179–81, 186–7
Janicaud, Dominique 197–8
Jenks, Chris 2, 59–60, 63–5, 77, 100
Johnson, Winnie 51, 54, 79, 81
Julius, Anthony 2, 3, 12, 13, 15, 53, 56, 62, 63, 79, 82, 90, 97, 99, 109, 112, 170

Kant, Immanuel 5–6, 8, 38–9; categorical imperative 38–9, 173
Kardon, Janet 109
Kelley, Mike 298
Kent, Sarah 71, 75, 77, 87, 174, 197
Kidscape 54
Kieran, Matthew 8, 9, 11, 45, 71–2, 80–1, 84, 183–5
Kilbride, John 58
Knight, G. Wilson 191
Kristeva, Julia 36, 98, 131, 141
Kundera, Milan 135, 149

Lacan, Jacques 98, 108, 194
Lamarque, Peter 190, 194
Lapper, Alison 32, 37, 38, 39–41, 46, 47, 50, 58
Lehmann, Ulrich 144
Levinas, Emmanuel 130, 135–7, 142, 144, 146–8, 155, 173, 174,
Levine, Sherrie 110, 111, 116, 117, 119
Lewis, Jim 22–5
Lingwood, James 26
Lippard, Lucy 91
Lorand, Ruth 7
Löwy, Michael, 48
Lubbock, Tom 57
Lucas, Sarah 19, 75,

Maloney, Martin 106, 110, 112, 113, 121, 126
Mann, Sally 116–20, 125
Mapplethorpe, Robert 25, 41, 74, 116, 117, 120, 125, 222n.; *Jesse Mc Bride* 116; *Rosie* 116
Marx, Karl 65
masturbation 75
McCarthy, Paul 2–3, 4, 6–8, 10, 98; *Bossy Burger* 6, 8
McGinn, Colin 30
McGrath, Melanie 129
merited response theory 79–84
Minotaure 101
Miro, Victoria 89, 97
Molyneux, John 54, 57
moralism 29–32, 43–4, 179, 180–3, *passim*
Morgan, Michael 148, 156
Morgan, Stuart 94–6
Morris, Jenny 37
Muehl, Otto 2
Muir, Gregor 126

Mulholland, Neil 56, 74
Mulvey, Laura 21
Murdoch, Iris 115

Nabokov, Vladimir 30; *Lolita* 30
Nietzsche, Friedrich 2, 98, 173, 174, 191; *Beyond Good and Evil* 98
Nitsch, Hermann 2, 3
Noddings, Nel 142, 174, 175
Norman, Richard 39, 127
Norris, David 89
Nussbaum, Martha C. 12, 37, 47, 123, 142, 155–7, 197

Olly and Suzi 170, 183; *Shark Bite* 170
Orgiastic Mystery Theatre 3
Orlan 9–11, 37–8
Orr, Deborah 47
Osborne, Peter 128

parrhesia (fearless speech) 151–7
PETA (People for the Ethical Treatment of Animals) 166
Picasso, Pablo 74; *Guernica* 57
pluralism 13
pornography 71–4, 75, 77, 98, 123, 125
postmodernism 1, 9, 66–7, 110–11, 122, 221n.
Preece, Robert 134, 143
pregnancy 48
psychoanalysis 96, 102–3, 107–9, 122
Pulp 17, 19

Quinn, Marc 14, 32, 33–43, 46–7, 50, 58; *Alison Lapper Pregnant* 32, 47–8, 50; *Self* 34

Ramkalawon, Jennifer 88, 94
Reade, Pauline 58
Reardon, Valerie 115–18
Regan, Tom 161, 168, 173
repression 3, 96, 99, 107
retail realism 87, 112
Richter, Gerhard 129
Riefenstahl, Leni 44, 49; *Triumph des Willens* 44, 49
Rodin, 74, 98
Rolé, Jacques 54, 81
Rose, Barbara 10
Rowlands, Mark 161, 173
Royal Academy of Arts 14, 53, 54

Saatchi, Charles 51, 129
Sade, Marquis de 98, 99
Salecl, Renata 137–8
Sartre, Jean-Paul 144, 145–8, 152, 155
Saville, Jenny 8
Schiele, Egon 74
Schopenhauer, Arthur 187
Self, Will 11, 36, 38, 46, 134, 231ff.
Sensation: Young British Art from the Saatchi Collection 1997/1999 14, 17, 53, 56, 57, 66, 68, 87, 129, 162, 165
Serrano, Andreas 9, 25, 41, 91; *Piss Christ* 91
Shakespeare, William 186, 191; *King Lear* 186, 192–4
shame 144–9, 154–7
Sherman, Cindy 8, 40
Siderfin, Naomi 54
Singer, Peter 14, 161, 168–73
Smithard, Paula 126, 128
social class 19–22
Solomon, Robert 14, 142
Sontag, Susan 26, 27, 49
Spector, Jack 108
Spenser, Liese 125
Stallabrass, Julian 22, 24, 56, 62, 71, 79, 81, 85, 106, 110, 125–6, 152, 190; *High Art Lite* 110, 125
Stanford, Peter 59
Sterbak, Jana 2
Stolnitz, Jerome 18, 111
sublimation 2, 4, 94, 96, 97, 112, 103, 107, 108, 109, 112, 120, 218n; de-sublimation 4, 94, 96–7, 107
sublime, the 176–9, 185–6
suicide 132–4

Taylor, Sue 101, 103, 108
Telfer, Elizabeth 39
Tirrell, Lynne 74
Townsend, Chris 128, 192
Tozer, John 67, 78

tragedy 186–96
Turk, Gavin 18
Turner, Christopher 97

Wallinger, Mark 19, 48, 54; *Ecce Homo* 48
Walton, Kendall 44
Warnock, Mary 145, 167, 168
Wearing, Gillian 206 n.
West, Ann 54, 59, 81
Weston, Edward 110, 117, 119
Wiener Actionismus 2–4, 10
Wilde, Oscar 28, 51
Williams, Bernard 142
Witkin, Joel-Peter 40
Wittgenstein, Ludwig 10, 194
Wyschogrod, Edith 136, 143

yBa 14
Yong Ping, Huang 170

Žižek, Slavoj 98, 107